Encyclopedia of Robust Control: Applied Principles

Volume IV

Encyclopedia of Robust Control: Applied Principles

Volume IV

Edited by **Zac Fredericks**

CLANRYE INTERNATIONAL

New Jersey

Published by Clanrye International,
55 Van Reypen Street,
Jersey City, NJ 07306, USA
www.clanryeinternational.com

Encyclopedia of Robust Control: Applied Principles
Volume IV
Edited by Zac Fredericks

International Standard Book Number: 978-1-63240-203-5 (Hardback)

Printed in the United States of America.

Contents

Preface

This book aims to highlight the current researches and provides a platform to further the scope of innovations in this area. This book is a product of the combined efforts of many researchers and scientists, after going through thorough studies and analysis from different parts of the world. The objective of this book is to provide the readers with the latest information of the field.

The purpose of this book is to provide some exemplary models and significant challenges faced in the domain of robust control design and applications. It comprises of research and discussion on some breakthrough applications in this domain such as sliding mode, robust PID, H-infinity, etc. These techniques have given new dimension to this genre of science and broadened the application spectra to even non-engineering systems. This book comprises of two sections, "Robust Control in Aircraft, Vehicle and Automotive Applications", and "Control of Structures, Mechanical and Electro-Mechanical Systems".

I would like to express my sincere thanks to the authors for their dedicated efforts in the completion of this book. I acknowledge the efforts of the publisher for providing constant support. Lastly, I would like to thank my family for their support in all academic endeavors.

Editor

Part 1

Robust Control in Aircraft, Vehicle and Automotive Applications

1

Advanced Control Techniques for the Transonic Phase of a Re-Entry Flight

Gianfranco Morani, Giovanni Cuciniello,
Federico Corraro and Adolfo Sollazzo
Italian Aerospace Research Centre (CIRA)
Italy

1. Introduction

New technological developments in space engineering and science require sophisticated control systems with both high performance and reliability. How to achieve these goals against various uncertainties and off-nominal scenarios has been a very challenging issue for control system design over the last years.
Several efforts have been spent on control systems design in aerospace applications, in order to conceive new control approaches and techniques trying to overcome the inherent limitations of classical control designs.
In fact, the current industrial practice for designing flight control laws is based on Proportional Integral Derivative (PID) controllers with scheduled gains. With this approach, several controllers are designed at various points in the operative flight envelope, considering local time-invariant linear models based on small perturbations of a detailed nonlinear aircraft model. Although these techniques are commonly used in control systems design, they may have inherent limitations stemming from the poor capability of guaranteeing acceptable performances and stability for flight conditions different from the selected ones, especially when the scheduling parameters rapidly change.
This issue becomes very critical when designing flight control system for space re-entry vehicles. Indeed, space reentry applications have some distinctive features with respect to aeronautical ones, mainly related to the lack of stationary equilibrium conditions along the trajectories, to the wide flight envelope characterizing missions (from hypersonic flight regime to subsonic one) and to the high level of uncertainty in the knowledge of vehicle aerodynamic parameters.
Over the past years, several techniques have been proposed for advanced control system development, such as Linear Quadratic Optimal Control (LQOC), Eigenstructure Assignment, Robust control theory, Quantitative feedback theory (QFT), Adaptive Model Following, Feedback Linearization, Linear Parameter Varying (LPV) and probabilistic approach. Hereinafter, a brief recall of the most used techniques will be given.
Linear Quadratic Optimal Control (LQOC) allows finding an optimal control law for a given system based on a given criterion. The optimal control can be derived using Pontryagin's maximum principle and it has been commonly applied in designing Linear Quadratic Regulator (LQR) of flight control system (see Xing, 2003; Vincent et al., 1994).

The Eigenstructure Assignment consists of placing the eigenvalues of a linear system using state feedback and then using any remaining degrees of freedom to align the eigenvectors as accurately as possible (Konstantopoulos & Antsaklis, 1996; Liu & Patton, 1996; Ashari et al., 2005). Nevertheless there are several limitations, since only linear systems are considered and moreover the effects of uncertainty have been not extensively studied.

Robust analysis and control theory is a method to measure performance degradation of a control system when considering system uncertainties (Rollins, 1999; Balas, 2005). In this framework a concept of structured singular value (i.e μ-Synthesis) is introduced for including structured uncertainties into control system synthesis as well as for checking robust stability of a system.

Adaptive Model Following (AMF) technique has the advantage of strong robustness against parameter uncertainty of the system model, if compared to classical control techniques (Bodson & Grosziewicz, 1997; Kim et al., 2003). The model following approach has interesting features and it may be an important part of an autonomous reconfigurable algorithm, because it aims to emulate the performance characteristics of a target model, even in presence of plant's uncertainties.

Another powerful nonlinear design is Feedback Linearization which transforms a generic non linear system into an equivalent linear system, through a change of variables and a suitable control input (Bharadwaj et al., 1998; Van Soest et al., 2006). Feedback linearization is an approach to nonlinear control design which is based on the algebraic transformation of nonlinear systems dynamics into linear ones, so that linear control techniques can be applied.

More recently an emerging approach, named Linear Parameter Varying (LPV) control, has been developed as a powerful alternative to the classical concept of gain scheduling (Spillman, 2000; Malloy & Chang, 1998; Marcos & Balas, 2004). LPV techniques are well suited to account for on-line parameter variations such that the controllers can be designed to ensure performance and robustness in all the operative envelope. In this way a gain-scheduling controller can be achieved without interpolating between several design points.

The main effort (and also main drawback) required by the above techniques is the modelling of a nonlinear system as a LPV system. Several techniques exist but they may require a huge effort for testing controller performances on the nonlinear system. Other modelling techniques try to overcome this problem at the expense of a higher computational effort.

Finally in the last decades, a new philosophy has emerged, that is, probabilistic approach for control systems analysis and synthesis (Calafiore et al., 2007; Tempo et al., 1999; Tempo et al., 2005). In this approach, the meaning of robustness is shifted from its usual deterministic sense to a probabilistic one. The new paradigm is then based on the probabilistic definition of robustness, by which it is claimed that a certain property of a control system is "almost" robustly satisfied, if it holds for "most" instances of uncertainties. The algorithms based on probabilistic approach, usually called randomized algorithms (RAs), often have low complexity and are associated to robustness bounds which are less conservative than classical ones, obviously at the expense of a probabilistic risk.

In this chapter the results of a research activity focused on the comparison between different advanced control architectures for transonic phase of a reentry flight are reported. The activity has been carried out in the framework of Unmanned Space Vehicle (USV) program of Italian Aerospace Research Centre (CIRA), which is in charge of developing unmanned space Flying Test Beds (FTB) to test advanced technologies during flight. The first USV

Dropped Transonic Flight Test (named DTFT1) was carried out in February 2007 with the first vehicle configuration of USV program (named FTB1) (see Russo et al., 2007 for details). For this mission, a conventional control architecture was implemented. DTFT1 was then used as a benchmark application for comparison among different advanced control techniques. This comparison aimed at choosing the most suited control technique to be used for the subsequent, more complex, dropped flight test, named DTFT2, successfully carried out on April 2010. To this end, three techniques were selected after a dedicated literature survey, namely:

- μ-Control with Fuzzy Logic Gain-Scheduling
- Direct Adaptive Model Following Control
- Probabilistic Robust Control Synthesis

In the next sections, the above techniques will be briefly described with particular emphasis on their application to DTFT1 mission. In sec. 5 the performance analysis carried out for comparison among the different techniques will be presented.

2. Fuzzy scheduled MU-controller

2.1 The H∞ control problem

The H∞ Control Theory (Zhou & Doyle, 1998) rises as response to the deficiencies of the classical Linear Quadratic Gaussian (LQG) control theory of the 1960s applications. The general problem formulation is described through the following equations:

$$\begin{bmatrix} z \\ y \end{bmatrix} = P(s)\begin{bmatrix} w \\ u \end{bmatrix} = \begin{bmatrix} P_{11} & P_{12} \\ P_{21} & P_{22} \end{bmatrix}\begin{bmatrix} w \\ u \end{bmatrix} \qquad (1)$$
$$u = K(s)y$$

where P is the nominal plant, u is the control variable, y is the measured variable, w is an exogenous signals (such as disturbances) and z is the error signal to be minimized. The generic control scheme is depicted in Fig 1.

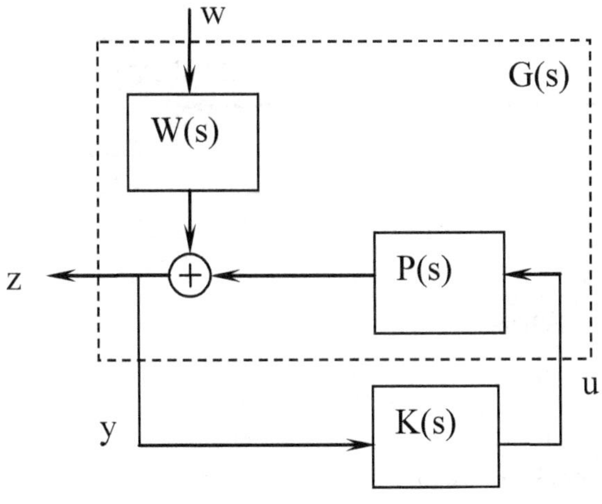

Fig. 1. Nominal Performance Scheme

It can be shown that closed-loop transfer function from w to z can be obtained via lower linear fractional transformation (Zhou & Doyle, 1998).
Therefore H_∞ control problem is to find a stabilizing controller, K, which minimizes

$$\left\|F_l(P,K)\right\|_\infty = \sup_\omega \bar{\sigma}\left(F_l(P,K)(j\omega)\right) = \gamma_M \tag{2}$$

where F_l is the lower linear fractional transformation from w to z and $\bar{\sigma}$ is the singular value of specified transfer function.
For what concerns Nominal Performance Problem, it is required that error z is kept as small as possible. To this end, a new generalized plant can be considered (see the dashed line). The weighting function penalizes the infinite-norm of new plant to achieve required performances.
In the same way, Robust Stability Problem can be solved applying Small Gain Theorem (Zhou & Doyle, 1998) to the following new generalized plant selected (see the dashed line):

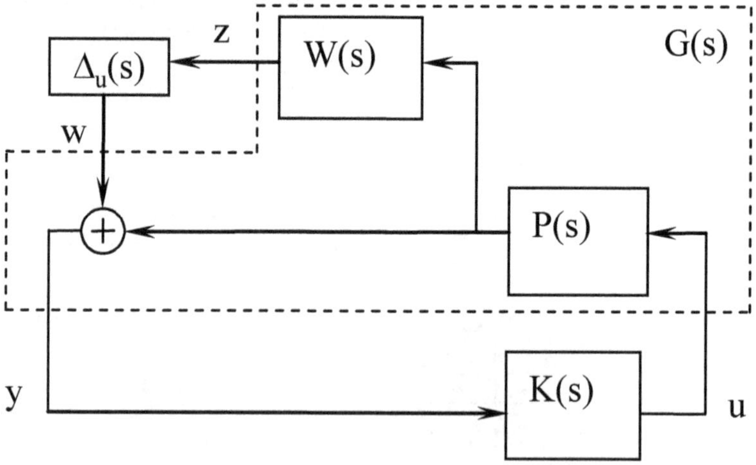

Fig. 2. Robust Stability Scheme

A more general problem to solve is Robust Performance Problem that takes into account both Nominal Performance and Robust Stability Problems. It is worth noting that a Nominal Performance Scheme allows to find a stabilizing controller that satisfies Small Gain Theorem in presence of a fictitious uncertainty block Δf(s) (with $\left\|\Delta_f(s)\right\|_\infty < 1/\gamma_M$). Hence a general scheme for Robust Performance Problem is the following one:

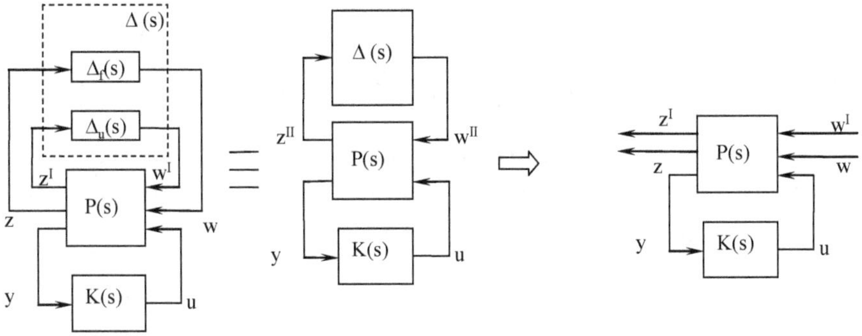

Fig. 3. Robust Performance Scheme

where:

$$\Delta(s) = \begin{bmatrix} \Delta_u(s) & 0 \\ 0 & \Delta_f(s) \end{bmatrix} \quad (3)$$

It is clear from the figures that all above problem formulations can be always rearranged to solve the same general H_∞ problem. It is worth noting that for what concerns Robust Performance Case, Δ(s) matrix has a diagonal block structure. Plant uncertainties can be structured like mixed (real and complex) uncertainties. Unfortunately H_∞ problem only deals with unstructured full complex Δ(s), so optimal (or sub-optimal) controller might be very conservative. μ-analysis and synthesis try to solve this issue by dealing with structured uncertainties.

2.2 μ-synthesis framework

The brief discussion of previous paragraph has shown how to design an H_∞ controller starting from a generalized plant. Required performances are achieved through optimal (or sub-optimal) controller by means of weighting functions of a generalized plant. In the same way, robust stability is achieved together with performances by solving Robust Performance Problem. Let $M = F_l(P,K)$, then a general scheme for μ-analysis is the following one:

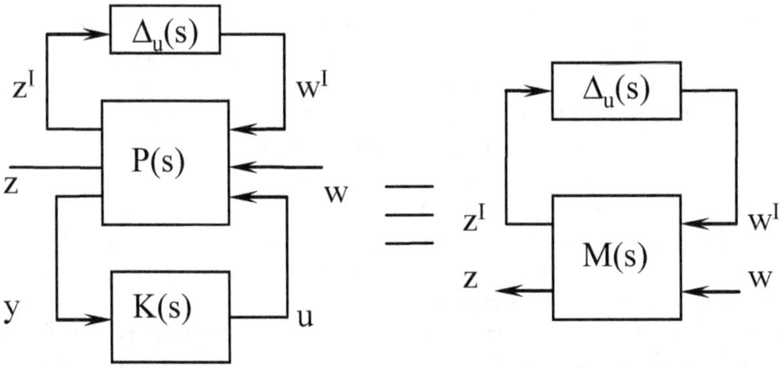

Fig. 4. μ-Analysis Scheme

Introducing structured singular value:

$$\mu_{\Delta}(M) := \frac{1}{\min\{\bar{\sigma}(\Delta) \ : \det(I - M\Delta) = 0\}} \tag{4}$$

(where Δ_u is the structured uncertainty mentioned earlier), for all $\Delta_u(s)$ with $\|\Delta_u(s)\|_\infty < 1/\beta$, and $\beta>0$, the loop of previous figure is internally stable and $\|F_l(M,\Delta_u)\|_\infty < \beta$ if and only if

$$\sup_{\omega \in R} \mu_{\Delta}(M(j\omega)) \leq \beta \tag{5}$$

Therefore, given a controller K(s), μ-bound β can be numerically computed. Finally μ-synthesis framework can be represented through the following scheme.

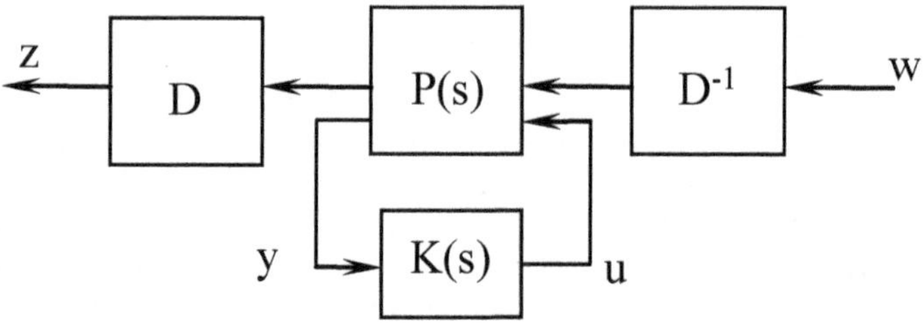

Fig. 5. μ-Synthesis via scaling

where *D* matrix allows scaling the process taking into account structured uncertainties from *z* to *w*. A commonly used methodology to solve the above problem is DK-iterations algorithm (Zhou & Doyle, 1998) that sequentially performs two parameter minimization: first minimizing over *K* with *D* fixed, then minimizing over *D* with *K* fixed, then again over *K*, and again over *D*, etc. The algorithm runs until a fixed bound is achieved and final *K* is the desired controller.

2.3 Fuzzy scheduling

Each controller developed using the technique described in the previous sections can be considered as a "local" controller, since it might not guarantee the same performances "far away" from design point (or outside a given region of flight envelope). If that region does not cover flight envelope of interest, a controller scheduling is necessary.

Many techniques and methodology have been investigated in literature (Nichols et al., 1993; Pedrycz & Peters, 1997; Hyde & Glover, 1993), but no one guarantees that scheduled controller provides robust performance to be achieved by closed loop system.

In (Pedrycz & Peters, 1997), authors present a general approach to a fuzzy interpolation of different LTI controllers. Although controllers are PID with different gains, the technique can be easily generalized to more complex LTI systems.

For what concerns application of fuzzy scheduling for the proposed DTFT application, a sort of fuzzy gain scheduling technique has been implemented using an approach similar to the one described in (Pedrycz & Peters, 1997).

Considering a system with dynamics described by the following equations:

$$\begin{aligned} \dot{x} &= f(x(t),u(t)) \\ y &= g(x(t),u(t)) \\ x &\in R^n, u \in R^r, y \in R^m \end{aligned} \tag{6}$$

and a family of equilibrium points (x_{ei}, y_{ei}, u_{ei}), with i=1, 2, ..., c. System linearization leads to the following linear system:

$$\begin{aligned} \dot{\tilde{x}} &= A_i\tilde{x} + B_i\tilde{u} \\ \tilde{y} &= C_i\tilde{x} + D_i\tilde{u} \end{aligned} \tag{7}$$

For each linearized model it is possible to design a local (linear) controller, L1, L2, …, Lc, on which the overall control laws will be based. Let Ω_1, Ω_2, .. Ω_c be fuzzy relations whose activation levels require specific control actions; the computations of control are then regulated by smooth, centre of gravity type of switching:

$$u = \frac{\sum_{i=1}^{c} Li\left(y * \frac{\Omega_i(x,u_{ei})}{\sum_{i=1}^{c}\Omega_i(x,u_{ei})} \right) * \Omega_i(x,u_{ei})}{\sum_{i=1}^{c}\Omega_i(x,u_{ei})} \tag{8}$$

3. Adaptive control system

Direct Adaptive Model Following (DAMF) is a Model Reference Control Strategy with strong robustness properties obtained through the use of direct adaptation of control loop gains in order to achieve a twofold objective: zero error between output of reference model and output of real plant and furthermore minimization of control effort. The proposed adaptation algorithm is based on Lyapunov theory. Hereinafter a brief mathematical description of the method, fully reported in (Kim et al., 2003), will be given. Starting from generic linear model of a plant:

$$\begin{aligned} \dot{x} &= Ax + Bu + d \\ y &= Cx \end{aligned} \tag{9}$$

where $x \in \Re^n$ is the state vector, $y \in \Re^l$ the output vector, $u \in \Re^m$ the control vector, $A \in \Re^{nxn}$, $B \in \Re^{nxm}$, $C \in \Re^{lxn}$ and the term d represents the trim data, reference system dynamics are written in term of desired input-output behaviour:

$$\dot{y}_m = A_m y_m + B_m r \tag{10}$$

where y_m is the desired output for the plant, r is the reference signal, A_m and B_m represent the reference linear system dynamics. Control laws structure is defined as:

$$u = C_0\left(G_0 x + v + r + K_0 y_m\right) \tag{11}$$

where G_0, C_0 and v are adaptive control gains, while K_0 is a feed-forward gain matrix off-line computed. It is possible to demonstrate that the following adaptation rules for control laws parameters:

$$\begin{aligned} \dot{G}_0 &= -\gamma_1 B_m^T P e x^T \\ \dot{C}_0 &= -\gamma_2 C_0 B_m^T P e u^T C_0 \\ \dot{v}_0 &= -\gamma_3 B_m^T P e \end{aligned} \tag{12}$$

imply the non-positiveness of Lyapunov candidate function derivative:

$$\dot{V} = -e^T P e \leq 0 \tag{13}$$

which guarantees the asymptotical stability for the error dynamic system (Kim et al., 2003). Matrix P is the solution of Lyapunov equation:

$$A_e^T P + P A_e = -Q; \quad \text{with } Q > 0 \tag{14}$$

With reference to the implementation of adaptive technique for DTFT1 benchmark application, detailed scheme of MIMO controller is reported in Fig. 6. The design parameters of both inner and outer loops consist of a few number of matrices. First of all, Reference Dynamics are expressed by means of two matrices A_m and B_m with limitation that B_m must be chosen invertible. Desired error dynamic is regulated by means of A_e. Through this matrix it is also possible to modify system capability to reject noise and disturbances, thus defining the shape of closed loop system bandwidth. The matrix Q in Eq. (14) is used to specify tracking performance requirements of output variables. Finally, parameters $\gamma 1$, $\gamma 2$ and $\gamma 3$ are used to regulate the adaptive capability of control gains. Large values imply quick adaptivity and vice versa.

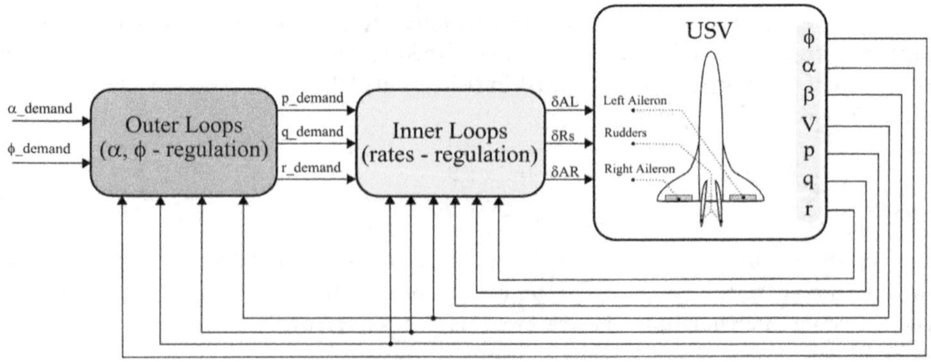

Fig. 6. The general scheme of control system architecture

Control architecture depicted in Fig. 6 is made of two MIMO control loops. The inner one is referred to the rates (p, q, r) regulation, while the outer one is used to control both angle of

attack (α) and roll angle (ϕ). Either MIMO controllers are designed with Adaptive Model Following (AMF) control technique above described.
In the following table a brief description of which variables have been used for the design of both inner and outer loops is given.

	y	x	r	u
inner loops	p, q, r	$v_{TAS}, \alpha, \beta, p, q, r$	$p_{DEM}, q_{DEM}, r_{DEM}$	$\delta_{AL}, \delta_{AR}, \delta_R$
outer loops	α, ϕ	$v_{TAS}, \alpha, \beta, \phi$	α_{DEM}, ϕ_{DEM}	$p_{DEM}, q_{DEM}, r_{DEM}$

Table 1. Controller Variables

4. Probabilistic robust controller

Within the stochastic paradigm for control system design/analysis, the meaning of robustness is moved from its well known deterministic sense to a probabilistic one. Indeed, it is claimed that a certain property of a control system is "almost" robustly satisfied, if it holds for "most" of the occurrences of uncertain variables. In other words, a risk that this property is violated by a set of uncertainties with small probability measure is considered acceptable.
Nevertheless, from a computational point of view, assessing probabilistic robustness of a given property may be more difficult than the deterministic case, since it requires the computation of a multi-dimensional probability integral. This problem is overcome by means of randomized algorithms which estimate performance probability by randomly sampling the uncertainty space, and computing bounds on the estimation error. Since estimated probability is itself a random quantity, this method always entails a certain risk of failure, i.e. there exists a nonzero probability of making an erroneous estimation. These algorithms have low complexity and are associated to robustness bounds which are less conservative than classical ones, obviously at the expense of a non deterministic result.
Randomization can be effectively used for control synthesis, by means of two different approaches. The first one aims at designing controllers that satisfy a given performance specification for most values of uncertainties, i.e. that are robust in a probabilistic sense, while the second one aims at finding a controller that maximizes the mean value of performance index, thus in the latter case the objective is to obtain a controlled system that guarantees the best performance on average (Tempo et al., 2005). For what concerns the use of this technique for DTFT1 benchmark application, the second approach has been used.
The approach used for controller synthesis was to look for a controller that (probabilistically) minimizes the mean value of the performance index, thus the objective was to obtain a controlled system that guarantees the best performance *on average*.
Performance function for the uncertain system is first defined:

$$\mathrm{u}(\Delta) : \Delta \rightarrow \Re \tag{15}$$

the above function gives a measure of system performance for a given value of uncertainty Δ. In this application the function u is the following Boolean function which represents the "failure" of a given controller, that is,

$$u(\Delta) = \begin{cases} 1 & \textit{if}\ \text{a given system property is not satisifed} \\ 0 & \text{otherwise} \end{cases} \tag{16}$$

Controller C_{opt} will be the one guaranteeing that the expected value of performance function u(Δ,C) is minimized:

$$C_{prob} = \arg \min_{c \in \mathbf{C}} E\left[\mathrm{u}(\Delta,C)\right] \tag{17}$$

An approximate solution can be obtained by means of randomized algorithms which are based on sampling both uncertainty set Δ and controller set C. To this end, two separate problem need to be solved: first, an estimate of the expected value is computed, then this estimate is minimized.

Computation of $E\left[\mathrm{u}(\Delta,C)\right]$ is carried out through randomization, that is, M independent, identically distributed (i.i.d.) controllers $C^1, C^2, \ldots, C^M \in \mathbf{C}$ are extracted according to their probability density function $f_C(C)$; an estimation of the minimum value is then given by:

$$\min_{i=1,2,\ldots,M} E\left[\mathrm{u}\left(\Delta,C^i\right)\right] \tag{18}$$

It is possible to demonstrate (Tempo et al., 2005) that, given $\varepsilon_1 \in [0,1]$, and $\delta \in [0,1]$, if

$$M \geq \frac{\log \frac{1}{\delta}}{\log \frac{1}{1-\varepsilon_1}} \tag{19}$$

then:

$$\mathrm{Prob}\left\{\mathrm{Prob}\left\{E\left[\mathrm{u}(\Delta,C)\right] \leq \min_{i=1,2,\ldots,M} E\left[\mathrm{u}\left(\Delta,C^i\right)\right]\right\} \leq \varepsilon_1\right\} \geq 1-\delta \tag{20}$$

As it can be noticed, computation of $E\left[\mathrm{u}\left(\Delta,C^i\right)\right]$ for each C^i requires the execution of a multidimensional integral, that is very difficult in general; also this problem is solved by randomization approach.

For what concerns estimation of the expected value $E\left[\mathrm{u}\left(\Delta,C^i\right)\right]$ of performance function, N i.i.d. samples $\Delta^1, \Delta^2, \ldots \Delta^N$ are extracted from **Δ**, according to their density function f_Δ; performance functions $\mathrm{u}(\Delta^1,C^1), \ldots, \mathrm{u}(\Delta^1,C^i)$ are then computed for a fixed controller $C^i \in \mathbf{C}$, and an estimation $\hat{E}_N\left[\mathrm{u}\left(\Delta,C^i\right)\right]$ of the expected value $E\left[\mathrm{u}\left(\Delta,C^i\right)\right]$ is given by:

$$\hat{E}_N\left[\mathrm{u}\left(\Delta,C^i\right)\right] = \frac{1}{N}\sum_{k=1}^{N} \mathrm{u}\left(\Delta^k,C^i\right) \tag{21}$$

It can be demonstrated (Tempo et al., 2005) that, if:

$$N \geq \frac{\log \frac{2}{\delta}}{2\varepsilon_2^2} \tag{22}$$

then:

$$\text{Prob}\left\{\left|E\left[\text{u}\left(\Delta,C^i\right)\right]-\hat{E}_N\left[\text{u}\left(\Delta,C^i\right)\right]\right|\le\varepsilon\right\}\ge 1-\delta \tag{23}$$

In order to compute a probabilistic controller, equations (20) and (23) must be put together. To this end, it can be shown that, for any $\varepsilon_1, \varepsilon_2 \in [0,1]$ and $\delta \in [0,1]$, if

$$M \ge \frac{\log\frac{1}{\delta}}{\log\frac{1}{1-\varepsilon_1}} \quad \text{and} \quad N \ge \frac{\log\frac{2M}{\delta}}{2\varepsilon_2^2} \tag{24}$$

then

$$\text{Prob}\left\{\text{Prob}\left\{E\left[\text{u}\left(\Delta,C\right)\right]\le \min_{i=1,2,\dots,M} \hat{E}_N\left[\text{u}\left(\Delta,C^i\right)\right]-\varepsilon_2\right\}\le\varepsilon_1\right\}\ge 1-\frac{\delta}{2} \tag{25}$$

The randomized probabilistic controller is given by:

$$\hat{C}_{NM} = \arg\min_{i=1,\dots,M}\frac{1}{N}\sum_{k=1}^{N}u\left(\Delta^k,C^i\right) \tag{26}$$

Eq. (25) states that the estimated minimum $\min_{i=1,2,\dots,M}\hat{E}_N\left[\text{u}\left(\Delta,C^i\right)\right]$ is "close" to the actual one $E\left[\text{u}\left(\Delta,C_{prob}\right)\right]$ within ε_2 in terms of probability, and this is guaranteed with an accuracy ε□ and a confidence level at least δ/2.

For what concerns the implementation of the above technique to the benchmark application, a fixed control system architecture (inherited from GNC system of DTFT1) has been chosen and its parameters have been optimized according to a stochastic technique. Since controller gains are scheduled with dynamic pressure, controller design have been carried out by optimizing scheduling parameters through stochastic synthesis.

In particular, once the controller structure is defined, stochastic optimization allows selecting the optimum controller parameters also accounting for all the uncertain parameters, mainly vehicle and environment ones. For each candidate vector of control parameters, success rate is computed according to a pre-specified figure of merit and the applied uncertainties. To this end, a first test is performed considering nominal conditions, i.e. no uncertainties applied. If the considered controller passes the test in nominal conditions, uncertainty region is sampled and, for each uncertainty sample, the nonlinear test is repeated and success rate is computed. For this application, the following test success criteria have been used:

- No instability (identified as commands oscillation along the trajectory) occurring during the trajectory.
- No Out-of-Range commands deflection (Max. ± 25° for the elevons, ± 20° for the rudder);
- Satisfactory tracking performances for tracked variables (1° RMS in α and β, 3° RMS in ϕ);
- Valid aerodynamic data during the trajectory (α ∈ [-5 ÷ 18°], β ∈ [-8 ÷ 8°]).

5. Numerical analysis

In this section the results of a numerical analysis carried out in order to compare performance and robustness of the developed control systems will be presented. The activity has been carried out in the framework of Unmanned Space Vehicle (USV) program of Italian Aerospace Research Centre (CIRA), which is in charge of developing unmanned space Flying Test Beds (FTB) to test advanced technologies during flight. The first USV Dropped Transonic Flight Test (named DTFT1) was accomplished in February 2007 with the first vehicle configuration of USV program (named FTB1) (Russo et al., 2007). In this mission, a conventional control architecture was implemented. DTFT1 was then used as a benchmark application for comparison among different advanced control techniques. This comparison aimed at choosing the most suited control technique to be used for subsequent dropped flight test, named DTFT2, carried out on April 2010.
In the figure below the trajectory of DTFT1 mission in the plane Mach-altitude is depicted.

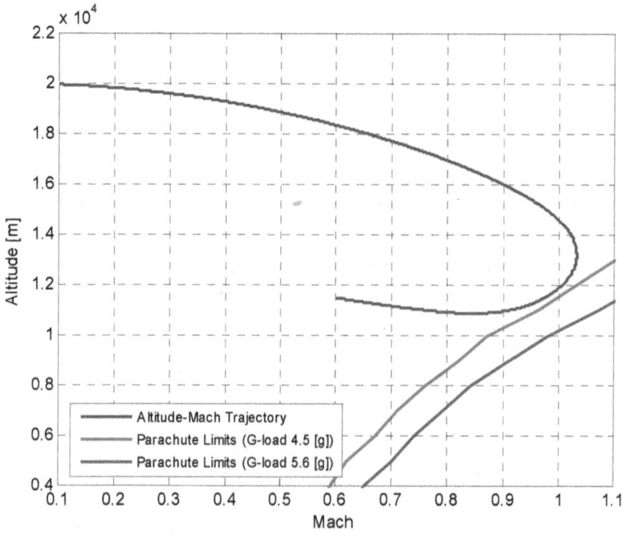

Fig. 7. Mach-Altitude Trajectory

For what concerns control performances, they are specified in the next table and they are valid only for Mach>0.7 (transonic regime):

Variable Tracked	Tracked Value [deg]	RMS Accuracy [deg]
Angle of Attack	7	1
Angle of Sideslip	0	1
Roll angle	0	3

Table 2. Tracked Variables

In order to compare the advanced controllers described in previous sections, the following scenarios have been identified:

- robustness to parametric uncertainties, namely aerodynamic ones
- robustness to initial state displacement
- robustness to navigation errors (sensor noise)
- robustness to actuator failures

Within this framework, control laws robustness is the capability of guaranteeing performances and stability of control systems in presence of above uncertainties.
Numerical evaluation reported in this section have been carried out using a complete 6 Dof model of FTB1 vehicle together with Atmospheric Model, wind model, Hydraulic Actuator System, Air Data System, Inertial Measurement System and control laws.
Parametric uncertainties have been accounted for by considering a particular aerodynamic configuration (hereafter called the worst configuration) which was identified as the aerodynamic uncertainty configuration leading to worst dynamic behaviour of FTB1 vehicle, in terms of stability, damping and control derivatives that mainly affect stability properties.
Two test cases, named C_0, and $\hat{C}_0$, have been accomplished with both nominal conditions (nominal initial state, zero navigation errors, no failure, etc.) and worst aerodynamic configuration respectively.
For what concerns robustness to initial state displacement, several off-nominal conditions in terms of Euler angles and angular rates have been considered (see the following table). Nominal DTFT1 initial state in terms of attitude, heading and angular rates is: $\phi_0 = 0$ deg, $\theta_0 = -90$ deg, $\psi = 0$ deg, $p = 0$ deg/s, $q = 0$ deg/s, $r = 0$ deg/s.

Initial State Displacement	ϕ_0 [deg]	θ_0 [deg]	ψ_0 [deg]	p_0 [deg/s]	q_0 [deg/s]	r_0 [deg/s]
I_1	-20	-89.9	0	-5	3	-3
I_2	20	-89.9	0	2	2	-2
I_3	20	-89.9	0	5	2	1
I_4	0	-85	0	-5	2	0

Table 3. Initial State Displacement

Furthermore for each case of the above table, nominal (case $C_1 - C_4$) and worst aerodynamic configuration (case $C_5 - C_8$) have been simulated.
For what concerns navigation errors, simulations have been performed with both nominal (case C_9) and worst aerodynamic configuration (case C_{10}) without any initial state have displacement.
As far as robustness to actuator failures is concerned, a rudder failure occurring after 30 s from vehicle's drop has been simulated, in particular a jam of the right rudder. It is worth noting that in this case (C_{11}) both initial state and aerodynamic configuration are nominal. All the benchmark scenarios are summarized in the following table.

Case	Aerodynamic Configuration	Initial State	Navigation Errors	Actuator Failure
C_0	Nominal	Nominal	No errors	No failure
$\hat{C}_0$	Worst-Aero 1	Nominal	No errors	No failure
C_1	Nominal	Off-nominal I_1	No errors	No failure
C_2	Nominal	Off-nominal I_2	No errors	No failure
C_3	Nominal	Off-nominal I_3	No errors	No failure
C_4	Nominal	Off-nominal I_4	No errors	No failure
C_5	Worst-Aero	Off-nominal I_1	No errors	No failure
C_6	Worst-Aero	Off-nominal I_2	No errors	No failure
C_7	Worst-Aero	Off-nominal I_3	No errors	No failure
C_8	Worst-Aero	Off-nominal I_4	No errors	No failure
C_9	Nominal	Nominal	Errors	No failure
C_{10}	Worst-Aero	Nominal	Errors	No failure
C_{11}	Nominal	Nominal	No errors	Right Rudder jamming at 30 s

Table 4. Benchmark Scenarios for Perfomance Evaluation

For what concerns robust performance indicators, tracking accuracy of trajectory has been defined as a performance parameter. Performance requirements are given in the table below:

Variable Tracked	RMS Tracking error [deg]
Angle of Attack	±1
Angle of Sideslip	±1
Roll angle	±3

Table 5. Tracking Performance requirements

In the next figures the results of scenarios C_0 and $\hat{C}_0$ are reported.

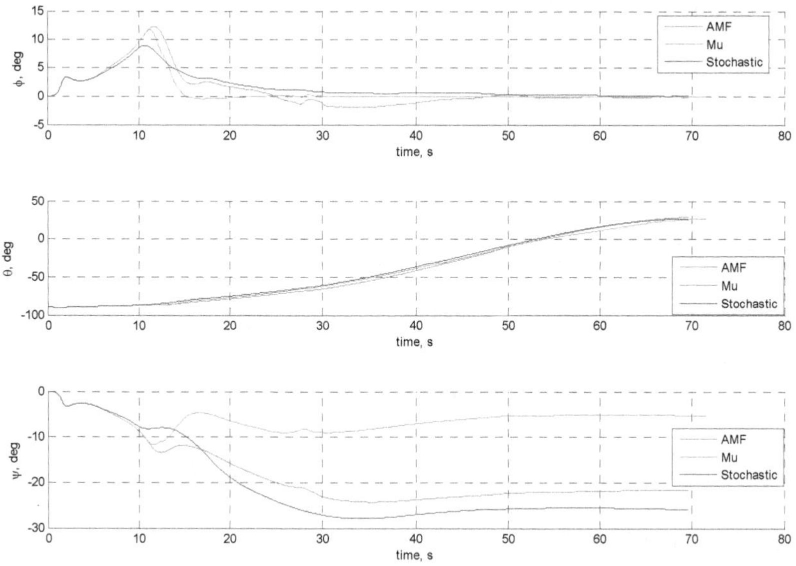

Fig. 8. Case C_0 -Euler Angles

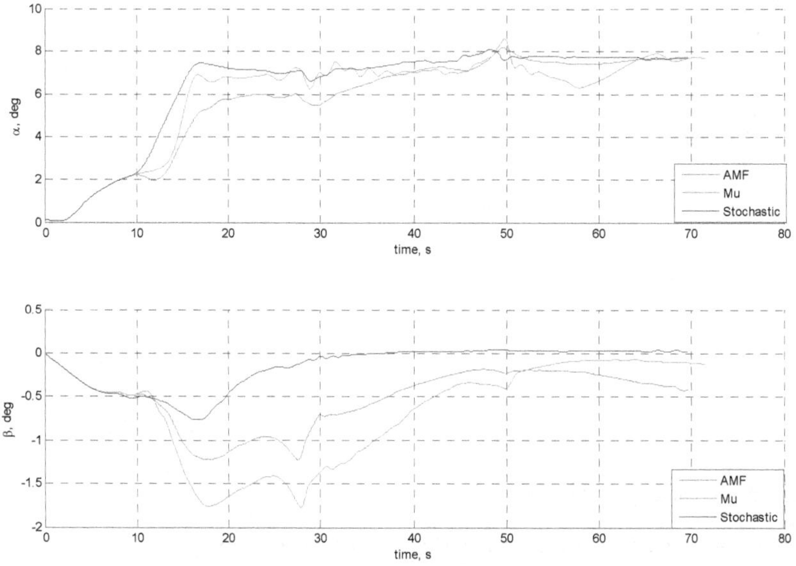

Fig. 9. Case C_0 -Incidence Angles

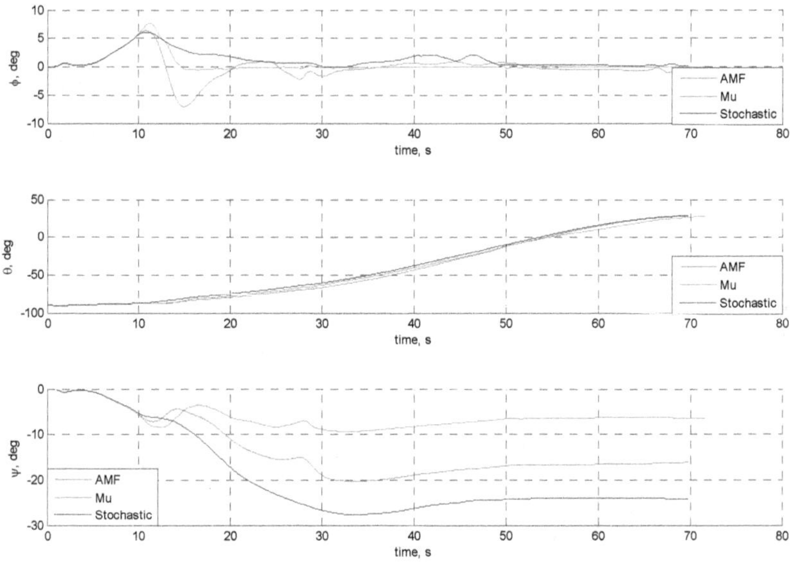

Fig. 10. Case $\hat{C}_0$ -Euler Angles

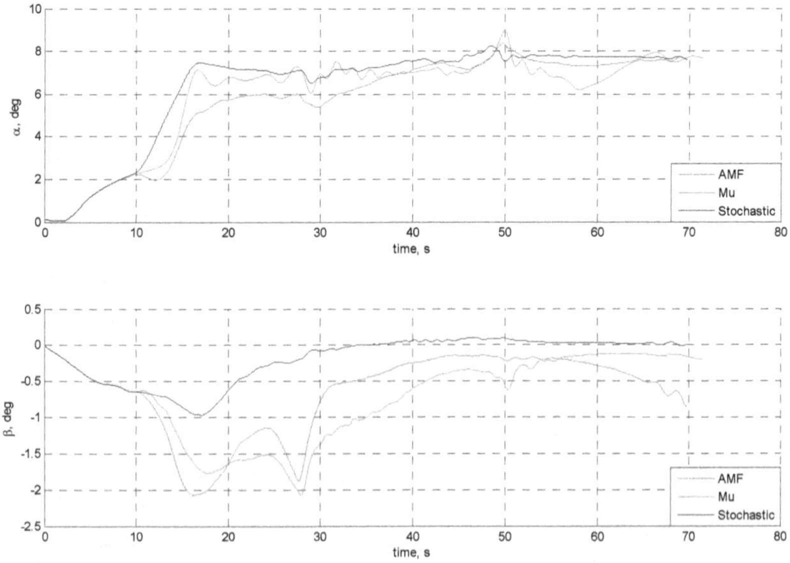

Fig. 11. Case $\hat{C}_0$ -Incidence Angles

As it can be seen from the figures, performances of all control algorithms are globally satisfactory. It is worth noting that Mu-controller shows a light unstable behaviour on sideslip angle around 50 s in worst case configuration, but it is however rapidly damped in few seconds. For what concerns uncertainties to initial state displacement, several cases have been considered with different attitude and angular velocity at vehicle drop. In the following figures, for sake of brevity, only the cases C_5 and C_8 are reported. They refer to initial state conditions I_1 and I_4 with worst aerodynamic configuration (see Table 4).

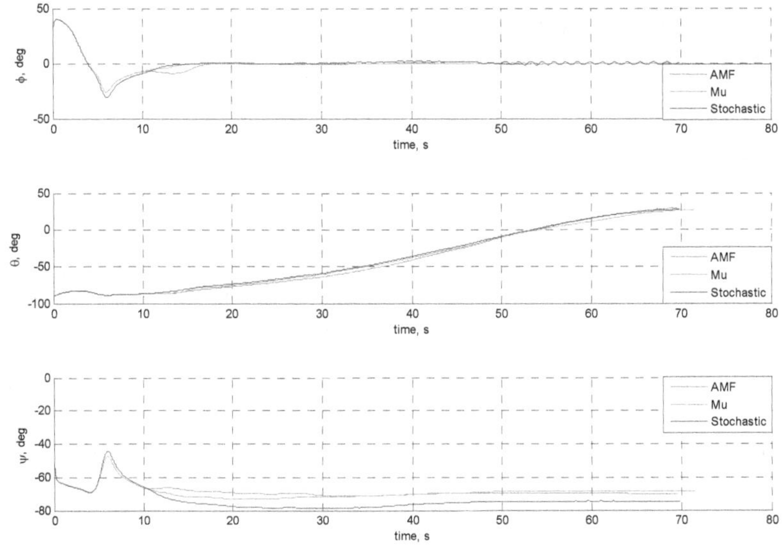

Fig. 12. Case C_5 -Euler Angles

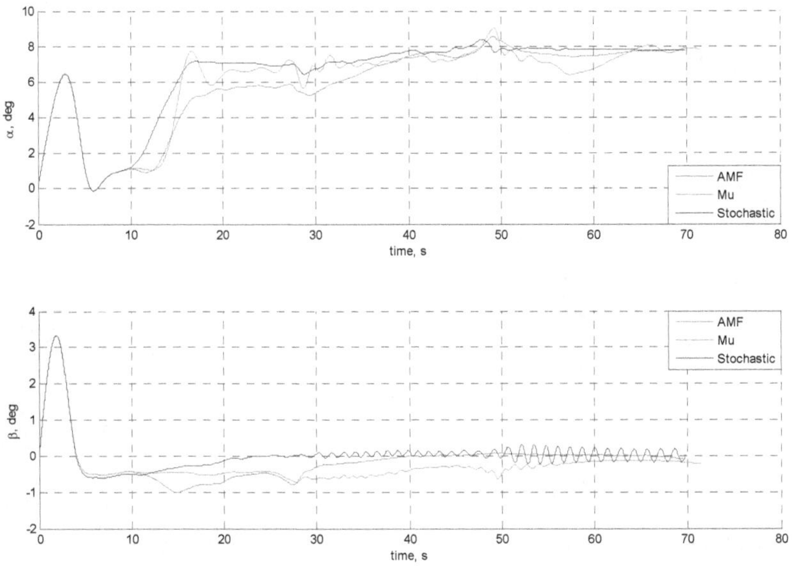

Fig. 13. Case C_5 -Incidence Angles

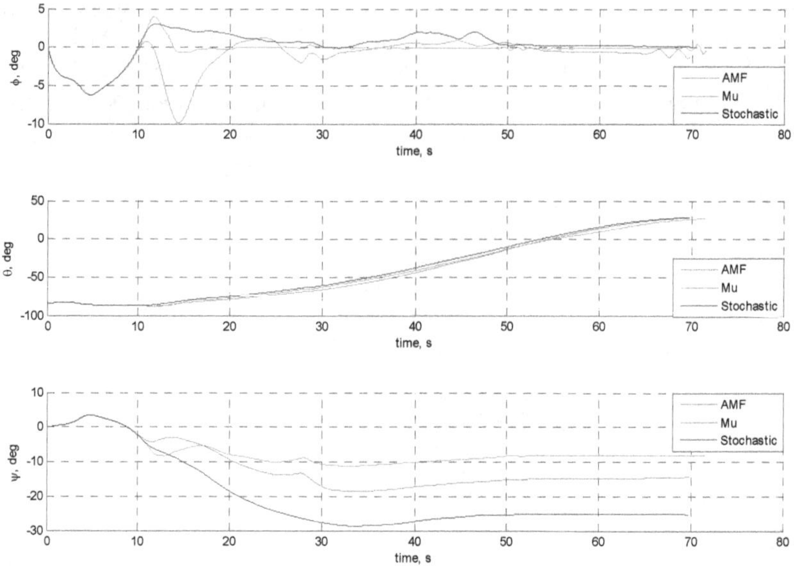

Fig. 14. Case C_8 -Euler Angles

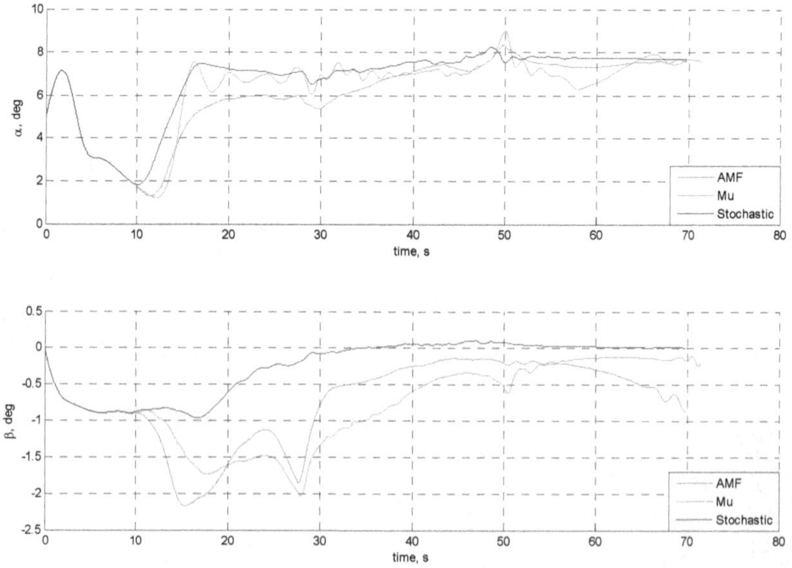

Fig. 15. Case C_8 -Incidence Angles

All controllers satisfactory work in presence of initial state displacement. In spite of a light oscillatory mode on sideslip and roll angles, stochastic controller guarantees very good performances for what concerns tracking of sideslip angle and angle of attack.

As mentioned earlier, in order to evaluate control algorithms capabilities to face disturbances such as navigation errors, two test cases have been considered, i.e. nominal and worst aerodynamic configuration (cases C_9 and C_{10}) without any initial state displacement. The comparison between controllers is reported in the following figure, only with reference to the case C_{10} for sake of simplicity.

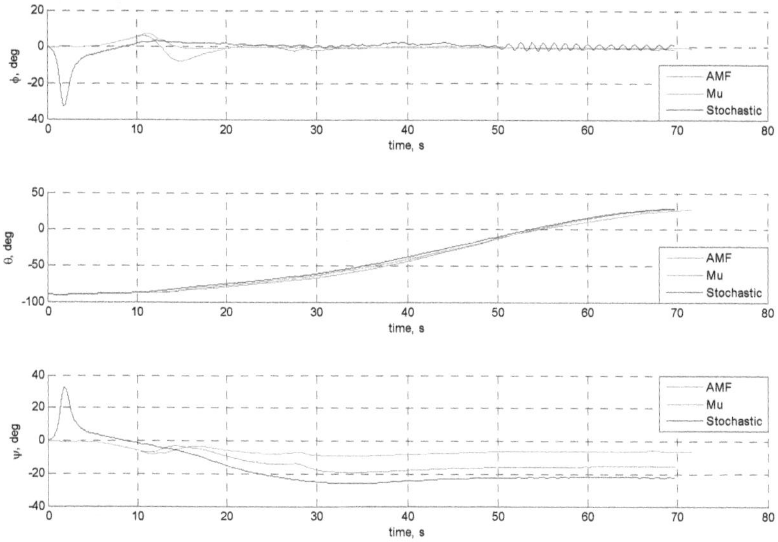

Fig. 16. Case C_{10} -Euler Angles

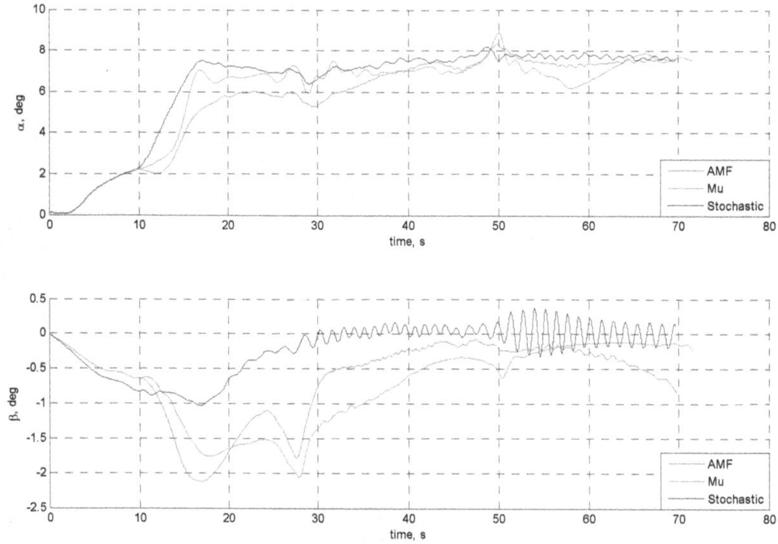

Fig. 17. Case C_{10} -Incidence Angles

Simulations show an acceptable robustness to sensor noise. A small effect on incidence angles, in terms of reduced damping, is shown by stochastic controller.
Finally algorithms robustness to an actuator failure has been evaluated. In particular a rudder jamming at t=30 s has been simulated.

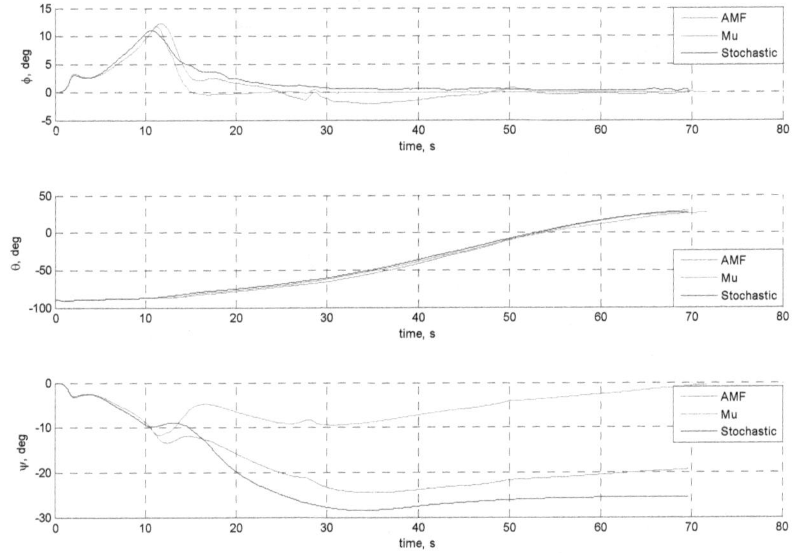

Fig. 18. Case C_{11} -Euler Angles

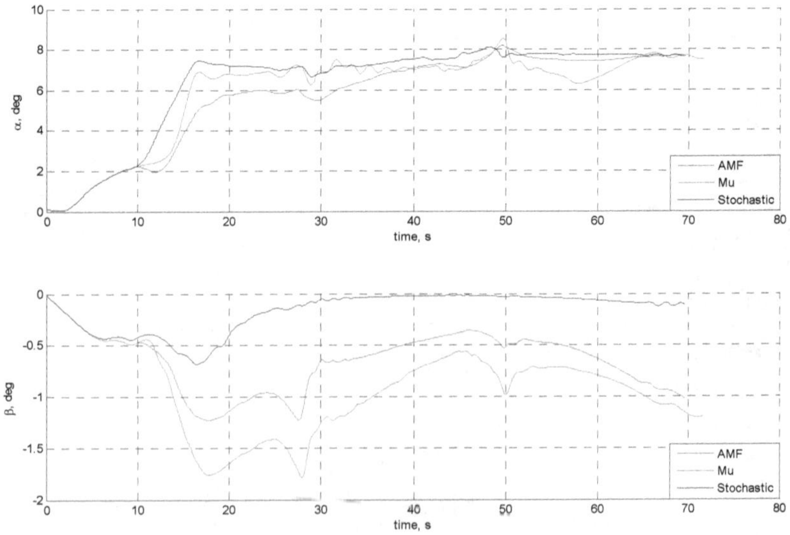

Fig. 19. Case C_{11} -Incidence Angles

The above figures show that rudder jam failure is well tolerated by all the controllers.
The following table summarizes the performances achieved by the controllers for all considered scenarios.

Case	**Adaptive Controller** AoA-AoS-Phi accuracy [deg]	**MU-Controller** AoA-AoS-Phi accuracy [deg]	**Stochastic Controller** AoA-AoS-Phi accuracy [deg]
C_0	0.87676 0.5969 0.72448	0.57129 0.88441 0.053638	0.21606 0.13512 0.61134
$\hat{C}_0$	0.90016 0.74635 0.59708	0.62284 0.91081 0.067061	0.24501 0.18806 0.8251
C_1	0.88835 0.26603 0.45265	0.5642 0.63046 0.061391	0.21624 0.066145 0.42644
C_2	0.88043 0.58375 0.75665	0.57188 0.97939 0.089979	0.21585 0.14444 0.64976
C_3	0.87282 0.62874 0.71016	0.57878 0.83847 0.038177	0.21536 0.13685 0.63915
C_4	0.86873 0.593 0.71128	0.53892 0.87025 0.05387	0.21588 0.13086 0.59952
C_5	0.91649 0.29559 0.35717	0.62481 0.40438 0.14435	0.2452 0.1115 1.1254
C_6	0.91255 0.75401 0.69885	0.62265 1.0448 0.13026	0.24415 0.20172 0.82289
C_7	0.89565 0.73756 0.66584	0.6301 0.84141 0.044825	0.24409 0.18635 0.76552
C_8	0.8919 0.74122 0.59849	0.59116 0.89455 0.10033	0.24443 0.18392 0.82521
C_9	0.87611 0.60085 0.7007	0.57183 0.88728 0.053653	0.22299 0.15436 0.61589
C_{10}	0.90059 0.74182 0.57556	0.62011 0.91444 0.061636	0.25904 0.23867 1.2075
C_{11}	0.8759 0.72793 0.80693	0.57115 1.0664 0.066715	0.20854 0.12598 0.65093

Table 6. Controller Perfromances

The comparison between the controllers has shown that:

1. Stochastic controller guarantees the best performances for what concerns the tracking of AoA and AoS and it always meets performance requirements. Anyway, it presents some light oscillations on lateral and directional dynamics in worst aerodynamic configuration.
2. μ-controller guarantees the best tracking performance in terms of roll angle, much better than required (3 deg error), but in some cases it fails to meet performance requirements on AoA and AoS (see C_6 and C_{11}).
3. Adaptive Controller guarantees almost good tracking performances even though they are never better than the other two controllers. In any case, performance requirements are always met.

Based on the above considerations, the controller obtained by means of stochastic synthesis was considered the most suited for the DTFT2 scopes, so it was selected (after a fine tuning) as a part of an advanced GNC system for DTFT2 mission, successfully carried out on April 2010.

In fact, despite the limitation of using an 'a priori' fixed control structure, control laws obtained though the stochastic synthesis have the following good features:

- excellent performances and good stability properties in spite of large uncertainties affecting the system;
- simple control structures while guaranteeing robust performances and stability as well as low computational effort and implementation simplicity.

6. Conclusions

Over the last decades many efforts have been spent to develop advanced control techniques for aerospace applications, aimed at overcoming limitations of commonly used control techniques, mainly lack of robustness against various uncertainties affecting the system to be controlled. The importance of a robust control system is readily understood when space reentry applications are considered. Indeed, these applications have some distinctive features, mainly related to the lack of stationary equilibrium conditions along the trajectories, to the wide flight envelope characterizing the missions (from hypersonic flight regime to subsonic one) and to the high level of uncertainty in the knowledge of vehicle aerodynamic parameters.

The development of an advanced control system having robustness capabilities is one of the goals of research activities carried out by Italian Aerospace Research Centre in the framework of USV program. In order to select a control strategy having the advantages above discussed, three candidate control techniques have been compared with the aim of selecting the most suited one for the second dropped flight test of USV program, named DTFT2, successfully carried out on April 2010. The three techniques are:

- μ-Controller with Fuzzy Logic Gain-Scheduling
- Direct Adaptive Model Following Control
- Probabilistic Robust Control Synthesis

In order to evaluate the robustness capabilities of proposed control algorithms, a numerical robustness analysis has been performed. Performances and stability of candidate control techniques have been evaluated in presence of several sources of uncertainties (aerodynamics, initial state, etc.) and failure scenarios.

Robustness analysis showed that all three techniques are well suited to accomplish robust control in USV DTFT1 mission, in presence of large parameters uncertainty (the vehicle mostly flies in transonic regime, where accurate aerodynamic prediction is very difficult to obtain).
Nevertheless the controller obtained by means of stochastic synthesis was selected as a part of on-board advanced GNC system for DTFT2 mission, due to its good performances and relatively simple implementation.

7. References

Ashari E. A. et al. (2005), Reconfigurable control system design using eigenstructure assignment: static, dynamic and robust approaches; International Journal of Control, vol. 78, No. 13, 10 September 2005, 1005-1016

Balas Gary J. (2005), Application of Robust Multivariable Control to Stability, Control Augmentation and Trajectory Tracking of Unmanned Space and Aerial Vehicle, CIRA Short course, 14-18 November 2005

Bharadwaj, S. Rao, Anil V., and Mease, Kenneth D. (1998), Entry Trajectory Tracking Law via Feedback Linearization, Journal of Guidance, Control, and Dynamics, Vol. 21, No. 5, September–October 1998

Bodson M., Groszkiewicz J.E. (1997), Multivariable Adaptive Algorithms for Reconfigurable Flight Control; IEEE Transactions on Control Systems Technology, vol. 5, No. 2, March 1997.

Calafiore G., Dabbene F., Tempo R. (2007), A survey of randomized algorithms for control synthesis and performance verification, Journal of Complexity 23 (2007), pp. 301-316

Hyde, A., Glover K. (1993), The Application of Scheduled H∞ Controllers to a VSTOL Aircraft, IEEE Transaction on Automatic Control, VOL. 38, NO. 7, July 1993. 1021-1039

Kim K., Lee K., Kim Y. (2003), Reconfigurable Flight Control System Design Using Direct Adaptive Method, Journal of Guidance, Control, and Dynamics, Vol. 26, N° 4, July-August 2003

Konstantopoulos K., Antsaklis P. (1996), Eigenstructure Assignment in Reconfigurable Control Systems, Technical Report of the ISIS group at the University of Notre Dame, ISIS-96-001, January, 1996

Liu, G. P. and Patton, R. J. (1996), Robust Parametric Eigenstructure Assignment, AIAA-96-3908

Malloy, D., and Chang, B.C. (1998), Stabilizing Controller Design for Linear Parameter-Varying Systems Using Parameter Feedback, Journal of Guidance, Control, and Dynamics, Vol. 21, No. 6, November–December 1998

Marcos, A., and Balas, Gary J. (2004), Development of Linear Parameter Varying Models for Aircraft, Journal of Guidance, Control, and Dynamics, Vol. 27, No. 2, March 2004

Nichols, A., Reichert, R. T., W. J. Rugh (1993), Gain Scheduling for H-infinity Controllers: A Flight Control Example, IEEE Transactions on Control Systems Technology, Vol. 1, No. 2, June 1993.

Pedrycz, W., Peters J. F. (1997), Hierarchical Fuzzy Controllers: Fuzzy Gain Scheduling, IEEE Intern. Conf. on SMC[C], 1997.1139-1143

Rollins L. (1999), Robust Control Theory, Carnegie Mellon University, 18-849b Dependable Embedded Systems, Spring 1999

Russo, G., et al. (2007), Unmanned Space Vehicle Program: DTFT in Flight Experiments, 18th ESA Symposium on European Rocket and Balloon Programmes and Related Research, Visby, Sweden, 2007.

Spillman, Mark S. (2000), Robust Longitudinal Flight Control Design Using Linear Parameter-Varying Feedback, Journal of Guidance, Control, and Dynamics, Vol. 23, No. 1, January–February 2000

Tempo R. and Dabbene F. (1999), Probabilistic Robustness Analysis and Design of Uncertain Systems, in Dynamical Systems Control, Coding, Computer Vision - New Trends, Interfaces, and Interplay, ed. by Picci G. and Gilliam D.S., Birkhauser Verlag, 1999

Tempo, R., Calafiore, G., Dabbene, F. (2005), Randomized Algorithms for Analysis and Control of Uncertain Systems ; New York: Springer-Verlag, 2005.

Van Soest, W. R., Chu, Q. P. and Mulder, J. A. (2006), Combined Feedback Linearization and Constrained Model Predictive Control for Entry Flight, Journal of Guidance, Control, and Dynamics, Vol. 29, No. 2, March–April 2006

Vincent, James H., Abbas Emami-Naeinjt and Nasser M. Khraishi (1994), Case Study Comparison of Linear Quadratic Regulator and H∞ Control Synthesis, Journal Of Guidance, Control, And Dynamics, Vol. 17, No. 5, September-October 1994

Xing, L. (2003), Comparison of Pole Assignment & LQR Design Methods for Multivariable Control for STATCOM, Thesis submitted to the Department of Mechanical Engineering, Florida State University

Zhou , K., and Doyle, John C. (1998), Essential Of Robust Control, Prentice Hal, 1998

2

Fault Tolerant Depth Control of the MARES AUV

Bruno Ferreira, Aníbal Matos and Nuno Cruz
INESC Porto and University of Porto
Portugal

1. Introduction

Control theory has been applied to several domains where practical considerations are relevant. Robotics is a notable example of this. In most cases, mobile robotic systems are governed such that their behavior obeys to a defined motion. However, during their operations, it is conceivable that faults could occur. Indeed, this assumption has to be made in order to predict a possible malfunction and to take an appropriate action according to the fault, improving the robustness and the reliability of the system. This work tackles the problem of fault detection, identification and automatic reconfiguration of an autonomous underwater vehicle (AUV). Although our emphasis will be directed to an AUV, the methods and the tools that are employed in this chapter can be easily extended to other engineering problems beyond robotics.

In this work, we will consider the MARES (Modular Autonomous Robot for Environment Sampling) (Fig. 1) Cruz & Matos (2008); Matos & Cruz (2009), a small-sized (1.5 meters long), torpedo shaped AUV weighting 32 kg, able to move at constant velocities up to 2.5 m/s. Its four thrusters provide four degrees of freedom (DOF), namely surge, heave, pitch and yaw. One of its main particularities is the capability to dive independently of the forward motion. The vertical through-hull thrusters provide heave and pitch controllability, while the horizontal ones ensure the surge and the yaw DOFs. The heave and pitch DOFs make the vertical plane control redundant when the vehicle is moving with surge velocities different from zero. In other words, the vehicle remains controllable if only one of these two DOFs is available. Such characteristic will be explored along this chapter in which the control of the nonlinear dynamics of the AUV Ferreira, Matos, Cruz & Pinto (2010); Fossen (1994) constitutes a challenging problem.

By taking advantage of the distribution of the actuators on the vehicle, it is possible to decouple the horizontal and the vertical motion. A common approach in such systems is to consider reduced models in order to simplify the analysis and the derivation of the control law (see Ferreira, Matos, Cruz & Pinto (2010); Teixeira et al. (2010) or Fossen (1994), for example). In general, for topedo-shaped vehicles, coupling effects due to composed motions (e.g., simultaneous sway and heave motions) are clearly smaller than the self effects of decomposed motion (e.g., effect of the heave motion on the heave dynamics) and can therefore be considered disturbances in the reduced model in which they are not included. Thus, a reduced model will be considered to deal with the vertical motion taking surge, heave and pitch rate as state components.

In order to make the detection and identification of possible faults, we present a method based on process monitoring by estimating relevant state variables of the system. See Frank & Ding (1997) for an overview on several techniques andZhang & Jiang (2002) for an application to a particular linear system. Wu et al. (2000) have developed an algorithm based on the two-stage

Fig. 1. MARES starting a typical mission in the ocean

Kalman filter to estimate deviations from expected input actuation for a linear system. Their approach consists in estimating the *loss of control effectiveness factors* that are added as entries of the state estimate, while guaranteeing that the corresponding estimate covariance lies in a defined interval. By imposing boundaries on the corresponding eigenvalues, it is possible to avoid impetuous corrections or to be insensitive to measurements. Inspired on the work by Zhang & Jiang (2002) and Wu et al. (2000), the present paper describes the implementation of an augmented state extended Kalman filter (ASEKF) to estimate the effectiveness of the control commands, detect and identify the possible faults.

The present work focuses on the vertical motion considering faults on the vertical thrusters. The method for accomodation of the faults consists in three main steps: fault detection, fault diagnosis and decision. Fault detection is responsible for creating a warning whenever an abrupt or an incipient fault happens, while fault diagnosis distinguishes and identifies the fault. In the presence of faults, a decision must be taken, adopting a suitable control law to stabilize the vertical motion. In the presence of faults in one of the vertical thrusters, the heave motion will no longer be controllable. Consequently, a control law derived for normal operation could be inadequate or even turn the feedback system unstable when such a fault occurs. An algorithm has to be developed in order to make the behavior of the robotic system tolerant to faults.

Making use of the pitch angle controllability, we will derive two control laws to drive the vehicle to a depth reference, possibly time variant. To achieve so, we make use of the Lyapunov theory, adopting the backstepping method Khalil (2002). Nevertheless, the presence of biases in steady state shifts the error at equilibrium away from zero. Those biases are commonly induced by unmodeled, neglected effects or external disturbances whose values are hard to observe or to estimate. The introduction of an integral term, under some assumptions, would solve the problem allowing the error to converge to zero as time goes to infinity. Based on the conditional integrators, extended by Singh & Khalil (2005) to more general control framework beyond sliding mode control Seshagiri & Khalil (2005), we present a control law that makes it possible to achieve asymptotic regulation of the vehicle depth error when operating with only one thruster. The method considers an integral component in the control law derived in the backstepping first step.

Beyond the derivation and the particularization of the mathematical tools used here, we demonstrate our approach by illustrating the work with real experiments, voluntarily inducing faults on the system, and analyze the behavior of the dynamic system under such conditions.

The organization of the chapter is as follow: the section 2 describes the MARES AUV and presents the main mathematical models under consideration here, namely the kinematic and the dynamic models. In section 3, we introduce the relevant concepts and formulate the ASEKF from a reduced model of the vertical dynamics and describe how to identify the fault. In section 4, we derive the control law to drive the depth error to zero making use of the tools described above. Finally, in 5, our solution is demonstrated through real experiments.

2. MARES

The MARES autonomous underwater vehicle was developed in 2006 at the Faculty of Engineering of the University of Porto (FEUP). Typical operations have been performed in the ocean and fresh water, collecting relevant data for surveys and environmental monitoring during several tens of missions to date. Its configuration was specially designed to dive vertically in the water column while its horizontal motion is controlled independently, resulting in truly decoupled vertical and horizontal motions. Such characteristic is particularly appreciated in missions where the operation area is restricted or precise positioning is required. Parallel to the missions to collect data, the MARES AUV has also been used as a testbed for intensive research being performed in several problems related to robotics, specially on localization and control. Thus, besides the typical applications, several missions have been conducted to test and to verify implemented algorithms.

Before presenting our method to detect a possible fault and to control the vehicle under such situation, let us first introduce the kinematics and dynamics concepts and equations. We assume an inertial earth-fixed frame $\{I\} = \{x_I, y_I, z_I\}$, where $x_I, y_I, z_I \in \mathbb{R}^3$ are orthonormal vectors (in the marine literature, they are often made coincident with north, east and down directions, respectively), and a body-fixed frame $\{B\} = \{x_B, y_B, z_B\}$, where $x_B, y_B, z_B \in \mathbb{R}^3$ are orthonormal vectors frequently refered to as surge, sway and heave directions, respectively (see Fig. 2). The absolute position and orientation of the vehicle is expressed in the inertial frame $\{I\}$ through the vector $\eta_c = [\eta_1, \eta_2]^T = [x, y, z, \phi, \theta, \psi]^T$, where $\eta_2 = [\phi, \theta, \psi]^T$ is the vector of euler angles with respect to x_I, y_I and z_I, and $[x, y, z]$ are the coordinate of the frame $\{B\}$ expressed in $\{I\}$. The vehicle's velocity, expressed in the body frame $\{B\}$, is given by $\nu_c = [u, v, w, p, q, r]^T$, where p, q and r are the angular velocities along x_B, y_B and z_B, respectively. The velocities in both referentials are related through the kinematic equation Fossen (1994)

$$\dot{\eta}_c = J(\eta_2)\nu_c, \tag{1}$$

where $\dot{\eta}_c$ denotes the time derivative of η and $J(\eta_2) = block\,diag[J_1, J_2]$ represents the rotation matrix, with $J_1, J_2 \in \mathbb{R}^{3\times3}$. Although this transformation is common in the literature to map vectors from a referential frame to another, it is not the only one. An alternative can be found in quaternions (see Zhang (1997), for an introduction and useful results), avoiding the singularity problems of the matrix J_2. However, in this chapter, we will assume that the values of the angles that make the matrix J_2 singular (and J, consequently) are not reached. Moreover, since the water currents present in the ocean and in the rivers do not influence the development of the present work, they will not be considered for simplicity.

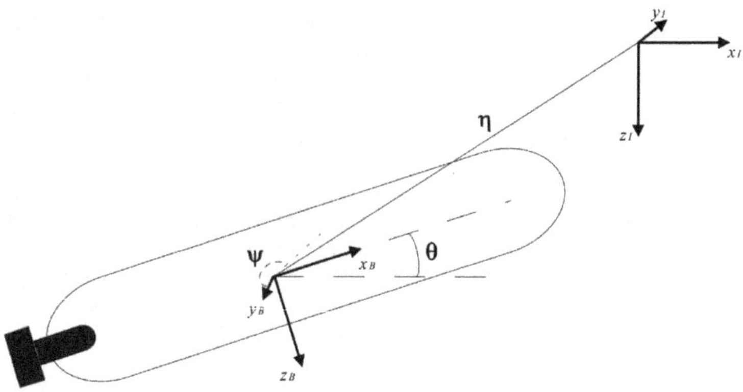

Fig. 2. Body frame and inertial frame referentials

As it is well known, rigid bodies moving in the three dimensional space are governed by nonlinear equations. For the particular case of underwater vehicles, such equations include the effect of the added mass, viscous damping, restoring and actuation forces and moments. Following the notation in Fossen (1994), the nonlinear second order, six dimensions equation is written as:

$$M_c\dot{\nu}_c = -C_c(\nu_c)\nu_c - D_c(\nu_c)\nu_c - g_c(\eta_c) + \tau_c \tag{2}$$

where $M_c \in \mathbb{R}^{6\times6}$ is the sum of the body inertia and added mass matrices, $C_c \in \mathbb{R}^{6\times6}$ results from the sum of the Coriolis and centrifugal terms from body inertia and added mass, $D_c \in \mathbb{R}^{6\times6}$ is the viscous damping matrix, $g_c \in \mathbb{R}^6$ is the vector of restoring forces and moments and $\tau_c \in \mathbb{R}^6$ is the vector of actuation forces and moments.

Such system is complex and the task of deriving control laws that ensure stability is not trivial, having led to order reduction in several works (see Ferreira, Matos, Cruz & IEEE (2010); Fossen (1994); Teixeira et al. (2010), for example). By taking advantage of the body shape symmetries and of the configuration of the actuators on the body, it is usual to decouple the complex motion in more elementary ones. However, this has consequences since some cross-coupling terms are eliminated but their influence is often small and can be neglected or considered disturbances. Such approach has been implemented in the MARES AUV and the corresponding performances were already demonstrated in Ferreira, Matos, Cruz & Pinto (2010). The current thruster configuration on the MARES makes it possible to decouple the motion into the vertical and the horizontal plane. Since the roll angle is stable (and $\phi \approx 0$) two reduced order models are extracted. See Ferreira, Matos, Cruz & Pinto (2010), for further details.

3. Fault detection and identification

Under normal operation, the vertical thrusters of MARES provide the capability to control almost independently the pitch and heave degrees of freedom (DOF). In the same way, the horizontal thrusters make possible the control on the surge and yaw DOFs. As it will be exposed later, the vehicle remains controllable if one of the vertical thrusters fails. As an aside, note that the same is not verified if one the two horizontal thrusters fails since the surge and the yaw motion can no longer be decoupled. The derivation of the control laws is left to the next section.

Several approaches for fault identification and detection have been proposed, commonly based on observation of the residuals Frank & Ding (1997) either by using state observers or by using accurate models. Our approach makes use of an extended Kalman filter to detect the faults, indirectly exploiting the residuals to estimate actuation bias variables additionally incorporated in the state. A similar approach was already carried out by Zhang & Jiang (2002) where they used a two stage Kalman filter to identify the faults on actuation of a linear system. The method presented here makes it possible not only to detect faults but also to identify the faulty actuator. By taking advantage of the cyclic predictions and corrections, the main idea behind our approach is to estimate the biases on the actuation (or deviation from the nominal value, commonly referred to as loss of control effectiveness factor in Wu et al. (2000); Zhang & Jiang (2002) whose values should theoretically equal zero when no fault is occuring.

3.1 Vertical plane dynamics

The implementation of the extended Kalman filter assumes the use of a reasonably accurate dynamics model that recreates mathematically the behavior of the system for the prediction step. As it was pointed out in the previous section, the use of the complete model of the vehicle dynamics is complex and computationally expensive. Thus, from 2, we derive the reduced model for the vertical motion, considering that cross-terms are negligible:

$$M\dot{\nu} = -C(\nu)\nu - D(\nu)\nu - g(\eta_2) + P_f \mathbf{f_t}(t) \tag{3}$$

where $\nu = [u, w, q]^T$ and

$$M = \begin{bmatrix} m - X_{\dot{u}} & 0 & -X_{\dot{q}} \\ 0 & m - Z_{\dot{w}} & -Z_{\dot{q}} \\ -M_{\dot{u}} & -M_{\dot{w}} & -M_{\dot{q}} \end{bmatrix}, \; C(\nu) = \begin{bmatrix} 0 & -mq & -Z_{\dot{w}}w - Z_{\dot{q}}q \\ -mq & 0 & X_{\dot{u}}u + X_{\dot{q}}q \\ Z_{\dot{w}}w + Z_{\dot{q}}q & -X_{\dot{u}}u - X_{\dot{q}}q & 0 \end{bmatrix},$$

$$D(\nu) = -\begin{bmatrix} X_{|u|u}|u| & 0 & X_{|q|q}|q| \\ 0 & Z_{|w|w}|w| & Z_{|q|q}|q| \\ M_{|u|u}|u| & M_{|w|w}|w| & M_{|q|q}|q| \end{bmatrix}, \; g(\eta_2) = -\begin{bmatrix} (W-B)\sin\theta \\ (B-W)\cos\theta \\ -z_{CB}B\sin\theta \end{bmatrix},$$

$$P_f = \begin{bmatrix} 1 & 1 & 0 & 0 \\ 0 & 0 & 1 & 1 \\ 0 & 0 & x_{ts} & x_{tb} \end{bmatrix}, \; \mathbf{f_t}(t) = \begin{bmatrix} f_p(t) \\ f_r(t) \\ f_s(t) \\ f_b(t) \end{bmatrix}.$$

The authors recommend Fossen (1994); Triantafyllou & Hover (2002) for details about the parameters above and their derivation, and Hoerner (1993); White (2008) for further details. Notice that $\mathbf{f_t}(t)$ is the vector of forces applied by the thrusters that are generated according to a given control law, and f_p, f_r, f_s and f_b are scalars that represents the force applied by the port, starboard, stern and bow thrusters, respectively. We assume that such forces can be directly measured during operation. The inclusion of the surge velocity is required in this reduced order model due to the nonnegligible influence it has on the vertical plane dynamics. The parameters used in the reduced model are listed in the table 1.

3.2 Augmented state extended Kalman filter formulation

Our final goal in this section is to detect and to identify a fault occuring on one of the vertical thrusters. To this end, one aims to quantify the loss of control effectiveness of the referred actuators: The effective force applied by the vertical thrusters may differ from the commanded one. We will consider that f_s and f_b are the commanded forces, which may not correspond

Parameter	Value	units	Description
m	$3.20 \cdot 10^{1}$	kg	Vehicle's mass
W	$3.14 \cdot 10^{2}$	N	Vehicle's weight
B	$3.16 \cdot 10^{2}$	N	Vehicle's bouyancy
z_{CB}	$-4.40 \cdot 10^{-3}$	m	z_B of CB w.r.t CG
$X_{\dot{u}}$	$-1.74 \cdot 10^{0}$	kg	Added mass longitudinal term
$X_{\dot{q}}$	$-3.05 \cdot 10^{-2}$	$kg \cdot m$	Added mass cross-term
$Z_{\dot{w}}$	$-4.12 \cdot 10^{1}$	kg	Added mass heave term
$Z_{\dot{q}}$	$-1.23 \cdot 10^{-1}$	$kg \cdot m$	Added mass cross-term
$M_{\dot{u}}$	$-3.05 \cdot 10^{-2}$	$kg \cdot m$	Added mass cross-term
$M_{\dot{w}}$	$-1.23 \cdot 10^{-1}$	$kg \cdot m$	Added mass cross-term
$M_{\dot{q}}$	$-6.07 \cdot 10^{0}$	$kg \cdot m^2$	Added mass pitch term
$X_{\|u\|u}$	$-1.04 \cdot 10^{1}$	$kg \cdot m^{-1}$	Drag longitudinal term
$X_{\|q\|q}$	$4.84 \cdot 10^{-2}$	$kg \cdot m$	Drag cross term
$Z_{\|w\|w}$	$-1.16 \cdot 10^{2}$	$kg \cdot m^{-1}$	Drag heave term
$Z_{\|q\|q}$	$-5.95 \cdot 10^{0}$	$kg \cdot m$	Drag cross-term
$M_{\|u\|u}$	$-2.11 \cdot 10^{-1}$	kg	Drag cross-term
$M_{\|w\|w}$	$-8.26 \cdot 10^{0}$	kg	Drag cross-term
$M_{\|q\|q}$	$-1.56 \cdot 10^{1}$	$kg \cdot m^2$	Drag pitch term
x_{ts}	$-3.21 \cdot 10^{-1}$	m	x_B of stern vertical thruster w.r.t CG
x_{tb}	$5.34 \cdot 10^{-1}$	m	x_B of bow vertical thruster w.r.t CG

Table 1. Reduced model terms

to the effective applied force. Like in many other problems in robotics, it is often difficult or even impossible to measure such forces. Measuring relative or absolute motion variables then becomes an alternative and the choice of the state to be observed is directly influenced by the variables that can be actually measured. Therefore, we propose the following model for the fault free ideal system:

$$\begin{aligned} \dot{\mathbf{x}} = \begin{bmatrix} \dot{\mathbf{x}}_1 \\ \dot{\mathbf{x}}_2 \end{bmatrix} = \begin{bmatrix} \dot{z} \\ \dot{\theta} \\ \dot{w} \\ \dot{q} \end{bmatrix} &= A_l(\mathbf{x})\mathbf{x} + f_u(\mathbf{x}, u) + f(\mathbf{x}, u, \mathbf{f_v}) + w^x(t) \\ y &= h(x) + v_n(t), \end{aligned} \tag{4}$$

where $w^x \in \mathbb{R}^4$ is a zero-mean Gaussian noise vector with autocorrelation matrix $Q^w(t)$, $\mathbf{x_1} = [z, \theta]^T$, $\mathbf{x_2} = [w, q]^T$, A_l and $f_u(\cdot)$ are easily derived from the kinematics model in 1 as

$$A_l(\mathbf{x}) = \begin{bmatrix} 0 & 0 & \cos\theta & 0 \\ 0 & 0 & 0 & 1 \\ 0 & 0 & 0 & 0 \\ 0 & 0 & 0 & 0 \end{bmatrix}, \quad f_u(\mathbf{x}, u) = \begin{bmatrix} -u\sin\theta \\ 0 \\ 0 \\ 0 \end{bmatrix},$$

assuming $\phi = 0$, and $f(\cdot)$ results from the dynamics model 3 as

$$f(\mathbf{x}, u, \mathbf{f_v}) = \begin{bmatrix} 0 \\ 0 \\ \dot{w} \\ \dot{q} \end{bmatrix} = S\dot{\nu} = SM^{-1}(-C(\nu)\nu - D(\nu)\nu - g(\mathbf{x_2}) + P_v\mathbf{f_v}(t)),$$

$$S = \begin{bmatrix} 0\,0\,0 \\ 0\,0\,0 \\ 0\,1\,0 \\ 0\,0\,1 \end{bmatrix}, \quad P_v = \begin{bmatrix} 0 & 0 \\ 1 & 1 \\ x_{ts} & x_{tb} \end{bmatrix}, \quad \mathbf{f_v} = \begin{bmatrix} f_s(t) \\ f_b(t) \end{bmatrix}.$$

Regarding the output y of 4, the dimension of the function $h(\mathbf{x})$ depends on the measurements and consequently on the on-board sensors. Here, we will assume we are able to observe the depth z, the pitch angle θ and the pitch rate q. Thus it results

$$h(\mathbf{x}) = C_h\mathbf{x}, \quad C_h = \begin{bmatrix} 1\,0\,0\,0 \\ 0\,1\,0\,0 \\ 0\,0\,0\,1 \end{bmatrix}.$$

The vector $v_n \in \mathbb{R}^3$ is the output noise, assumed to be zero-mean, Gaussian noise with autocorrelation matrix R^v.

Notice that $\mathbf{x_2}$ is the vector containing the last two entries of the velocity vector ν, i.e., $\nu = [u, \mathbf{x_2}]$. For simplicity of notation, in the expressions above we wrote ν instead of $[u, \mathbf{x_2}]$. Recall that we assumed that u is a measured variable, or at least, it can be accurately estimated. Indeed, it could be included in the state in 4 but the complexity of this latter would increase without advantages in the approach.

In order to model the possible loss of control effectiveness, let us define $\gamma = [\gamma_s, \gamma_b]^T$ as the vector of loss of control effectiveness factors, adopting the same notation as in Wu et al. (2000). Introducing these multiplicative factors in 4, the augmented state model results in

$$\begin{aligned} \dot{\mathbf{x}} &= A_l(\mathbf{x})\mathbf{x} + f_u(\mathbf{x}, u) + f(\mathbf{x}, u, \mathbf{f_v}) + E(\mathbf{f_v})\gamma + w^x(t) \\ \dot{\gamma} &= w^\gamma(t) \\ y &= C_h x + v_n(t), \end{aligned} \tag{5}$$

where $w^\gamma \in \mathbb{R}^2$ is a zero-mean, Gaussian noise vector with autocorrelation matrix Q^γ, uncorrelated with w^x, and

$$E(\mathbf{f_v}) = SM^{-1}P_v\,\mathrm{diag}(\mathbf{f_v}).$$

As it can be seen in 5, γ is assumed to be driven only by the noise w^γ. This comes from the fact that, in real scenarios, it is impossible to predict how the fault and, consequently, how γ evolve. In such situation, the most appropriate is to model the evolution with a noise vector w^γ with a sufficiently large autocorrelation (see Wu et al. (2000)), whose entries can play an important role in the design of the augmented state estimator, as it will be seen later on.

Making $s = [\mathbf{x}^T, \gamma^T]^T$, we rewrite 5 on the form

$$\begin{aligned} \dot{s} &= A_s(s)s + f_{us}(s, u) + f_s(s, u, \mathbf{f_v}) + E_s(\mathbf{f_v})s + w_s(t) \\ y &= C_s s + v_n(t). \end{aligned} \tag{6}$$

where

$$A_s = \begin{bmatrix} A_l & 0_{4\times2} \\ 0_{2\times4} & 0_{2\times2} \end{bmatrix}, \ f_{us} = \begin{bmatrix} f_u \\ 0_{2\times1} \end{bmatrix}, \ f_s = \begin{bmatrix} f \\ 0_{2\times1} \end{bmatrix},$$

$$E_s = \begin{bmatrix} 0_{4\times4} & E \\ 0_{2\times4} & 0_{2\times2} \end{bmatrix}, \ w_s = \begin{bmatrix} w^x \\ w^\gamma \end{bmatrix} \ C_s = \begin{bmatrix} C_h & 0_{3\times2} \end{bmatrix}.$$

The discrete time representation of 6 follows

$$s_{k+1} = A_{sk}(s_k)s_k + f_{usk}(s_k, u_k) + f_{sk}(s_k, u_k, \mathbf{f}_{\mathbf{v}k}) + E_{sk}(\mathbf{f}_{\mathbf{v}k})s_k + w_{sk} \tag{7}$$

$$y_{k+1} = C_s s_{k+1} + v_{k+1},$$

where β_k represents the discrete time equivalent vector, or matrix, β at time t_k.
We assume that the process noise w_{sk} and the output noise v_k are uncorrelated, i.e., $E\{w_{sk}v_k^T\} = 0$. The autocorrelation of the process noise and of the output are respectively given by

$$E\{w_{sk}w_{sk}^T\} = Q_k = \begin{bmatrix} Q_k^x & 0 \\ 0 & Q_k^\gamma \end{bmatrix}, \quad E\{v_k v_k^T\} = R_k. \tag{8}$$

The formulation of a Kalman filter assumes the use of a model of the process which is a mathematical representation of the dynamics. However, the mathematical translation of the dynamics of a given system may be inaccurate or may not describe entirely its behavior. This is the case in hydrodynamics, where the models are complex, difficult to extract. Moreover, there is no complete theory that allows for determining an accurate model and calculations of parameters mostly rely on empirical or semi-empirical formulas.
Hence, we define $\hat{\beta}$ as the estimate of the generic vector, or matrix, β. The augmented state extended Kalman filter formulation follows now directly from Gelb (1974). During the prediction stage, the state estimate and the covariance matrix evolve according to

$$\hat{s}_{k+1|k} = \hat{A}_{\hat{s}k}(\hat{s}_k)\hat{s}_k + \hat{f}_{usk}(\hat{s}_k, \hat{u}_k) + \hat{f}_{sk}(\hat{s}_k, \hat{u}_k, \mathbf{f}_{\mathbf{v}k}) + \hat{E}_{\hat{s}k}(\mathbf{f}_{\mathbf{v}k})\hat{s}_k \tag{9}$$

$$P_{k+1|k} = F_k P_k F_k^T + Q_k, \tag{10}$$

where F_k stands for the Jacobian of $\dot{s}$ evaluated at $\hat{s}_k$:

$$F_k = \frac{\partial \dot{s}}{\partial s}_{|s=\hat{s}_k}.$$

The so-called Kalman gain and the updates of the estimate and of the covariance matrix are respectively given by

$$K_{k+1} = P_{k+1|k}C_s^T(C_s P_{k+1|k} C_s^T + R_k)^{-1} \tag{11}$$

$$\hat{s}_{k+1|k+1} = s_{k+1|k} + K_{k+1}(y_{k+1} - C_s s_{k+1|k}) \tag{12}$$

$$P_{k+1|k+1} = (I - K_{k+1}C_s)P_{k+1|k}. \tag{13}$$

From the state estimate, it is now possible to extract the vector γ_k, whose entries constitute the base to determine whether a fault has occured or not.
As it was stated earlier, the autocorrelation matrix Q_k^γ can play a significant role to avoid divergence or guarantee faster convergence of the estimate of the loss of control effectiveness

factors. For the sake of clarity, from 10 and 13 we can decompose P_k as

$$P_k = \begin{bmatrix} P_k^x & P_k^{\gamma x} \\ P_k^{x\gamma} & P_k^{\gamma} \end{bmatrix}$$

Thus, from 10 and 13, we can conclude

$$P_{k+1|k}^{\gamma} = P_{k|k}^{\gamma} + Q_k^{\gamma}$$

$$P_{k+1|k+1}^{\gamma} \leq P_{k+1|k}^{\gamma}$$

where we used the fact that $P_{k+1|k} > 0$. Hence, the autocorrelation matrix Q_k^{γ} can be set such that P^{γ} lies in an interval, preventing state corrections to be excessive, when P^{γ} is too large, or to be insufficient with slow convergence, when P^{γ} is too small. Taking the eigenvalues λ^{γ} of P^{γ} as measures, we propose the following function

$$Q^{\gamma} = \begin{cases} diag(q_{\gamma}, q_{\gamma}) & , \text{ if } \max(\lambda_1^{\gamma}, \lambda_2^{\gamma}) < \lambda_{max} \\ 0 & , \text{ if } \max(\lambda_1^{\gamma}, \lambda_2^{\gamma}) \geq \lambda_{max} \end{cases} \tag{14}$$

where q_{γ} is the autocorrelation of $\gamma_i, i = 1, 2$ and λ_{max} is a preset maximum constant.

3.3 Fault identification

The loss control effectiveness factors provide an estimate of the performances of the actuators. Ideally, a fault would be identified whenever the absolute value of one of the factors would rise above a preset threshold. However, model uncertainties will be directly reflected in these factors. Even in normal operation, with the actuators working perfectly, the loss of control effectiveness factors may diverge from zero, reflecting, for example, the effect of a damping force greater than the modeled. As these errors are frequently commited on the overall model, their effects are verified on all actuators either by increasing or decreasing the loss of control effectiveness factors. Hence, for the present case, a reasonable measure of the malfunction of one of the thrusters is given by the difference of the corresponding loss of control effectiveness factor estimate. On the other hand, taking a decision about the malfunction of a given thruster should also be based on the confidence of the factor estimate, which can be indirectly taken from the eigenvalues λ^{γ} of P_k^{γ}, avoiding taking decisions on transient state, while considerable corrections on the state are being performed. Thus, we propose the following measure for fault detection:

$$\delta = \frac{|\gamma_s - \gamma_b|}{f_{\lambda}(\lambda_1^{\gamma} + \lambda_2^{\gamma})}. \tag{15}$$

where f_{λ} is a monotically increasing function of its argument.
Whenever δ is greater than a preset threshold, a fault is detected and the identification is made according to the greater λ, i.e., if $\gamma_s > \gamma_b$ then the stern thruster is faulty and vice-versa.

4. Control of MARES

In the presence of a faulty vertical thruster, the reconfiguration of the actuation is required. Otherwise, keeping the same actuation will likely lead to instability or to other pratical problems such as thruster dammage or large battery consumption, for example. Therefore, the control law for normal operation could be inadequate and another control law must take

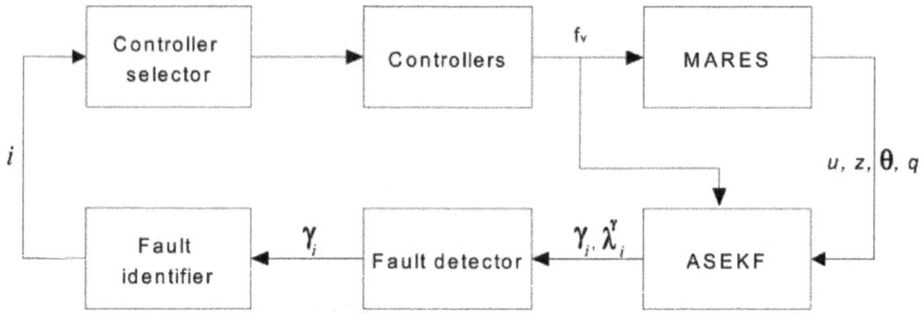

Fig. 3. Operation of the fault overall fault detection and recovery algorithm

over. In this section, we first start by deriving such controller and present the main concepts behind the derivation of the control for normal operation in order to make the result section clear.

4.1 Control under fault

We consider now the scenario in which only one of the vertical thrusters is available to control the motion of the vehicle. Under such situation, the heave DOF is no longer controllable but the depth is still controllable by manipulating pitch. Based on the Lyapunov theory we will derive a controller that makes it possible to control the vehicle's depth, while assuming that the absolute value of the surge velocity is sufficiently large to compensate the vehicle's flotation. The derivation of the controller employs the well know backstepping method as well as conditional integrators to achieve asymptotic regulation.

As the final goal in this section is to control the vehicle depth, we will assume that roll angle is null ($\phi = 0$), resulting:

$$\dot{z} = -u \sin\theta + w \cos\theta \tag{16}$$

Let us introduce the error variable $e_z = z - z_d$, which we want to drive to zero, and the quadratic Lyapunov function:

$$V_1 = \frac{1}{2} e_z^2, \tag{17}$$

whose time derivative results

$$\dot{V}_1 = e_z \dot{e}_z = e_z(-u \sin\theta + w \cos\theta - \dot{z}_d). \tag{18}$$

Although u, θ and z are measured by sensors or estimated, it is hard to accurately compute w due to model uncertainties and measurement noise. Thus we will assume that it constitutes a disturbance acting on the system, shifting the equilibrium point $e_z = 0$ to an uncertain value. Throughout the following developments, we will consider that the surge velocity is maintained constant in order to simplify our approach. Indeed, in most missions the surge velocity is intended to be constant along the trajectory. Moreover, the limited actuation on the vertical thruster makes the pitch angular velocity to lie in a bounded interval. Hence, from the vertical dynamics, we can assume that there exists an upper bound on the absolute value of $w \in [-w_{max}, w_{max}]$.

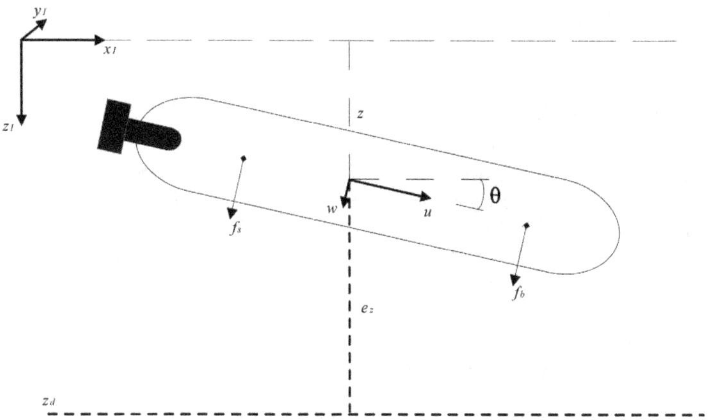

Fig. 4. Depth control by actuating either f_s or f_b

Inspired by Singh & Khalil (2005), let us suppose we are able to handle θ directly through the virtual control law

$$\theta = \theta_d(e_z) = \arcsin\Big[-\frac{1}{u}(\dot{z}_d - \alpha(e_z)\varphi(\frac{e_z}{\mu}))\Big], \tag{19}$$

where $\varphi(\cdot) : \mathbb{R} \to \mathbb{R}$ is the continuous infinitely differentiable sigmoid function

$$\varphi(x) = \frac{2}{1 + e^{-\varsigma x}} - 1, \tag{20}$$

which verifies $x\varphi(x) > 0$, $x \neq 0$, and $\alpha(\cdot) > 0$ is a continuous function left to be determined later. Of course, handling θ directly and instantaneously is not realistic and such assumption will be lifted next. In opposition to Singh & Khalil (2005), we have selected a sigmoid function φ instead of a saturated linear function due to the differentiability characteristic. Let us take take $\varsigma = 2$, which will make $\varphi(\cdot)$ equal to the hyperbolic tangent function.
Assuming z_d sufficiently smooth, $u > 0$ and imposing

$$-\frac{1}{u}(\dot{z}_d - \alpha(e_z)\varphi(\frac{e_z}{\mu})) \leq 1, \tag{21}$$

the time derivative of the Lyapunov function in 18 results

$$\begin{aligned} \dot{V}_1 &= e_z\Big(-\alpha(e_z)\varphi(\frac{e_z}{\mu}) + w\cos\theta\Big) \\ &\leq -e_z\alpha(e_z)\varphi(\frac{e_z}{\mu}) + |e_z|w_{max}, \end{aligned} \tag{22}$$

where we used the fact that $|\cos\theta| \leq 1$ and w be bounded. By choosing appropriately $\alpha(\cdot)$ and $\varphi(\cdot)$, the system can now be made pratically stable (see Singh & Khalil (2005)). Hence, let us define $\varepsilon \in (0, 1)$ and take $\mu = \frac{1}{\tanh^{-1}(\varepsilon)}$, then choosing $\alpha(e_z) = K_z$, $K_z \in (\frac{w_{max}}{\varepsilon}, u + \dot{z}_d]$, such that it satisfies 21, it comes

$$\dot{V}_1 < 0, \ ||e_z|| > 1$$
$$\dot{V}_1 \leq -e_z\alpha(e_z)\varphi(\frac{e_z}{\mu}) + |e_z|w_{max}, \ ||e_z|| \leq 1.$$

Thus, the system is made pratically stable and the invariant set for which the error tends to can be made arbitrarily small by handling μ. However, a too small μ induces chattering phenomena which are intended to be minimal.
Taking into account that V_1 is a strictly increasing function of e_z from the last inequalities, we can state that the error enters a positively invariant set $\Omega = \{e_z \leq 1\}$. However, due to non-null disturbances considered above, asymptotic stability can not be achieved. Therefore, following the same idea as in Singh & Khalil (2005), the conditional integrator is now introduced to obtain asymptotic convergence to the origin $e_z = 0$. Modifiyng the control law in 19 to include an integral component, it results

$$\theta_d(e_z) = \arcsin\Big[-\frac{1}{u}(\dot{z}_d - \alpha(e_z)\varphi(\frac{e_z+\sigma}{\mu}))\Big], \tag{23}$$

where

$$\dot{\sigma} = -\gamma\sigma + \mu\varphi(\frac{e_z+\sigma}{\mu}), \ \gamma > 0, \ \sigma(t_0) = 0.$$

Since $|\phi(x)| < 1, \ \forall x \in \mathbb{R}$, it is easy to check that $\sigma \leq \frac{\mu}{\gamma}$. In order to guarantee convergence to zero, one has to set γ and μ such that the maximum absolute value of the integral satisfies$|\sigma| > \mu|\varphi^{-1}(\frac{w_{max}}{K_z})|$. Although conservative, this will allow the integral component to compensate the disturbance effect. By applying theorem 1 in Singh & Khalil (2005), convergence to $e_z = 0$ as $t \to \infty$ is ensured.
So far, we have considered that we are able to handle θ directly, which is not true, as it was stated before. Thus, based on the backstepping method Khalil (2002), let us introduce the new error variable $e_\theta = \theta - \theta_d$ and the new augmented Lyapunov function as follows

$$V_2 = V_1 + \frac{1}{2}e_\theta^2, \tag{24}$$

whose time derivative results

$$\dot{V}_2 = \dot{V}_1 + e_\theta(\dot{\theta} - \dot{\theta}_d), \tag{25}$$

with

$$\dot{\theta}_d = -\frac{\ddot{z}_d - K_z\frac{\partial}{\partial t}\varphi(\frac{e_z+\sigma}{\mu})}{\left(u^2 - (\dot{z}_d - K_z\varphi(\frac{e_z+\sigma}{\mu}))^2\right)^{1/2}}.$$

Then by imposing

$$\dot{\theta} = q_d = \dot{\theta}_d - K_\theta e_\theta, \ \ K_\theta > 0, \tag{26}$$

the time derivative of the augmented Lyapunov function satisfies $\dot{V}_2 \leq \dot{V}_1 - K_\theta e_\theta^2$. Taking into account the previous result about the convergence of e_z to zero and the fact that V_1 is a class $\mathcal{K}_\infty$ function, we can deduce that $V_2 \to 0$ as $t \to \infty$.
Nevertheless, we are not able to handle $\dot{\theta}$ directly and, as it can be seen from 1 and 2, a last step is required. Hence, we define $e_q = q - q_d = S_q\nu - q_d$, with $S_q = [0,0,1]$, as the pitch rate

error variable as well as the new augmented Lyapunov function:

$$V_3 = V_2 + \frac{1}{2}e_q^2. \tag{27}$$

Considering 3, the time derivative results

$$\begin{aligned} \dot{V}_3 &= \dot{V}_2 + e_q(S_q\dot{\nu} - q_d) \\ &= \dot{V}_2 + e_q(S_qM^{-1}(-C(\nu)\nu - D(\nu)\nu - g(\eta_2) + P_if_{pi}) - \dot{q}_d). \end{aligned} \tag{28}$$

where P_i and f_{pi}, $i = \{s, b\}$, are given as functions of the actuator configuration. When the vehicle is operating with only one thruster, either stern or bow thruster, P_i and f_{pi} are respectively given by

$$P_s = \begin{bmatrix} 1 & 1 & 0 \\ 0 & 0 & 0 \\ 0 & 0 & x_{ts} \end{bmatrix}, \quad P_b = \begin{bmatrix} 1 & 1 & 0 \\ 0 & 0 & 0 \\ 0 & 0 & x_{tb} \end{bmatrix}, \quad f_{ps} = \begin{bmatrix} f_p \\ f_r \\ f_s \end{bmatrix}, \quad f_{pb} = \begin{bmatrix} f_p \\ f_r \\ f_b \end{bmatrix}.$$

Note that P_i takes the form $P = [P_h|P_{vi}]$, where $P_h \in \mathbb{R}^{3\times 2}$ is the submatrix composed by the first two columns of P_i and $P_{vi} \in \mathbb{R}^{3\times 1}$ is the last column of P_i. Further, let us decouple the input vector into $f_{pi} = [f_h^T, f_i^T]^T$, where $f_h \in \mathbb{R}^2$ is composed by the first two entries of f_{pi} and f_i is the last entry of this latter, which we can manipulate directly. By considering the decoupled form of P_i, we can rewrite 28 as

$$\dot{V}_3 = \dot{V}_2 + e_q(S_qM^{-1}(-C(\nu)\nu - D(\nu)\nu - g(\eta_2) + P_hf_h + P_{vi}f_i) - \dot{q}_d).$$

Clearly $S_qM^{-1}P_hf_h = 0$, which means that the horizontal thrusters have no direct influence on the pitch dynamics (see the entries of P_s and P_b).
Finally, defining the proportional gain $K_q > 0$ and choosing the control law

$$f_i = (S_qM^{-1}P_{vi})^{-1}(S_qM^{-1}(C(\nu)\nu + D(\nu)\nu + g(\eta)) + \dot{q}_d - K_qe_q), \quad i = \{s, b\}, \tag{29}$$

the time derivative of the Lyapunov function 28 becomes

$$\dot{V}_3 = \dot{V}_2 - K_qe_q^2. \tag{30}$$

Therefore, the convergence of the error e_z to zero is then guaranteed by setting the input f_i according to the control law 29. Note that Equation 29 gives the two control laws for either actuating with only stern or bow thruster, being different on the entries of P_{vi} only.

4.2 Control without fault

Under normal operation, the two through-hull thrusters provide controllability on the heave and the pitch DOFs. We will not give emphasis to the derivation of this controller since it was previously derived in Ferreira, Matos, Cruz & Pinto (2010). We aim at exposing the main concepts that led to the control law, in order to better understand the results of the next section. The controller was derived using common backstepping with no integral terms.
In opposition to the previous subsection, the errors considered for the control with the two thrusters are bidimensional vectors. Naturally, the error vector for vertical position comes

$$e'_p = \begin{bmatrix} z - z_d \\ \theta - \theta_d \end{bmatrix},$$

assuming that $\theta, \theta_d \neq \pi/2$. Following the same method as previously, a first Lyapunov function is defined as a quadratic function of the error e_p and its time derivative is made negative definite by adequately choosing $\dot{z}$ and $\dot{\theta}$ as virtual control variables to achieve asymptotic stability.
A new augmented Lyapunov function is then introduced by adding a quadratic term of the error

$$e'_v = \begin{bmatrix} w - w_d \\ q - q_d \end{bmatrix},$$

and, from the reduced dynamics model 3, the control law for the two vertical thrusters $f_{pv} = \chi(e'_p, e'_v, u, \eta_2) \in \mathbb{R}^2$ is determined such that the time derivative of the augmented Lyapunov function is made negative definite.

5. Experiments and results

To validate the method described in the previous sections, several experimental tests were conducted. The results will be presented in a decoupled way in order to facilitate the exposition and the analysis. First, the results obtained from the ASEKF will be exposed for the system under normal operation with induced faults. Then the performances of the controller derived in the previous section will be presented.

5.1 Fault detection

Several tests were performed in order to verify the behavior of the fault detection and identification algorithm. Under normal operation, we have intentionally induced faults in the thrusters with the aim of analyzing the behavior of our approach. The following graphs expose the evolution of some of the most relevant variables referred in section 3. The model errors and uncertainties were not corrected so that we could observe behaviors similar to those occuring with real faults. Although not explicitly written, the units of the loss of control effectiveness factors, their difference, the eigenvalues of the corresponding covariance matrix as well as the fault measure are dimensionless, while angles and linear distances are expressed in radians and meters, respectively.
The fault in one of the thruster can be simulated by a conteracting force in the same axis of force application, with an opposite direction. The following tests were carried out such that a force with an opposite direction was applied in an axis near the axis of force application along all the operation or along part of it. The fault measure computed and exposed in the graphs below was set, according to 15, equal to

$$\delta = \frac{|\gamma_s - \gamma_b|}{\sqrt{\lambda_1^\gamma + \lambda_2^\gamma}}.$$

Fig. 5 presents the evolution of the state estimate in normal operation without conteracting forces. It can be seen in Fig. 5(a), however, that the loss of control effectiveness factors are non-null, in opposition to what would be expected. Indeed, such behavior is due to errors of model parameters, neglected dynamics effects, discretization errors as well as linearization in the extended Kalman filter formulation. Nevertheless, it can be seen they are limited and their differences in Fig. 5(b) are confined to a well defined interval. This effect is unavoidable since deviations of the mathematical model will be directly reflected in the loss of control effectiveness factors.
On the other hand, the eigenvalues of the submatrix P^γ (Fig. 5(c)) are monotically increasing along the operation due to the reduced actuation, and consequently poor observability. In

fact, the vertical thrusters are mainly compensating the difference between the weight and the bouyancy of the vehicle, which is less than 1.5 Newton, well below the maximum actuation (24N in each thruster). Although it is not shown in the graph, the eigenvalues would stabilize after some more time of operation.

In Fig. 6, the graphs show the evolution of the variables during the operation for which 1.5N and 2.5N of force are opposing the vertical bow and stern thrusters, respectively. It can be seen that the eigenvalues (Fig. 6(c)) reach their "steady stade" after 40 seconds. In this case, the controller compensates the effects of the opposition force by increasing the actuation, which, in turn, makes the observability better than in the previous case (compare Fig. 6(c) with Fig. 5(c)). Regarding the loss of control effectiveness factors, one can observe that the bow thruster is more affected by the added forces than the stern one when compared with Fig. 5(a). This behavior is explained by the fact that the opposition forces were applied asymetrically with respect to the center of gravity of the vehicle.

In Fig. 7 and Fig. 8, we present the same variables as in the previous figures, but now with a disturbance occuring at time $t = 60s$, approximately. The graphs in Fig. 7 are related to the disturbance applied in the stern thruster while the graphs in Fig. 8 corresponds to the disturbance in the bow thruster. Comparing the results in Fig. 5 and Fig. 6 with those in Fig. 7 and Fig. 8, the occurence of faults in the last two experiences is evident through simple analysis of Fig. 7(b) and Fig. 8(b).

By comparing the results exposed in Fig. 5(d), 6(d), 7(d), 8(d), we can conclude that setting the threshold $\delta_{th} = 7$ would adequatly detect the occurence of a fault, while ensuring a sufficiently large margin to avoid false dectections. The choice of such threshold has to be made according to the sensitivity desired for the detections of faults which must be mainly related to the accuracy of the model.

The identification is made according to the stated before, being the thruster with bigger $|\gamma|$ the one that is identified as faulty. In both situations (Fig. 7(a) and Fig. 8(a)), the faulty thruster is easily identifiable. Still, practical considerations have to be made at this stage: One can observe that δ reaches larger values in the initial transient instants due to small eigenvalues, which could lead to false detections (depending on the threshold). To avoid so, a possibility would be integrating the value of δ when it is above the threshold, while using a forgetting factor, and defining another threshold for the value of the integral. Nonetheless, the simple method with the threshold defined above would be sufficient for the present work, as it can be seen from the experiments.

On the other hand, the relation between the actuation amplitude and the eigenvalues of the matrix P^{γ} is now notable in Fig. 7(c) and Fig. 8(c). With the application of the disturbance, the controller increases the actuation and, as a consequence, the observability is made greater (see 7(c) and 8(c)).

5.2 Control

The control laws derived in section 4 were implemented in MARES and tested in real conditions. The results of the operations are shown in this section, being the analysis of the performances of the controllers the main topic. The vehicle missions were programed such that it navigates at a constant depth reference with a given constant orientation. We must highlight that several unconsidered disturbances have acted on the vehicle during operations: The vehicle was subject to more bouyancy than the assumed in the mathematical model; the fedback depth measurement is actually performed in the nose of MARES instead of the vehicle's center of gravity. Such disturbances induce undesired effects on the controllers. However, the following figures show the robustness of our approach. The variables shown in the graphs have the following units correspondence: Depth is expressed in meters, the pitch angle is expressed in radians while the surge velocity is expressed in meters per second.

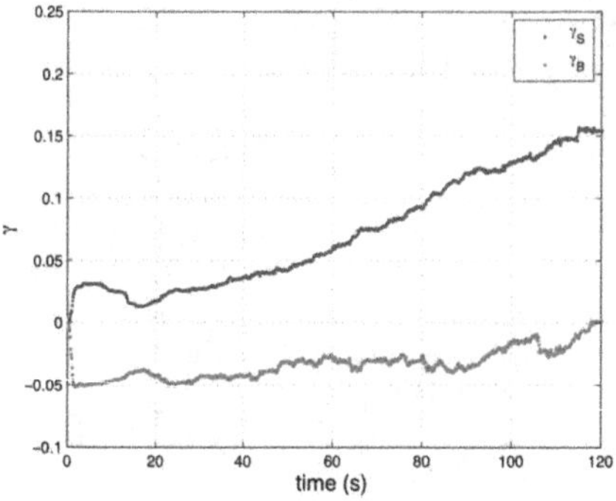

(a) Control effectiveness factors

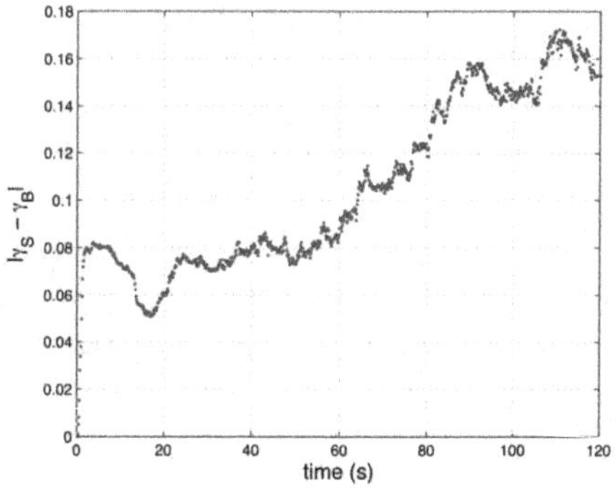

(b) Difference of control effectiveness factors

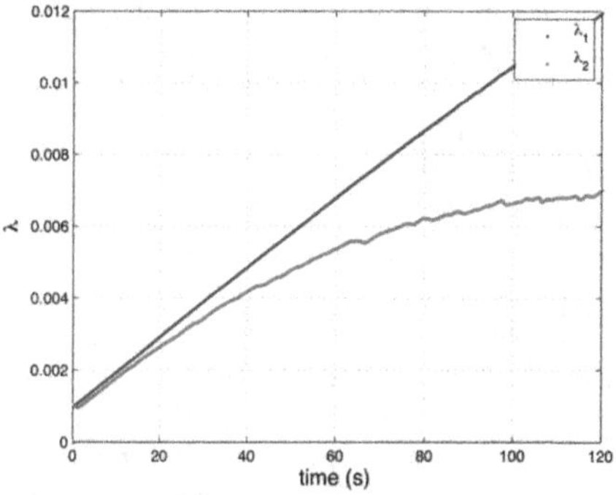

(c) Eigenvalues

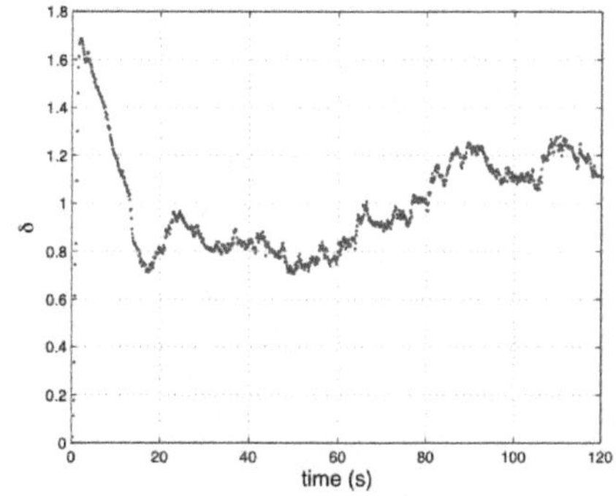

(d) Fault measure

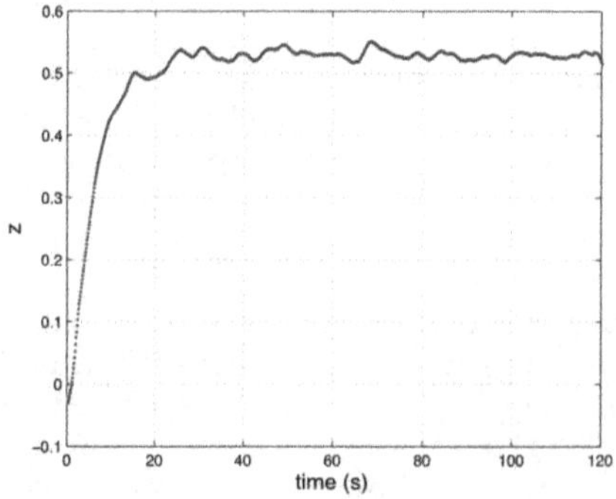

(e) Depth

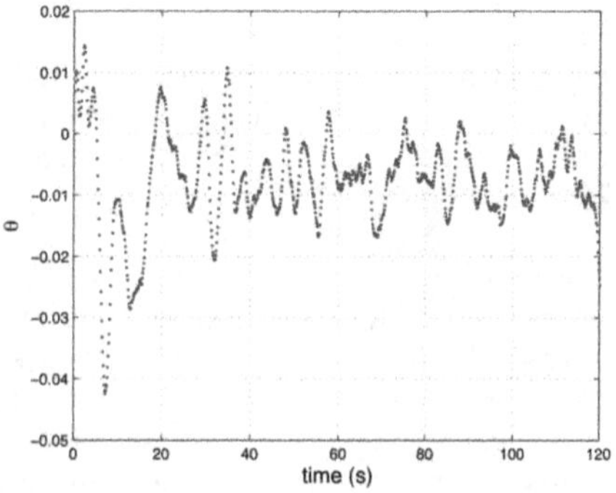

(f) Pitch angle

Fig. 5. MARES under normal operation (no faults)

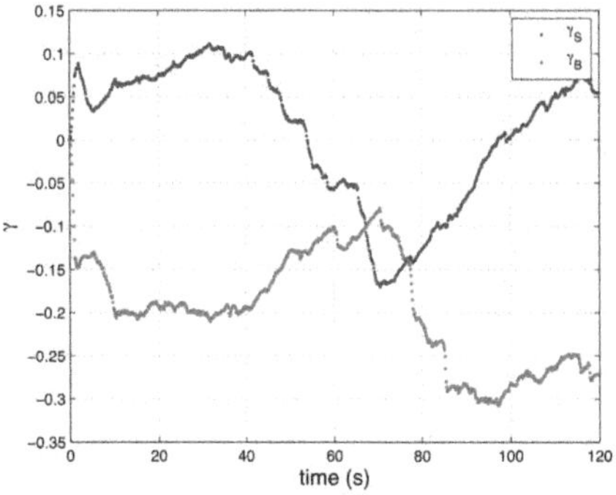

(a) Control effectiveness factors

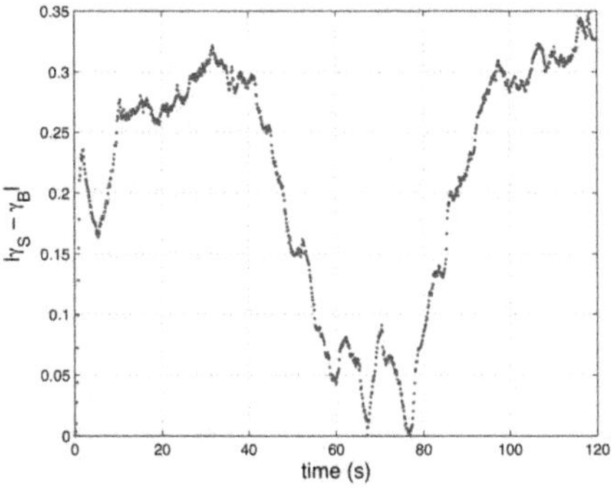

(b) Difference of control effectiveness factors

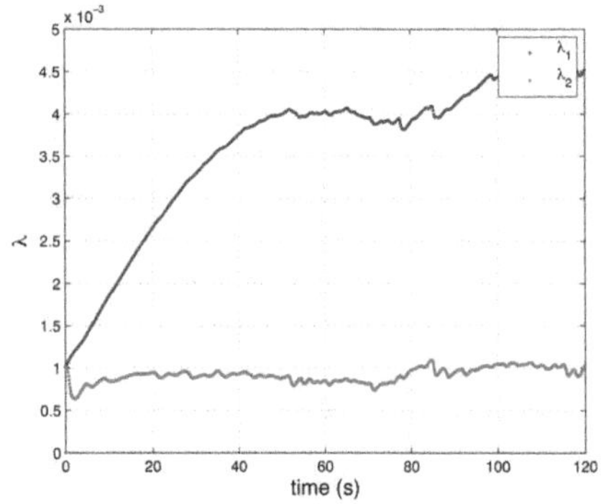

(c) Eigenvalues

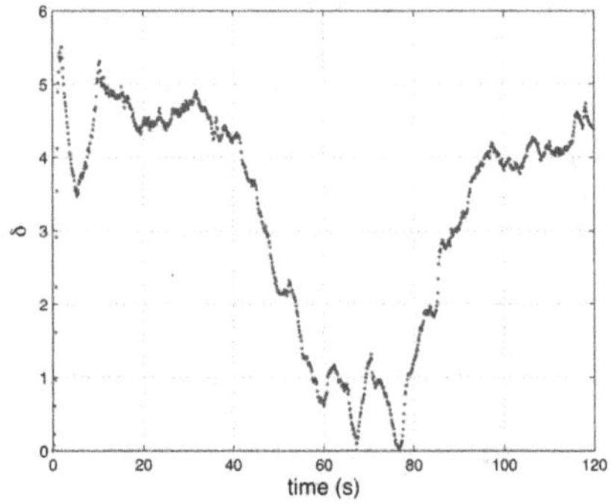

(d) Fault measure

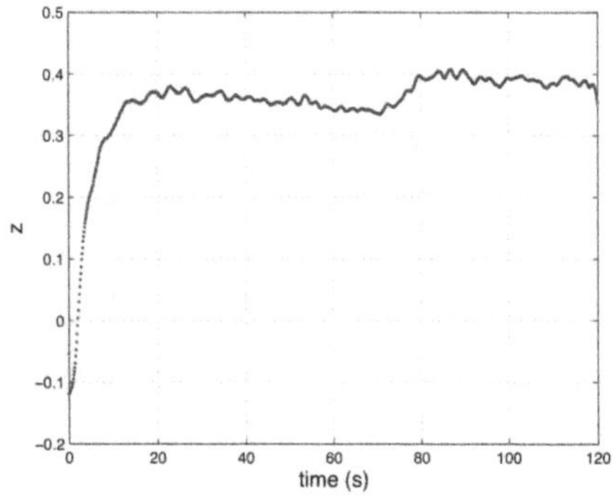

(e) Depth

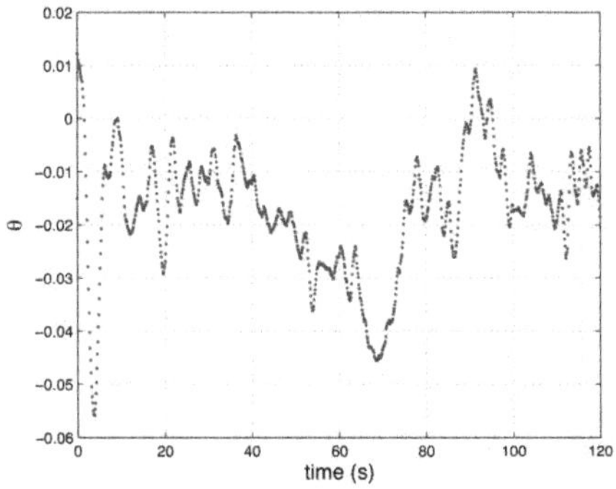

(f) Pitch angle

Fig. 6. MARES with constant disturbances: bouyancy added in the nose and the tail asymetrically

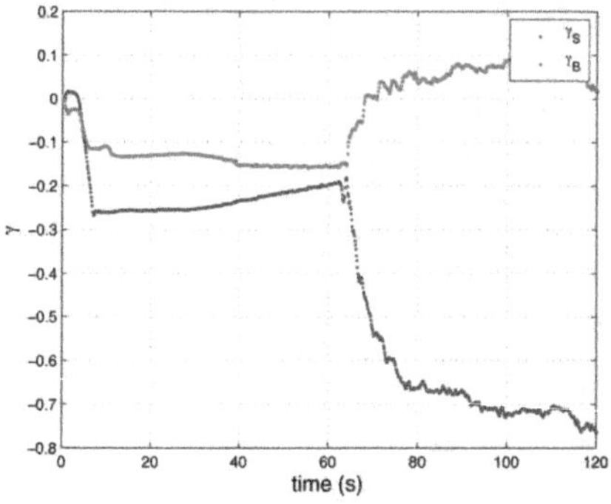

(a) Control effectiveness factors

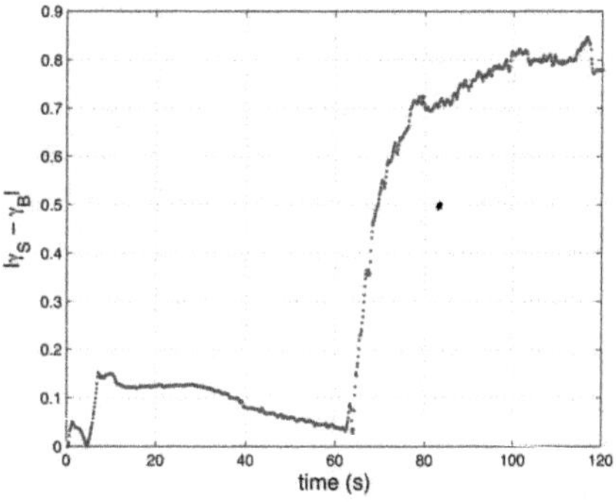

(b) Difference of control effectiveness factors

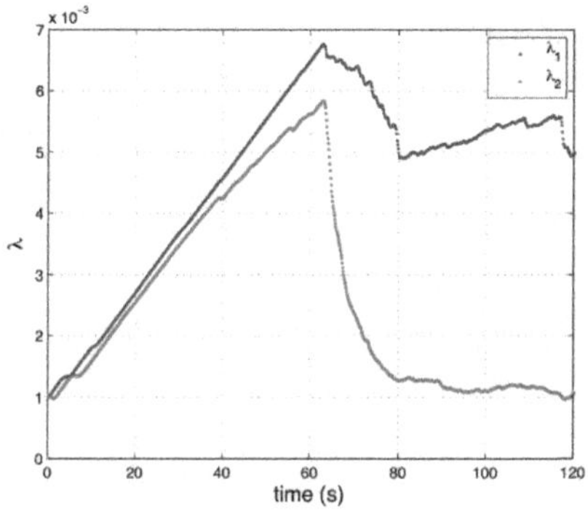

(c) Eigenvalues

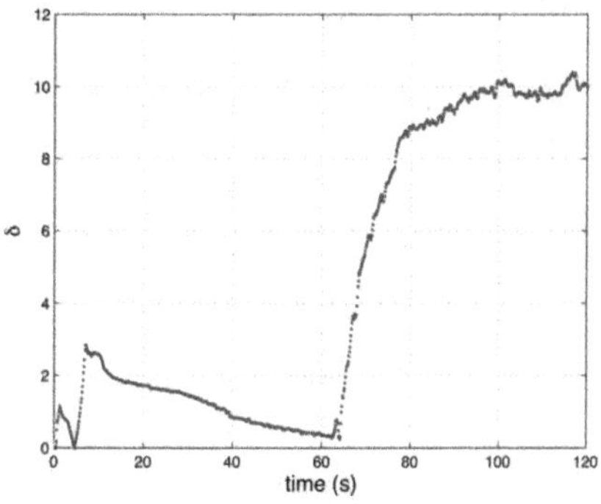

(d) Fault measure

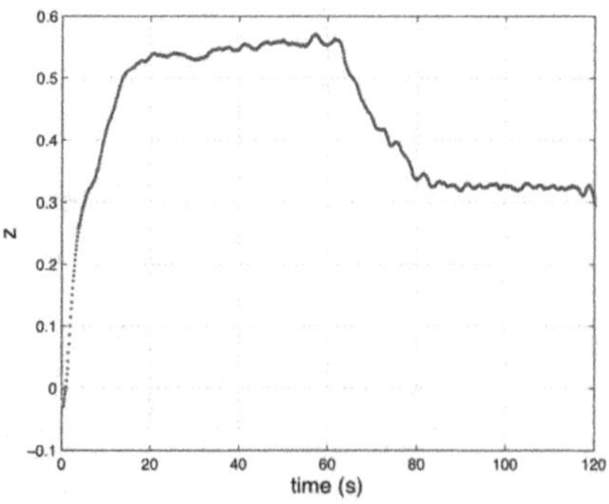

(e) Depth

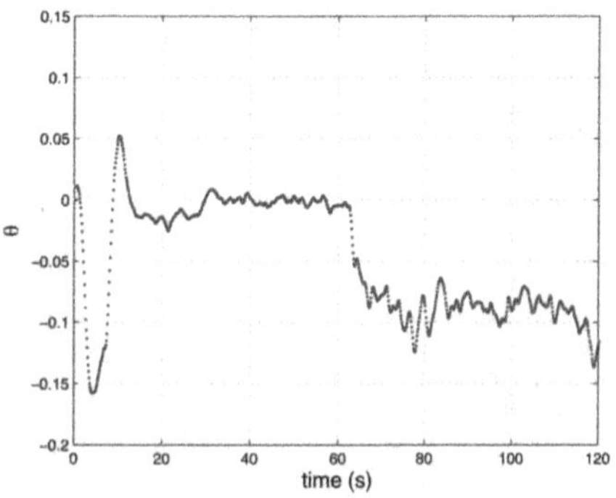

(f) Pitch angle

Fig. 7. MARES with disturbance in the stern thruster at $t = 60s$ approximately

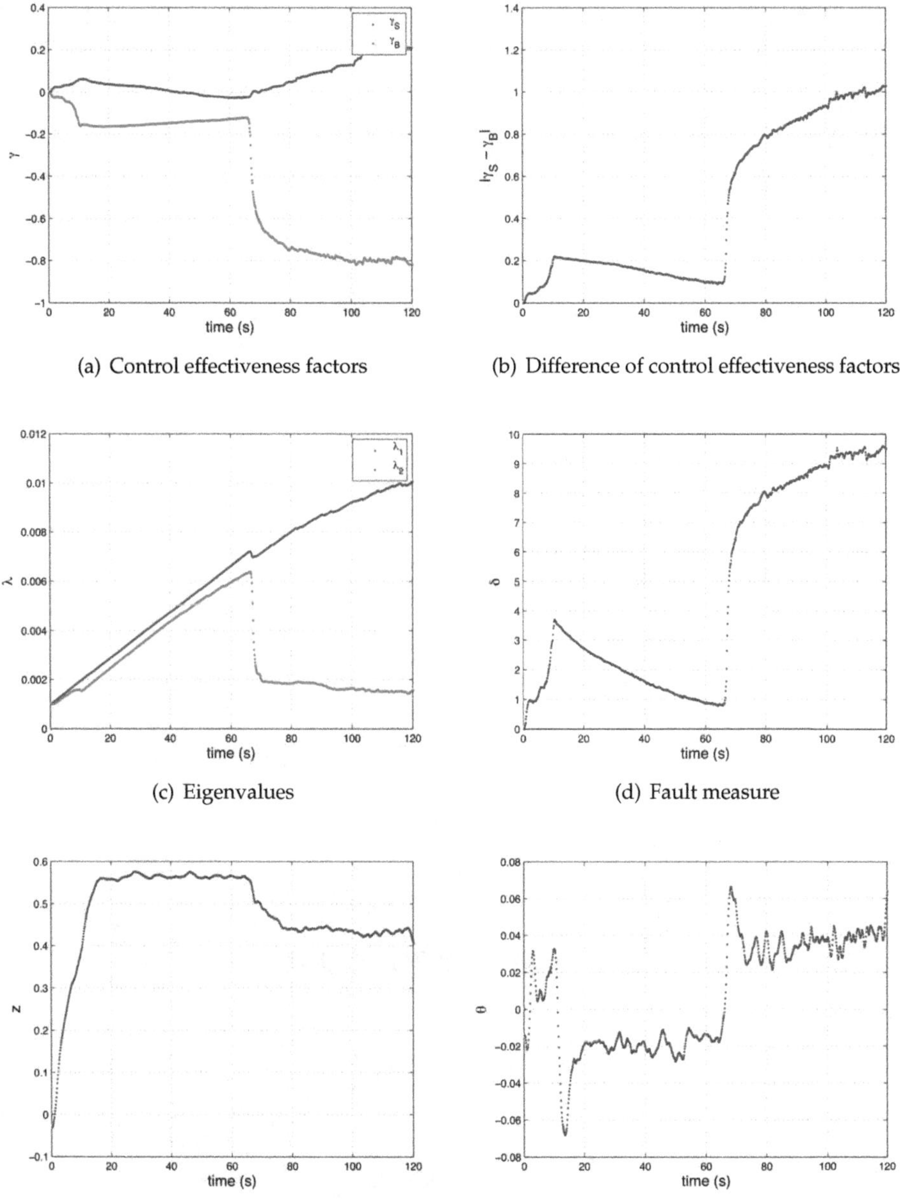

(a) Control effectiveness factors

(b) Difference of control effectiveness factors

(c) Eigenvalues

(d) Fault measure

(e) Depth

(f) Pitch angle

Fig. 8. MARES with disturbance in the bow thruster at $t = 60s$ approximately

Figures 9 to 11 show the results obtained during the operation of the controllers. The missions were set so that the vehicle starts diving with the two vertical thrusters simultaneously controlling pitch and depth, with surge velocity $u = 0$. At time $t = 20s$, a fault is simulated

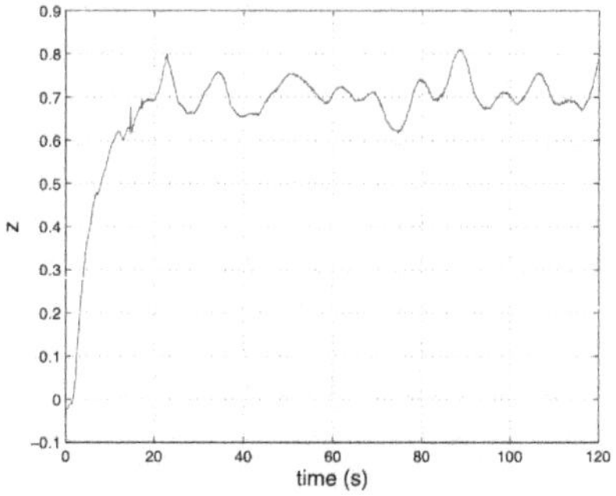

(a) Depth

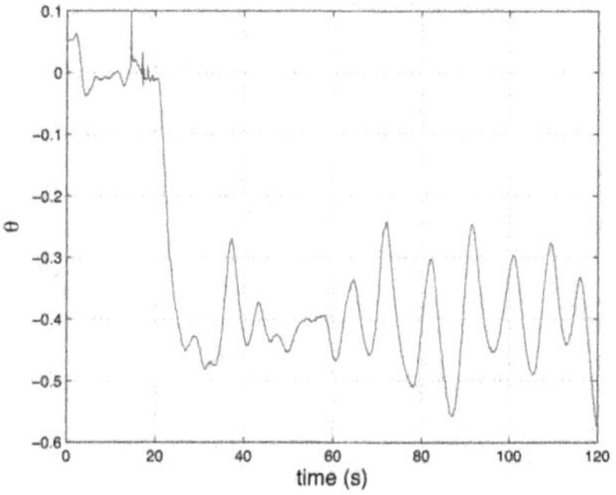

(b) Pitch angle

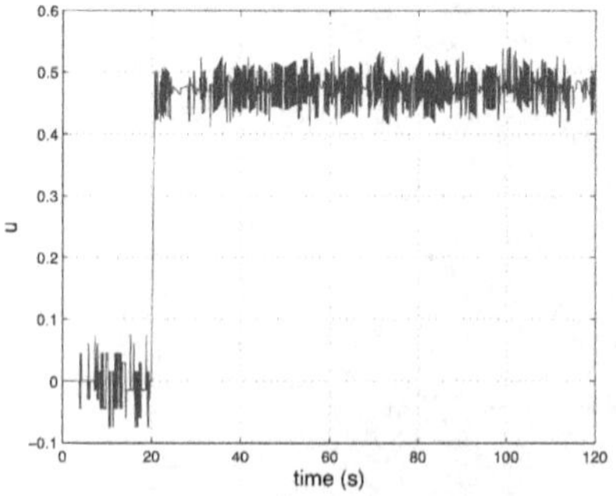

(c) Surge velocity

Fig. 9. MARES controlling depth with bow and horizontal thrusters only ($z_d = 0.7$ m)

and one of the controllers for degraded mode with only one vertical thruster starts operating. The figures show the results for different surge velocities and for the two controllers.
The Fig. 9 shows the variables directly measured from the sensors for a mission with a depth reference $z_d = 0.7$m, only with bow thruster. One can verify that the depth (9(a)) is reasonably close the reference and the small oscillation is due to natural disturbances that the vehicle

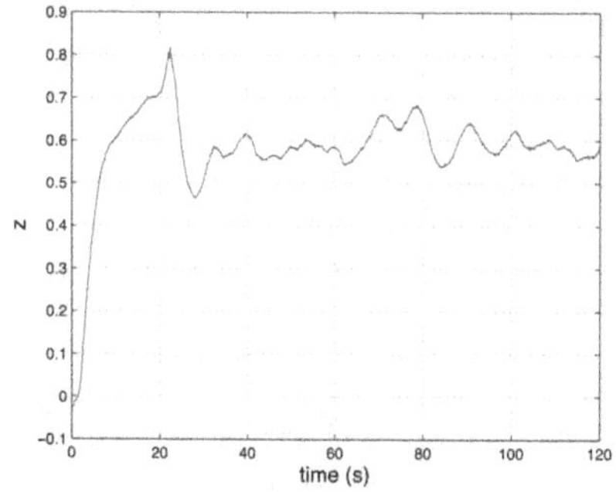

(a) Depth

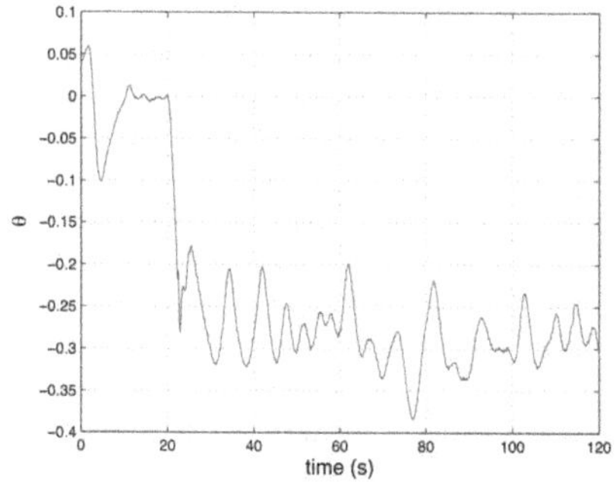

(b) Pitch angle

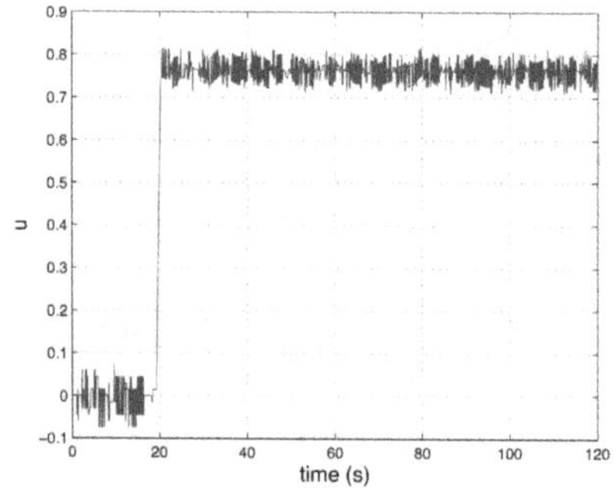

(c) Surge velocity

Fig. 10. MARES controlling depth with bow and horizontal thrusters only ($z_d = 0.6$ m)

founds in practical operations. Moreover, the commanded forces are affected by delays and thruster model is subject to uncertainties, which certainly influence the behavior.
On the other hand, the Fig. 11(a) shows that the oscillation amplitude is bigger than in Fig. 9(a) and 9(a), having been induced by more disturbances. Moreover, for stern-only control,

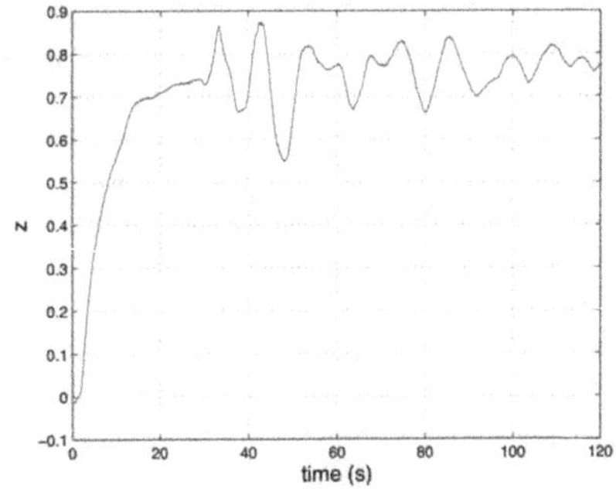

(a) Depth

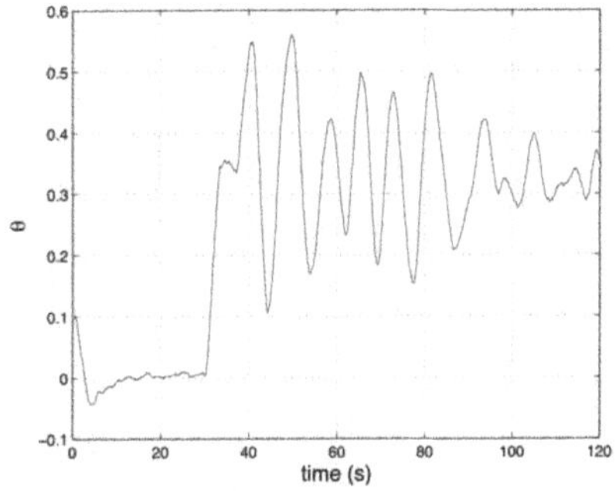

(b) Pitch angle

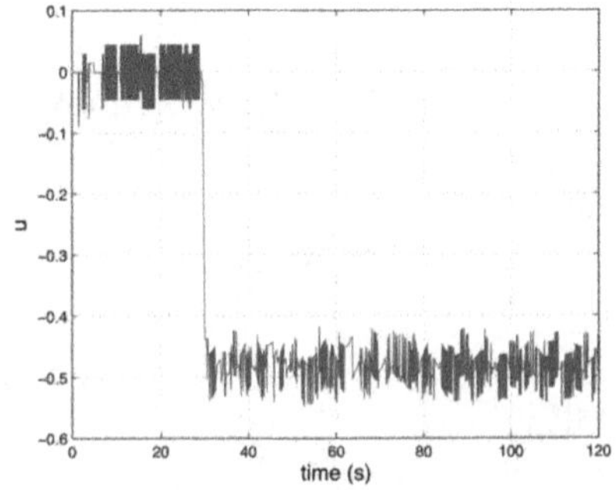

(c) Surge velocity

Fig. 11. MARES controlling depth with stern and horizontal thrusters only ($z_d = 0.8$ m)

more actuation is needed for the same pitch angle, in steady state. Such behavior is originated by the smaller distance at which the stern thruster is placed relatively to the center of gravity, comparing to the bow thruster (see Table 1).
Figures 9 to 11 show the robustness of the control laws, independently of the surge velocity. Even in the presence of unconsidered disturbances naturally induced by the environment, the graphs 9(a), 10(a) and 11(a) demonstrate that the controllers provide satisfactory results in real operation.

6. Conclusions

In this work, we have presented a complete method for fault detection, identification and automatic reconfiguration of the MARES AUV. Although we have focused on this particular system, the concepts and ideas can easily be extended to other problems, even beyond robotics.
Based on the dynamics and kinematics models, we have formulated a filter to estimate possible actuation biases. The augmented state extended Kalman filter was chosen to handle the problem, contemplating a reduced order model to simplify the analysis and the formulation. Bias variables were introduced in the state to be estimated as loss of control effectiveness factors whose values reflect the commanded underactuation/overactuation. Along with these estimated variables, the eigenvalues of the corresponding submatrix in the state estimate covariance matrix were taken to define a fault measure. Such measure was then used to generate a fault detection warning through comparison of its value with a given threshold. Finally, the faulty thruster is identified through analysis of the biases amplitude.
When a fault occurs and the corresponding thruster is set off, a suitable control law has to take over to ensure that the on-going mission succeed. To achieve so, we have defined two control laws for which we have based the derivation on Lyapunov theory and on backstepping method and further applied conditional integrators in order to drive the vehicle depth to a given reference with a null error in steady state.
At last, we demonstrated the performances of the developed method through real experiments in which we verified the operation of both estimator and controllers. Even in the presence of unconsidered disturbances, naturally induced by the environment, we have demonstrated that the controllers provide satisfactory results for several surge velocities and different thruster configurations.

7. Acknowledgement

Bruno Ferreira was supported by the Portuguese Foundation for Science and Technology through the Ph.D. grant SFRH/BD/60522/2009.

8. References

Cruz, N. A. & Matos, A. C. (2008). The MARES auv, a modular autonomous robot for environment sampling, *Oceans 2008, Vols 1-4*, Oceans-IEEE, IEEE, New York, pp. 1996–2001.

Ferreira, B., Matos, A., Cruz, N. & IEEE (2010). Single beacon navigation: Localization and control of the mares auv, *Oceans 2010*, Oceans-IEEE, IEEE, New York.

Ferreira, B., Matos, A., Cruz, N. & Pinto, M. (2010). Modeling and control of the MARES autonomous underwater vehicle, *Marine Technology Society Journal* 44(2): 19–36.

Fossen, T. I. (1994). *Guidance and Control of Ocean Vehicles*, John Whiley & Sons Ltd.

Frank, P. M. & Ding, X. (1997). Survey of robust residual generation and evaluation methods in observer-based fault detection systems, *Journal of Process Control* 7(6): 403–424.

Gelb, e. A. (1974). *Optimal applied estimation*, MIT Press.
Hoerner, S. F. (1993). *Fluid dynamics drag: theoretical, experimental and statistical information*, Published by the author, Bakerfield, CA.
Khalil, H. (2002). *Nonlinear Systems*, 3 edn, Prentice Hall, Michigan State University, East Lansing.
Matos, A. & Cruz, N. (2009). MARES - navigation, control and on-board software, *in* A. V. Inzartsev (ed.), *Underwater Vehicles*, InTech.
Seshagiri, S. & Khalil, H. K. (2005). Robust output feedback regulation of minimum-phase nonlinear systems using conditional integrators, *Automatica* 41(1): 43–54.
Singh, A. & Khalil, H. K. (2005). Regulation of nonlinear systems using conditional integrators, *International Journal of Robust and Nonlinear Control* 15(8): 339–362. 930VR
Teixeira, F. C., Aguiar, A. P. & Pascoal, A. (2010). Nonlinear adaptive control of an underwater towed vehicle, *Ocean Engineering* 37(13): 1193–1220.
Triantafyllou, M. S. & Hover, F. S. (2002). Maneuvering and control of marine vehicles, *Technical report*, Massachussets Institute of Technology.
White, F. M. (2008). *Fluid Mechanics*, 5 edn, McGraw Hill, Boston.
Wu, N. E., Zhang, Y. M. & Zhou, K. M. (2000). Detection, estimation, and accommodation of loss of control effectiveness, *International Journal of Adaptive Control and Signal Processing* 14(7): 775–795.
Zhang, F. Z. (1997). Quaternions and matrices of quaternions, *Linear Algebra and Its Applications* 251: 21–57.
Zhang, Y. M. & Jiang, J. (2002). Active fault-tolerant control system against partial actuator failures, *IEEE Proceedings-Control Theory and Applications* 149(1): 95–104.

3

Sliding Mode Approach to Control Quadrotor Using Dynamic Inversion

Abhijit Das, Frank L. Lewis and Kamesh Subbarao
Automation and Robotics Research Institute
The University of Texas at Arlington
USA

1. Introduction

Nowadays unmanned rotorcraft are designed to operate with greater agility, rapid maneuvering, and are capable of work in degraded environments such as wind gusts etc. The control of this rotorcraft is a subject of research especially in applications such as rescue, surveillance, inspection, mapping etc. For these applications, the ability of the rotorcraft to maneuver sharply and hover precisely is important (Koo and Sastry 1998). Rotorcraft control as in these applications often requires holding a particular trimmed state; generally hover, as well as making changes of velocity and acceleration in a desired way (Gavrilets, Mettler, and Feron 2003). Similar to aircraft control, rotorcraft control too involves controlling the pitch, yaw, and roll motion. But the main difference is that, due to the unique body structure of rotorcraft (as well as the rotor dynamics and other rotating elements) the pitch, yaw and roll dynamics are strongly coupled. Therefore, it is difficult to design a decoupled control law of sound structure that stabilizes the faster and slower dynamics simultaneously. On the contrary, for a fixed wing aircraft it is relatively easy to design decoupled standard control laws with intuitively comprehensible structure and guaranteed performance (Stevens and F. L. Lewis 2003). There are many different approaches available for rotorcraft control such as (Altug, Ostrowski, and Mahony 2002; Bijnens et al. 2005; T. Madani and Benallegue 2006; Mistler, Benallegue, and M'Sirdi 2001; Mokhtari, Benallegue, and Orlov 2006) etc. Popular methods include input-output linearization and back-stepping. The 6-DOF airframe dynamics of a typical quadrotor involves the typical translational and rotational dynamical equations as in (Gavrilets, Mettler, and Feron 2003; Castillo, Lozano, and Dzul 2005; Castillo, Dzul, and Lozano 2004). The dynamics of a quadrotor is essentially a simplified form of helicopter dynamics that exhibits the basic problems including under-actuation, strong coupling, multi-input/multi-output, and unknown nonlinearities. The quadrotor is classified as a rotorcraft where lift is derived from the four rotors. Most often they are classified as helicopters as its movements are characterized by the resultant force and moments of the four rotors. Therefore the control algorithms designed for a quadrotor could be applied to a helicopter with relatively straightforward modifications. Most of the papers (B. Bijnens et al. 2005; T. Madani and Benallegue 2006; Mokhtari, Benallegue, and Orlov 2006) etc. deal with either input-output linearization for decoupling pitch yaw roll or back-stepping to deal with the under-actuation problem. The problem of coupling in the yaw-pitch-roll of a helicopter, as well as the problem of coupled dynamics-kinematic underactuated system, can be solved by back-stepping (Kanellakopoulos, Kokotovic, and Morse 1991; Khalil 2002; Slotine and Li 1991). Dynamic inversion (Stevens and F. L. Lewis 2003; Slotine and Li 1991; A. Das et al. 2004) is effective in the control of both linear and nonlinear systems and involves an inner inversion loop (similar to feedback linearization) which results in tracking if the residual or internal dynamics is stable. Typical usage requires the selection of the output control variables so that the internal dynamics is guaranteed to be stable. This implies that the tracking control cannot always be guaranteed for the original outputs of interest.

The application of dynamic inversion on UAV's and other flying vehicles such as missiles, fighter aircrafts etc. are proposed in several research works such as (Kim and Calise 1997; Prasad and Calise 1999; Calise et al. 1994) etc. It is also shown that the inclusion of dynamic neural network for estimating the dynamic inversion errors can improve the controller stability and tracking performance. Some other papers such as (Hovakimyan et al. 2001; Rysdyk and Calise 2005; Wise et al. 1999; Campos, F. L. Lewis, and Selmic 2000) etc. discuss the application of dynamic inversion on nonlinear systems to tackle the model and parametric uncertainties using neural nets. It is also shown that a reconfigurable control law can be designed for fighter aircrafts using neural net and dynamic inversion. Sometimes the inverse transformations required in dynamic inversion or feedback linearization are computed by neural network to reduce the inversion error by online learning.

In this chapter we apply dynamic inversion to tackle the coupling in quadrotor dynamics which is in fact an underactuated system. Dynamic inversion is applied to the inner loop, which yields internal dynamics that are not necessarily stable. Instead of redesigning the output control variables to guarantee stability of the internal dynamics, we use a sliding mode approach to stabilize the internal dynamics. This yields a two-loop structured tracking controller with a dynamic inversion inner loop and an internal dynamics stabilization outer loop. But it is interesting to notice that unlike normal two loop structure, we designed an inner loop which controls and stabilizes altitude and attitude of the quadrotor and an outer loop which controls and stabilizes the position (x,y) of the quadrotor. This yields a new structure of the autopilot in contrast to the conventional loop linear or nonlinear autopilot.

Section 2 of this chapter discusses the basic quadrotor dynamics which is used for control law formulation. Section 3 shows dynamic inversion of a nonlinear state-space model of a quadrotor. Sections 4 discuss the robust control method using sliding mode approach to stabilize the internal dynamics. In the final section, simulation results are shown to validate the control law discussed in this chapter.

2. Quadrotor dynamics

Fig. 1 shows a basic model of an unmanned quadrotor. The quadrotor has some basic advantage over the conventional helicopter. Given that the front and the rear motors rotate counter-clockwise while the other two rotate clockwise, gyroscopic effects and aerodynamic torques tend to cancel in trimmed flight. This four-rotor rotorcraft does not have a swash-plate (P. Castillo, R. Lozano, and A. Dzul 2005). In fact it does not need any blade pitch control. The collective input (or throttle input) is the sum of the thrusts of each motor (see Fig. 1). Pitch movement is obtained by increasing (reducing) the speed of the rear motor while reducing (increasing) the speed of the front motor. The roll movement is obtained similarly using the lateral motors. The yaw movement is obtained by increasing (decreasing) the speed of the front and rear motors while decreasing (increasing) the speed of the lateral motors (Bouabdallah, Noth, and Siegwart 2004).

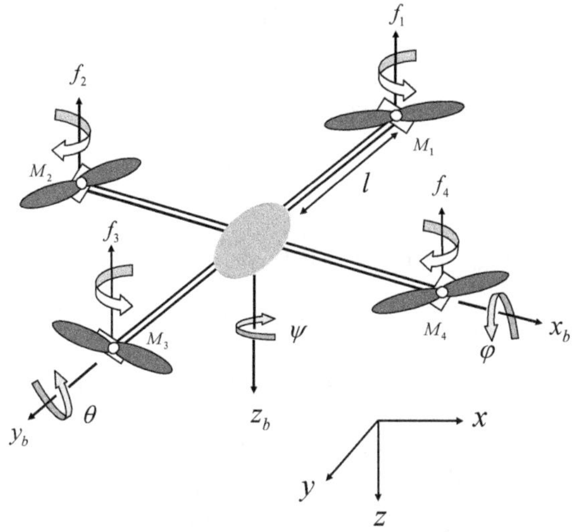

Fig. 1. A typical model of a quadrotor helicopter

In this section we will describe the basic state-space model of the quadrotor. The dynamics of the four rotors are relatively much faster than the main system and thus neglected in our case. The generalized coordinates of the rotorcraft are $q = (x, y, z, \psi, \theta, \varphi)$, where (x, y, z) represents the relative position of the center of mass of the quadrotor with respect to an inertial frame $\Im$, and (ψ, θ, φ) are the three Euler angles representing the orientation of the rotorcraft, namely yaw-pitch-roll of the vehicle.

Let us assume that the transitional and rotational coordinates are in the form $\xi = (x, y, z)^T \in R^3$ and $\eta = (\psi, \theta, \varphi) \in R^3$. Now the total transitional kinetic energy of the rotorcraft will be $T_{trans} = \frac{m}{2}\dot{\xi}^T\dot{\xi}$ where m is the mass of the quadrotor. The rotational kinetic energy is described as $T_{rot} = \frac{1}{2}\dot{\eta}^T J\dot{\eta}$, where matrix $J = J(\eta)$ is the auxiliary matrix expressed in terms of the generalized coordinates η. The potential energy in the system can be characterized by the gravitational potential, described as $U = mgz$. Defining the Lagrangian $L = T_{trans} + T_{rot} - U$, where $T_{trans} = (m/2)\dot{\xi}^T\dot{\xi}$ is the translational kinetic energy, $T_{rot} = (1/2)\omega^T I\omega$ is the rotational kinetic energy with ω as angular speed, $U = mgz$ is the potential energy, z is the quadrotor altitude, I is the body inertia matrix, and g is the acceleration due to gravity.

Then the full quadrotor dynamics is obtained as a function of the external generalized forces $F = (F_\xi, \tau)$ as

$$\frac{d}{dt}\frac{\partial L}{\partial \dot{q}} - \frac{\partial L}{\partial q} = F \tag{1}$$

The principal control inputs are defined as follows. Define

$$F_R = \begin{pmatrix} 0 \\ 0 \\ u \end{pmatrix} \tag{2}$$

where u is the main thrust and defined by

$$u = f_1 + f_2 + f_3 + f_4 \tag{3}$$

and f_i's are described as $f_i = k_i \omega_i^2$, where k_i are positive constants and ω_i are the angular speed of the motor i. Then F_ξ can be written as

$$F_\xi = \overline{R} F_R \tag{4}$$

where $\overline{R}$ is the transformation matrix representing the orientation of the rotorcraft as

$$\overline{R} = \begin{pmatrix} c_\theta c_\psi & s_\psi s_\theta & -s_\theta \\ c_\psi s_\theta s_\varphi - s_\psi c_\varphi & s_\psi s_\theta s_\varphi + c_\psi c_\varphi & c_\theta s_\varphi \\ c_\psi s_\theta c_\varphi + s_\psi s_\varphi & s_\psi s_\theta c_\varphi - c_\psi s_\varphi & c_\theta c_\varphi \end{pmatrix} \tag{5}$$

The generalized torque for the η variables are

$$\tau = \begin{pmatrix} \tau_\psi \\ \tau_\theta \\ \tau_\varphi \end{pmatrix} \tag{6}$$

where

$$\tau_\psi = \sum_{i=1}^{4} \tau_{M_i} = c(f_1 - f_2 + f_3 - f_4) \tag{7}$$

$$\tau_\theta = (f_2 - f_4) l \tag{8}$$

$$\tau_\varphi = (f_3 - f_1) l \tag{9}$$

Thus the control distribution from the four actuator motors of the quadrotor is given by

$$\begin{pmatrix} u \\ \tau_\varphi \\ \tau_\theta \\ \tau_\psi \end{pmatrix} = \underbrace{\begin{pmatrix} 1 & 1 & 1 & 1 \\ -l & 0 & l & 0 \\ 0 & l & 0 & -l \\ c & -c & c & -c \end{pmatrix}}_{C} \underbrace{\begin{pmatrix} f_1 \\ f_2 \\ f_3 \\ f_4 \end{pmatrix}}_{\underline{f}} \tag{10}$$

where l is the distance from the motors to the center of gravity, τ_{M_i} is the torque produced by motor M_i, and c is a constant known as force-to-moment scaling factor. So, if a required thrust and torque vector are given, one may solve for the rotor force using (10).

The final dynamic model of the quadrotor is described by (11)-(14),

$$m\ddot{\xi} + \begin{pmatrix} 0 \\ 0 \\ mg \end{pmatrix} = F_R \tag{11}$$

$$J(\eta)\ddot{\eta} + \frac{d}{dt}\{J(\eta)\}\dot{\eta} - \frac{1}{2}\frac{\partial}{\partial\eta}(\dot{\eta}^T J(\eta)\dot{\eta}) = \tau \tag{12}$$

$$J(\eta)\ddot{\eta} + \frac{d}{dt}\{J(\eta)\}\dot{\eta} - \bar{C}(\eta,\dot{\eta}) = \tau \tag{13}$$

$$J(\eta)\ddot{\eta} + C(\eta,\dot{\eta}) = \tau \tag{14}$$

where, $F_R = u\begin{pmatrix} -\sin\theta \\ \cos\theta\sin\varphi \\ \cos\theta\cos\varphi \end{pmatrix}$, auxiliary Matrix $\{J(\eta)\} = J = T_\eta^T I T_\eta$ with

$$T_\eta = \begin{pmatrix} -\sin\theta & 0 & 1 \\ \cos\theta\sin\psi & \cos\psi & 0 \\ \cos\theta\cos\psi & -\sin\psi & 0 \end{pmatrix}.$$

Now finally the dynamic model of the quadrotor in terms of position (x,y,z) and rotation (φ,θ,ψ) is written as,

$$\begin{pmatrix} \ddot{x} \\ \ddot{y} \\ \ddot{z} \end{pmatrix} = \begin{pmatrix} 0 \\ 0 \\ -g \end{pmatrix} + \frac{1}{m}\begin{pmatrix} -\sin\theta \\ \cos\theta\sin\varphi \\ \cos\theta\cos\varphi \end{pmatrix} u \tag{15}$$

$$\begin{pmatrix} \ddot{\varphi} \\ \ddot{\theta} \\ \ddot{\psi} \end{pmatrix} = f(\varphi,\theta,\psi) + g(\varphi,\theta,\psi)\tau \tag{16}$$

where,

$$f(\varphi,\theta,\psi) = \begin{pmatrix} \dot{\theta}\dot{\psi}\left(\frac{I_y - I_z}{I_x}\right) - \frac{J_p}{I_x}\dot{\theta}\Omega \\ \dot{\varphi}\dot{\psi}\left(\frac{I_z - I_x}{I_y}\right) + \frac{J_p}{I_y}\dot{\varphi}\Omega \\ \dot{\varphi}\dot{\theta}\left(\frac{I_x - I_y}{I_z}\right) \end{pmatrix}, g(\varphi,\theta,\psi) = \begin{pmatrix} \frac{l}{I_x} & 0 & 0 \\ 0 & \frac{l}{I_y} & 0 \\ 0 & 0 & \frac{l}{I_z} \end{pmatrix}, u \in R^1 \text{ and } \tau = \begin{bmatrix} \tau_\varphi \\ \tau_\theta \\ \tau_\psi \end{bmatrix} \in R^3 \text{ are the}$$

control inputs, $I_{x,y,z}$ are body inertia, J_p is propeller/rotor inertia and $\Omega = \omega_2 + \omega_4 - \omega_1 - \omega_3$. Thus, the system is the form of an under-actuated system with six outputs and four inputs.

Comment 2.1: *In this chapter we considered a generalized state space model of quadrotor derived from Lagrangian dynamics. Design autopilot with actual Lagrangian model of quadrotor is discussed in* (Abhijit Das, Frank Lewis, and Kamesh Subbarao 2009).

3. Partial feedback linearization for Quadrotor model

Dynamic inversion (Stevens and F. L. Lewis 2003) is an approach where a feedback linearization loop is applied to the tracking outputs of interest. The residual dynamics, not directly controlled, is known as the internal dynamics. If the internal dynamics are stable, dynamic inversion is successful. Typical usage requires the selection of the output control variables so that the internal dynamics is guaranteed to be stable. This means that tracking cannot always be guaranteed for the original outputs of interest.

In this chapter we apply dynamic inversion to the system given by (15) and (16) to achieve station-keeping tracking control for the position outputs (x,y,z,ψ). Initially we select the convenient output vector $y_{di}=(z,\varphi,\theta,\psi)$ which makes the dynamic inverse easy to find. Dynamic inversion now yields effectively an inner control loop that feedback linearizes the system from the control $u_{di}=(u,\tau_\varphi,\tau_\theta,\tau_\psi)$ to the output $y_{di}=(z,\varphi,\theta,\psi)$. Note that the output contains attitude parameters as well as altitude of the quadrotor.

Note however that y_{di} is not the desired system output. Moreover, dynamic inversion generates a specific internal dynamics, as detailed below, which may not always be stable. Therefore, a second outer loop is designed to generate the required values for $y_{di}=(z,\varphi,\theta,\psi)$ in terms of the values of the desired tracking output (x,y,z,ψ). An overall Lyapunov proof guarantees stability and performance. The following background is required. Consider a nonlinear system of the form

$$\dot{q}=f(q,u_q) \tag{17}$$

where $u_q\in R^m$ is the control input and $q\in R^n$ is state vector. The technique of designing the control input u using dynamic inversion involves two steps. First, one finds a state transformation $z=z(q)$ and an input transformation $u_q=u_q(q,v)$ so that the nonlinear system dynamics is transformed into an equivalent linear time invariant dynamics of the form

$$\dot{z}=az+bv \tag{18}$$

where $a\in R^{n\times n}, b\in R^{n\times m}$ are constant matrices with v is known as new input to the linear system. Secondly one can design v easily from the linear control theory approach such as pole placement etc. To get the desired linear equations (18), one has to differentiate outputs until input vector u_{di} appears. The procedure is known as dynamic inversion.

3.1 Dynamic inversion for inner loop

The system, (15)→(16) is an underactuated system if we consider the states $(x,y,z,\varphi,\theta,\psi)$ as outputs and $u_{di}=\begin{bmatrix}u & \tau_\varphi & \tau_\theta & \tau_\psi\end{bmatrix}^T$ as inputs. To overcome these difficulties we consider four outputs $y_{di}=(z,\varphi,\theta,\psi)$ which are used for feedback linearization. Differentiating the output vector twice with respect to the time we get from (15) and (16) that,

$$\ddot{y}_{di} = M_{di} + E_{di}u_{di} \tag{19}$$

where,

$$M_{di} = \begin{bmatrix} -g \\ \dot{\theta}\dot{\psi}\left(\dfrac{I_y - I_z}{I_x}\right) - \dfrac{J_P}{I_x}\dot{\theta}\Omega \\ \dot{\varphi}\dot{\psi}\left(\dfrac{I_z - I_x}{I_y}\right) + \dfrac{J_P}{I_y}\dot{\varphi}\Omega \\ \dot{\varphi}\dot{\theta}\left(\dfrac{I_x - I_y}{I_z}\right) \end{bmatrix} \in \Re^4, \; E_{di} = \begin{bmatrix} -(1/m)\cos\theta\cos\varphi & 0 & 0 & 0 \\ 0 & \dfrac{l}{I_x} & 0 & 0 \\ 0 & 0 & \dfrac{l}{I_y} & 0 \\ 0 & 0 & 0 & \dfrac{l}{I_z} \end{bmatrix} \in \Re^{4\times 4}$$

The number $(r = 8)$ of differentiation required for an invertible E_{di} is known as the relative degree of the system and generally $r < n = 12$; if $r = n$ then full state feedback linearization is achieved if E_{di} is invertible. Note that for multi-input multi-output system, if number of outputs is not equal to the number of inputs (under-actuated system), then E_{di} becomes non-square and is difficult to obtain a feasible linearizing input u_{di}.
It is seen that for non-singularity of E_{di}, $0 \le \theta, \varphi < 90^\circ$. The relative degree of the system is calculated as 8 whereas the order of the system is 12. So, the remaining dynamics $(= 4)$ which does not come out in the process of feedback linearization is known as internal dynamics. To guarantee the stability of the whole system, it is mandatory to guarantee the stability of the internal dynamics. In the next section we will discuss how to control the internal dynamics using a PID with a feed-forward acceleration outer loop. Now using (19) we can write the desired input to the system

$$u_{di} = E_{di}^{-1}(-M_{di} + v_{di}) \tag{20}$$

which yields

$$\ddot{y}_{di} = v_{di} \tag{21}$$

where, $v_{di} = \begin{pmatrix} v_z & v_\varphi & v_\theta & v_\psi \end{pmatrix}^T$. This system is decoupled and linear. The auxiliary input v_{di} is designed as described below.

3.2 Design of linear controller

Assuming the desired output to the system is $y_d = \begin{pmatrix} z_d & \varphi_d & \theta_d & \psi_d \end{pmatrix}^T$, the linear controller v_{di} is designed in the following way

$$v_{di} = \begin{bmatrix} v_z \\ v_\varphi \\ v_\theta \\ v_\psi \end{bmatrix} = \begin{bmatrix} \ddot{z}_d - K_{1_z}(\dot{z} - \dot{z}_d) - K_{2_z}(z - z_d) \\ \ddot{\varphi}_d - K_{1_\varphi}(\dot{\varphi} - \dot{\varphi}_d) - K_{2_\varphi}(\varphi - \varphi_d) \\ \ddot{\theta}_d - K_{1_\theta}(\dot{\theta} - \dot{\theta}_d) - K_{2_\theta}(\theta - \theta_d) \\ \ddot{\psi}_d - K_{1_\psi}(\dot{\psi} - \dot{\psi}_d) - K_{2_\psi}(\psi - \psi_d) \end{bmatrix} \tag{22}$$

where, $K_{1_\varphi}, K_{2_\varphi}, ...$ etc. are positive constants so that the poles of the error dynamics arising from (23) and (24) are in the left half of the $s-$plane. For hovering control, z_d and ψ_d are chosen depending upon the designer choice.

3.3 Defining sliding variable error

Let us define the state error $e_1 = \left(z_d - z \quad \varphi_d - \varphi \quad \theta_d - \theta \quad \psi_d - \psi\right)^T$ and a sliding mode error as

$$r_1 = \dot{e}_1 + \Lambda_1 e_1 \tag{23}$$

where, Λ_1 is a diagonal positive definite design parameter matrix. Common usage is to select Λ_1 diagonal with positive entries. Then, (23) is a stable system so that e_1 is bounded as long as the controller guarantees that the filtered error r_1 is bounded. In fact it is easy to show (F. Lewis, Jagannathan, and Yesildirek 1999) that one has

$$\|e_1\| \le \frac{\|r_1\|}{\sigma_{\min}(\Lambda_1)}, \|\dot{e}_1\| \le \|r_1\| \tag{24}$$

Note that $\dot{e}_1 + \Lambda_1 e_1 = 0$ defines a stable sliding mode surface. The function of the controller to be designed is to force the system onto this surface by making r_1 small. The parameter Λ_1 is selected for a desired sliding mode response

$$e_1(t) = e_1^{-\Lambda_1 t} e_1(0) \tag{25}$$

We now focus on designing a controller to keep $\|r_1\|$ small. From (23),

$$\dot{r}_1 = \ddot{e}_1 + \Lambda_1 \dot{e}_1 \tag{26}$$

Adding an integrator to the linear controller given in (22), and now we can rewrite (22) as

$$v_{di} = \ddot{y}_{di_d} + K_1 \dot{e}_1 + K_2 e_1 + K_3 \int_0^t r_1 dt \tag{27}$$

where, $y_{di_d} = \left[\ddot{z}_d, \ddot{\varphi}_d, \ddot{\theta}_d, \ddot{\psi}_d\right]^T$ and $K_i = diag(K_{i_z}, K_{i_\varphi}, K_{i_\theta}, K_{i_\psi}) > 0$, $i = 1,2,3,4$.

Now using equation (20) and (27) we can rewrite the equation (19) in the form of error dynamics as

$$\ddot{e}_1 + K_1 \dot{e}_1 + K_2 e_1 + K_3 \int_0^t r_1 dt = 0 \tag{28}$$

Thus equation (26) becomes

$$\dot{r}_1 = -K_1 \dot{e}_1 - K_2 e_1 - K_3 \int_0^t r_1 dt + \Lambda_1 \dot{e}_1 \tag{29}$$

If we choose $K_1 = (\Lambda_1 + R), K_2 = \Lambda_1 R$, then equation (29) will look like

$$\dot{r}_1 = -R r_1 - K_3 \int_0^t r_1 dt \tag{30}$$

Note that $R > 0$ is also a diagonal matrix.

4. Sliding mode control for internal dynamics

The internal dynamics (Slotine and Li 1991) for the feedback linearizes system given by

$$\ddot{x} = -\frac{u}{m}\sin\theta \tag{31}$$

$$\ddot{y} = \frac{u}{m}\cos\theta\sin\varphi \tag{32}$$

For the stability of the whole system as well as for the tracking purposes, x, y should be bounded and controlled in a desired way. Note that the altitude z of the rotorcraft a any given time t is controlled by (20),(22).
To stabilize the zero dynamics, we select some desired θ_d and φ_d such that (x, y) is bounded. Then that (θ_d, φ_d) can be fed into (22) as a reference. Using Taylor series expansion about some nominal values θ_d^* , φ_d^* and considering up to first order terms

$$\begin{aligned} \sin\theta_d &= \sin\theta_d^* + \cos\theta_d^*(\theta_d - \theta_d^*) \\ \cos\theta_d &= \cos\theta_d^* - \sin\theta_d^*(\theta_d - \theta_d^*) \\ \sin\varphi_d &= \sin\varphi_d^* + \cos\varphi_d^*(\varphi_d - \varphi_d^*) \end{aligned} \tag{33}$$

Using (33) on (31) we get

$$\ddot{x} = -\frac{u}{m}\left\{\sin\theta_d^* + \cos\theta_d^*(\theta_d - \theta_d^*)\right\} \tag{34}$$

$$\ddot{y} = \frac{u}{m}\left\{\cos\theta_d^* - \sin\theta_d^*(\theta_d - \theta_d^*)\right\}\left\{\sin\varphi_d^* + \cos\varphi_d^*(\varphi_d - \varphi_d^*)\right\} \tag{35}$$

For hovering of a quadrotor, assuming the nominal values $\theta_d^* \approx 0$, $\varphi_d^* \approx 0$, (31) and (32) becomes

$$\ddot{x} = -\frac{u}{m}\theta_d \tag{36}$$

$$\ddot{y} = \frac{u}{m}\varphi_d \tag{37}$$

Define the state error

$$e_2 = \begin{pmatrix} x_d - x & y_d - y \end{pmatrix}^T \tag{38}$$

and the sliding mode error for the internal dynamics as

$$r_2 = \dot{e}_2 + \Lambda_2 e_2 \tag{39}$$

where, Λ_2 is a diagonal positive definite design parameter matrix with similar characteristic of Λ_1. Also

$$\|e_2\| \le \frac{\|r_2\|}{\sigma_{\min}(\Lambda_2)}, \|\dot{e}_2\| \le \|r_2\| \tag{40}$$

Therefore according to (40), designing a controller to keep $\|r_2\|$ small will guarantee that $\|e_2\|$ and $\|\dot{e}_2\|$ are small. Differentiating r_2 we get

$$\dot{r}_2 = \ddot{e}_2 + \Lambda_2 \dot{e}_2 \tag{41}$$

Let the choice of the control law is as follows

$$\theta_d = \frac{m}{u}\left[-\ddot{x}_d - c_{11}(\dot{x}_d - \dot{x}) - c_{12}(x_d - x) - c_{13}\int_0^t r_2 dt - \beta_x \operatorname{sgn}(r_2)\right], \beta_x > 0 \tag{42}$$

$$\varphi_d = \frac{m}{u}\left[\ddot{y}_d + c_{21}(\dot{y}_d - \dot{y}) + c_{22}(y_d - y) + c_{23}\int_0^t r_2 dt + \beta_y \operatorname{sgn}(r_2)\right], \beta_y > 0 \tag{43}$$

where, $\begin{bmatrix} c_{11} & 0 \\ 0 & c_{21} \end{bmatrix} = C_1 > 0$, $\begin{bmatrix} c_{12} & 0 \\ 0 & c_{22} \end{bmatrix} = C_2 > 0$, $\begin{bmatrix} c_{13} & 0 \\ 0 & c_{23} \end{bmatrix} = C_3 > 0$ and $\begin{bmatrix} \beta_x & 0 \\ 0 & \beta_y \end{bmatrix} = \beta > 0$.

Combining the equations (36) to (43)

$$\ddot{e}_2 + C_1\dot{e}_2 + C_2 e_2 + C_3\int_0^t r_2 dt + \beta \operatorname{sgn}(r_2) = 0 \tag{44}$$

Therefore

$$\dot{r}_2 = -C_1\dot{e}_2 - C_2 e_2 - C_3\int_0^t r_2 dt - \beta \operatorname{sgn}(r_2) + \Lambda_2 \dot{e}_2 \tag{45}$$

Let

$$C_1 = \Lambda_2 + S_0 \tag{46}$$

$$C_2 = \Lambda_2 S_0 \tag{47}$$

Therefore

$$\dot{r}_2 = -(\Lambda_2 + S_0)\dot{e}_2 - \Lambda_2 S_0 e_2 - C_3\int_0^t r_2 dt - \beta \operatorname{sgn}(r_2) + \Lambda_2 \dot{e}_2 \tag{48}$$

$$\dot{r}_2 = -S_0 r_2 - C_3\int_0^t r_2 dt - \beta \operatorname{sgn}(r_2) \tag{49}$$

5. Controller structure and stability analysis

The overall control system has two loops and is depicted in Fig. 2. The following theorem details the performance of the controller.

Definition 5.1: *The equilibrium point x_e is said to be uniformly ultimately bounded (UUB) if there exist a compact set $S \subset R^n$ so that for all $x_0 \in S$ there exist a bound B and a time $T(B,x_0)$ such that $\|x(t)-x_e(t)\| \le B \forall t \ge t_0 + T$.*

Theorem 5.1: *Given the system as described in (15) and (16) with a control law shown in Fig. 2. and given by (20), (27), (42), (43). Then, the tracking errors r_1 and r_2 and thereby e_1 and e_2 are UUB if (53) and (54) are satisfied and can be made arbitrarily small with a suitable choice of gain parameters. According to the definition given by (23) of r_1 and (39) of r_2, this guarantees that e_1 and e_2 are UUB since*

$$\begin{aligned} \|e_1\| &\le \frac{\|r_1\|}{\sigma_{\min}(\Lambda_1)} \le \frac{b_{r_1}}{\sigma_{\min}(\Lambda_1)} \qquad b_{r_1} > 0 \\ \|e_2\| &\le \frac{\|r_2\|}{\sigma_{\min}(\Lambda_2)} \le \frac{b_{r_2}}{\sigma_{\min}(\Lambda_2)} \qquad b_{r_2} > 0 \end{aligned} \tag{50}$$

where $\sigma_{\min}(\Lambda_i)$ is the minimum singular value of $\Lambda_i, i = 1,2$.

Proof: Consider the Lyapunov function

$$L = \frac{1}{2}r_1^T P_1 r_1 + \frac{1}{2}r_2^T Q_1 r_2 + \frac{1}{2}\left[\int_0^t r_1^T dt\right] P_2 \left[\int_0^t r_1 dt\right] + \frac{1}{2}\left[\int_0^t r_2^T dt\right] Q_2 \left[\int_0^t r_2 dt\right] \tag{51}$$

with symmetric matrices $P_1, P_2, Q_1, Q_2 > 0$

Therefore, by differentiating L we will get the following

$$\begin{aligned} \dot{L} = &-r_1^T P_1 R r_1 - r_1^T P_1 K_3 \int_0^t r_1 dt + r_1 P_2 \int_0^t r_1 dt - r_2^T Q_1 S_0 r_2 - \\ & r_2^T Q_1 C_3 \int_0^t r_2 dt + r_2^T Q_2 \int_0^t r_2 dt - r_2^T Q_1 \beta \operatorname{sgn}(r_2) \end{aligned} \tag{52}$$

Define,

$$P_2 = P_1 K_3 \tag{53}$$

$$Q_2 = Q_1 C_3 \tag{54}$$

then integration term vanishes.

$$\dot{L} = -r_1^T P_1 R r_1 - r_2^T Q_1 S_0 r_2 - r_2^T Q_1 \beta \operatorname{sgn}(r_2) \tag{55}$$

The Equation (55) can be written as

$$\dot{L} \le -\sigma_{\max}(P_1 R) r_1^2 - \sigma_{\max}(Q_1 S_0) r_2^2 - \sigma_{\max}(Q_1 \beta)|r_2| \le 0 \tag{56}$$

where, $\sigma_{\max}(\cdot)$ denotes the maximum singular value. ■

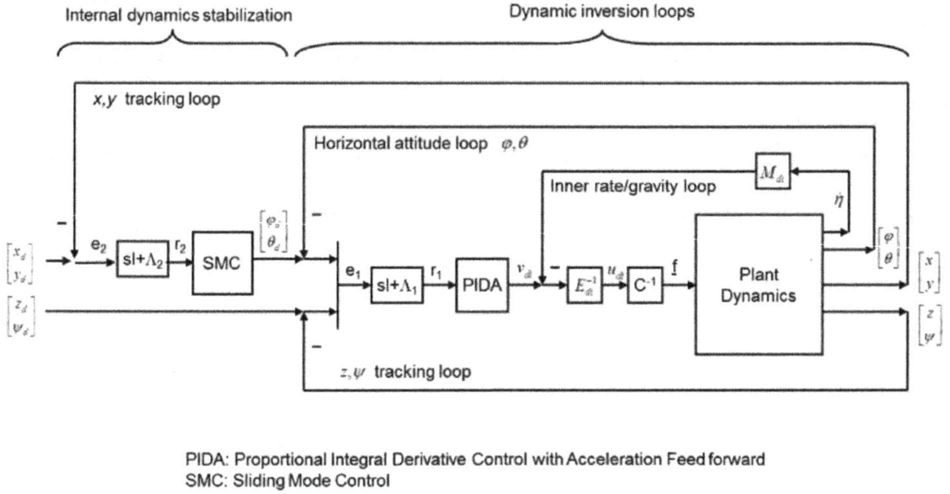

Fig. 2. Control configuration

Comment 5.1: *Equations* (31)-(32) *can also be rewritten* as

$$\ddot{x} = -\frac{u}{m}\theta_d - \frac{u}{m}(-\tilde{\theta}) \tag{57}$$

$$\ddot{y} = \frac{u}{m}\varphi_d - \frac{u}{m}\tilde{\varphi} \tag{58}$$

where $\tilde{\theta} = \theta_d - \sin\theta$ *and* $\tilde{\varphi} = \varphi_d - \cos\theta\sin\varphi$ *. According to* (A. Das, K. Subbarao, and F. Lewis 2009) *there exist a robustifying term* V_r *which would modify the* v_{di} *as*

$$v_{di} = \begin{bmatrix} v_z \\ v_\varphi \\ v_\theta \\ v_\psi \end{bmatrix} = \begin{bmatrix} \ddot{z}_d - K_{1_z}(\dot{z} - \dot{z}_d) - K_{2_z}(z - z_d) \\ \ddot{\varphi}_d - K_{1_\varphi}(\dot{\varphi} - \dot{\varphi}_d) - K_{2_\varphi}(\varphi - \varphi_d) \\ \ddot{\theta}_d - K_{1_\theta}(\dot{\theta} - \dot{\theta}_d) - K_{2_\theta}(\theta - \theta_d) \\ \ddot{\psi}_d - K_{1_\psi}(\dot{\psi} - \dot{\psi}_d) - K_{2_\psi}(\psi - \psi_d) \end{bmatrix} + V_r \tag{59}$$

and thereby one can easily show that $\dot{L} \le 0$ *by suitbale choice of* V_r *. For this book chapter we considered the Eq. (36),(37), whcih in fact a simpler version of (31),(32). But we belive, for designing autopilot for quadrotor, the proposed mehtod discussed in this chapter can be used without loss of any genreality.*

6. Simulation results

6.1 Rotorcraft parameters

Simulation for a typical quadrotor is performed using the following parameters (SI unit):

$$M_1 = \begin{bmatrix} 1 & 0 & 0 \\ 0 & 1 & 0 \\ 0 & 0 & 1 \end{bmatrix}; \qquad J = \begin{bmatrix} 5 & 0 & 0 \\ 0 & 5 & 0 \\ 0 & 0 & 15 \end{bmatrix}; \qquad g = 9.81 .$$

6.2 Reference trajectory generation

As outlined in Refs (Hogan 1984; Flash and Hogan 1985), a reference trajectory is derived that minimizes the jerk (rate of change of acceleration) over the time horizon. The trajectory ensures that the velocities and accelerations at the end point are zero while meeting the position tracking objective. The following summarizes this approach:

$$\dot{x}_d(t) = a_{1_x} + 2a_{2_x} t + 3a_{3_x} t^2 + 4a_{4_x} t^3 + 5a_{5_x} t^4 \tag{60}$$

Differentiating again,

$$\ddot{x}_d(t) = 2a_{2_x} + 6a_{3_x} t + 12a_{4_x} t^2 + 20a_{5_x} t^3 \tag{61}$$

As we indicated before that initial and final velocities and accelerations are zero; so from Eqs. (60) and (61) we can conclude the following:

$$\begin{bmatrix} d_x \\ 0 \\ 0 \end{bmatrix} = \begin{bmatrix} 1 & t_f & t_f^2 \\ 3 & 4t_f & 5t_f^2 \\ 6 & 12t_f & 20t_f^2 \end{bmatrix} \begin{bmatrix} a_{3_x} \\ a_{4_x} \\ a_{5_x} \end{bmatrix} \tag{62}$$

Where, $d_x = \left(x_{d_f} - x_{d_0}\right) / t_f^3$. Now, solving for coefficients

$$\begin{bmatrix} a_{3_x} \\ a_{4_x} \\ a_{5_x} \end{bmatrix} = \begin{bmatrix} 1 & t_f & t_f^2 \\ 3 & 4t_f & 5t_f^2 \\ 6 & 12t_f & 20t_f^2 \end{bmatrix}^{-1} \begin{bmatrix} d_x \\ 0 \\ 0 \end{bmatrix} \tag{63}$$

Thus the desired trajectory for the x direction is given by

$$x_d(t) = x_{d_0} + a_{3_x} t^3 + a_{4_x} t^4 + a_{5_x} t^5 \tag{64}$$

Similarly, the reference trajectories for the y and z directions are gives by Eq. (65) and Eq. (66) respectively.

$$y_d(t) = y_{d_0} + a_{3_y} t^3 + a_{4_y} t^4 + a_{5_y} t^5 \tag{65}$$

$$z_d(t) = z_{d_0} + a_{3_z} t^3 + a_{4_z} t^4 + a_{5_z} t^5 \tag{66}$$

The beauty of this method lying in the fact that more demanding changes in position can be accommodated by varying the final time. That is acceleration/torque ratio can be controlled smoothly as per requirement. For example,

Let us assume at $t = 0$, $x_{d_0} = 0$ and at $t = 10$ sec, $x_{d_f} = 10$. Therefore $d_x = 0.01$ and the trajectory is given by Eq. (67) and shown in Fig. 3 for various desired final positions.

$$x_d(t) = 0.1t^3 - 0.015t^4 + 0.0006t^5 \tag{67}$$

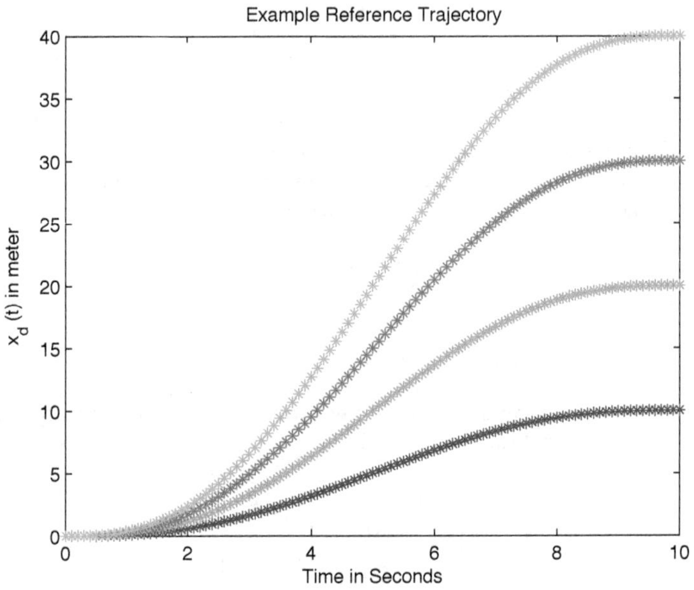

Fig. 3. Example trajectory simulation for different final positions

6.3 Case 1: From initial position at $(0,5,10)$ to final position at $(20,-5,0)$

Figure 4 describes the controlled motion of the quadrotor from its initial position $(0,5,10)$ to final position $(20,-5,0)$ for a given time (20 seconds). The actual trajectories $x(t), y(t), z(t)$ match exactly their desired values $x_d(t), y_d(t), z_d(t)$ respectively nearly exactly. The errors along the three axes are also shown in the same figure. It can be seen that the tracking is almost perfect as well as the tracking errors are significantly small. Figure 5 describes the attitude of the quadrotor φ, θ along with their demands φ_d, θ_d and attitude errors in radian. Again the angles match their command values nearly perfectly. Figure 6 describes the control input requirement which is very much realizable. Note that as described before the control requirement for yaw angle is $\tau_\psi = 0$ and it is seen from Fig. 6.

6.4 Case 2: From initial position at $(0,5,10)$ to final position at $(20,5,10)$

Figures 7-8 illustrates the decoupling phenomenon of the control law. Fig. 7 shows that $x(t)$ follows the command $x_d(t)$ nearly perfectly unlike $y(t)$ and $z(t)$ are held their initial values. Fig. 8 shows that the change in x does not make any influence on φ. The corresponding control inputs are also shown in Fig. 9 and due to the full decoupling effect it is seen that τ_φ is almost zero.

The similar type of simulations are performed for y and z directional motions separately and similar plots are obtained showing excellent tracking.

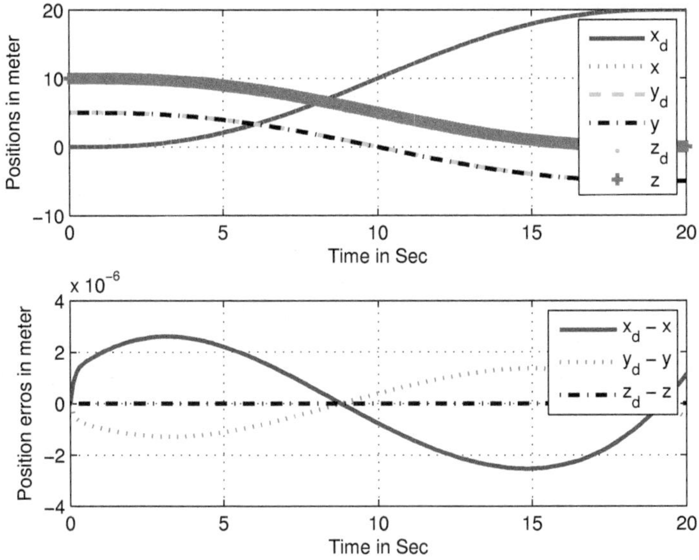

Fig. 4. Three position commands simultaneously

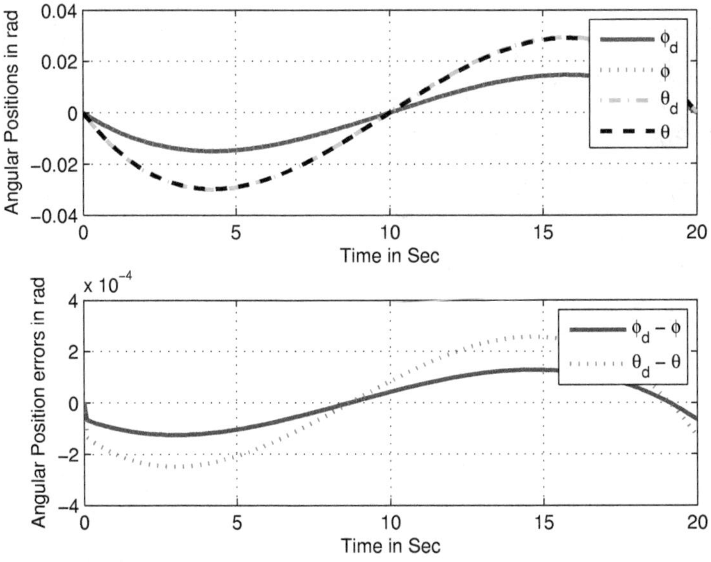

Fig. 5. Resultant angular positions and errors

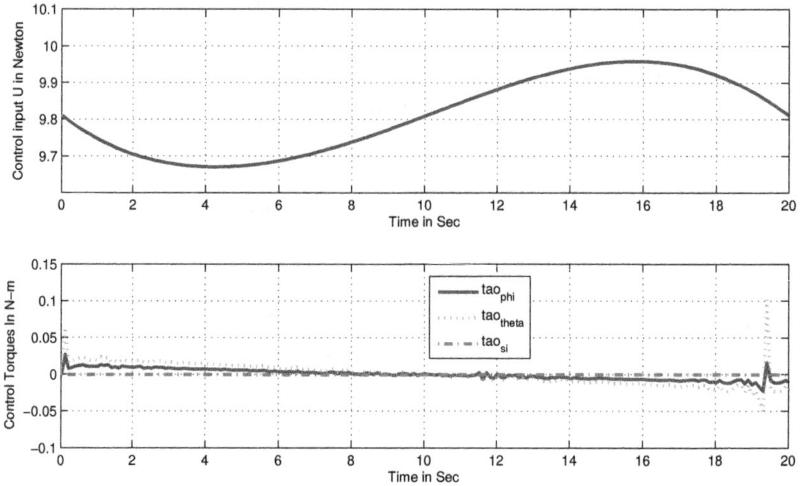

Fig. 6. Input commands for Case I

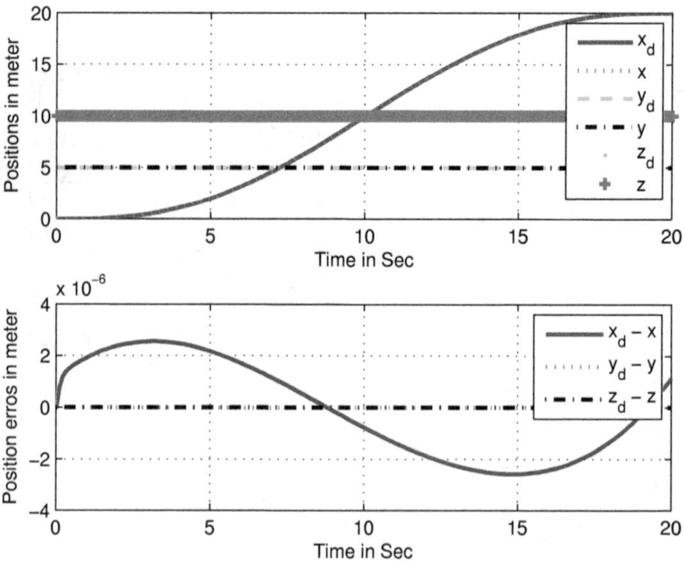

Fig. 7. Plots of position and position tracking errors for x command only

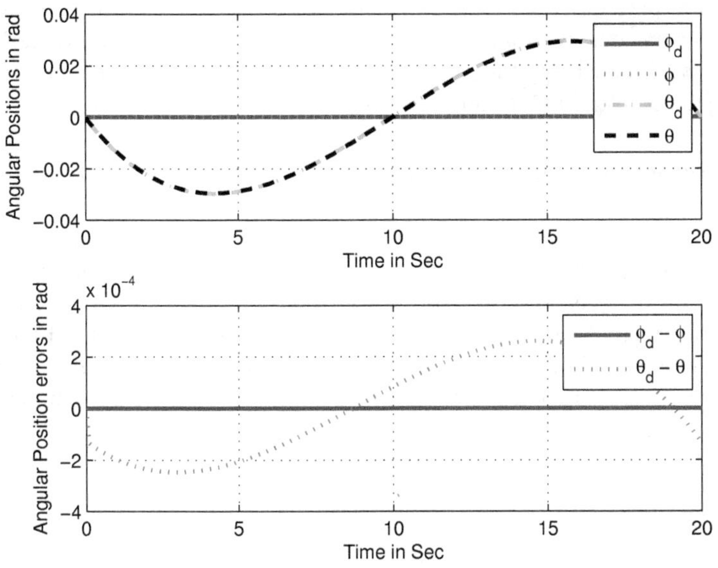

Fig. 8. Angular variations due to change in x

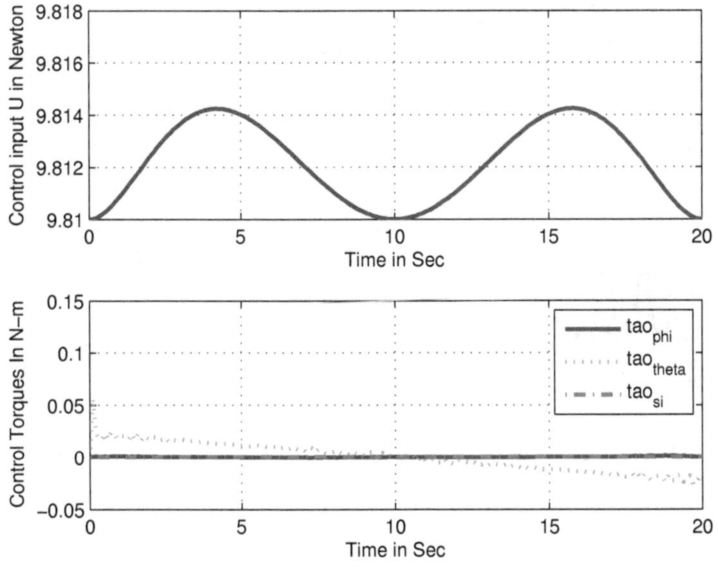

Fig. 9. Input commands for variation in x (Case II)

6.5 Simulation with unmodeled input disturbances

The simulation is performed to verify its robustness properties against unmodeled input disturbances. For this case we simulate the dynamics with high frequency disturbance 0.1* $\sin(5t)$ (1% of maximum magnitude of force) for force channel and $0.01\sin(5t)$ (~15% of maximum angular acceleration) for torque channel.

6.6 Case-3: From initial position at $(0,5,10)$ to final position at $(20,-5,0)$ with disturbance

Fig. 10-11 describes the motion of the quadrotor from its initial position $(0,5,10)$ to final position $(20,-5,0)$ for a given time (20 seconds) with input disturbances. It can be seen from Fig 10 that the quadrotor can track the desired position effectively without any effect of high input disturbances. From Fig 10 and Fig 11, it is also seen that the position errors are bounded and small. Fig. 12 shows the bounded variation of control inputs in presence of disturbance. Similar tracking performance is obtained for other commanded motion.

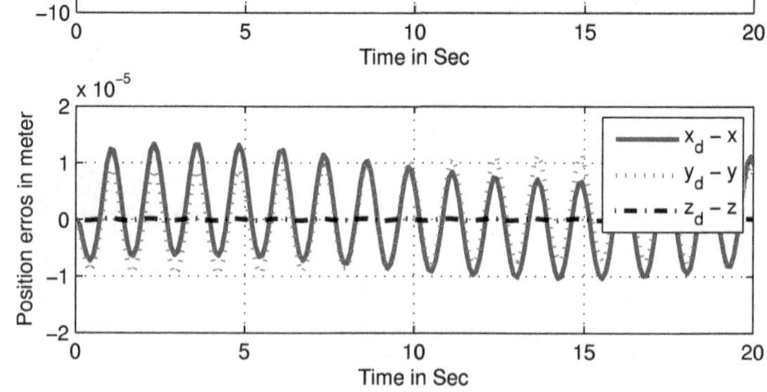

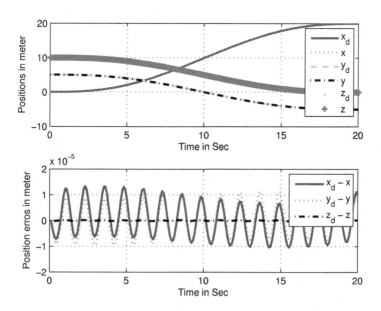

Fig. 10. Position tracking – Simultaneous command in x, y and z + Input disturbances

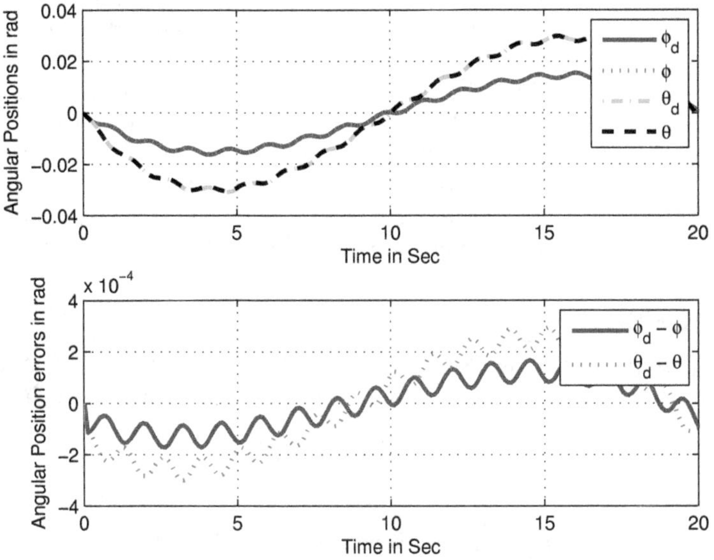

Fig. 11. Angular variations, errors and velocities (with input disturbances)

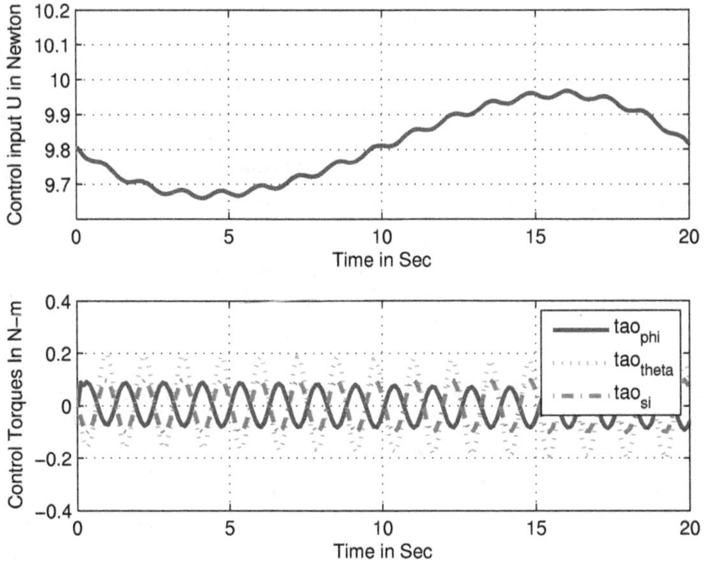

Fig. 12. Force and torque input variations (with input disturbances)

7. Conclusion

Sliding mode approach using input-output linearization to design nonlinear controller for a quadrotor dynamics is discussed in this Chapter. Using this approach, an intuitively structured controller was derived that has an outer sliding mode control loop and an inner feedback linearizing control loop. The dynamics of a quadrotor are a simplified form of helicopter dynamics that exhibits the basic problems including under-actuation, strong coupling, multi-input/multi-output. The derived controller is capable of deal with such problems simultaneously and satisfactorily. As the quadrotor model discuss in this Chapter is similar to a full scale unmanned helicopter model, the same control configuration derived for quadrotor is also applicable for a helicopter model. The simulation results are presented to demonstrate the validity of the control law discussed in the Chapter.

8. Acknowledgement

This work was supported by the National Science Foundation ECS-0801330, the Army Research Office W91NF-05-1-0314 and the Air Force Office of Scientific Research FA9550-09-1-0278.

9. References

Altug, Erdinc, James P. Ostrowski, and Robert Mahony. 2002. Control of a Quadrotor Helicopter Using Visual Feedback ID - 376. In . Washington DC, Virginia, June.

B. Bijnens, Q. P. Chu, G. M. Voorsluijs, and J. A. Mulder. 2005. AIAA Guidance, Navigation, and Control Conference and Exhibit. In . San Francisco, California.

Bijnens, B., Q. P. Chu, G. M. Voorsluijs, and J. A. Mulder. 2005. Adaptive Feedback Linearization Flight Control for a Helicopter UAVID - 199.

Bouabdallah, Samir, AndrÂ´e Noth, and Roland Siegwart. 2004. International Conference on Intelligent Robots and Systems. In , 3:2451-2456. Sendal, Japan: IEEE.

Calise, A. J., B. S. Kim, J. Leitner, and J. V. R. Prasad. 1994. Helicopter adaptive flight control using neural networks. In . Lake Buena Vista, FL.

Campos, J., F. L. Lewis, and C. R. Selmic. 2000. Backlash Compensation in Discrete Time Nonlinear Systems Using Dynamic Inversion by Neural Networks. In . San Francisco, CA.

Castillo, P., A. Dzul, and R. Lozano. 2004. Real-time Stabilization and Tracking of a Four-Rotor Mini Rotorcraft. *IEEE Transaction on Control System Technology* 12: 510-516.

Castillo, P., R. Lozano, and A. Dzul. 2005. *Modelling and Control of Mini Flying Machines.* Springer-Verlag.

Das, A., T. Garai, S. Mukhopadhyay, and A. Patra. 2004. Feedback Linearization for a Nonlinear Skid-To-Turn Missile Model. *First India annual conference, Proceedings of the IEEE INDICON 2004*: 586-589.

Das, A., K. Subbarao, and F. Lewis. 2009. Dynamic inversion with zero-dynamics stabilisation for quadrotor control. *Control Theory & Applications, IET* 3, no. 3 (March): 303 - 314.

Das, Abhijit, Frank Lewis, and Kamesh Subbarao. 2009. Backstepping Approach for Controlling a Quadrotor Using Lagrange Form Dynamics. *Journal of Intelligent and Robotic Systems* 56, no. 1-2 (4): 127-151. doi:10.1007/s10846-009-9331-0.

Flash, T., and N. Hogan. 1985. The Coordination of Arm Movements: an Experimentally Confirmed Mathematical Model. *Journal of Neuro Science* 5: 1688-1703.

Gavrilets, V., B. Mettler, and E. Feron. 2003. Dynamic Model for a Miniature Aerobatic Helicopter. *MIT-LIDS report* LIDS-P-2580.

Hogan, N. 1984. Adaptive Control of Mechanical Impedance by Coactivation of Antagonist Muscles. *IEEE Transaction of Automatic Control* 29: 681-690.

Hovakimyan, N., F. Nardi, A. J. Calise, and H. Lee. 2001. Adaptive Output Feedback Control of a Class of Nonlinear Systems Using Neural Networks. *International Journal of Control* 74: 1161-1169.

Kanellakopoulos, I., P. V. Kokotovic, and A. S. Morse. 1991. Systematic Design of Adaptive Controllers for Feedback Linearizable Systems. *IEEE Transaction of Automatic Control* 36: 1241-1253.

Khalil, Hassan K. 2002. *Nonlinear Systems*. 3rd ed. Upper Saddle River, N.J: Prentice Hall.

Kim, B. S., and A. J. Calise. 1997. Nonlinear flight control using neural networks. *Journal of Guidance Control Dynamics* 20: 26-33.

Koo, T. J., and S. Sastry. 1998. Output tracking control design of a helicopter model based on approximate linearization. In *Proceedings of the 37th Conference on Decision and Control*. Tampa, Florida: IEEE.

Lewis, F., S. Jagannathan, and A. Yesildirek. 1999. *Neural Network Control of Robot Manipulators and Nonlinear Systems*. London: Taylor and Francis.

Mistler, V., A. Benallegue, and N. K. M'Sirdi. 2001. Exact linearization and non- interacting control of a 4 rotors helicopter via dynamic feedback. In *10th IEEE Int. Workshop on Robot-Human Interactive Communication*. Paris.

Mokhtari, A., A. Benallegue, and Y. Orlov. 2006. Exact Linearization and Sliding Mode Observer for a Quadrotor Unmanned Aerial Vehicle. *International Journal of Robotics and Automation* 21: 39-49.

P. Castillo, R. Lozano, and A. Dzul. 2005. Stabilization of a Mini Rotorcraft Having Four Rotors. *IEEE Control System Magazine* 25: 45-55.

Prasad, J. V. R., and A. J. Calise. 1999. Adaptive nonlinear controller synthesis and flight evaluation on an unmanned helicopter. In . Kohala Coast-Island of Hawaii, USA.

Rysdyk, R., and A. J. Calise. 2005. Robust Nonlinear Adaptive Flight Control for Consistent Handling Qualities. *IEEE Transaction of Control System Technology* 13: 896-910.

Slotine, Jean-Jacques, and Weiping Li. 1991. *Applied Nonlinear Control*. Prentice Hall.

Stevens, B. L., and F. L. Lewis. 2003. *Aircraft Simulation and Control*. Wiley and Sons.

T. Madani, and A. Benallegue. 2006. Backstepping control for a quadrotor helicopter. In . Beijing, China.

Wise, K. A., J. S. Brinker, A. J. Calise, D. F. Enns, M. R. Elgersma, and P. Voulgaris. 1999. Direct Adaptive Reconfigurable Flight Control for a Tailless Advanced Fighter Aircraft. *International Journal of Robust and Nonlinear Control* 9: 999-1012.

4

Robust Control Design for Automotive Applications: A Variable Structure Control Approach

Benedikt Alt and Ferdinand Svaricek
University of the German Armed Forces Munich
Germany

1. Introduction

The steady rise in fuel prices and the increased awareness on climate issues led and still lead to considerable efforts in the development of automotive engines and drivetrains (Guzzella & Sciarretta (2005)). Thus, fuel savings and emission reduction are of general interest and obviously as important as improved riding comfort or driveability.

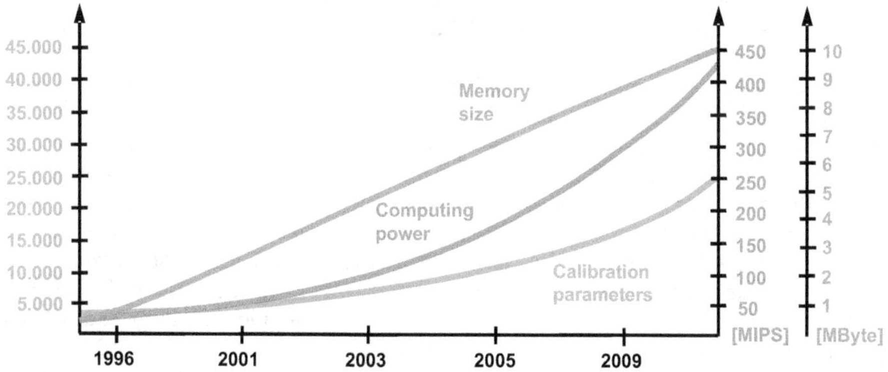

Fig. 1. Evolution of memory size, computing power and number of calibration parameters of an automotive engine control unit from 1996 to 2009 (ETAS GmbH (2010))

However, it is hard to find a suitable trade-off between all of these requirements and many resulting solutions lead to increased complexity of the vehicle systems. This is in particular true for common automotive combustion engines where the number of free calibration parameters of the corresponding electronic control unit (ECU) software has been increased up to five times during the last fifteen years (see Figure 1). From today's state of the art it takes up to five calibration engineers one whole year to finish all the calibration work on a series-production engine (Reif (2007)). Consequently, this time consuming calibration results in considerable development cost. Since the complexity of future drivetrains (e.g. battery electric vehicles or hybrid electric vehicles) will be drastically increased (Ehsani et al. (2010)) an ongoing rise on development cost is inevitable. However, with this effect cars may become unaffordable to many customers in the near future. Thus, novel control design strategies have to be introduced such that today's and future calibration work is minimized.

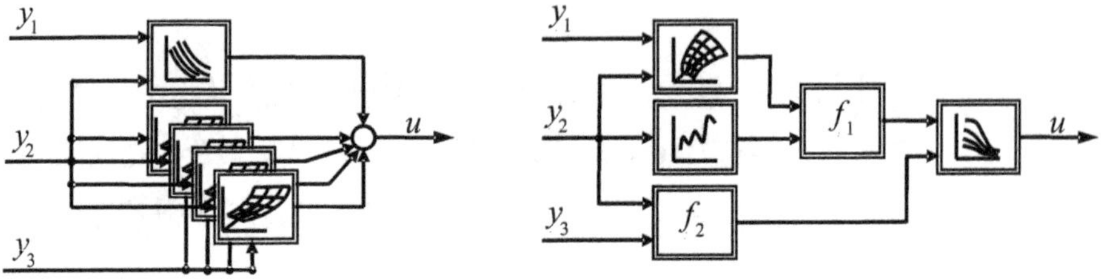

Fig. 2. Comparison of black box approach (left) and model based approach (right) for control design in ECU software development

Since several years common black box control design approaches are more and more replaced with model based design strategies (see Figure 2). Here, the corresponding control parameters are referred to a single subsystem of the plant and no longer to the entire process. Thus, each parameter has a clear physical meaning and any model uncertainties or unknown load torque disturbances can be systematically incorporated within the control design process. With this strategy a considerable reduction of calibration efforts can be achieved (Schopp et al. (2010)). However, the efforts for the design of a suitable process model have to be taken into account as well, since it is not easy to find a trade-off between model accuracy and complexity. Thus, it becomes clear that model based control design strategies are not the unique solution to minimize the development cost on ECU software. Often the desired reduction of efforts is less than expected. To overcome this major drawback a combination of model based and robust control design strategies is proposed since it is the best way to reduce the modeling and calibration efforts similarly (Alt (2010)).

Among robust control design methods the class of variable structure controllers (especially sliding mode controllers (SMCs)) is well known for their low burden on model accuracy. Regarding the operating range of a common combustion engine it is well known that the operating range of sliding mode control is enlarged compared to conventional solutions with gain scheduling techniques and heuristically tuned PI or PID controllers even if simple linear system models are used for control design (Edwards & Spurgeon (1998)). Hence, the total number of required operating points can be considerably reduced thus leading to less calibration efforts (see Figure 3). Moreover, sliding mode control shows good robustness properties against a wide class of model uncertainties and external disturbances including environmental influences, aging and tolerance effects (Hung et al. (1993); Utkin (1977)).

Due to its discontinuous nature a high frequency oscillation may arise and deteriorate the performance of closed-loop systems with SMCs (Utkin et al. (2009)). These so called chattering effects take usually place if the plant includes actuator dynamics which cannot be neglected (e.g. electromechanical actuators) or if the discretization effects affect the overall system behaviour. To alleviate the chattering phenomenon several control design approaches have been investigated. Among these control design methods second order sliding modes (SOSM) controllers attract great attention since they guarantee excellent robustness properties and even better accuracy compared to conventional SMCs (Alt et al. (2009a); Bartolini et al. (1998); Butt & Bhatti (2009); Khan et al. (2001); Levant (1993)).

In this contribution a SOSM based control strategy will be applied to a typical automotive control design task, namely the idle speed control (ISC) of a spark ignition (SI) engine (Alt

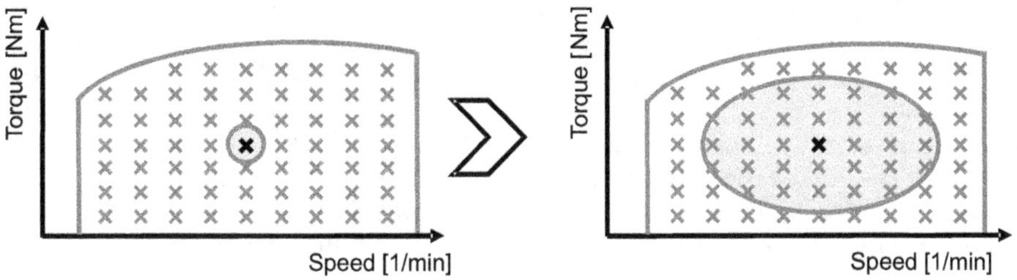

Fig. 3. Operating ranges of heuristically tuned PI or PID controller (left) and SMC controller (right)

et al. (2009b)). For this purpose a short introduction on SMCs and SOSM based controllers will be given. Here, the robustness properties will be analyzed and it will be shown how chattering effects can be alleviated efficiently. Then, the ISC control design task will be outlined and a corresponding simulation model will be introduced and validated on a research vehicle. Finally, the SOSM based control design approach will be applied to the ISC problem. Since the control parameters remain fixed no gain scheduling technique is necessary. Thus, the overall design and calibration efforts are considerably reduced compared to the series-production solution. However, representative nonlinear simulation and experimental results show impressively that the proposed controller is still able to satisfy all current ISC design requirements.

2. Sliding mode control and second order sliding mode control

Sliding mode control theory has attracted great interest among scientists and control engineers within the last decades. The resulting control laws can be applied but are not restricted to affine nonlinear single input single output (SISO) systems

$$\begin{aligned} \dot{\mathbf{x}}(t) &= \mathbf{f}\left(\mathbf{x}(t)\right) + \mathbf{g}\left(\mathbf{x}(t)\right) u(t) + \mathbf{z}(\mathbf{x}(t)) \\ y(t) &= h\left(\mathbf{x}(t)\right) \end{aligned} \tag{1}$$

where $\mathbf{x} = \mathbf{x}(t) \in \mathbb{R}^n$, $u = u(t) \in \mathbb{R}$ and $y = y(t) \in \mathbb{R}$. The system nonlinearities $\mathbf{f} \in \mathbb{R}^n$, $\mathbf{g} \in \mathbb{R}^n$ and $h \in \mathbb{R}$ are considered to be sufficiently smooth (Bartolini et al. (1998)). The discontinuous structure of these sliding mode controllers allows to switch between different system structures (or components) such that a new type of system motion, called sliding mode, exists in a dedicated manifold $\sigma(\mathbf{x}) = 0$. In particular the corresponding system trajectory moves onto this sliding manifold in finite time which leads to better system performance than the asymptotic behaviour of e.g. linear control systems. After reaching the manifold $\sigma(\mathbf{x}) = 0$ the system motion is uniquely characterized from the design of the sliding manifold and independent to any of the corresponding subsystems. Thus, once the system trajectory reached the sliding manifold its motion is insensitive to model uncertainties and disturbances that satisfy the so-called matching conditions (see Drazenovic (1969)). Here, the term matching conditions means that all these model uncertainties and disturbances enter the system through the control channel.

Regarding the overall control gain of the sliding mode control law the aforementioned robustness properties are easy to understand. As soon as the system trajectory reaches the sliding manifold the corresponding sliding variable $\sigma(\mathbf{x})$ is equal to zero. Since $\sigma(\mathbf{x})$ appears in the denominator of the overall control gain $k = \frac{u}{\sigma}$ this variable is drastically increased. In practice that means that the discontinuous control law acts directly with its maximum but finite control input if the system motion on the sliding manifold is affected. Due to that high gain effect the robustness properties of the sliding mode control system are similar to a closed-loop system with high-gain control law (Khalil (1996)). On the contrary to this class of nonlinear controllers the corresponding sliding mode control input doesn't suffer from unrealistic large control efforts. Instead it is well known that this control input is bounded by a finite value as shown in Figure 4. In the remainder of this section the following second

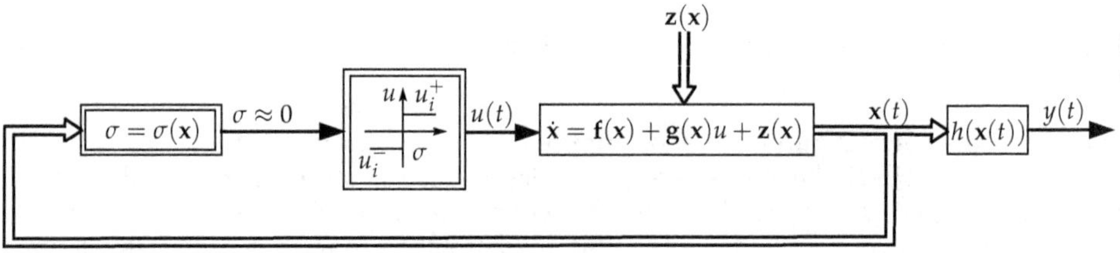

Fig. 4. Nonlinear single input single output (SISO) system with sliding mode controller, high gain effect with good robustness properties against matched model uncertainties and external disturbances after the system trajectory has reached the sliding manifold

order system

$$\begin{aligned} \dot{x}_1 &= x_2 \,, \\ \dot{x}_2 &= a^2 u \end{aligned} \tag{2}$$

with $a > 0$ is considered to explain the design of first order and second order sliding mode control laws. First, a so-called first order sliding mode control law (Perruquetti & Barbot (2002)) is given that guarantees the existence and the reachability (Edwards & Spurgeon (1998)) of the sliding motion in the entire state space:

$$u_{smc} = -\delta \, |x_1| \, \mathrm{sgn}\left(\sigma\left(x_1, x_2\right)\right) = \begin{cases} \delta \, |x_1| & \text{for} \quad \sigma\left(\mathbf{x}\right) < 0 \\ -\delta \, |x_1| & \text{for} \quad \sigma\left(\mathbf{x}\right) > 0 \end{cases} . \tag{3}$$

As soon as the system trajectory reaches the sliding manifold $\sigma(\mathbf{x}) = 0$ the control input u_{smc} shows a switching effect with infinite frequency. Of course, this infinite fast switching effect cannot occur in practical applications since each actuator has a limited bandwith and the corresponding control laws are calculated with finite sampling rates. Thus, the intended ideal sliding motion is also not realizable and the system trajectory oscillates around the given manifold as shown in Figure 5. These so-called chattering effects have to be alleviated in practical applications since chattering may lead to high power loss or even damages on the actuators or the overall system (Utkin et al. (2009)). Thus, the alleviation of chattering effects has been also intensively studied in the last decades (Bartolini et al. (1998); Hung et al. (1993); Utkin (1977); Utkin et al. (2009); Young et al. (1999)). Here, the so-called boundary layer approach (Edwards & Spurgeon (1998)) represents an efficient solution for many practical applications. However, it is well known that this alleviation approach suffers from reduced robustness properties since the system trajectory is no longer able to reach the sliding manifold exactly. Instead it can only be guaranteed that the trajectory moves within a dedicated boundary layer around the sliding manifold.

Another interesting approach for the alleviation of chattering effects can be found within the class of second order sliding mode (SOSM) controllers (Bartolini et al. (1998); Levant (1993);

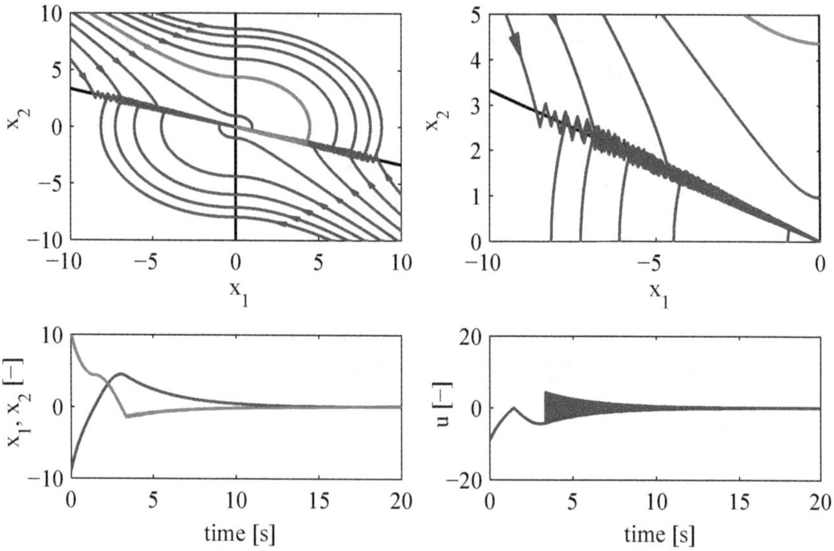

Fig. 5. Nonlinear simulation results for example in (2) with first order sliding mode control law in (3), sampling time $t_s = 20$ ms, phase portrait of closed-loop system (up, left), zoom-in of phase portrait (up, right), system states x_1 (blue) and x_2 (red), (low, left) and control input u (low, right)

Utkin et al. (2009)). The corresponding design of this specific control law which is referred to super twisting algorithm (STA) is briefly discussed in the remainder of this section. For this purpose the class of affine nonlinear SISO systems is considered as already introduced in (1). Additionally, it is assumed that the system trajectory should reach the sliding manifold $\dot{\sigma} = \sigma = 0$ in finite time and that the relative degree of this system is one, i.e. the control input appears in the first time derivative of the sliding variable $\sigma(\mathbf{x})$. Although this assumption looks restrictive it has been shown in Alt (2010) that many systems in the field of automotive, electric drive or robotic systems fulfill this requirement. Finally, the first and second order time derivatives of $\sigma(\mathbf{x})$ have to be calculated for the following control design steps:

$$\begin{aligned} \dot{\sigma} &= \frac{\partial}{\partial t}\sigma + \frac{\partial}{\partial \mathbf{x}}\sigma\left(\mathbf{f}(\mathbf{x}) + \mathbf{g}(\mathbf{x})u + \mathbf{z}(\mathbf{x})\right), \\ \ddot{\sigma} &= \underbrace{\frac{\partial}{\partial t}\dot{\sigma} + \frac{\partial}{\partial \mathbf{x}}\dot{\sigma}\left(\mathbf{f}(\mathbf{x}) + \mathbf{g}(\mathbf{x})u + \mathbf{z}(\mathbf{x})\right)}_{\phi(\mathbf{x})} + \underbrace{\frac{\partial}{\partial u}\dot{\sigma}}_{\gamma(\mathbf{x})}\dot{u}\,. \end{aligned} \tag{4}$$

From $\dot{\sigma}$ and $\ddot{\sigma}$ it can be clearly seen that the lumped model uncertainties and external disturbances $\mathbf{z}(\mathbf{x})$ appear within $\phi(\mathbf{x})$ and $\gamma(\mathbf{x})$. However, no detailed knowledge of these nonlinear relationships is required for the following control design steps. Instead it turned out to be sufficient to introduce dedicated lower and upper bounds $|\phi(\mathbf{x})| < \Phi$ and $0 < \Gamma_m < \gamma(\mathbf{x}) < \Gamma_M$ on $\phi(\mathbf{x})$ and $\gamma(\mathbf{x})$, respectively to cope with the matched model uncertainties and external disturbances where $\Phi, \Gamma_m, \Gamma_M \in \mathbb{R}^+$. Thus, the robustness properties are considered to be similar to those of a closed-loop system with first order sliding mode control law.

For a better general understanding the reduction of the chattering effects can be related to the additional integrator within the well-known form of the super twisting algorithm (Fridman & Levant (2002)) control law

$$u_{sta} = u_{sta,1} + u_{sta,2}\,,$$
$$\dot{u}_{sta,1} = \begin{cases} -u_{sta} & \text{for } |u_{sta}| > 1 \\ -W\text{sgn}\,(\sigma) & \text{for } |u_{sta}| \leq 1\,, \end{cases} \tag{5}$$
$$u_{sta,2} = \begin{cases} -\lambda\,|\sigma_0|^{\rho}\,\text{sgn}\,(\sigma) & \text{for } |\sigma| > \sigma_0 \\ -\lambda\,|\sigma|^{\rho}\,\text{sgn}\,(\sigma) & \text{for } |\sigma| \leq \sigma_0\,. \end{cases}$$

Thus, the discontinuous first order sliding mode control law in (3) is replaced by a continuous alternative. However, the resulting implementation and calibration efforts are increased with regards to practical applications.

For the calculation of the control gains W, λ and ρ the first order time derivative $\dot{u}_{sta}$ of the control variable from (5) has to be inserted in the right hand side of the second order time derivative $\ddot{\sigma}$ in (4) where $|u_{sta}| \leq 1$ and $|\sigma| \leq \sigma_0$:

$$\ddot{\sigma} = \phi\,(\mathbf{x}) - \gamma\,(\mathbf{x}) \left(W\text{sgn}\,(\sigma) + \rho\lambda \frac{\dot{\sigma}}{|\sigma|^{1-\rho}} \right)\,. \tag{6}$$

Considering the lower and upper bounds Φ, Γ_m and Γ_M of $\phi\,(\mathbf{x})$ and $\gamma\,(\mathbf{x})$, the right hand side of $\ddot{\sigma}$ turns from an ordinary differential equation into a differential inclusion (Emelyanov et al. (1996); Levant (1993)):

$$\ddot{\sigma} \in [\Gamma_m W - \Phi, \Gamma_M W - \Phi] - [\Gamma_m, \Gamma_M] + \rho\lambda \frac{\dot{\sigma}}{|\sigma|^{1-\rho}}\,. \tag{7}$$

With regards to the calibration of the control gains W, λ and ρ it can be clearly seen from (7) that no unique bounds can be given such that the system trajectory reaches $\dot{\sigma} = \sigma = 0$ in finite time. However, with some further dedicated assumptions some more conservative bounds (Fridman & Levant (2002)) on W, λ and ρ can be introduced to satisfy this stringent condition:

$$W > \frac{\Phi}{\Gamma_m}\,,$$
$$\lambda^2 \geq \frac{4\Phi\,\Gamma_M\,(W + \Phi)}{\Gamma_m^2\,\Gamma_m\,(W - \Phi)}\,, \tag{8}$$
$$0 < \rho \leq 0.5\,.$$

Here, it has to be noted that the assumptions on these conservative bounds for deriving W, λ and ρ may vary from reference to reference (see Levant (1993; 1998)). In practice, these sufficient conditions on W, λ and ρ are often used to simplify the heuristic calibration process (Bartolini et al. (1999)).

Finally, the introductory example in (2) is considered to show the efficiency of the super twisting algorithm in terms of chattering alleviation purposes. The corresponding simulation results are depicted in Figure 6 and it can be clearly seen that the system trajectories reach the sliding manifold $\dot{\sigma} = \sigma = 0$ in finite time. Additionally, the chattering effects are considerably reduced.

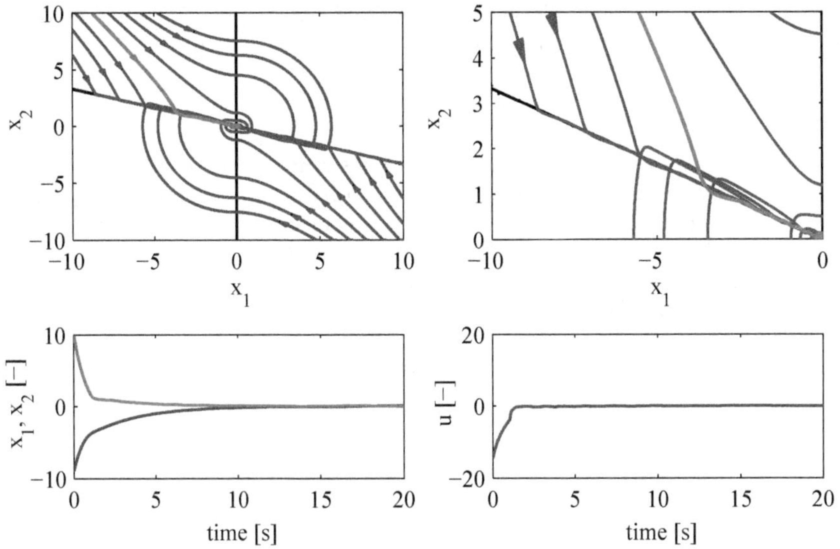

Fig. 6. Nonlinear simulation results for example in (2) with second order sliding mode control law in (5), sampling time $t_s = 20$ ms, phase portrait of closed-loop system (up, left), zoom-in of phase portrait (up, right), system states x_1 (blue) and x_2 (red), (low, left) and control input u (low, right)

3. Nonlinear engine model

In this section a mathematical model of the spark ignition (SI) engine is briefly discussed. In the remainder of this contribution this engine model will basically be used as a nonlinear simulation model and thus as virtual engine test rig. It incorporates both the overall system dynamics of the engine and the torque structure of current engine management systems. For modeling purposes of the engine a continuous time mean value modeling approach turned out to be sufficient at idle condition (Guzzella & Sciarretta (2005)). This means, that all internal processes of the engine are spread out over one combustion period and differences from cylinder to cylinder are neglected. Thus, it is sufficient to take only the electronic throttle with its position controller, the intake manifold and the rotational dynamics of the crankshaft into account:

$$\begin{aligned} \dot{\alpha}_{thr} &= -\frac{1}{\tau_{thr}}\alpha_{thr} + \frac{1}{\tau_{thr}}\alpha_{thr,u} \,, \\ \dot{p}_{im} &= \frac{R\theta_{im}}{V_{im}}(\dot{m}_{thr} - \dot{m}_{cc}) \,, \\ \dot{N} &= \frac{30}{\pi J}(T_{ind} - T_{loss} - T_{load}) \,, \end{aligned} \tag{9}$$

where τ_{thr} represents the time constant of the closed loop behaviour of the electronic throttle. The variables $\dot{m}_{thr} = \dot{m}_{thr}(p_{im}, \alpha_{thr,u})$ and $\dot{m}_{cc} = \dot{m}_{cc}(p_{im}, N)$ denote the air mass flow rates into the intake manifold and the combustion chamber, respectively. For the calculation of the indicated torque $T_{ind} = T_{ind}(\dot{m}'_{cc}, T_{ign,u}(t - \tau_d))$ per combustion cycle the air mass flow rate into the combustion chamber has to be related to the crank-angle domain based software features of the electronic control unit:

$$\dot{m}'_{cc} = \frac{120}{N_{cc}N}\dot{m}_{cc} . \tag{10}$$

Additionally, the physical actuator inputs (throttle position $\alpha_{thr,u}$ and ignition setting $\alpha_{ign,SP}$) are transformed into torque demands $T_{air,u}$ and $T_{ign,u}$ on the air path and on the ignition path, respectively. In general the torque demand $T_{ign,u}$ is considered as only control input acting directly on the indicated torque T_{ind} and hence on the engine speed N. The remaining control input $T_{air,u}$ on the air path influences however the maximum brake torque $T_{bas} = T_{bas}(\dot{m}_{cc}, N)$. Thus both control inputs affect also the torque reserve

$$T_{res} = T_{bas} - T_{ind} . \tag{11}$$

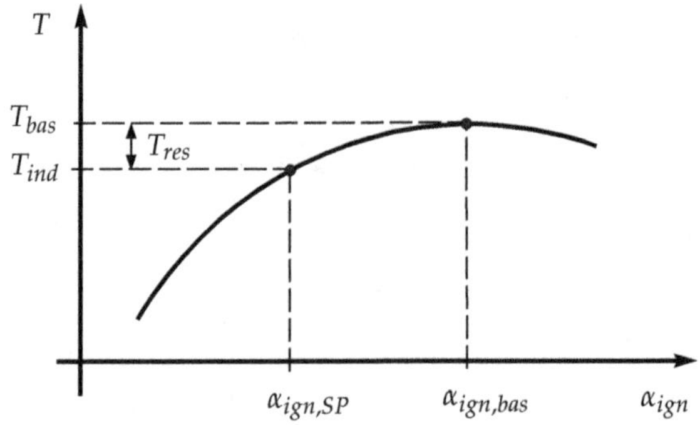

Fig. 7. Engine torque over spark ignition setting α_{ign} with fixed intake manifold mass flow $\dot{m}_{thr} = \dot{m}_{thr}(p_{im}, \alpha_{thr,u})$, this characteristic is also known as spark sweep

As seen in Figure 7 the torque reserve T_{res} represents the amount of torque that is available on the ignition path. Hence there exists a unidirectional coupling between the torque demands on the air and the ignition path and the system outputs because the air path is able to adjust the dynamic actuator constraints on the ignition path. With equations (9), (10), (11) and the ECU related software structure from Alt (2010) a nonlinear state space representation can be derived, where $\mathbf{x} = [\alpha_{thr}\ p_{im}\ N]^T$, $\mathbf{u} = \left[T_{ign,u}\ T_{air,u}\right]^T$ and $\mathbf{y} = [N\ T_{res}]^T$:

$$\begin{bmatrix} \dot{x}_1 \\ \dot{x}_2 \\ \dot{x}_3 \end{bmatrix} = \begin{bmatrix} f_1(x_1, x_2, x_3, u_2) \\ f_{21}(x_2, x_3) + f_{22}(x_1) \\ f_{31}(x_2, x_3) + f_{32}(u_1) \end{bmatrix} ,$$
$$\begin{bmatrix} y_1 \\ y_2 \end{bmatrix} = \begin{bmatrix} x_3 \\ h_{21}(x_2, x_3, u_2) - h_{22}(x_2, x_3, u_1) \end{bmatrix} . \tag{12}$$

The structure of the overall nonlinear engine model is shown in Figure 8. Here, it can be clearly seen that there exists a unidirectional coupling between the control inputs $T_{ign,u}$, $T_{air,u}$ and the outputs N and T_{res}. In the remainder of this paper the nonlinear model (12) is used as a

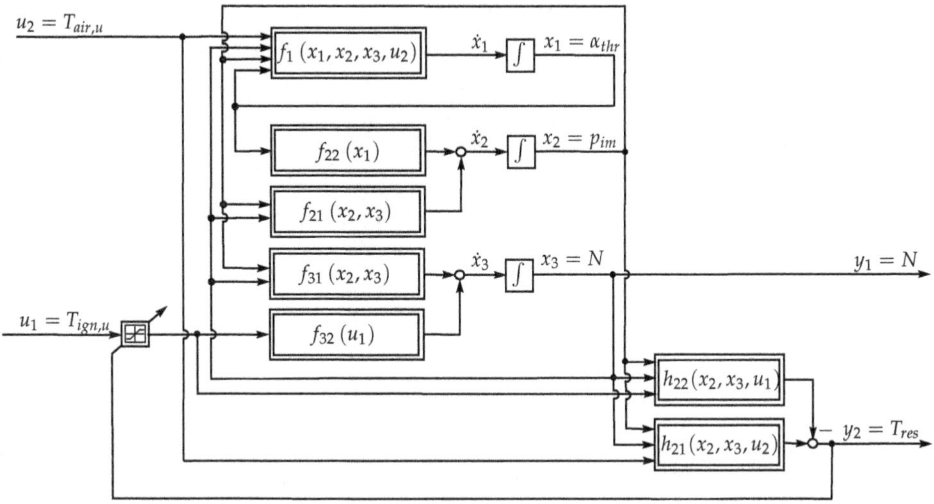

Fig. 8. Structure of nonlinear engine model

virtual test rig for the simulation studies. To show the performance of the proposed modeling approach a validation process has been carried out on a series-production vehicle with a 2.0l SI engine and a common rapid control prototyping system. Since the validation should cover the whole idle operating range different engine speed setpoints have to be considered. In Figure 9 and 10 two representative examples are shown where the corresponding engine speed setpoint $N_{SP} = 800\,1/\text{min}$ is situated in the middle of the idle operating range. For identification purposes a step in the torque demand $T_{air,u}$ on the air path and a step in the torque demand $T_{ign,u}$ on the ignition path are applied to the system. In the first case the maximum torque T_{bas} of the engine is increased while the indicated torque T_{ind} remains nearly the same. Due to the unidirectional coupling the engine speed N is not affected. In the second case the engine speed N and the torque reserve are both affected due to the step demand on the control input $T_{ign,u}$. From both Figures it can be also seen that there exists a good matching between the outputs of the simulation model and the real plant measurements.

4. Idle speed control design

In this section a decoupling controller is proposed that will be able to hold the engine speed N and the torque reserve T_{res} at their reference values N_{SP} and $T_{res,SP}$, respectively. Whenever the engine runs at idle condition and the reference value of the torque reserve $T_{res,SP}$ is greater than zero, this ISC controller will be active. The corresponding control structure is shown in Figure 11. Here, it can be seen that the novel ISC controller includes two individual feedback controllers and a decoupling compensation.

First, the design of the decoupling compensation is shown which will improve the driver's impression on the engine quality. In particular he should not registrate any influence on the engine speed N when changes in the reference value of the torque reserve $T_{res,SP}$ occur. As seen in (12) the unilateral coupling between the control inputs $T_{ign,u}$, $T_{air,u}$ and the outputs N and T_{res} has to be taken into account such that any influence on the engine speed N vanishes. This decoupling compensation is based on a linear time invariant (LTI) model that can either

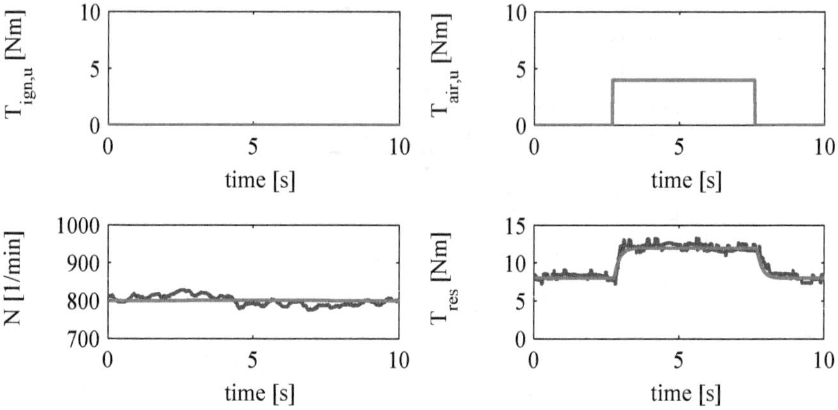

Fig. 9. Experimental results for validation of the nonlinear engine model, step on the air path torque demand: Control input $T_{ign,u}$ (up, left), control input $T_{air,u}$ (up, right), engine speed N (low, left), torque reserve T_{res} (low, right), experimental results (blue), simulation results (red)

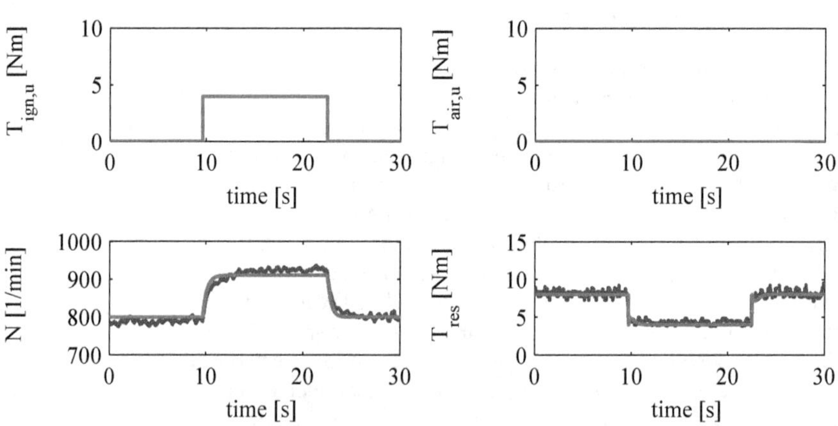

Fig. 10. Experimental results for validation of the nonlinear engine model, step on the ignition path torque demand: Control input $T_{ign,u}$ (up, left), control input $T_{air,u}$ (up, right), engine speed N (low, left), torque reserve T_{res} (low, right), experimental results (blue), simulation results (red)

be derived using analytical linearization or by system identification methods (Ljung (1999)). In many automotive control problems the latter techniques are more common since often no detailed nonlinear mathematical model is available. Instead test rig measurements are easily accessible. For this reason the remainder of the work is also based on identification methods. The resulting LTI models are generally valid in the neighbourhood of given operating points. Here, the required test rig measurements are taken from the validated nonlinear simulation model of (12) for the sake of simplicity. The aforementioned operating point with its reference values for the engine speed $N_{SP,0} = 800\,1/\text{min}$ and the torque reserve $T_{res,SP,0} = 8\,\text{Nm}$ represents a good choice for the following control design steps since it is situated in the middle

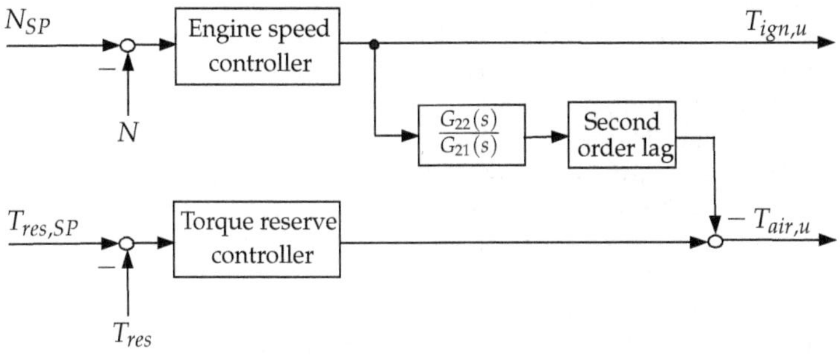

Fig. 11. Block diagram of the decoupling controller at idle condition

of the range at idle condition. If the behaviour of the nonlinear engine model at this operating point has to be described with a LTI model it is clear that the unidirectional coupling structure is still conserved. Hence, the LTI model can be written as

$$\begin{aligned} N(s) &= G_{12}(s)T_{ign,u}(s)\,, \\ T_{res}(s) &= G_{21}(s)T_{air,u}(s) + G_{22}(s)T_{ign,u}(s)\,. \end{aligned} \tag{13}$$

The operating point dependent continuous time transfer functions $G_{12}(s)$, $G_{21}(s)$ and $G_{22}(s)$ are calculated from various step responses using MATLAB's System Identication Toolbox (Ljung (2006)):

$$\begin{aligned} G_{12}(s) &= \frac{246.4}{s + 2.235}\,, \\ G_{21}(s) &= \frac{4.618}{s + 4.625}\,, \\ G_{22}(s) &= \frac{-26.14s - 91.07}{s^2 + 45.03s + 90.9}\,. \end{aligned} \tag{14}$$

The parameters of $G_{12}(s)$, $G_{21}(s)$ and $G_{22}(s)$ are calculated numerically using a maximum likelihood criterion. That means the underlying identification algorithm is based on continuous time low order transfer functions and it includes an iterative estimation method that minimizes the prediction errors. From the LTI model in (13) it can be seen that the transfer function

$$G_{Ds}(s) = \frac{G_{22}(s)}{G_{21}(s)} \tag{15}$$

helps to compensate the influence of the torque demand $T_{ign,u}$ on the torque reserve T_{res} efficiently. Hence, the decoupled system with its inputs $T_{ign,u}$ and $T_{air,u}$ can be controlled by two feedback controllers which are designed independently of each other. Since the dynamics of the air path are generally much slower than the dynamics on the ignition path a second order lag is additionally introduced to smooth the transient behaviour of the decoupling compensation in (15), see Figure 11. The corresponding damping of this filter and its natural frequency have to be determined experimentally.

For the design of both feedback controllers linear control theory would be generally sufficient as shown in current series-production applications or even in Kiencke & Nielsen (2005). Nevertheless, it is well known that classical linear controllers often do their job only in the neighbourhood of an operating point and the control parameters have to be scheduled over the entire operating range. This leads to time-consuming calibration efforts. In this work the potential of sliding mode control theory will be particularly analyzed with regards to reduced calibration efforts. Hence, both feedback controllers are designed using a second order sliding modes (SOSM) control design approach that has already been introduced in Section 2. This so-called super twisting algorithm (STA) has been developed to control systems with relative degree one in order to avoid chattering effects. Furthermore, it does not need any information on the time derivative of the sliding variable. For these reasons the super twisting algorithm has become very popular in recent years and it has been adopted to many real world control applications so far (Alt et al. (2009a); Butt & Bhatti (2009); Perruquetti & Barbot (2002)). In the following steps the control law for the engine speed N is derived while the engine runs at idle and the condition $T_{res} > 0$ holds true. This control law includes two major parts:

$$
\begin{aligned}
u_N &= u_{N,1} + u_{N,2}\,,\\
\dot{u}_{N,1} &= \begin{cases} -u_{N,1} & \text{for } |u_{N,1}| > 1 \\ -W_{N,1}\text{sgn}(\sigma_N) & \text{for } |u_{N,1}| \le 1\,, \end{cases}\\
u_{N,2} &= -\lambda_{N,1}\,|\sigma_N|^{\rho_{N,1}}\,\text{sgn}(\sigma_N)\,,
\end{aligned}
\tag{16}
$$

where $\sigma_N = 0$ with $\sigma_N = N - N_{SP}$ represents the engine speed related sliding manifold.

For the application of the super twisting algorithm it has to be guaranteed that the considered system has relative degree one. For this purpose the time derivative

$$
\dot{\sigma}_N = f_{31}(x_2, x_3) + f_{32}(u_1) - \dot{N}_{SP} \tag{17}
$$

is calculated using the nonlinear model in (12). Here, it can be clearly seen that the control input u_1 appears in $f_{32}(u_1)$ and thus in the first time derivative of σ_N. Thus, the aforementioned relative degree one condition is fulfilled for this case and the super twisting algorithm can be applied. For the calibration of the control gains $W_{N,1}$, $\lambda_{N,1}$ and $\rho_{N,1}$ sufficient conditions for finite time convergence to the sliding surface $\sigma_N = 0$ are derived in Levant (1993). Here, it is shown that starting from an initial value $\sigma_{N,0}$ at an arbitrary time instant $t_{N,0}$ the variable σ_N converges to $\sigma_N = 0$ if the following sufficient conditions (Fridman & Levant (2002); Levant (1993; 1998)) on $W_{N,1}$, $\lambda_{N,1}$ and $\rho_{N,1}$ are satisfied:

$$
\begin{aligned}
W_{N,1} &> \frac{\Phi_{N,1}}{\Gamma_{N,m1}}\,,\\
\lambda_{N,1}^2 &\ge \frac{4\Phi_{N,1}}{\Gamma_{N,m1}^2}\,\frac{\Gamma_{N,M1}(W_{N,1} + \Phi_{N,1})}{\Gamma_{N,m1}(W_{N,1} - \Phi_{N,1})}\,,\\
0 &< \rho_{N,1} \le 0.5\,.
\end{aligned}
\tag{18}
$$

Here, the variables $\Gamma_{N,m1}$ and $\Gamma_{N,M1}$ denote lower and upper limitations of the nonlinear relationship $f_{31}(x_2, x_3) - \dot{N}_{SP}$, where

$$0 < \Gamma_{N,m} \leq f_{31}(x_2, x_3) - \dot{N}_{SP} \leq \Gamma_{N,M} \,. \tag{19}$$

Additionally, the variable $\Phi_{N,1}$ represents an upper bound for all effects which appear in case of model uncertainties due to the inversion of $f_{32}(u_1)$:

$$|f_{32}(f_{32}^{*}(u_1))| \leq \Phi_{N,1} \,. \tag{20}$$

Here, $f_{32}^{*}(u_1)$ denotes the nominal value of $f_{32}(u_1)$. Hence, the design of the engine speed controller is complete. The design of the torque reserve controller runs similarly to (16). The corresponding control law includes also an integral and a nonlinear part:

$$\begin{aligned} u_{Tres} &= u_{Tres,1} + u_{Tres,2} \,, \\ \dot{u}_{Tres,1} &= \begin{cases} -u_{Tres,1} & \text{for } |u_{Tres,1}| > 1 \\ -W_{Tres,1}\text{sgn}(\sigma_{Tres}) & \text{for } |u_{Tres,1}| \leq 1 \,, \end{cases} \\ u_{Tres,2} &= -\lambda_{Tres,1} \, |\sigma_{Tres}|^{\rho_{Tres,1}} \, \text{sgn}(\sigma_{Tres}) \,. \end{aligned} \tag{21}$$

where $\sigma_{Tres} = 0$ with $\sigma_{Tres} = T_{res} - T_{res,SP}$ represents the torque reserve related sliding manifold.

For the application of the super twisting algorithm it has to be again guaranteed that the considered system has relative degree one. For this purpose the time derivative

$$\dot{\sigma}_{Tres} = \frac{\partial h_2}{\partial x_2} f_{21}(x_2, x_3) + \frac{\partial h_2}{\partial x_2} f_{22}(x_1) - \dot{T}_{res,SP} \,. \tag{22}$$

is calculated using the nonlinear relationship from (12) while the corresponding time derivative of T_{res} is simplified to

$$\dot{T}_{res} \approx \frac{\partial h_2}{\partial x_2} \dot{x}_2 \,. \tag{23}$$

From (22) it can be clearly seen that the state x_1 appears in the nonlinear relationship $\frac{\partial h_2}{\partial x_2} f_{22}(x_1)$ and thus in the first time derivative of σ_{Tres}. However, to satisfy the relative degree one condition the dynamics of the subordinated electronic throttle control loop $\dot{x}_1 = f_1(x_1, x_2, x_3, u_2)$ in (12) have to be neglected for the following control design steps. This assumption is justified since the time lag of the subordinated throttle control loop is ten times smaller than the remaining ones of the SI engine model. With this simplification the state $x_1 = \alpha_{thr}$ is assumed to be equal to the control input $\alpha_{thr,SP}$ of the subordinated closed-loop system.

Under these conditions the time derivative of the torque reserve related sliding surface is given with

$$\dot{\sigma}_{Tres} = \frac{\partial h_2}{\partial x_2} f_{21}(x_2, x_3) + \frac{\partial h_2}{\partial x_2} f_{22}(f_{22}^{*(-1)}(u_2)) - \dot{T}_{res,SP} \,. \tag{24}$$

With this assumption the corresponding system fulfills the relative degree one condition. Thus, the super twisting algorithm can be also applied to the torque reserve controller.

Regarding the control gains $W_{Tres,1}$, $\lambda_{Tres,1}$ und $\rho_{Tres,1}$ it has to be guaranteed similar to the engine speed controller that starting from an initial value $\sigma_{Tres,0}$ at an arbitrary time instant

$t_{Tres,0}$ the sliding variable σ_{Tres} converges to $\sigma_{Tres} = 0$ in finite time. For this purpose the following sufficient conditions (Fridman & Levant (2002); Levant (1993; 1998)) have to be fulfilled:

$$\begin{aligned} W_{Tres,1} &> \frac{\Phi_{Tres,1}}{\Gamma_{Tres,m1}}, \\ \lambda^2_{Tres,1} &\geq \frac{4\Phi_{Tres,1}}{\Gamma^2_{Tres,m1}} \frac{\Gamma_{Tres,M1}(W_{Tres,1} + \Phi_{Tres,1})}{\Gamma_{Tres,m1}(W_{Tres,1} - \Phi_{Tres,1})}, \\ 0 &< \rho_{Tres,1} \leq 0.5\,. \end{aligned} \tag{25}$$

Here, the variables $\Gamma_{Tres,m1}$ and $\Gamma_{Tres,M1}$ denote lower and upper limitations of the nonlinear relationship $\frac{\partial h_2}{\partial x_2} f_{21}(x_2, x_3) - \dot{T}_{res,SP}$:

$$0 < \Gamma_{Tres,m} \leq \frac{\partial h_2}{\partial x_2} f_{21}(x_2, x_3) - \dot{T}_{,res,SP} \leq \Gamma_{Tres,M}\,. \tag{26}$$

The variable $\Phi_{Tres,1}$ represents similar to $\Phi_{N,1}$ an upper bound for all effects which appear due to possible model uncertainties that are related to the inversion of $f_{22}(u_2)$:

$$\left| \frac{\partial h_2}{\partial x_2} f_{22}(f_{22}^{*(-1)}(T_{air,u})) \right| \leq \Phi_{Tres,1}\,. \tag{27}$$

Here, $f^*_{22}(u_2)$ denotes the nominal value of $f_{22}(u_2)$. Note that, in practice the engine speed control and the torque control loops are affected by model uncertainties and external disturbances leading to imperfect decoupling properties of the multivariable system. Nevertheless, it is well known from literature (Alt et al. (2009a); Bartolini et al. (1999); Levant (1993; 1998)) that the sliding surfaces $\sigma_N = 0$ and $\sigma_{Tres} = 0$ can still be reached in this case. Thus, the engine speed control and the torque reserve control loops are supposed to be robust against any disturbances due to improper decoupling. Finally, it has been shown in Alt (2010) that this multivariable control design approach leads to better performance and less calibration efforts than a similar approach without decoupling compensation.

5. Nonlinear simulation and experimental results

This section illustrates the efficiency and the robustness properties of the proposed decoupling controller. For this purpose some representative nonlinear simulation and experimental results are shown. All the simulations are based on the nonlinear engine model of Alt (2010) with a controller sampling time of $t_s = 10$ ms. The experimental results include representative field test data with a 2.0l series-production vehicle and a common rapid control prototyping system.

In the first scenario the disturbance rejection properties of the closed-loop system are evaluated. For this purpose an additional load torque of $T_{load} = 8$ Nm (e.g. power steering) is applied to the engine at $t_1 = 4$ s and removed again at $t_2 = 9$ s. From Figure 12 it can be seen that due to this load torque the engine speed N and the torque reserve T_{res} drop below their reference values while the corresponding transients stay below $\Delta N = 40$ 1/min and $\Delta T_{res} = 8$ Nm, respectively. However, the proposed idle speed controller steers both variables back to their reference values $N_{SP} = 800$ 1/min and $T_{res,SP} = 8$ Nm within less than 2 s.

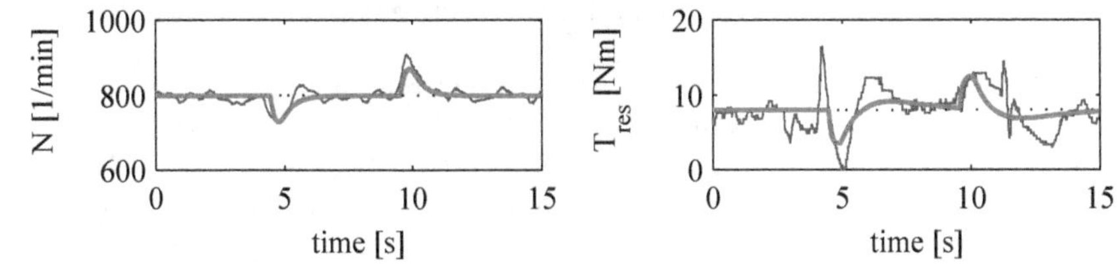

Fig. 12. Nonlinear simulation and experimental results for super twisting algorithm based decoupling controller, disturbance rejection properties: Engine speed N (left), torque reserve T_{res} (right), experimental results (blue), simulation results (red)

When disabling the load torque similar effects take place. Considering the engine speed N it can also clearly be seen that there exists a good matching between the nonlinear simulation data and the experimental measurements. For the torque reserve T_{res} this matching is less perfect since this variable is much more prone to unmodelled dynamics and tolerance effects that have not been considered in the nonlinear simulation model. This effect will be further evaluated in Section 6. In a second representative scenario the engine speed reference value

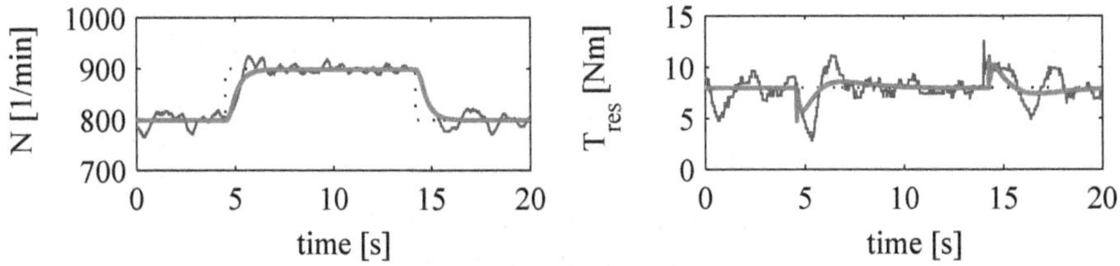

Fig. 13. Nonlinear simulation and experimental results for super twisting algorithm based decoupling controller, tracking of an engine speed reference step profile: Engine speed N (left), torque reserve T_{res} (right), experimental results (blue), simulation results (red)

N_{SP} is increased at $t_1 = 4$ s and lowered again at $t_2 = 14$ s. The corresponding simulation results are shown in Figure 13. Regarding the step response of the engine speed N it can be clearly seen that no overshoot occurs and the settling times are within less than 2 s and thus reasonable small. Additionally, the torque reserve T_{res} shows only small deviations due to the

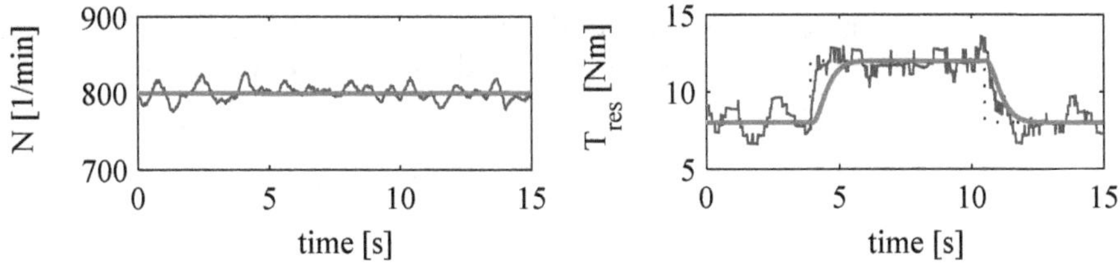

Fig. 14. Nonlinear simulation and experimental results for super twisting algorithm based decoupling controller, tracking of a torque reserve reference step profile: Engine speed N (left), torque reserve T_{res} (right), experimental results (blue), simulation results (red)

step changes on the engine speed N and it returns to its reference value $T_{res,SP}$ within a short settling time.
Similar results can be seen from Figure 14 where the torque reserve reference value $T_{res,SP}$ is increased at $t_1 = 3$ s and lowered again at $t_2 = 14$ s. During these changes on the torque reserve T_{res} the minimization of any effects on the engine speed N is considered as most important design criteria since this behaviour would affect the driver's comfort. From Figure 14 it can be clearly seen that the proposed idle speed controller is able to fulfill this requirement as specified. As known from existing series-production ISC controllers this overall performance can not be achieved using classical linear control design approaches without gain scheduling. Finally, the step response of the torque reserve T_{res} is also without any overshoot and faster than that for the engine speed N.

6. Robustness analysis

After the first experimental studies the robustness properties of the closed-loop system have to be analyzed in detail. For the sake of simplicity this analysis will be performed using the validated nonlinear simulation model from Alt (2010). Here, a representative disturbance rejection scenario is used to illustrate the major effects of model uncertainties on the closed-loop system performance. This simulation scenario includes an external load torque disturbance of $T_{load} = 10$ Nm which is applied to the engine at $t_1 = 10$ s and removed again at $t_2 = 20$ s. The overall robustness analysis covers variations of $\pm$ 10 % in up to 19 different characteristic maps of the nonlinear simulation model. In particular, the system nonlinearities f_1, f_{21}, f_{22}, f_{31}, f_{32} and $h_2 = h_2(h_{21}, hh22)$ are varied one after another using multiplicative uncertainty functions:

$$\begin{aligned}
f_1 &= d_{1,\pm} \cdot f_{1,nom} \quad \text{mit} \quad d_{1,\pm} \in [0.9, 1.1]\,, \\
f_{21} &= d_{21,\pm} \cdot f_{21,nom} \quad \text{mit} \quad d_{21,\pm} \in [0.9, 1.1]\,, \\
f_{22} &= d_{22,\pm} \cdot f_{22,nom} \quad \text{mit} \quad d_{22,\pm} \in [0.9, 1.1]\,, \\
f_{31} &= d_{31,\pm} \cdot f_{31,nom} \quad \text{mit} \quad d_{31,\pm} \in [0.9, 1.1]\,, \\
f_{32} &= d_{32,\pm} \cdot f_{32,nom} \quad \text{mit} \quad d_{32,\pm} \in [0.9, 1.1]\,, \\
h_2 &= d_{2,\pm} \cdot h_{2,nom} \quad \text{mit} \quad d_{2,\pm} \in [0.9, 1.1]\,.
\end{aligned} \tag{28}$$

Furthermore, the intake-to-torque-production delay τ_d has been increased up to 4 times to cope with any signal communication problems

$$\tau_d = \tau_{d,nom} + \Delta\tau_d \quad \text{with} \quad \Delta\tau_d = 20\ \text{ms}. \tag{29}$$

All these nonlinear simulation results are depicted in Figure 15.
In a second step all resulting deviations $\text{dev}(N)$ and $\text{dev}(T_{res})$ on the nominal behaviour of the engine speed and the torque reserve are scaled with the reference values of the operating point ($N_{SP,0} = 800$ 1/min, $T_{res,SP,0} = 8$ Nm):

$$\text{dev}(N(t)) = \frac{|\max(\Delta N_{\pm}(t)) - \Delta N_{nom}(t)|}{N_{SP}} \cdot 100\,, \tag{30}$$

$$\text{dev}(T_{res}(t)) = \frac{|\max(\Delta T_{res\pm}(t)) - \Delta T_{res,nom}(t)|}{T_{res,SP}} \cdot 100\,, \tag{31}$$

where $\Delta N_{nom}(t) = |N_{SP}(t) - N_{nom}(t)|$ and $\Delta T_{res,nom}(t) = |T_{res,SP}(t) - T_{res,nom}(t)|$ represent the resulting errors to the corresponding reference values N_{SP} and $T_{res,SP}$ while the engine

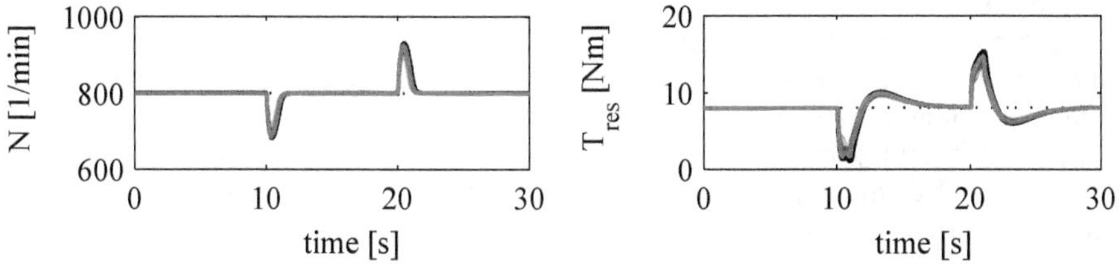

Fig. 15. Simulation results of engine speed N (left) and torque reserve T_{res} (right) for load torque disturbance rejection scenario with multiplicative variations on the system nonlinearities and the intake-to-torque production delay

operates in nominal condition. In Figure 16 the calculated deviations $\text{dev}(N)$ and $\text{dev}(T_{res})$ are shown for all 20 variations with strongest impact $\max(\Delta N_{\pm}(t)) = |N_{SP}(t) - N_{\pm}(t)|$ and $\max(\Delta T_{res,\pm}(t)) = |T_{res,SP}(t) - T_{res,\pm}(t)|$ on the closed-loop system.

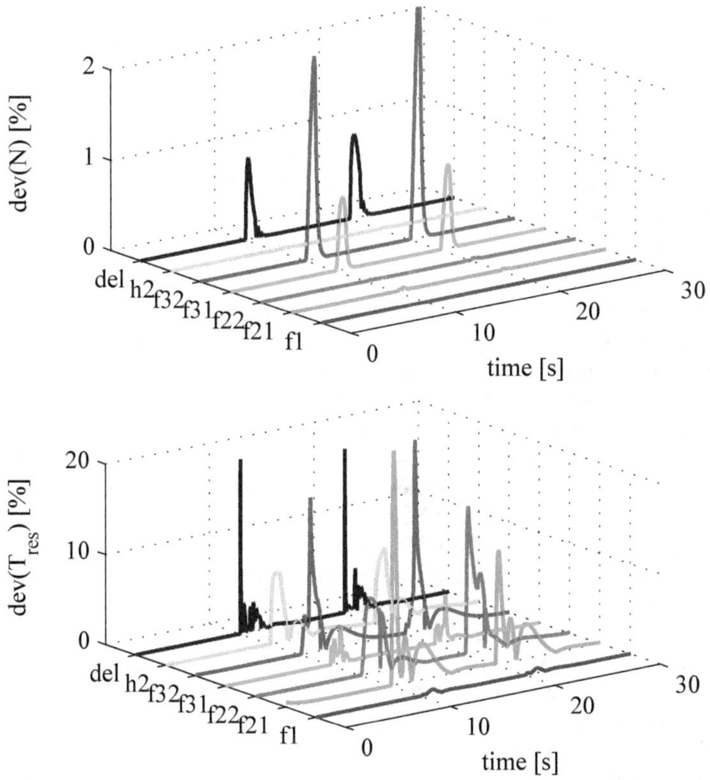

Fig. 16. Simulation results of engine speed deviations $\text{dev}(N)$ (up) and torque reserve deviations $\text{dev}(T_{res})$ (low) for load torque disturbance rejection scenario with multiplicative variations on the system nonlinearities and the intake-to-torque production delay

From Figure 16 it can be seen that the engine speed deviation dev(N) is bounded with about 1 % while the deviation dev(T_{res}) on the torque reserve is bounded with about 15 %. This large peak deviation on the torque reserve seems to be not reasonable since the impact on the system parameters is bounded with only 10 %. However, it has to be noted that the calibration of the controllers allows to find a trade off between the accuracy on N and T_{res} and thus to penalize the engine speed error more than the torque reserve error. Since the comfort and the driver's impression on the engine quality are mainly affected by deviations on the engine speed it becomes clear that large control errors on N should be more penalized than deviations on T_{res}. Keeping this effect in mind it can be anyhow summarized that the proposed control framework shows good robustness properties despite any uncertainties in the system parameters, e.g. aging, tolerance effects or environmental influences.

7. Conclusion and future work

The paper deals with the idle speed control problem which represents an interesting multivariable control design application in the field of modern automotive spark ignition engines. In idle condition the engine speed and the torque reserve should be held at their reference values. The key design requirements include the decoupling of the underlying multivariable system and the improvement of the robustness properties against unknown load torque disturbances and tolerance effects. In the first step a nonlinear engine model is introduced that includes both the main dynamics of the engine internal processes and also the major parts of the torque structure of current engine management systems. The resulting nonlinear simulation model is validated on a series-production vehicle and it is used as a virtual engine test rig. Then, a decoupling control framework is introduced that is able to hold the idle engine speed and the torque reserve at their reference values despite external load torque disturbances or even uncertainites in the system parameters or the intake-to-torque-production delay.

The multivariable control framework consists of two independent feedback controllers and a decoupling compensation. Each of these two controllers is based on a second order sliding modes control design method that is also known as super twisting algorithm. The decoupling compensation is based on an identified linear time invariant model of the plant that is valid around a given operating point which is situated in the middle of the idle operating range. Here, the required LTI model is deduced from test rig measurements using system identification methods. The efficiency of the proposed control framework is shown by nonlinear simulation results. It can be seen that the controller shows good performance for the large signal behaviour although it is only designed for the neigbourhood of the given operating point. Nonlinear simulation and experimental results show as well that the proposed controller is able to handle a wide operating range at idle condition while the control gains remain unchanged. Hence, the proposed control framework is easier to calibrate since the number of control parameters is severly reduced compared to classical series-production control design methods using gain scheduling techniques. The efficiency and the robustness properties against system uncertainties and variations in the intake-to-torque production delay are evaluated by extended simulation studies. Current research includes the application of this second order sliding modes based multivariable design approach in the field of other automotive control design tasks (i.e. hybrid electric vehicles) and aerospace applications (i.e. smart aeroengines).

8. Acknowledgment

This work has been supported by IAV GmbH Gifhorn in Germany. The authors express their gratitude to Jan Peter Blath and Matthias Schultalbers for their support.

9. References

Alt, B. (2010). *Modellbasierte Regelung ausgewählter Komponenten im Antriebsstrang eines Kraftfahrzeugs mit Ottomotor*, PhD thesis, Universität der Bundeswehr München, Germany.

Alt, B., Blath, J., Svaricek, F. & Schultalbers, M. (2009a). Control of idle engine speed and torque reserve with higher order sliding modes, *Proceedings of the Multi-Conference on Systems and Control, Saint Petersburg, Russia*.

Alt, B., Blath, J., Svaricek, F. & Schultalbers, M. (2009b). Multiple sliding surface control of idle engine speed and torque reserve with dead start assist control, *IEEE Transactions on Industrial Electronics*, Vol. 56: 3580 – 3592.

Bartolini, G., Ferrara, A., Levant, A. & Usai, E. (1999). On second order sliding mode controllers, *in* K. Young & U. Özgüner (eds), *Variable structure systems, sliding mode and nonlinear control*, Springer, London, Berlin, Heidelberg.

Bartolini, G., Ferrara, A. & Usai, E. (1998). Chattering avoidance by second order sliding mode control, *IEEE Transactions on Automatic Control*, Vol. 43, No. 2: 241 – 246.

Butt, Q. & Bhatti, A. (2009). Estimation of gasoline-engine parameters using higher order sliding mode, *IEEE Transactions on Industrial Electronics*, Vol. 55, No. 11: pp. 3891 – 3898.

Drazenovic, B. (1969). The invariance conditions in variable structure systems, *Automatica*, Vol. 5, No. 3: pp. 287 – 295.

Edwards, C. & Spurgeon, S. (1998). *Sliding mode control, theory and applications*, Taylor and Francis Ltd. London, UK.

Ehsani, M., Gao, Y. & Emadi, A. (2010). *Modern electric, hybrid electric and fuel cell vehicles*, CRC Press, Boca Raton, London, New York.

Emelyanov, S., Korovin, S. & Levant, A. (1996). Higher-order sliding modes in control systems, *Computational Mathematics and Modeling*, Vol. 7: pp. 294 – 318.

ETAS GmbH (2010).
URL: *http://www.etas.com/de/products/applications calibrating automotive electronics.php*

Fridman, L. & Levant, A. (2002). Higher-order sliding modes, *in* W. Perruquetti & J. Barbot (eds), *Sliding mode control in engineering*, Marcel Dekker Inc., New York, Basel.

Guzzella, L. & Sciarretta, A. (2005). *Vehicle propulsion systems, Introduction to modeling and optimization*, Springer, Berlin, Heidelberg, New York.

Hung, J., Gao, W. & Hung, J. (1993). Variable structure control: a survey, *IEEE Transactions on Industrial Electronics*, Vol. 40, No. 1: 2 – 22.

Khalil, H. (1996). *Nonlinear Systems, 3rd edition*, Prentice Hall, Upper Saddle River, NJ, USA.

Khan, M., Spurgeon, S. & Bhatti, A. (2001). Robust speed control of an automotive engine using second order sliding modes, *Proceedings of the European Control Conference 2001, Porto, Portugal*.

Kiencke, U. & Nielsen, L. (2005). *Automotive control systems for engine, driveline and vehicle - 2nd edition*, Springer, Berlin, Heidelberg, New York.

Levant, A. (1993). Sliding order and sliding accuracy in sliding mode control, *International Journal of Automatic Control*, Vol. 58, No. 6: 1247 – 1263.

Levant, A. (1998). Robust exact differentiation via sliding mode technique, *Automatica*, Vol. 34: 379 – 384.

Ljung, L. (1999). *System identification - theory for the user*, Prentice Hall, Upper Saddle River, NJ, USA.

Ljung, L. (2006). *System identification toolbox for use with Matlab*, The Mathworks Inc., Natick, MA, USA.

Perruquetti, W. & Barbot, J. (2002). *Sliding mode control in engineering*, Marcel Dekker Inc. New York, Basel.

Reif, K. (2007). *Automobilelektronik*, Vieweg & Teubner, Wiesbaden, Germany.

Schopp, G., Burkhardt, T., Dingl, J., Schwarz, R. & Eisath, C. (2010). Funktionsentwicklung und Kalibration für aufgeladene Motoren - Modellbasiert vom Konzept bis zur Serie, *in* R. Isermann (ed.), *Elektronisches Management motorischer Antriebe*, Vieweg & Teubner, Wiesbaden, Germany.

Utkin, V. (1977). Variable structure systems with sliding modes, *IEEE Transactions on Automatic Control*, Vol. 22: 212 – 222.

Utkin, V., Guldner, J. & Shi, J. (2009). *Sliding mode control in electromechanical systems*, CRC Press, Boca Raton, London, New York.

Young, K., Utkin, V. & Özgüner, . (1999). A control engineer's guide to sliding mode control, *IEEE Transactions on Control Systems Technology*, Vol. 7, No. 3: pp. 328 – 342.

5

Robust Active Suspension Control for Vibration Reduction of Passenger's Body

Takuma Suzuki and Masaki Takahashi
Keio University
Japan

1. Introduction

An automotive performance has improved from the demand of ride comfort and driving stability. Many research have proposed various control system design methods for active and semi-active suspension systems. These studies evaluated the amount of reduced vibration in the vehicle body, i.e., the vertical acceleration in the center-of-gravity (CoG) of the vehicle's body (Ikeda *et al.*, 1999; Kosemura *et al.*, 2008; Itagaki *et al.*, 2008). However, any passengers always do not sit in the CoG of the vehicle body. In the seated position that is not the CoG of the vehicle body, vertical acceleration is caused by vertical, roll and pitch motion of the vehicle. In nearly the resonance frequency of the seated human, the passenger's vibration becomes larger than the seated position's vibration of the vehicle body due to the seated human dynamics.

The seated human dynamics and human sensibility of vibration are cleared by many researchers. So far some human dynamics model has been proposed (Tamaoki *et al.*, 1996, 1998, 2002; Koizumi *et al.*, 2000). Moreover, some of them are standardized in ISO (ISO-2631-1, 1997; ISO-5982, 2001). At the research as for automotive comfort with the passenger-vehicle system, M.Oya et al. proposed the suspension control method considering the passenger seated position in the half vehicle model (Oya *et al.*, 2008). G.J. Stein et al. evaluated passenger's head acceleration at some vehicle velocities and some road profiles (Guglielmino *et al.*, 2008). There are few active suspension control design methods which are positively based on a passenger's dynamics and the seating position. These methods can be expected to improve the control performance.

In this paper, new active suspension control method is developed to reduce the passenger's vibration. Firstly, a vehicle and passenger model including those dynamics at seated position is constructed. Next, a generalized plant that uses the vertical acceleration of the passenger's head as one of the controlled output is constructed to design the linear H_∞ controller. In this paper, this proposed method defines as "Passenger Control". "Passenger Control" means passenger's vibration control. Moreover, in an active suspension control, it is very important to reduce the vibration at the condition of the limited actuating force. Then, we design two methods which are "Vehicle CoG Control", and "Seat Position Control", and compare the proposed method with two methods. "Vehicle CoG Control" means vibration control of vehicle. "Seat Position Control" means vibration control of seat position. Finally, several simulations are carried out by using a full vehicle model which has active suspension system. From the result, it was confirmed that in nearly the resonance frequency of a passenger's head in the vertical direction, "Passenger Control" is effective in reducing a passenger's vibration better than "Vehicle CoG Control" and "Seat Position Control". The numerical simulation results show that the proposed method has the highest control performance which is vibration reduction of the passenger's head per generated force by the active suspension. Moreover, the results show that the proposed method has robustness for the difference in passenger's vibration characteristic.

2. Modeling

2.1 Modeling of the vehicle

Figure 1 shows a full vehicle model which is equipped with an active suspension between each wheel and the vehicle body. The weight of the vehicle body is supported by the spring. We assume that a vehicle model is a generic sedan car as shown in Table 1. The equations of motion which are, bounce, roll, pitch and each unsprung motion are as follows:

$$M_b \ddot{z}_{cg} = \sum_{i=1}^{4} f_{si}, \tag{1}$$

$$I_r \ddot{\phi} = \frac{T_f}{2}\left(f_{s1} - f_{s2}\right) + \frac{T_r}{2}\left(f_{s3} - f_{s4}\right) + M_b g H_r \phi, \tag{2}$$

$$I_p \ddot{\theta} = -L_f\left(f_{s1} + f_{s2}\right) + L_r\left(f_{s3} + f_{s4}\right) + M_b g H_p \theta, \tag{3}$$

$$M_{ti} \ddot{z}_{ui} = -F_{di} + K_t z_{ti} \quad (i = 1, \cdots, 4). \tag{4}$$

where H_r is the distance from a roll center to the CoG of the vehicle body, and H_p is the distance from a pitch center to the CoG of the vehicle body. These parameters are constant. The spring coefficients of each wheel are different from each other, and were set to $K_{1,2} = K_f$, $K_{3,4} = K_r$, z_{si} means a suspension stroke of each wheel, z_{ti} means deformation of the each tire.

$$\begin{aligned}
z_{s1} &= z_{cg} + T_f/2\phi - L_f\theta - z_{u1} \\
z_{s2} &= z_{cg} - T_f/2\phi - L_f\theta - z_{u2} \\
z_{s3} &= z_{cg} + T_r/2\phi + L_r\theta - z_{u3} \\
z_{s4} &= z_{cg} - T_r/2\phi + L_r\theta - z_{u4} \\
z_{ti} &= z_{ri} - z_{ui} \quad (i = 1, \cdots, 4)
\end{aligned} \tag{5}$$

The spring and damping forces which act between the wheels and the vehicle body, are given by the following equation.

$$F_{di} = -K_i z_{si} - C_i(t)\dot{z}_{si} \quad (i = 1, \cdots, 4) \tag{6}$$

2.2 Modeling of the passenger

Various models of a seated human have been proposed so far. In this paper, the passenger's motion is expressed to the seated human model shown in Fig. 2. Therefore, it is easy to understand the passenger's motion. To the seated position, Ps, the body part has three

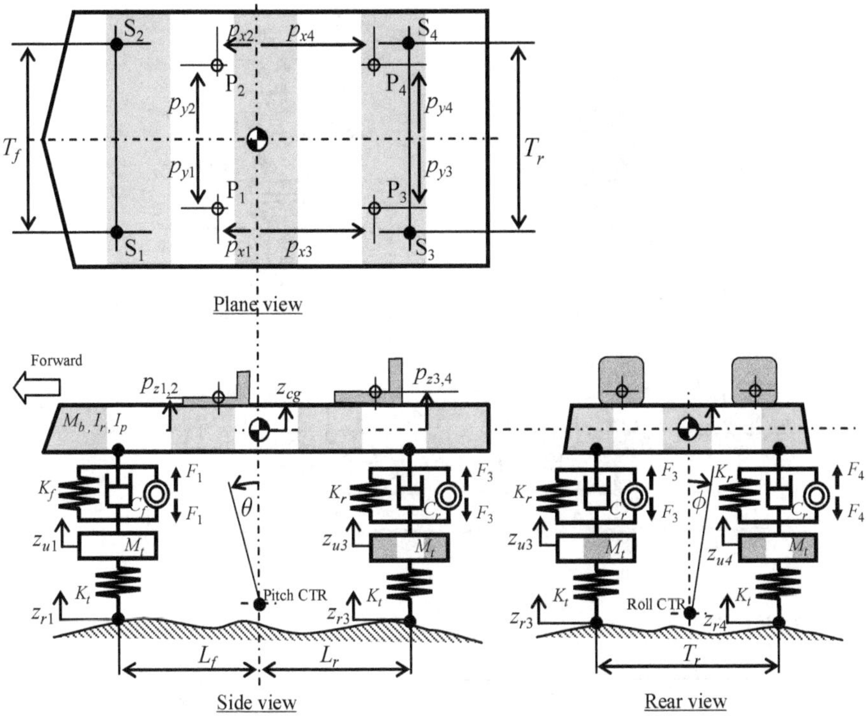

Fig. 1. Full vehicle model

Symbol	Value		Symbol	Value	
M_b	1900	kg	T_f	1.53	m
M_t	50	kg	T_r	1.50	m
I_r	600	kgm^2	H_r	0.45	m
I_p	3000	kgm^2	H_p	0.53	m
K_f	33×10^3	N/m	$p_{x1,2}$	0.04	m
K_r	31×10^3	N/m	p_{y1}	0.4	m
K_t	260×10^3	N/m	p_{y2}	-0.4	m
L_f	1.34	m	$p_{z1,2}$	-0.045	m
L_r	1.46	m			

Table 1. Specification of vehicle mode

degree of freedom (DOF) which is longitudinal, lateral, and vertical motions. The head has 3 DOF. First, the head moves up and down to the body parts. Second, the head rotates around the point, Pp, at the pitch direction. Third, the head rotates around the point, Pr, at the roll direction. Thus the passenger model has a total of 6 DOF. Between the each part, it has a spring and a damper. The equation of motion of the passenger model is as follows.

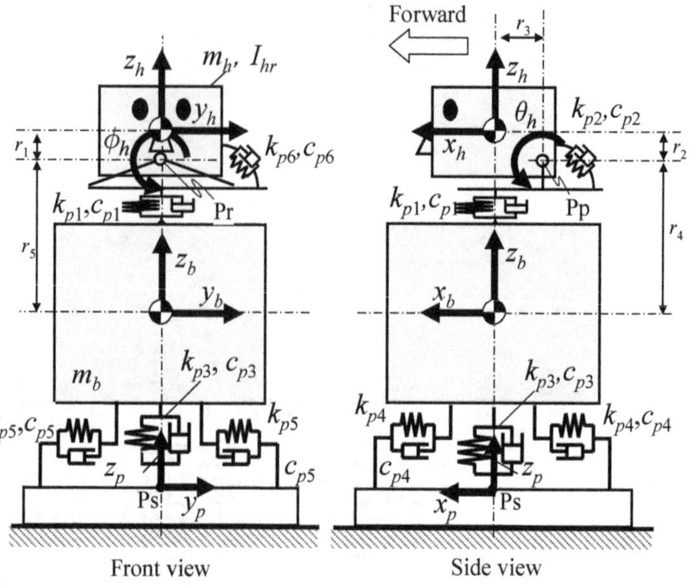

Fig. 2. Passenger model

i	k_{pi} [N/m]	c_{pi} [N/m/s]	r_{pi} [m]
1	40000	2000	0.1
2	15*	0.9**	0.1
3	96000	1120	0.05
4	22500	600	0.2
5	2000	400	0.3
6	20*	1.2**	0.3

Table 2. Specification of passenger model (*:Nm/rad, **:Nm/rad/s)

$$m_{bh}\ddot{x}_b = 2k_{p4}\left(x_p - x_b\right) + 2c_{p4}\left(\dot{x}_p - \dot{x}_b\right) + \left(-c_{p2}\dot{\theta}_h - k_{p2}\theta_h\right)/r_4 \tag{7}$$

$$m_{bh}\ddot{y}_b = 2k_{p5}\left(y_p - y_b\right) + 2c_{p5}\left(\dot{y}_p - \dot{y}_b\right) - \left(-c_{p6}\dot{\phi}_h - k_{p6}\phi_h\right)/r_5 \tag{8}$$

$$\begin{aligned} m_b\ddot{z}_b &= k_{p3}\left(z_p - z_b\right) + c_{p3}\left(\dot{z}_p - \dot{z}_b\right) - \left[k_{p1}\left(z_b - z_h\right) + c_{p1}\left(\dot{z}_b - \dot{z}_h\right)\right] \\ &\quad + \left(-c_{p2}\dot{\theta}_h - k_{p2}\theta_h\right)/r_3 \end{aligned} \tag{9}$$

$$m_h\ddot{z}_h = k_{p1}\left(z_b - z_h\right) + c_{p1}\left(\dot{z}_b - \dot{z}_h\right) - \left(-c_{p2}\dot{\theta}_h - k_{p2}\theta_h\right)/r_3 \tag{10}$$

$$\begin{aligned} I_{hr}\ddot{\phi}_h &= -c_{p6}\dot{\phi}_h - k_{p6}\phi_h \\ &+ m_{hbh}r_1\left[2k_{p5}\left(y_p - y_b\right) + 2c_{p5}\left(\dot{y}_p - \dot{y}_b\right) - \left(-c_{p6}\dot{\phi}_h - k_{p6}\phi_h\right)/r_5\right] \end{aligned} \tag{11}$$

$$\begin{aligned} I_{hp}\ddot{\theta}_h &= -c_{p2}\dot{\theta}_h - k_{p2}\theta_h + \left[k_{p1}\left(z_b - z_h\right) + c_{p1}\left(\dot{z}_b - \dot{z}_h\right)\right]r_3 \\ &- m_{hbh}r_2\left[2k_{p4}\left(x_p - x_b\right) + 2c_{p4}\left(\dot{x}_p - \dot{x}_b\right) + \left(-c_{p2}\dot{\theta}_h - k_{p2}\theta_h\right)/r_4\right] \end{aligned} \tag{12}$$

Where,

$$m_{bh} = m_b + m_h, \quad m_{hbh} = \frac{m_b}{m_b + m_h}.$$

Each parameter of the passenger model is set to m_b = 45 kg, m_h = 7.5 kg, I_{hr} = 8.3×10^{-2} kgm^2, I_{bp} = 5.0 kgm^2, and I_{hp} = 5.5×10^{-2} kgm^2 based on the adult male's height and weight data. In addition, the acceleration of the passenger's head is derived from a geometric relation.

$$\begin{aligned} \ddot{x}_h &= \ddot{x}_b + \ddot{\theta}_h/r_2 \\ \ddot{y}_h &= \ddot{y}_b + \ddot{\phi}_h/r_1 \end{aligned} \tag{13}$$

As shown in Table 2, the spring, the damper, and length were adjusted to conform the passenger model and an experimental data which was reported in previous research shown in Figs. 3 and 4 (Tamaoki *et al.*, 1996, 1998). The results shown in Figs. 3(c) and 4(c) demonstrate that the gain characteristics of the model were nearly equal to the experimental ones. However, as shown in Figs. 3(b) and 4(b), there were some differences in the high-frequency band for the phase properties. To reduce these differences, the passenger model must be made more complex, but this necessitates the use of a higher order control system. Because the purpose of our controller is to reduce the vertical vibration of the passengers in comparison with the lateral vibration, we designed it using this passenger model.

2.3 Vehicle-passenger model

In this section, the passenger for the vehicle model was assumed to sit in the front-left seat in designing the control system to reduce passenger vibration and motion. The vehicle-passenger model is shown in Fig. 5. The passenger model is set to the vehicle model in a front-left seat to design the controller. The translational motion of the position of the seat and the motion of the vehicle have the following relation;

$$\begin{aligned} x_{p1} &= \left(H_p + p_{1z}\right)\theta \\ y_{p1} &= -\left(H_r + p_{1z}\right)\phi \\ z_{p1} &= z_{cg} + p_{1y}\phi - p_{1x}\theta \end{aligned} \tag{14}$$

The equation of state of the vehicle-passenger model is defined as the following equation.

$$\dot{x}(t) = A_p x(t) + B_{p1}w(t) + B_{p2}u(t) \tag{15}$$

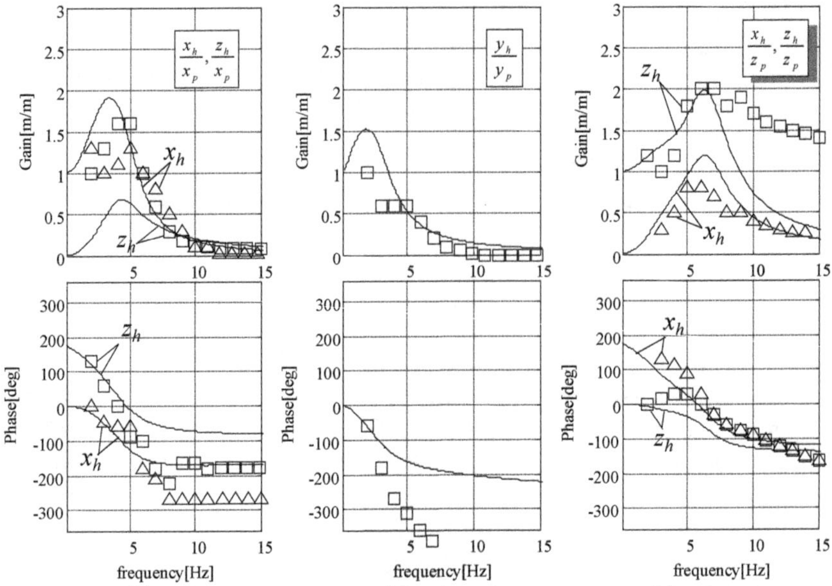

(a) x_p input (b) y_p input (c) z_p input

Fig. 3. Transfer function from seat to the head (Translational motion, Dot: Experiment (Tamaoki *et al.*, 1998), Line: model)

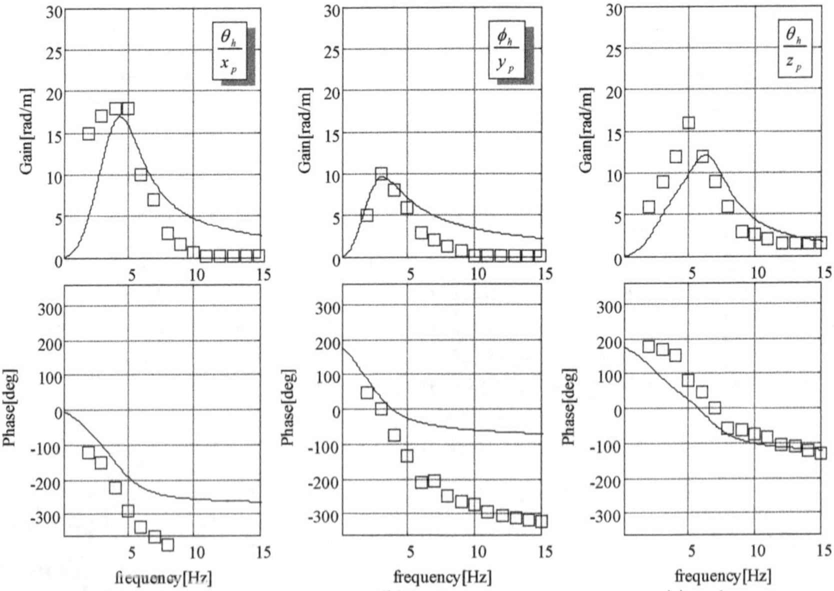

(a) x_p input (b) y_p input (c) z_p input

Fig. 4. Transfer function from seat to the head (Rotational motion, Dot: Experiment (Tamaoki *et al.*, 1996), Line: Model)

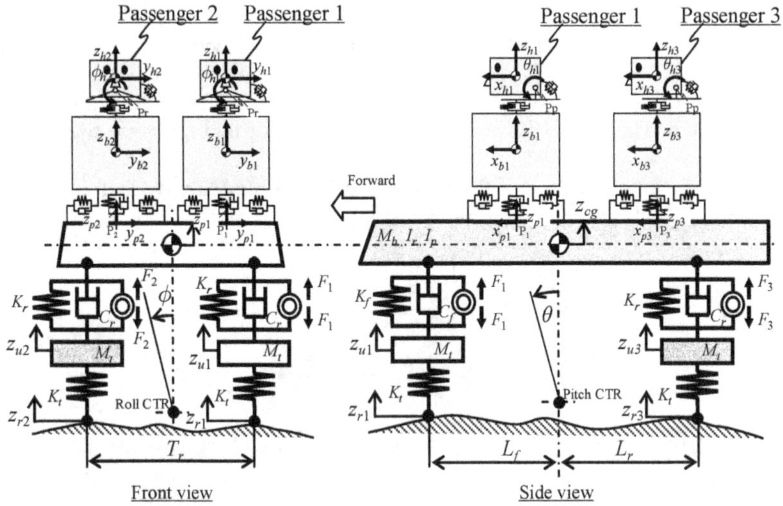

Fig. 5. Vehicle-passenger model

Where,

$$x(t)=\left[z_{u1}\,z_{u2}\,z_{u3}\,z_{u4}\,z_{cg}\,\phi\,\theta\,\dot{z}_{u1}\,\dot{z}_{u2}\,\dot{z}_{u3}\,\dot{z}_{u4}\,\dot{z}_{cg}\dot{\phi}\,\dot{\theta}\,x_{b1}\,y_{b1}\,z_{b1}\,z_{h}\,\phi_{h1}\,\theta_{h1}\,\dot{x}_{b1}\,\dot{y}_{b1}\,\dot{z}_{b1}\,\dot{z}_{h}\,\dot{\phi}_{h1}\,\dot{\theta}_{h1}\right]^T$$
$$w(t)=\left[z_{r1}\,z_{r2}\,z_{r3}\,z_{r4}\right]^T$$
$$u(t)=\left[F_1\,F_2\,F_3\,F_4\right]^T$$

3. Design of controller

3.1 Disturbance accommodating control

We found that feedforward control of disturbance information in the finite frequency range and feedback control improve performance (Okamoto *et al.*, 2000). The power spectral density of the actual velocity of disturbances had flat characteristics in a low frequency, and decreased according to frequency at a region of high frequency. We assumed that it regarded as the colored noise formed by shaping filter which has a transfer function with low-pass characteristics. This filter of the each wheel is based on the road condition which defined by ISO (ISO-8608, 1995). The filter is as follows:

$$Q_{di}\begin{cases}\dot{x}_{di}(t)=A_{di}x_{di}(t)+B_{di}w_{gi}(t)\\ w_i(t)=C_{di}x_{di}(t) \qquad (i=1,\cdots,4)\end{cases}$$
$$\frac{w_i(s)}{w_{gi}(s)}=\frac{\varpi_d^{\,2}}{s^2+2\xi_d\varpi_d s+\varpi_d^{\,2}} \qquad (i=1,\cdots,4) \tag{16}$$

where, w_{gi} is road input of the each wheel, w_i is road input of the vehicle-passenger model of the generalized plant to design the controller as shown in Fig. 6. It was referred to as $\varpi_d = 50\times 2\pi$ and $\xi_d = 0.706$.

3.2 Disturbance accommodating H_∞ control.

The feedforward control of disturbances resulted in worse accuracy outside the assumed frequency (Okamoto *et al.*, 2000). Furthermore, because each resonance frequency of the vehicles, passenger, and tire differs, the control system design considering each resonance frequency is needed. Therefore, the control system was designed by using the H_∞ method in the control theory.

We integrated each state variable of the road disturbance model and frequency weights for controlled values. The frequency weights are as follows:

$$Q_{wi}\begin{cases}\dot{x}_{wi}(t)=A_{wi}x_{wi}(t)+B_{wi}z_{pi}(t)\\ z_{gi}(t)=C_{wi}x_{wi}(t) \qquad (i=1,\cdots,4)\end{cases}. \qquad (17)$$

$$\frac{z_{gi}(s)}{z_{pi}(s)}=K_{wi}W_i(s) \qquad (i=1,\cdots,4)$$

where, z_{pi} is controlled value of the vehicle-passenger model, z_{gi} is controlled value of the generalized plant. Figure 6 shows a block diagram of the generalized plant to design the controller, and the state-space form of the generalized plant is as follows:

$$\begin{aligned}\dot{x}_g(t)&=A_gx_g(t)+B_{g1}w_g(t)+B_{g2}u(t)\\ z_g(t)&=C_{g1}x_g(t) \qquad\qquad +D_{g12}u(t)\ .\\ y_g(t)&=C_{g2}x_g(t)+D_{g21}w_g(t)\end{aligned} \qquad (18)$$

H_∞ norm of the transfer function from disturbance $w_g(t)$ to controlled value $z(t)$ is expressed by the following equation.

$$\left\|G_{z_gw_g}\right\|_\infty=\sup_w\frac{\left\|z_g\right\|_2}{\left\|w_g\right\|_2} \qquad (19)$$

$$\min_u\left\|G_{z_gw_g}\right\|_\infty=:\gamma^* \qquad (20)$$

where, γ^* is a minimum of H_∞ norm of the generalized plant realized with H_∞ controller. The controller is the following equation (Glover & Doyle, 1988).

$$\begin{aligned}\dot{x}_k(t)&=A_kx_k(t)+B_ky(t)\\ u(t)&=C_kx_k(t)\end{aligned} \qquad (21)$$

The measured outputs, $y(t)$, are four vertical accelerations of the wheel position of the vehicle body. The controlled values, $z(t)$, are vertical acceleration of the passenger's head, vertical velocity of the sprung, tire deformation, and actuating force. Frequency weight W_i, shown in Fig. 7 was determined by trial and error.

A bandpass filter, W_1, that had a peak frequency equal to the resonance frequency of the passenger's head was used based on sensitivity curves (ISO-2631-1, 1997), such as that being standardized by ISO and shown in Fig. 8. In order to prevent the increase of response in each resonance, a low pass filter W_2 and a bandpass filter W_3 are used. Moreover, to prevent steady control input and minimize energy consumption, a high pass filter, W_4, was used.

We compare the proposal method and two generalized control methods to verify the control performance. As one of the generalized control methods, the controller in which the one of the controlled values is vertical acceleration of the body CoG (Vehicle CoG Control), is designed. Another is that one of the controlled values is vertical acceleration of a seated position (Seat Position Control). The design of two generalized control methods are changed the controlled value z_1 into the vertical acceleration of CoG of the vehicle body and seated position, respectively. Frequency weights, $W_1(s)$, $W_2(s)$, $W_3(s)$, $W_4(s)$, K_{w2} = 400, K_{w3} = 5000, and K_{w4} = 1.31, use the same value also in the three methods. The following section describes K_{w1}.

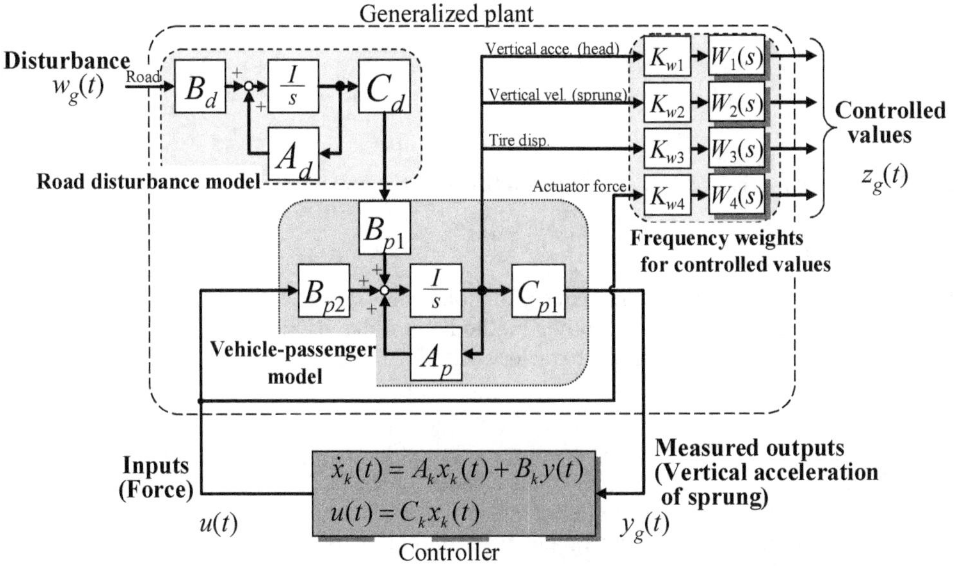

Fig. 6. Generalized plant for "Passenger Control"

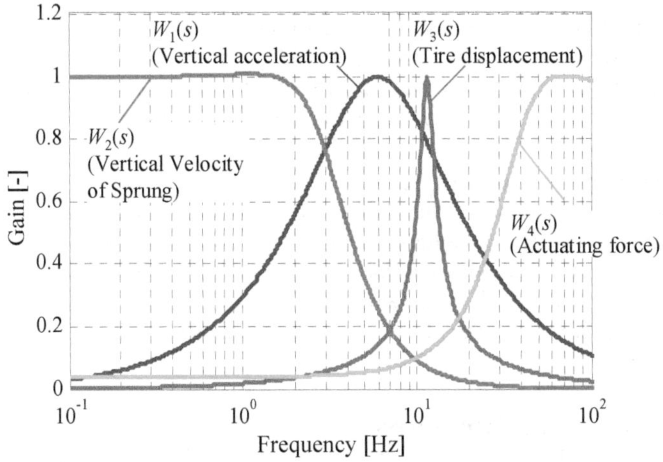

Fig. 7. Frequency weights for controlled value

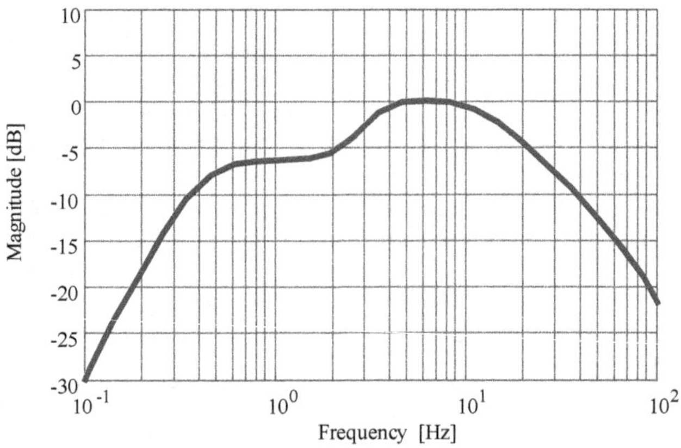

Fig. 8. Sensitivity curve of vertical vibration (ISO-2631-1, 1997)

4. Simulation

In this section, two kinds of numerical simulations were carried out. One is to verify control performance in comparison with other methods. Another is to verify robustness for the difference in passenger's vibration characteristic.

4.1 Assumption

We verified the effectiveness of the proposed method by using the vehicle-passenger model with H_∞ controller. We used MATLAB (The Math Work Inc.) for the calculations, and the Runge-Kutta method for the differential equations. The computational step size is 1 ms. In addition, it assumes that we perform the evaluation in an ideal condition, and the model to design the controller and the model for evaluation are same models.

4.2 Driving condition

It assumes that the PSD characteristic of the road surface is C class defined by ISO (ISO-8608, 1995). The vehicle speed is 16.6 m/s (60 km/h). The vehicle runs the straight for 10 seconds, and the input of the road surface to each wheel is independent. Figure 9 shows the PSD of the road disturbance. Figure 10 shows the road displacement.

4.3 Design of the frequency weight K_{w1}

In each method, if the evaluation function of acceleration is raised, it is clear that each acceleration set as the controlled value is reduced, and the actuating force increases. To set the same actuating force, frequency weight K_{w1} of each method was adjusted so that RMS value of the actuating force of the four wheels sets to 1000 N. The each frequency weight, K_{w1}, of "Vehicle CoG Control", "Seat Position Control" and "Passenger Control" is 244, 315, and 78 respectively.

4.4 Difference of vehicle-passenger model

In the numerical simulation, there are some diffidence in the vehicle-passenger model as shown in Table 3. In sections 4.5.1 and 4.5.2, passenger models sit in the front-left seat and front-right seat. In section 4.5.2, some specifications of the passenger model are different from the generalized plant to design controller.

4.5 Results

4.5.1 Comparison with the "Vehicle CoG Control" and "Seat Position Control"

Figure 11 shows the time histories of the vehicle and the passenger 1's vertical acceleration for 3 second. In this paper, passenger 1 sits a front-left seat, and passenger 2 sits a front-right. In the acceleration of the vehicle body, it was confirmed that there is few differences among the three methods. On the other hand, in the acceleration of the passenger's head, the proposed method is the smallest, and it was confirmed that the proposed method is effective for the passenger's vibration reduction.

The actuating force of each wheel in each method is shown in Fig. 12. In the Vehicle CoG Control, the actuating force of all wheels is generated in the same direction. In the other method, the actuating force of the left/right wheel is generated in a different direction. Therefore, the vertical accelerations of the seated position and the passenger's head are reduced by controlling the roll motion of the vehicle body.

Figure 13 shows the Lissajous figure of lateral and vertical accelerations of the seated position, the passenger's body and the head part respectively. This figure is seen from the front of vehicle. In upper-right figure of Fig. 13 (c), the proposed method has control effect which vertical acceleration of the passenger 1's head is reduced in comparison with "Vehicle CoG Control". Moreover, the proposed method has not only the vibration reduction effect of the passenger 1's head, but also the vertical acceleration reduction effect of the passenger 1's body.

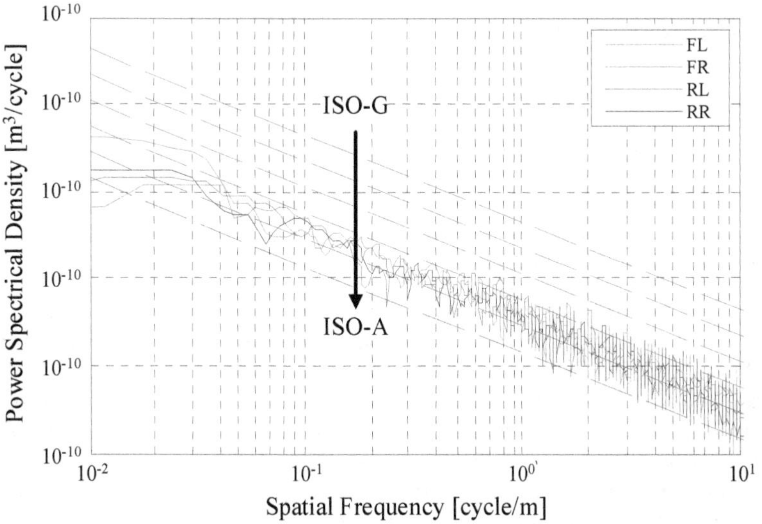

Fig. 9. PSD of road surface profile

Figure 14 shows power spectrum density (PSD) of the vertical acceleration of the passenger's head in each method, and actuating force. In the frequency band of 4-7 Hz with resonance of a passenger's head, although the proposed method has the vibration reduction effect better than other methods. On the other hand, PSD of the actuating force does not necessarily have the highest value in the frequency band. In this frequency band, the proposed method can reduce the passenger's vibration by the limited actuating force.

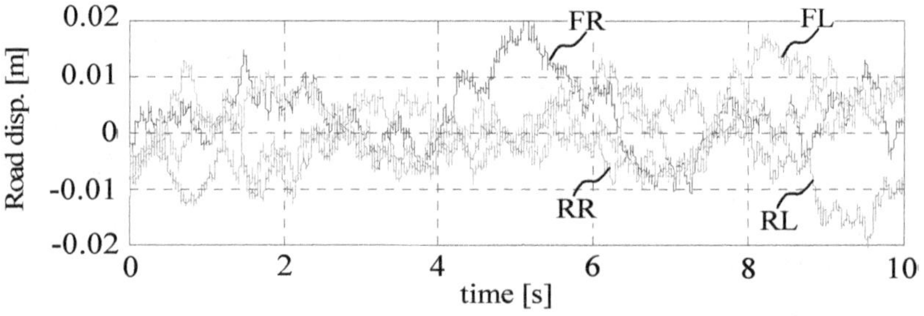

Fig. 10. Road displacement

	Generalized plant to design controller	Simulation model	
		Section 4.5.1	Section 4.5.2
Vehicle	Fig. 1, Table 1	←	←
Passenger	Fig. 2, Table 2	←	Table 4
Seated position	•Front-left	•Front-left •Front-right	←

Table 3. Vehicle-passenger model

In each frequency band, the sensitivity of the vertical acceleration for the human is defined by sensitivity curves (ISO-2631, 1997). In this paper, we estimate the root mean square (RMS) value which is added the sensitivity compensation expressed by a high order transfer function (Rimel & Mansfield, 2007). Figure 15 shows the ratio of the RMS value of each vertical acceleration to those values of "Vehicle CoG Control". In the passenger 1, it was confirmed that the proposed method can reduce the RMS value of the passenger 1's head (head 1). Moreover, in the passenger 2, it was confirmed that the RMS value of the passenger 2's head (head 2) is not increased by the proposed method, and the proposed method had the vibration reduction effect equivalent to the generalized control methods.

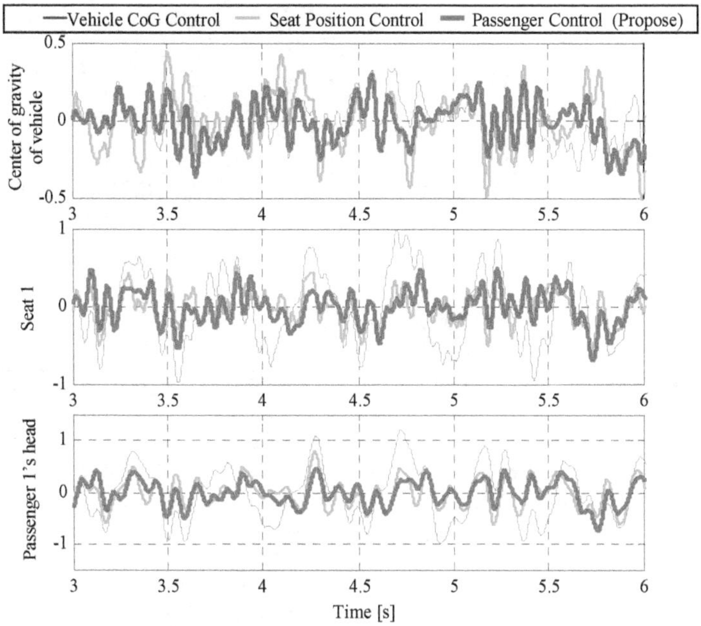

Fig. 11. Vehicle and passenger's behavior (Vertical acceleration, unit : m/s^2)

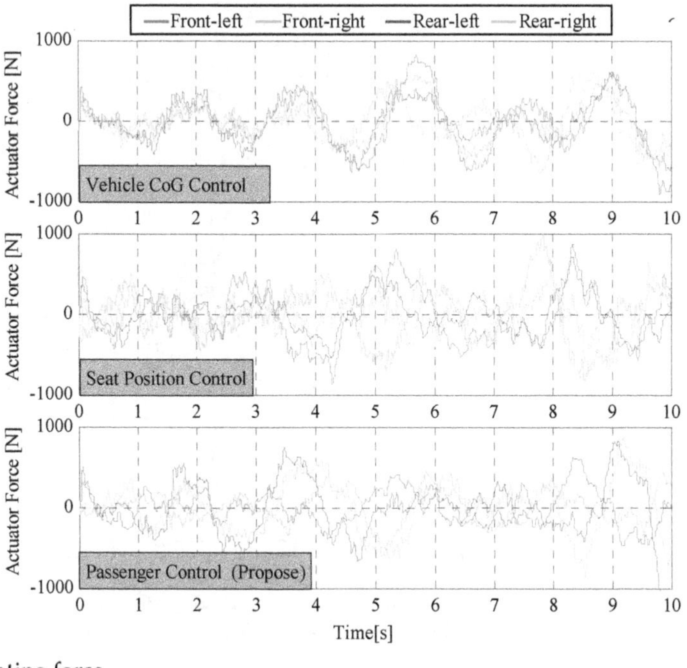

Fig. 12. Actuating force

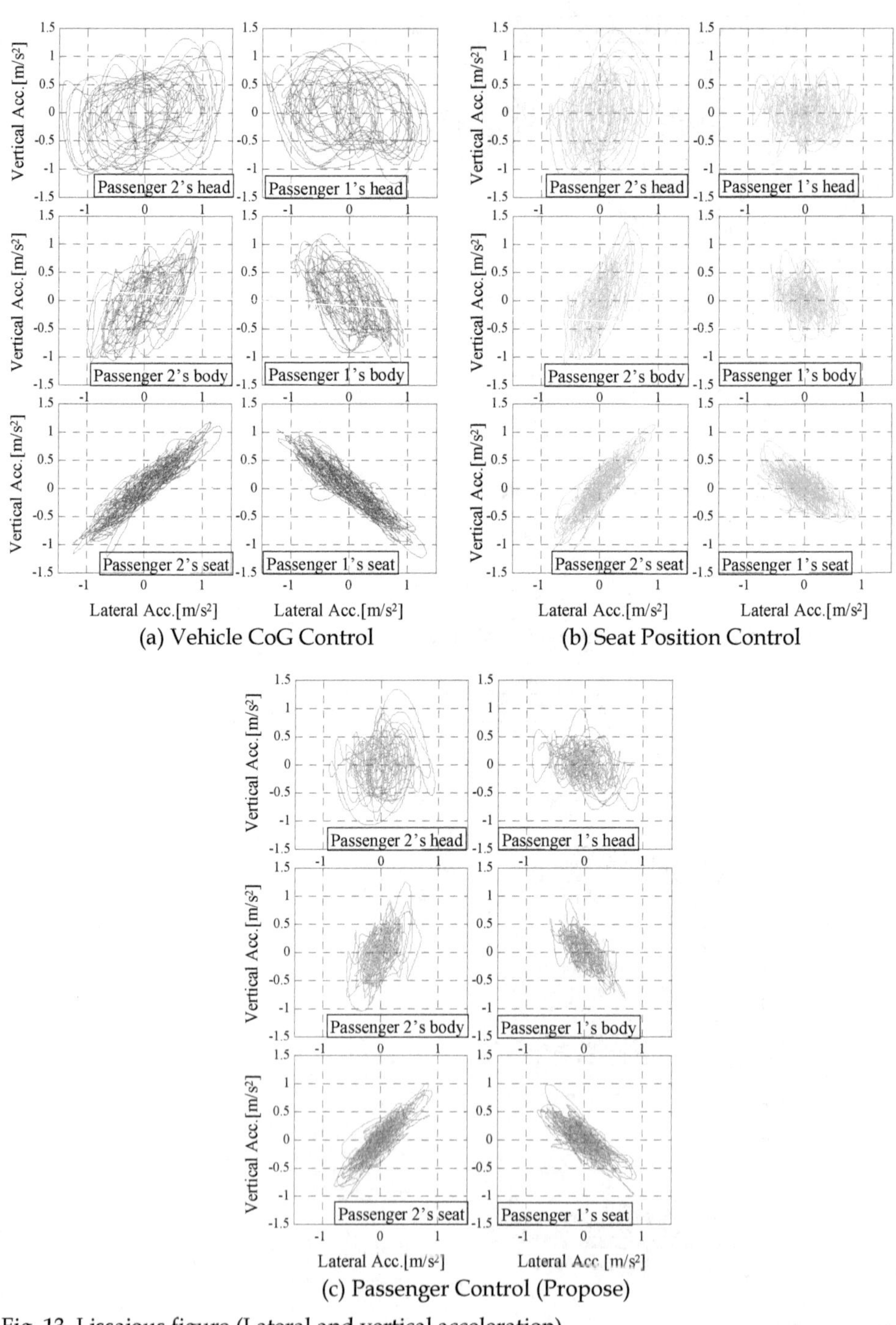

Fig. 13. Lissajous figure (Lateral and vertical acceleration)

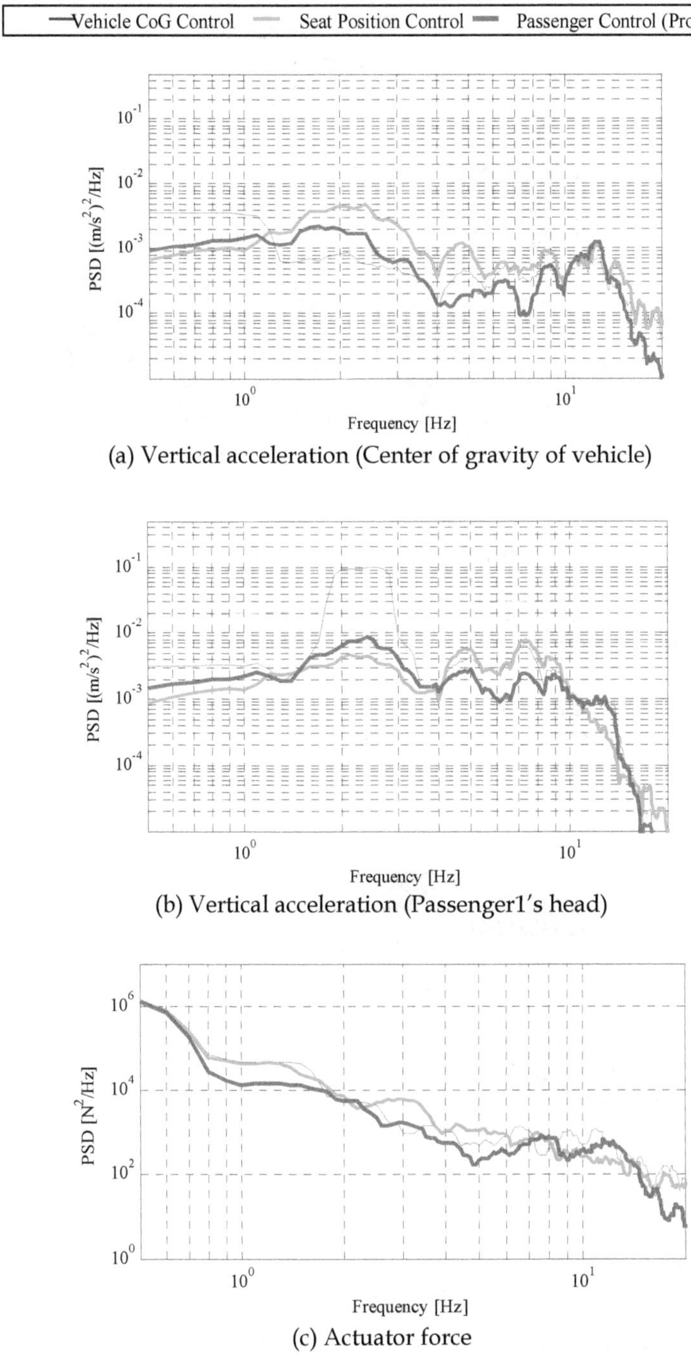

Fig. 14. Power spectral density

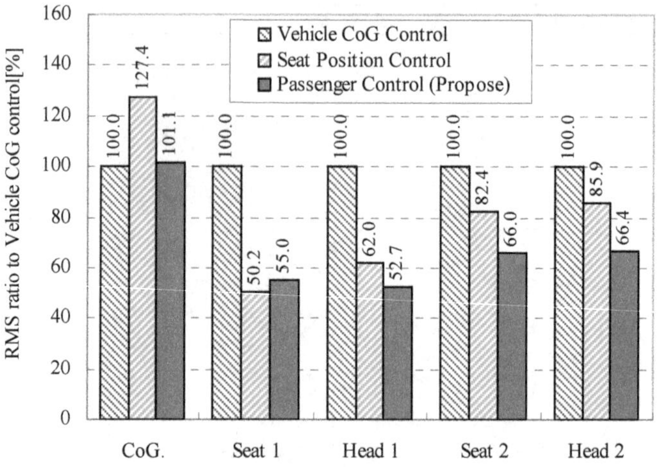

Fig. 15. RMS value of vertical acceleration

From these results, it was confirmed that the proposed method can effectively reduce passenger's vibration by using H_∞ control which including the dynamics of human body and seated position. By means of setting the passenger' motion to one of the amounts of evaluation function, the proposed method can directly control the passenger's vibration.

4.5.2 Comparison with the different passenger model

In this section, the robust performance against the difference in a passenger's vibration characteristic is verified. In previous research, there are many reports about seated human

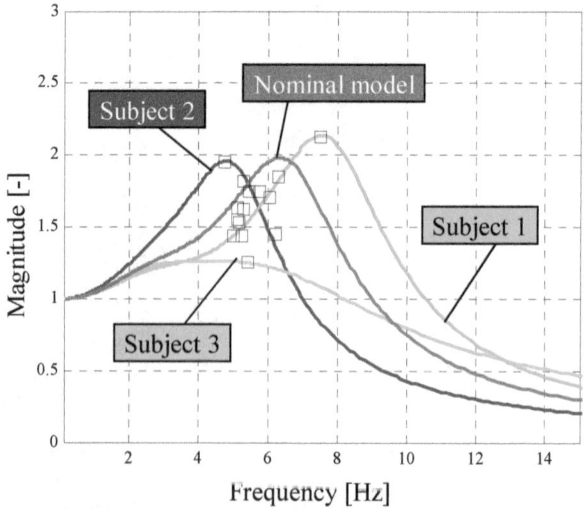

Fig. 16. Frequency response from seat to the head (Vertical motion, dot : Experiment (Varterasian & Thompson, 1977), Line : Model)

dynamics. Varterasian & Thompson reported the seated human dynamics from a large person to a small person(Varterasian & Thompson, 1977). Robust performance is verified by supposition that such person sits in the vehicle. Figure 16 shows the frequency response from vertical vibration of seat to vertical vibration of the head. Dot is 15 subjects' resonance peak. In this section, three outstanding subjects' data of their report is modeled in the vibration characteristic of vertical direction. The damper and spring were adjusted to conform the passenger model and an experimental data. The characteristic of the passenger model of three outstanding subjects are shown in Table 4.

	k_{p3} [N/m]	c_{p3} [N/m/s]
Nominal model	960000	1120
Subject 1	1320000	1150
Subject 2	576000	960
Subject 3	960000	2550

Table 4. Difference of specifications

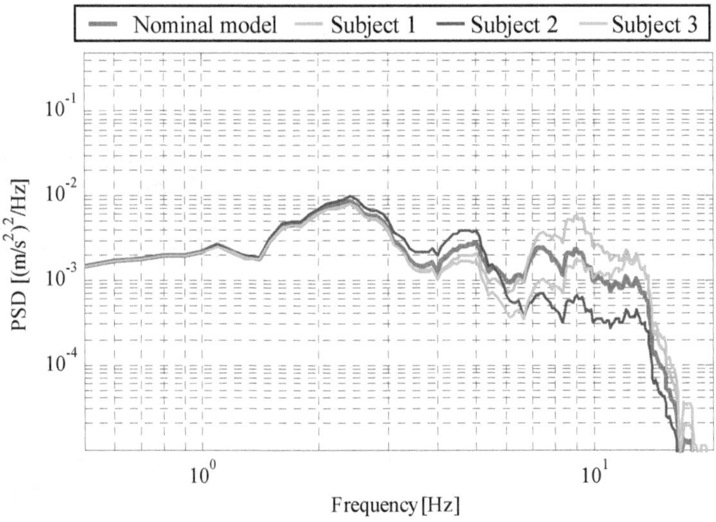

Fig. 17. PSD of vertical acceleration (Passenger 1's head)

The numerical simulation is carried out on the same road surface conditions as the section 4.5.1. Figure 17 shows PSD of the vertical acceleration of the passenger 1's head and Fig. 18

shows RMS value. In PSD of 7 Hz or more, RMS value of vertical acceleration of subject 1's head becomes higher than the nominal model. Moreover, RMS of subject 1 is the highest. On the other hand, RMS of subjects 2 and 3 is reduced in comparison with the nominal model. The physique of subject 1 differs from other subjects. When such a person sits, the specified controller should be designed. From these results, the proposed method has robustness for the passenger of the general physique.

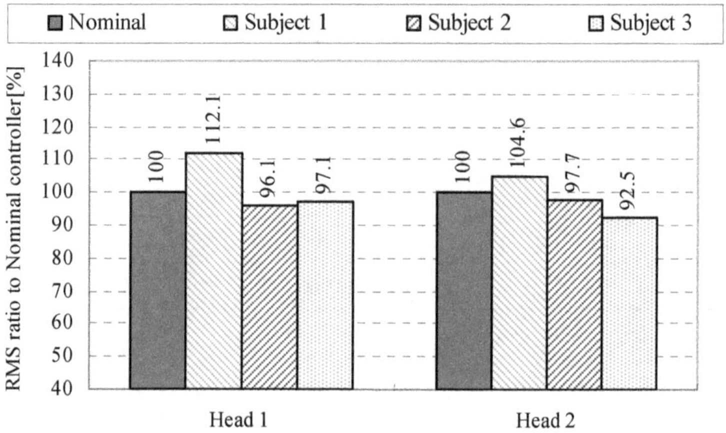

Fig. 18. RMS value of vertical acceleration of passenger 1's head

5. Conclusion

This study aims at establishing a control design method for the active suspension system in order to reduce the passenger's vibration. In the proposed method, a generalized plant that uses the vertical acceleration of the passenger's head as one of the controlled output is constructed to design the linear H_∞ controller. In the simulation results, when the actuating force is limited, we confirmed that the proposed method can reduce the passenger's vibration better than two methods which are not include passenger's dynamics. Moreover, the proposed method has robustness for the difference in passenger's vibration characteristic.

6. Acknowledgment

This work was supported in part by Grant in Aid for the Global Center of Excellence Program for "Center for Education and Research of Symbiotic, Safe and Secure System Design" from the Ministry of Education, Culture, Sport, and Technology in Japan.

7. References

Ikeda, S.; Murata, M.; Oosako, S. & Tomida, K. (1999). Developing of New Damping Force Control System -Virtual Roll Damper Control and Non-liner H_∞ Control-, *Transactions of the TOYOTA Technical Review*, Vol.49. No.2, pp.88-93

Kosemura, R.; Takahashi, M. & and Yoshida, K. (2008). Control Design for Vehicle Semi-Active Suspension Considering Driving Condition, *Proceedings of the Dynamics and Design Conference 2008*, 547, Kanagawa, Japan, September, 2008

Itagaki, N.; Fukao, T.; Amano, M.; Ichimaru, N.; Kobayashi, T. & Gankai, T. (2008). Semi-Active Suspension Systems based on Nonlinear Control, *Proceedings of the 9th International Symposium on Advanced Vehicle Control 2008*, pp. 684-689, Kobe, Japan, October, 2008

Tamaoki, G.; Yoshimura, T. & Tanimoto, Y. (1996). Dynamics and Modeling of Human Body Considering Rotation of the Head, *Proceedings of the Dynamics and Design Conference 1996*, 361, pp. 522-525, Fukuoka, Japan, August, 1996

Tamaoki, G.; Yoshimura, T. & Suzuki, K. (1998). Dynamics and Modeling of Human Body Exposed to Multidirectional Excitation (Dynamic Characteristics of Human Body Determined by Triaxial Vibration Test), *Transactions of the Japan Society of Mechanical Engineers, Series C*, Vol.64, No.617, pp. 266-272

Tamaoki, G. & Yoshimura, T. (2002). Effect of Seat on Human Vibrational Characteristics, *Proceedings of the Dynamics and Design Conference 2002*, 220, Kanazawa, Japan, October, 2002

Koizumi, T.; Tujiuchi, N.; Kohama, A. & Kaneda, T. (2000). A study on the evaluation of ride comfort due to human dynamic characteristics, *Proceedings of the Dynamics and Design Conference 2000*, 703, Hiroshima, Japan, October, 2000 ISO-2631-1 (1997). Mechanical vibration and shock–Evaluation of human exposure to whole-body vibration -, *International Organization for Standardization* ISO-5982 (2001). Mechanical vibration and shock -Range of idealized value to characterize seated body biodynamic response under vertical vibration, *International Organization for Standardization*

Oya, M.; Tsuchida, Y. & Qiang, W. (2008). Robust Control Scheme to Design Active Suspension Achieving the Best Ride Comfort at Any Specified Location on Vehicles, *Proceedings of the 9th International Symposium on Advanced Vehicle Control 2008*, pp.690-695, Kobe, Japan, October, 2008

Guglielmino, E.; Sireteanu, T.; Stammers, C. G.; Ghita, G. & Giuclea, M. (2008). *Semi-Active Suspension Control -Improved Vehicle Ride and Road Friendliness*, Springer-Verlag, ISBN- 978-1848002302, London

Okamoto, B. and Yoshida, K. (2000). Bilinear Disturbance-Accommodating Optimal Control of Semi-Active Suspension for Automobiles, *Transactions of the Japan Society of Mechanical Engineers, Series C*, Vol.66, No.650, pp. 3297-3304

Glover, K. & Doyle, J.C. (1988). State-space Formula for All Stabilizing Controllers that Satisfy an H_∞-norm Bound and Relations to Risk Sensitivity, *Journal of the Systems and Control letters*, 11, pp.167-172

ISO-8608 (1995). Mechanical vibration -Road surface profiles - Reporting of measured data, *International Organization for Standardization*

Rimel, A.N. & Mansfield, N.J. (2007). Design of digital filters for Frequency Weightings Required for Risk Assessment of workers Exposed to Vibration, *Transactions of the Industrial Health*, Vol.45, No.4, pp. 512-519

Varterasian, H. H. & Thompson, R. R. (1977). The Dynamic Characterristics of Automobiles Seats with Human Occupants, *SAE Paper*, No. 770249

6

Modelling and Nonlinear Robust Control of Longitudinal Vehicle Advanced ACC Systems

Yang Bin[1], Keqiang Li[2] and Nenglian Feng[1]
[1]*Beijing University of Technology*
[2]*Tsinghua University*
China

1. Introduction

Safety and energy are two key issues to affect the development of automotive industry. For the safety issue, the vehicle active collision avoidance system is developing gradually from a high-speed adaptive cruise control (ACC) to the current low-speed stop and go (SG), and the future research topic is the ACC system at full-speed, namely, the advanced ACC (AACC) system. The AACC system is an automatic driver assistance system, in which the driver's behavior and the complex traffic environment ranging are taken into account from high-speed to low-speed. By combining the function of the high-speed ACC and low-speed SG, the AACC system can regulate the relative distance and the relative velocity adaptively between two vehicles according to the driving condition and the external traffic environment. Therefore, not only can the driver stress and the energy consumption caused by the frequent manipulation and the traffic congestion both be reduced effectively at the urban traffic environment, but also the traffic flow and the vehicle safety will be improved on the highway.

Taking the actual traffic environment into account, the velocity of vehicle changes regularly in a wide range and even frequently under SG conditions. It is also subject to various external resistances, such as the road grade, mass, as well as the corresponding impact from the rolling resistance. Therefore, the behaviors of some main components within the power transmission show strong nonlinearity, for instance, the engine operating characteristics, automatic transmission switching logic and the torque converter capacity factor. In addition, the relative distance and the relative velocity of the inter-vehicles are also interfered by the frequent acceleration/deceleration of the leading vehicle. As a result, the performance of the longitudinal vehicle full-speed cruise system (LFS) represents strong nonlinearity and coupling dynamics under the impact of the external disturbance and the internal uncertainty. For such a complex dynamic system, many effective research works have been presented. J. K. Hedrick et al. proposed an upper+lower layered control algorithm concentrating on the high-speed ACC system, which was verified through a platoon cruise control system composed of multiple vehicles [1-3]. K. Yi et al. applied some linear control methods, likes linear quadratic (LQ) and proportional-integral-derivative (PID), to design the upper and lower layer controllers independently for the high-speed ACC system [4]. In ref.[5], Omae designed the model matching control (MMC) vehicle high-speed ACC system based on the H-*infinity* (H_{inf}) robust control method. To achieve a tracking control between the relative distance and the relative velocity of the inter-vehicles, A. Fritz proposed a nonlinear vehicle model for the high-speed ACC system with four state variables in refs.[6, 7], and designed a variable structure control (VSC) algorithm based on the feedback linearization. In ref. [8], J.E. Naranjo used the fuzzy theory to design a coordinate control algorithm between the throttle actuator and the braking system. It has been verified on an ACC and SG cruise system. Utilizing the model predictive control (MPC) method, D. Coron designed an ACC control system for a SMART Car [9]. G. N. Bifulco applied the human artificial intelligence to study an ACC control algorithm with anthropomorphic function [10]. U. Ozguner investigated the impact of inter-vehicles communications on the performance of vehicle cruise control system [11]. J. Martinez, et al. proposed a reference model-based method, which has been applied to the ACC and SG system, and achieved an expected tracking performance at full-speed condition [12]. Utilizing the idea of hierarchical design method, P. Venhovens proposed a low-speed SG cruise control system, and it has been verified on a BMW small sedan [13]. Y. Yamamura developed an SG control method based on an existing framework of the ACC control system, and applied it to the SG cruise control [14]. Focusing on the low-speed condition of the heavy-duty vehicles, Y. Bin et al. derived a nonlinear model [15, 16] and applied the theory of nonlinear disturbance decoupling (NDD) and LQ to the low-speed SG system [17, 18].

In the previous research works, the controlled object (i.e. the dynamics of the controlled vehicle) was almost simplified as a linear model without considering its own mass, gear position and the uncertainty from external environment (likes, the change of the road grade). Furthermore, the analysis of the disturbance from the leading vehicle's acceleration/ deceleration was not paid enough consideration, which has become a bottleneck in limiting the enhancement of the control performance. To summarize, based on a detailed analysis of the impact from the practical high/low speed operating condition, the uncertainty of complex traffic environment, vehicle mass, as well as the change of gear shifting to the vehicle dynamic, an innovative LFS model is proposed in this study, in which the dynamics of the controlled vehicle and the inter-vehicles are lumped together within a more accurate and reasonable mathmatical description. For the uncertainty, strong nonlinearity and the strong coupling dynamics of the proposed model, an idea of the step-by-step transformation and design is adopted, and a disturbance decoupling robust control (DDRC) method is proposed by combining the theory of NDD and VSC. On the basis of this method, it is possible to weaken the matching condition effectively within the invariance of VSC, and decouple the system from the external disturbance completely while with a simplified control structure. By this way, an improved AACC system for LFS based on the DDRC method is designed. Finally, a simulation in view of a typical vehicle moving scenario is conducted, and the results demonstrate that the proposed control system not only achieves a global optimization by means of a simplified control structure, but also exhibits an expected dynamic response, high tracking accuracy and a strong robustness regarding the external disturbance from the leading vehicle's frequent acceleration/deceleration and the internal uncertainty of the controlled vehicle.

2. LFS model

The LFS is composed of a leading vehicle and a controlled vehicle, and the block diagram is shown in Figure 1. The controlled vehicle is a heavy-duty truck, whose power transmission is composed of an engine, torque converter, automatic transmission and a final drive. The brake system is a typical one with the assistance of the compressed air. On-board millimetric wave radar is used to detect the information from the inter-vehicles (i.e., the relative distance and the relative velocity), which is installed in the front-end frame bumper of the controlled vehicle.

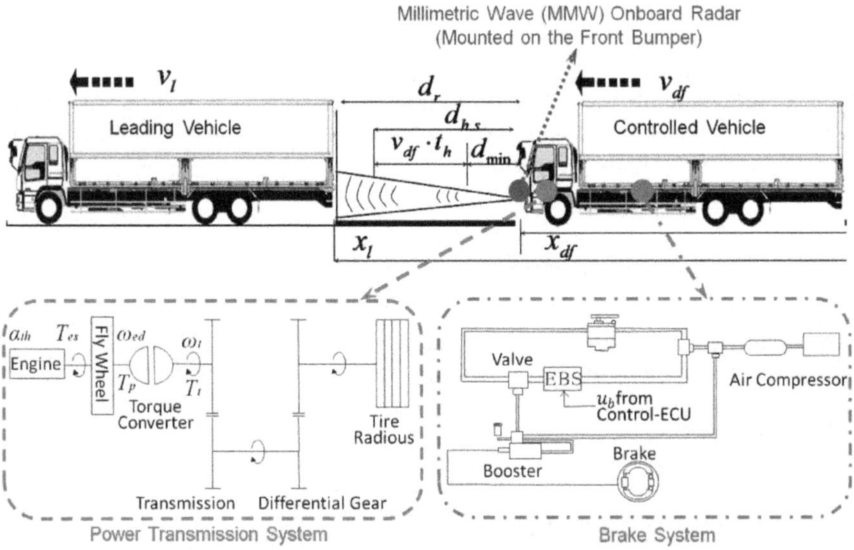

Fig. 1. Block diagram of LFS

x_l, x_{df}, v_l, v_{df} are absolute distance (m) and velocity (m/s) between the leading vehicle and the controlled vehicle, respectively. $d_r = x_l - x_{df}$ is an actual relative distance between the two vehicles. Desired relative distance can be expressed as $d_{h,s} = d_{min} + v_{df} t_h$, where, d_{min}=5m, t_h=2s. $v_r = v_l - v_{df}$ is an actual relative velocity. The purpose of LFS is to achieve the tracking of the inter-vehicles relative distance/relative velocity along a desired value. Therefore, a dynamics model of LFS at low-speed condition has been derived in ref. [15], which consists of two parts. The first part is the longitudinal dynamics model of the controlled vehicle, in which the nonlinearity of some main components, such as the engine, torque converter, etc, is taken into account. However, this model is only available at the following strict assumptions:

- the vehicle moves on a flat straight road at a low speed (<7m/s)
- assume the mass of vehicle body is constant
- the automatic transmission gear box is locked at the first gear position
- neglect the slip and the elasticity of the power train

The second part is the longitudinal dynamics model of the inter-vehicles, in which the disturbance from frequent accelartion/deccelartion of the leading vehicle is considered.

In general, since the mass, road grade and the gear position of the automatic transmission change regularly under the practical driving cycle and the traffic environment, the longitudinal dynamics model of the controlled vehicle in ref. [15] can only be used in some way to deal with an ideal traffic environment (i.e., the low-speed urban condition). In view of the uncertainties above, in this section, a more accurate longitudinal dynamics model of the controlled vehicle is derived for the purpose for high-speed and low-speed conditions (that is, the full-speed condition). After that, it will be integrated with a longitudinal dynamics model of the inter-vehicles, and an LFS dynamics model for practical applications can be obtained in consideration of the internal uncertainty and the external disturbance. It is a developed model with enhanced accuracy, rather than a simple extension in contrast with ref. [15].

2.1 Longitudinal dynamics model of the controlled vehicle

Based on the vehicle multi-body dynamics theory [19], modeling principles, and the above assumptions, two nominal models of the longitudinal vehicle dynamics are derived firstly according to the driving/braking condition:

The driving condition:

$$\dot{X} = F_{av}(X) + G_{av}(X)\alpha_{th} \Rightarrow \begin{bmatrix} \dot{x}_1 \\ \dot{x}_2 \end{bmatrix} = \begin{bmatrix} f_{av1}(X) \\ f_{av2}(X) \end{bmatrix} + \begin{bmatrix} g_{av1}(X) \\ g_{av2}(X) \end{bmatrix} \alpha_{th} \tag{1}$$

where two state variables are $x_1=\omega_t$ (turbine speed (r/min)) and $x_2=\omega_{ed}$ (engine speed (r/min)); a control variable is a_{th} (percentage of the throttle angle (%)); definitions of nonlinear items $f_{av1}(X)$, $f_{av2}(X)$, $g_{av1}(X)$ and $g_{av2}(X)$ are presented in Appendix (1).

The braking condition:

$$\dot{X} = F_{dv}(X) + G_{dv}(X)u_b \Rightarrow \begin{bmatrix} \dot{x}_1 \\ \dot{x}_2 \\ \dot{x}_3 \end{bmatrix} = \begin{bmatrix} f_{dv1}(X) \\ f_{dv2}(X) \\ f_{dv3}(X) \end{bmatrix} + \begin{bmatrix} g_{dv1}(X) \\ g_{dv2}(X) \\ g_{dv3}(X) \end{bmatrix} u_b \tag{2}$$

where $x_3=a_b$ is a braking deceleration (m/s^2); u_b is a control variable of the desired input voltage of EBS (V); definitions of nonlinear items $f_{dv1}(X)$~$f_{dv3}(X)$ and $g_{dv1}(X)$~$g_{dv3}(X)$ are presented in Appendix (2).

As mentioned earlier, models (1) and (2) are available based upon some strict assumptions. In view of the actual driving condition and complex traffic environment, some uncertainties which this heavy-duty vehicle may possibly encounter can be presented as follows:

1. variation of the mass $10{,}000\text{kg} \le M \le 25{,}000\text{kg}$
2. variation of the road grade $-3° \le \varphi_s \le 3°$
3. gear position shifting of the automatic transmission $i_{g1}=3.49$, $i_{g2}=1.86$, $i_{g3}=1.41$, $i_{g4}=1$, $i_{g5}=0.7$, $i_{g6}=0.65$.
4. mathematical modeling error from the engine, torque converter and the heat fade efficiency of the braking system.

Considering the uncertainties above, two longitudinal dynamics models of the controlled vehicle differ from Eqs. (1) and (2) are therefore expressed as

Driving condition:

$$\dot{X} = \left[F_{av}(X) + \Delta F_{av}(X)\right] + \left[G_{av}(X) + \Delta G_{av}(X)\right]\alpha_{th} \tag{3}$$

Braking condition:

$$\dot{X} = \left[F_{dv}(X) + \Delta F_{dv}(X)\right] + \left[G_{dv}(X) + \Delta G_{dv}(X)\right]u_b \tag{4}$$

where $\Delta F_{av}(X), \Delta G_{av}(X), \Delta F_{dv}(X), \Delta G_{dv}(X)$ are system uncertain matrixes relative to the nominal model. They are influenced by various factors, and are described as

$$\Delta F_{av}(X)=\begin{bmatrix}\Delta f_{av1}\\ \Delta f_{av2}\end{bmatrix},\ \Delta G_{av}(X)=\begin{bmatrix}\Delta g_{av1}\\ \Delta g_{av2}\end{bmatrix}, \Delta F_{dv}(X)=\begin{bmatrix}\Delta f_{dv1}\\ \Delta f_{dv2}\\ \Delta f_{dv3}\end{bmatrix},\ \Delta G_{dv}(X)=\begin{bmatrix}\Delta g_{dv1}\\ \Delta g_{dv2}\\ \Delta g_{dv3}\end{bmatrix}.$$

In terms of multiple factors of the uncertain matrixes, it is difficult to estimate the upper and lower boundaries of Eqs. (3) and (4) precisely by using the mathematical analytic method. Therefore, a simulation model of the heavy-duty vehicle is created at first by using the MATLAB/Simulink software, which will be used to estimate the upper and lower boundaries of the uncertain matrixes. To determine the upper and lower boundaries, an analysis on extreme driving/breaking conditions of models (3) and (4) is.

At first, the analysis of Eq. (3) indicates that with the increase of the mass M, road grade φ_s and the gear position, the item of $f_{av1}(X)$ converges reversely to its minimum value relative to the nominal condition (at a given ω_t, ω_{ed}). Similarly, the extreme operating condition for the maximum value of $f_{av1}(X)$ can be obtained. The analysis above can be applied equally to other items of Eq. (3), and can be summarized as the following two extreme conditions:

(a1) If the vehicle mass is M=10,000kg, the road grade is φ_s=-3° and the automatic transmission is locked at the first gear position, then the upper boundary of Δf_{av1} can be estimated.

(a2) If the vehicle mass is M=25,000kg, the road grade is φ_s=-3° and the automatic transmission is shifted to the third gear position (supposing that the gear position can not be shifted up to the sixth gear position, since it should be subject to a known gear shift logic under a given actual traffic condition), then the lower boundary of Δf_{av1} can be estimate.

On the analysis of Eq. (4), two extreme conditions corresponding to the upper and lower boundaries can also be obtained:

(b1) If the vehicle mass is M=10,000kg, the road grade is φ_s=-3°, the braking deceleration is a_b=0m/s^2 and the gear position is locked at the first gear position, then the upper boundary of Δf_{dv1} can be estimated.

(b2) If the vehicle mass is M=25,000kg, the road grade is φ_s=3°, the braking deceleration is a_b=-2m/s^2 (assuming it as the maximum braking deceleration commonly used) and the gear position is locked at the third gear position, then the lower boundary of Δf_{dv1} can be estimated.

By the foregoing analysis, the extreme and nominal operating conditions will be simulated respectively by using the simulation model of the heavy-duty vehicles. In order to activate entire gear positions of the automatic transmission, the vehicle is accelerated from 0m/s to the maximum velocity by inputting a engine throttle percentage of 100%. After that, the throttle angle percentage is closed to 0%, and the velocity is slowed down gradually in the following two patterns:

1. according to the requirement of (b1) condition, the vehicle is slowed down until stop by the use of the engine invert torque and the road resistance.
2. according to the requirement of (b2) condition, the vehicle is slowed down until stop through an adjoining of a deceleration a_b=-2m/s^2 generated by the EBS, as well as the sum of the engine invert torque and the road resistance.

According to the above extreme conditions (a1), (a2), (b1), (b2), the variation range of each uncertainty can be obtained by simulation, as shown in Figures 2 and 3. For removing the influence from the gear position, the *x*-coordinates in Figures 2 and 3 have been transferred into a universal scale of the engine speed.
For instance (see solid line in Figure 2), during the increase of the engine speed in condition (a1), the upper boundary of the item Δf_{av1} increases gradually, while the items Δf_{av2}, Δg_{av2} change trivially. As to the increase of the engine speed in condition (a2) (see dashed line in Figure 2), the lower boundary of the item Δf_{av1} increases rapidly at the beginning, and then drops slowly. The minimum value appears approximately at the slowest speed of the engine (i.e., the idle condition). The items Δf_{av2}, Δg_{av2} decrease during the engine speed increases.

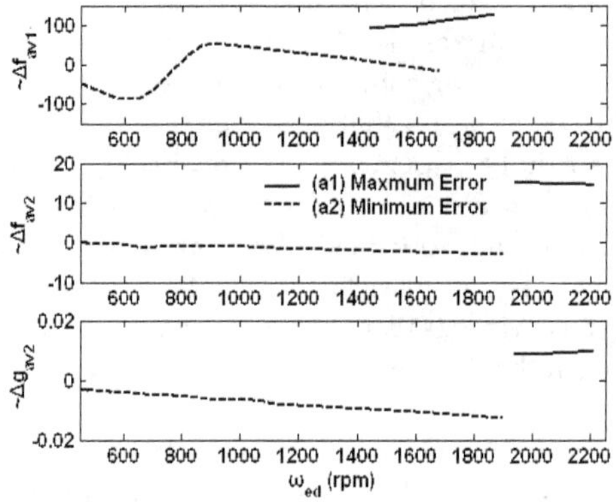

Fig. 2. Changes of uncertain items under driving condition

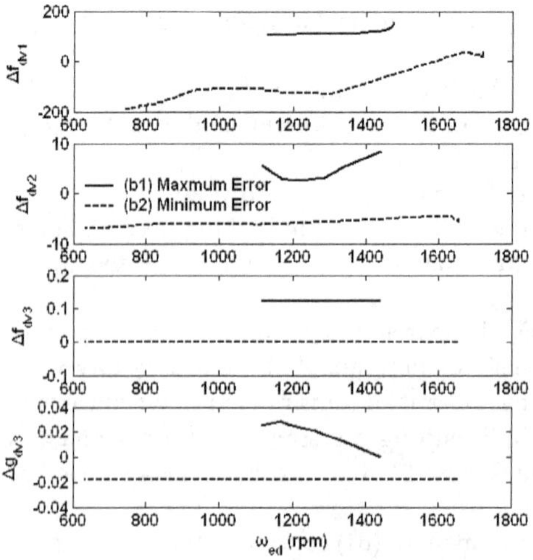

Fig. 3. Changes of uncertain items under braking condition

From the above simulation results, it is easy to calculate the upper and lower boundaries of the uncertain matrixes in Eqs. (3) and (4):

Driving condition:

$$-86 \le \Delta f_{av1} \le 127, \quad -2.75 \le \Delta f_{av2} \le 15, \quad \Delta g_{av1} = 0, \quad -0.0127 \le \Delta g_{av2} \le 0.001.$$

Braking condition:

$$-188 \le \Delta f_{dv1} \le 155, \quad -7 \le \Delta f_{dv2} \le 8.45, \quad 0 \le \Delta f_{dv3} \le 0.124, \quad \Delta g_{dv1} = \Delta g_{dv2} = 0,$$
$$-0.0174 \le \Delta g_{dv3} \le 0.029$$

where a unit of $\Delta f_{a^*}, \Delta f_{d^*}$ is $\mathrm{r/min^2}$, two units of $\Delta g_{a^*}, \Delta g_{d^*}$ are $\mathrm{r}/\left(\mathrm{min}^2 \cdot \%\right)$ and $\mathrm{m}/\left(\mathrm{s}^3 \cdot \mathrm{V}\right)$, respectively.

To verify the proposed models, some profiles are prepared in Figure 4 according to the aforementioned extreme conditions. They include the throttle angle percentage, EBS desired braking voltage and the road grade containing two values of $\pm 3°$. Figures 5 and 6 are the

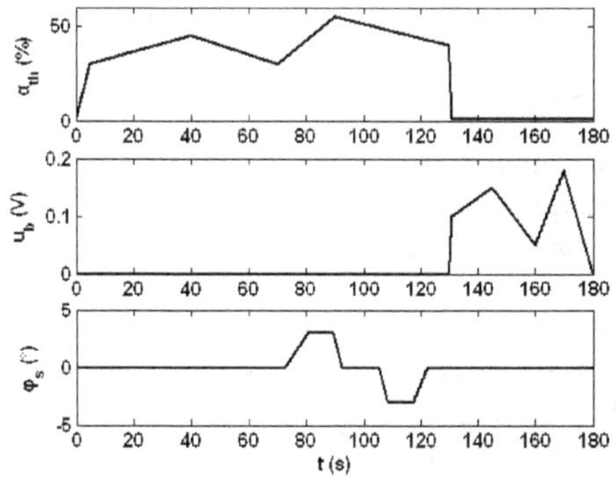

Fig. 4. Profiles of throttle angle percentage, EBS desired braking voltage and road grade

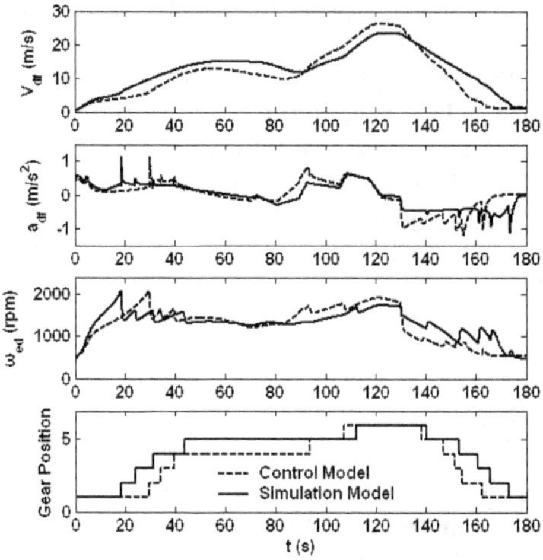

Fig. 5. Comparison results between control and simulation models (10,000kg)

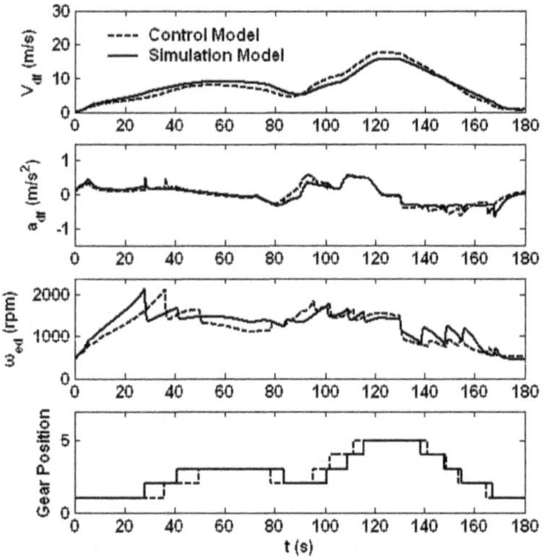

Fig. 6. Comparison results between control and simulation models (25,000kg)

comparison results corresponding to 10,000kg and 25,000kg, respectively. The dashed lines and the solid lines are the results of the control models (3) and (4) and the simulation models, respectively. It can be seen from the comparison results that the control models (3) and (4) are able to approximate the simulation models very closely, even in the case of a wide variation ranges of the velocity (0m/s~28m/s), mass (10,000kg~25,000kg) and the gear positions of the automatic transmission (1~6 gears). Because the models (3) and (4) only present the longitudinal dynamics of the controlled vehicle, the inter-vehicles dynamics has to be considered furthermore such that a completed dynamics model of the LFS at full-speed can be obtained.

2.2 Longitudinal dynamic model of the inter-vehicles

For the purposes of vehicular ACC or SG cruise control system design, many well-known achievements on the operation policy for the inter-vehicles relative distance and velocity have been intense studied [20, 21]. Focusing on the AACC system, the operation policy for the inter-vehicles relative distance and relative velocity should be determined so as to

- maintain desirable spacing between the vehicles
- ensure string stability of the convoy

Inspired by previous research [1], [2], [7] on the design of upper level controller, the operation policy of inter-vehicles relative distance and relative velocity can be defined as

$$\begin{aligned} \varepsilon_d &= d_{h,s} - d_r = \left(d_{\min} + v_{df}t_h\right) - \left(x_l - x_{df}\right) \\ \varepsilon_v &= a_{df}t_h - v_r = a_{df}t_h - \left(v_l - v_{df}\right) \end{aligned} . \quad (5)$$

where a_{df} is a controlled vehicle acceleration (m/s^2); ε_d is a tracking error of the longitudinal relative distance (m); ε_v is a tracking error of the longitudinal relative velocity (m/s).

As the illustration of the vehicle longitudinal AACC system (see Figure 1), it should be noted that an item $a_{df}t_h$ is introduced to define the inter-vehicles relative velocity ε_v so as to fit the dynamical process from one stable state to another one. In contrast to Eq. (5), conventional operation policy of inter-vehicles relative velocity is often defined as $\varepsilon_v = v_l - v_{df}$, which only focuses on the static situation of invariable velocity following. However, on account of the dynamic situation of acceleration/deceleration, the previously investigation [15, 16] has demonstrated that it is dangerous and uncomfortable for the AACC system to track a vehicle in front still adopted conventional operation policy. Therefore, an item of $a_{df}t_h$ is proposed to capture accurately the human driver's longitudinal behavior aiming at this situation. Generally, Eq. (5) can be regarded as the dynamical operation policy.

The accuracy of Eq. (5) is validated by the following experimental tests, which is carried out under complicated down-town traffic conditions in terms of five skillful adult drivers (including four males and one female). Two cases including an acceleration tracking and a deceleration approaching are considered. In the case of acceleration tracking, the driver is closing up a leading vehicle without initial error of relative distance and relative velocity. Then, the driver adjusts his/her velocity to the one of the vehicle in front. The headway distance aimed at by the driver during the tracking is essentially depending on the driver's desire of safety. In the case of deceleration approaching, the driver is closing down a leading vehicle with constant velocity. The driver brakes to reestablish the minimal headway distance, and then follow the leading vehicle with the same velocity. The experimental data presented in Figure 7 are the mean square value of five drivers' results. The comparison results confirm that Eq. (5) shows a sufficient agreement with practical driver manipulation, which can be adopted in the design of vehicle longitudinal AACC system.

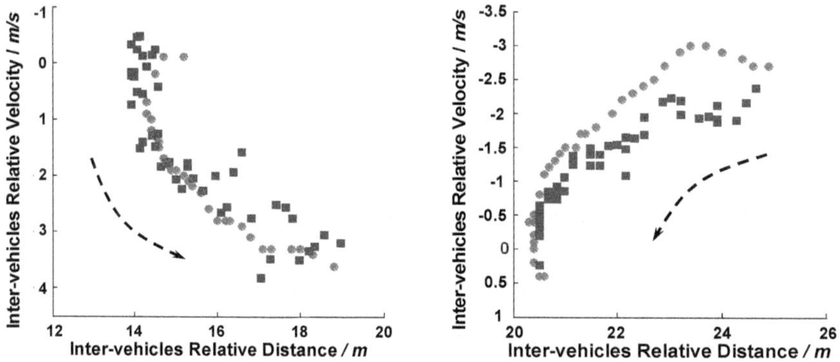

■Operation Policy •Experimental Data

(a) Acceleration tracking condition (b) Deceleration approaching condition

Fig. 7. Comparison results between experimental data and operation policy

By virtue of the operation policy (5), the mathematical model of inter-vehicles longitudinal dynamics is created

$$
\begin{aligned}
\dot{\varepsilon}_d &= \varepsilon_v = a_{df}t_h - \left(v_l - v_{df}\right) \\
\dot{\varepsilon}_v &= \dot{a}_{df}t_h - \left(\dot{v}_l - \dot{v}_{df}\right)
\end{aligned}
\quad . \tag{6}
$$

where $\dot{v}_l$ is a leading vehicle acceleration (m/s[2]), which is generally limited within an extreme acceleration/deceleration condition, i.e., $-2\text{m}/\text{s}^2 \le \dot{v}_l \le 2\text{m}/\text{s}^2$.

Although the inter-vehicles dynamics is considered in Eq. (6), the dynamics of the controlled vehicle that has great impact on the performance of entire system has been ignored instead. Actually, two aforementioned models are interrelated and coupled mutually in the LFS. To overcome the disadvantages of the existing independent modeling method, a more accurate model will be proposed in the following to describe the dynamics of the LFS reasonably. In this model, the longitudinal vehicle dynamics models (3) and (4) with uncertainty and the longitudinal inter-vehicles dynamic model (6) are both taken into account. As a result, a control system can be designed on this platform, and an optimal tracking performance with better robustness can also be achieved.

2.3 LFS dynamics model

Firstly, take the time derivative of the state variable $\dot{\omega}_t$ in Eq. (3), and obtain $\ddot{\omega}_t$. After that, $\dot{\omega}_t, \ddot{\omega}_t$ are substituted into Eq. (6) by virtue of the relationship $a_{df} = \alpha_n \dot{\omega}_t = \frac{2\pi r_t}{60 i_g i_0} \dot{\omega}_t$. Finally, an LFS dynamics model for the driving condition is derived according to Eqs. (3) and (6). It is a combination of the dynamics between the controlled vehicle and the inter-vehicles, as well as the uncertainty from actual driving conditions.

$$\dot{\mathbf{X}} = \left[\mathbf{F}_a(\mathbf{X}) + \Delta\mathbf{F}_a(\mathbf{X})\right] + \left[\mathbf{G}_a(\mathbf{X}) + \Delta\mathbf{G}_a(\mathbf{X})\right]\alpha_{th} + \mathbf{P}_a(\mathbf{X})w$$
$$\Leftrightarrow \begin{cases} \dot{\varepsilon}_d = f_{a1} \\ \dot{\varepsilon}_v = (f_{a2} + \Delta f_{a2}) + (g_{a1} + \Delta g_{a1})\alpha_{th} + p_{a1}\dot{v}_l \\ \dot{\omega}_t = f_{a3} + \Delta f_{a3} \\ \dot{\omega}_{ed} = (f_{a4} + \Delta f_{a4}) + (g_{a2} + \Delta g_{a2})\alpha_{th} \end{cases} \tag{7}$$

where $\mathbf{X} = \begin{bmatrix}\varepsilon_d & \varepsilon_v & \omega_t & \omega_{ed}\end{bmatrix}^T$ is a vector of the state variables, $w = \dot{v}_l$ is a disturbance variable, and α_{th} is a control variable. The definition of each item in Eq. (7) can be referred to Appendix (2).

Similarly, an LFS dynamics model for the braking condition is achieved:

$$\dot{\mathbf{X}} = \left[\mathbf{F}_d(\mathbf{X}) + \Delta\mathbf{F}_d(\mathbf{X})\right] + \left[\mathbf{G}_d(\mathbf{X}) + \Delta\mathbf{G}_d(\mathbf{X})\right]u_b + \mathbf{P}_d(\mathbf{X})w$$
$$\Leftrightarrow \begin{cases} \dot{\varepsilon}_d = f_{d1} \\ \dot{\varepsilon}_v = (f_{d2} + \Delta f_{d2}) + (g_{d1} + \Delta g_{d1})u_b + p_{d1}\dot{v}_l \\ \dot{\omega}_t = f_{d3} + \Delta f_{d3} \\ \dot{\omega}_{ed} = f_{d4} + \Delta f_{d4} \\ \dot{a}_b = (f_{d5} + \Delta f_{d5}) + (g_{d2} + \Delta g_{d2})u_b \end{cases} \tag{8}$$

where $\mathbf{X} = \begin{bmatrix}\varepsilon_d & \varepsilon_v & \omega_t & \omega_{ed} & a_b\end{bmatrix}^T$ is a vector of the state variables, u_b is a control variable. The definition of each item in Eq. (8) can be referred to Appendix (4).

According to the analysis of the extreme driving/braking conditions in 2.1, an approximate ranges of the upper and lower boundaries regarding uncertain items in Eqs. (7) and (8) can be calculated through simulation.

Driving condition:

$$-104 \le \Delta f_{a2} \le 203, -0.031 \le \Delta g_{a1} \le 0.0027$$

Braking condition:

$$-192 \le \Delta f_{d2} \le 174, -0.0153 \le \Delta g_{d1} \le 0.022$$

where an unit of Δf_* is m/s^2, units of $\Delta g_{a1}, \Delta g_{d1}$ are m/(s^2·%) and m/(s^2·V), respectively.
The analysis of the dynamics models (7) and (8) indicates that the LFS is an uncertain affine nonlinear system, in which the strong nonlinearities and the coupling properties caused by the disturbance and the uncertainty are represented. These complex behaviors result in more difficulties while implementing the control of the LFS, since the state variables ε_d, ε_v are influenced significantly by the nonlinearity, uncertainty, as well as the disturbance from the leading vehicle's acceleration/deceleration. However, because the longitudinal dynamics of the controlled vehicle and the inter-vehicles can be described and integrated into a universal frame of the state space equation accurately, this would be helpful for the purpose of achieving a global optimal and a robust control for the LFS.
The LFS AACC system intends to implement the accurate tracking control of the inter-vehicles relative distance/relative velocity under both high-speed and crowded traffic environments. Thus, the system should be provided with strong robustness in view of the complex external disturbance and the internal uncertainty, as well as the capability to eliminate the impact from the system's strong nonlinearity at low-speed. Focusing on the LFS, refs. [22-27] presented an NDD method to eliminate the disturbance effectively, which was, however, limited to some certain affine nonlinear systems. Utilizing the invariance of the sliding mode in VSC, the control algorithm proposed in refs. [28, 29] can implement the completely decoupling of all state variables from the disturbance and the uncertainty. But, it is not a global decoupling algorithm, and should also be submitted to some strict matching conditions. Refs. [30-34] studied the input-output linearization on an uncertain affine nonlinear system, but did not discuss the disturbance decoupling problem. On a nonlinear system with perturbation, ref. [35] gave the necessary and sufficient condition for the completely disturbance decoupling problem, but did not present the design of the feedback controller. To avoid the disadvantages of those control algorithms mentioned above, a DDRC method combining the theory of NDD and VSC is proposed in regard to the complex dynamics of the LFS.

3. DDRC method

The basic theory of DDRC method is inspired by the idea of the step-by-step transformation and design. First, on account of a certain affine nonlinear system with disturbance, the NDD theory based on the differential geometry is used to implement the disturbance decoupling and the input-output linearization. Hence, a linearized subsystem with partial state variables is given, in which the invariance matching conditions of the sliding mode can be discussed easily via VSC theory, and then a VSC controller can be deduced. Finally, two methods will be integrated together such that a completely decoupling of the system from the external disturbance, and a weakened invariance matching condition with a simplified control system structure are obtained.

3.1 NDD theory on certain affine nonlinear system

At first, consider a certain dynamics model of the LFS, where uncertain items of $\Delta F_a(X)$, $\Delta G_a(X)$, $\Delta F_d(X)$ and $\Delta G_d(X)$ are considered as zero. Hence, a certain affine nonlinear system can be simplified as

$$\begin{cases} \dot{\boldsymbol{X}} = \boldsymbol{F}(\boldsymbol{X}) + \boldsymbol{G}(\boldsymbol{X})u + \boldsymbol{P}(\boldsymbol{X})w \\ y = h(\boldsymbol{X}) \end{cases} \tag{9}$$

where $\boldsymbol{X} \in R^n$ and u, w, $y \in R$ are system state variable, control variable, disturbance variable and output variable, respectively, $\boldsymbol{F}$, $\boldsymbol{G}$, $\boldsymbol{P}$, h are differentiable functions of $\boldsymbol{X}$ with corresponding dimensions.

The basic theory of NDD is trying to seek a state feedback, and construct a closed-loop system as follows

$$\begin{cases} \dot{\boldsymbol{X}} = \boldsymbol{F}(\boldsymbol{X}) + \boldsymbol{G}(\boldsymbol{X})\alpha(\boldsymbol{X}) + \boldsymbol{G}(\boldsymbol{X})\beta(\boldsymbol{X})v + \boldsymbol{P}(\boldsymbol{X})w = \tilde{\boldsymbol{F}}(\boldsymbol{X}) + \tilde{\boldsymbol{G}}(\boldsymbol{X})v + \boldsymbol{P}(\boldsymbol{X})w \\ y = h(\boldsymbol{X}) \end{cases} \tag{10}$$

If there is an invariant distribution $\Delta(\boldsymbol{X})$ that exists over $\tilde{\boldsymbol{F}}(\boldsymbol{X}), \tilde{\boldsymbol{G}}(\boldsymbol{X})$, and satisfies

$$span\{\boldsymbol{P}\} \subset \Delta(\boldsymbol{X}) \subset \Omega^{\perp}(\boldsymbol{X}) \tag{11}$$

where

$$\Omega(\boldsymbol{X}) = \begin{bmatrix} dh(\boldsymbol{X}) & dL_{\boldsymbol{F}}h(\boldsymbol{X}) & \cdots & dL_{\boldsymbol{F}}^{r-1}h(\boldsymbol{X}) \end{bmatrix}^T .$$

Then, the output y can be decoupled from the disturbance w, and we have a r-dimension coordinate transformation

$$\boldsymbol{Z} = \boldsymbol{\psi}(\boldsymbol{X}) = [z_1, \cdots, z_r]^T = \left[h(\boldsymbol{X}), \cdots, L_{\boldsymbol{F}}^{r-1}h(\boldsymbol{X})\right]^T \tag{12}$$

as well as an n-r-dimension coordinate transformation

$$\boldsymbol{\mu} = \boldsymbol{\phi}(\boldsymbol{X}) = \left[\mu_1(\boldsymbol{X}), \cdots, \mu_{n-r}(\boldsymbol{X})\right]^T \tag{13}$$

where $\boldsymbol{\mu}$ satisfies

$$d\mu_i(\boldsymbol{X})\boldsymbol{G}(\boldsymbol{X}) = 0, \quad \forall \boldsymbol{X} \in U, \quad i = 1, \cdots, n-r \tag{14}$$

In this way, the original closed-loop system (9) can be modified as a following form over the new coordinate

$$\begin{aligned} \dot{z}_i &= z_{i+1} \qquad 1 \le i \le r-1 \\ \dot{z}_r &= v \end{aligned} \tag{15}$$

$$\dot{\boldsymbol{\mu}} = \boldsymbol{Q}(\boldsymbol{Z}, \boldsymbol{\mu}) + \boldsymbol{K}(\boldsymbol{Z}, \boldsymbol{\mu})w \tag{16}$$

Obviously, Eq. (15) is a linearized decoupling subsystem, while Eq. (16) is a nonlinear internal dynamic subsystem subject to the disturbance. The invariant distribution $\Delta(X)$ is defined as $\left[\tilde{F},\Delta\right](X) \subset \Delta(X)$, L is a Lie derivative, defined as $L_F G = \left(\frac{\partial G}{\partial X}\right) F$, r is a relative degree, defined as $L_G L_F^{r-1} h(X) \neq 0$ [36], $*^{\perp}$ is an orthogonal of" $*$ "[37]. Eq. (10) is a necessary and sufficient condition of the disturbance decoupling problem, which can be expressed in the equivalent form

$$\Omega(X)P(X) = 0 \tag{17}$$

State feedback is

$$u = \alpha(X) + \beta(X)v = \frac{-L_F^r h(X) + v}{L_G L_F^{r-1} h(X)} \tag{18}$$

If the disturbance w is measurable, the following state feedback can be considered

$$u = \alpha(X) + \beta(X)v + \gamma(X)w = \frac{-L_F^r h(X) + v - L_P L_F^{r-1} h(X) w}{L_G L_F^{r-1} h(X)} \tag{19}$$

In this way, a weakened necessary and sufficient condition of the disturbance decoupling problem is achieved as

$$\Omega(X)\left[G(X)\gamma + P(X)\right] = 0 \tag{20}$$

As a result, some existing linear control methods (likes, LQ, pole placement) can be used to implement the pole placement over the linearized decoupling subsystem. In the following, the NDD theory is used to discuss the VSC problem of the affine nonlinear systems under the impact of the uncertainty.

3.2 VSC of uncertain affine nonlinear systems based on NDD

Considering Eqs. (7) and (8) with uncertainty, they can be simplified as a more general forms for the analysis, i.e.,

$$\begin{cases} \dot{X} = \left[F(X) + \Delta F(X)\right] + \left[G(X) + \Delta G(X)\right]u + \left[P(X) + \Delta P(X)\right]w \\ y = h(X) \end{cases} \tag{21}$$

where F, G, P, h indicate the certain part of the system, and they are defined as Eq. (8), ΔF, ΔG, ΔP indicate the uncertain part correspondingly.
At first, take first derivative of the output variable $y=h(X)$:

$$\begin{aligned} \dot{z}_1 &= \frac{dy}{dt} \\ &= \frac{\partial h(X)}{\partial X}\left[F(X) + G(X)u + P(X)w\right] + \frac{\partial h(X)}{\partial X}\left[\Delta F(X) + \Delta G(X)u + \Delta P(X)w\right] \\ &= \left[L_F h(X) + L_G h(X)u + L_P h(X)w\right] + \left[L_{\Delta F} h(X) + L_{\Delta G} h(X)u + L_{\Delta P} h(X)w\right] \end{aligned} \tag{22}$$

Obviously, if

$$L_{\Delta F}h(X) = L_{\Delta G}h(X) = L_{\Delta P}h(X) = 0 \tag{23}$$

then according to the definition of the relative degree and Eq. (17), Eq. (22) becomes

$$\dot{z}_1 = L_F h(X) = z_2 \tag{24}$$

Differentiate Eq. (24) again yields

$$\begin{aligned}\dot{z}_2 &= \frac{dL_F h(X)}{dt}\\ &= \frac{\partial L_F h(X)}{\partial X}\left[F(X) + G(X)u + P(X)w\right] + \frac{\partial L_F h(X)}{\partial X}\left[\Delta F(X) + \Delta G(X)u + \Delta P(X)w\right]\\ &= \left[L_F^2 h(X) + L_G L_F h(X)u + L_P L_F h(X)w\right] + \left[L_{\Delta F} L_F h(X) + L_{\Delta G} L_F h(X)u + L_{\Delta P} L_F h(X)w\right]\end{aligned} \tag{25}$$

which in turn deduces

$$L_{\Delta F}L_F h(X) = L_{\Delta G}L_F h(X) = L_{\Delta P}L_F h(X) = 0 \tag{26}$$

By the definition of relative degree and Eq. (17), Eq. (25) becomes

$$\dot{z}_2 = L_F^2 h(X) = z_3 \tag{27}$$

After differentiating r times, we find that

$$\begin{aligned}\dot{z}_r &= L_G L_F^{r-1}h(X)u + L_F^r h(X) + L_{\Delta F}L_F^{r-1}h(X) + L_{\Delta G}L_F^{r-1}h(X)u + L_{\Delta P}L_F^{r-1}h(X)w\\ &= \left[L_{\Delta F}L_F^{r-1}h(X) + \alpha(X)L_{\Delta G}L_F^{r-1}h(X)\right] + \left[1 + \beta(X)L_{\Delta G}L_F^{r-1}h(X)\right]v + L_{\Delta P}L_F^{r-1}h(X)w\end{aligned} \tag{28}$$

Based on the above proof, the disturbance decoupling problem of uncertain affine nonlinear systems can be solved, if there exist VSC matching conditions such that

$$\text{(c1)}\ L_{\Delta F}L_F^i h(X) = 0, L_{\Delta G}L_F^i h(X) = 0, L_{\Delta P}L_F^i h(X) = 0,\ L_{\Delta P}L_F^i h(X) = 0, (0 \le i \le r-2)$$

$$\text{(c2)}\ \left\|\Delta F(X)\right\| \le f_m, \left\|\Delta G(X)\right\| \le g_m, \left\|\Delta P(X)\right\| \le p_m,\ \left\|w\right\| \le w_m$$

where $\|\bullet\|$ is a norm of the vector or matrix of "•", that is $\left\|\left(a_{ij}\right)_{n\times n}\right\| = \max_{1\le i\le n}\sum_{j=1}^{n}\left|a_{ij}\right|$; f_m, g_m, p_m, w_m are perturbation boundaries of the corresponding given matrixes.

Summing up the definition of the relative degree, matching conditions (c1) and the coordinate transformation **Z**=ψ(**X**), we obtain a closed-loop system over the new coordinate by substituting the state feedback (18) or (19) into Eq. (21), which has the form

$$\begin{aligned}\dot{z}_i &= z_{i+1}, \qquad 1 \le i \le r-1,\\ \dot{z}_r &= \left[L_{\Delta F}L_F^{r-1}h(X) + \alpha(X)L_{\Delta G}L_F^{r-1}h(X)\right] + \left[1 + \beta(X)L_{\Delta G}L_F^{r-1}h(X)\right]v + L_{\Delta P}L_F^{r-1}h(X)w\end{aligned} \tag{29}$$

$$\dot{\mu} = Q(Z,\mu) + \Delta Q(Z,\mu) + \Delta R(Z,\mu)v + \left[K(Z,\mu) + \Delta K(Z,\mu)\right]w \tag{30}$$

It can be noticed from Eq. (29) that for the state variables z_i of the first r-1 dimensions, the linearization and the disturbance decoupling have been achieved, except for the remaining z_r (Eq. (30)). By virtue of the invariance of the sliding mode in VSC [28], it will be used in consequence to eliminate the disturbance and the uncertainty on z_r.
Based on the VSC theory [28], a switching function is designed easily by taking advantage of the linearized decoupling subsystem (29) over the new coordination

$$S_Z = S(\boldsymbol{Z}) = \boldsymbol{C}[z_1 \cdots z_r]^T \tag{31}$$

where $\boldsymbol{C}=[c_1,\ldots,c_{r-1},1]$ is a normal constant coefficient matrix to be determined. Once the system is controlled towards the sliding mode, it satisfies

$$S_Z = \boldsymbol{C}[z_1 \cdots z_r]^T = 0 \tag{32}$$

yielding the following reduced-order equation

$$\dot{z}_i = z_{i+1}, \qquad 1 \le i \le r-1 \tag{33}$$

Clearly, a desired dynamic performance of each state variable in Eq. (33) can be achieved by configuring the coefficient $\boldsymbol{C}$.
As the desired dynamic performance of the sliding mode has already been achieved, an appropriate VSC law is to be defined so as to ensure the desired sliding mode occurring within a finite time. It is convenient to differentiate the switching function (31), and derive the following equation in terms of Eq. (29)：

$$\dot{S}_Z = \boldsymbol{A}_{S_Z} + \Delta\boldsymbol{A}_{S_Z} + \left(\boldsymbol{B}_{S_Z} + \Delta\boldsymbol{B}_{S_Z}\right)v + \Delta\boldsymbol{C}_{S_Z} w \tag{34}$$

where

$$\boldsymbol{A}_{S_Z} = \sum_{i=1}^{r-1} c_i \dot{z}_i, \Delta\boldsymbol{A}_{S_Z} = \boldsymbol{\varphi}\cdot\Delta\boldsymbol{F} + \alpha\boldsymbol{\varphi}\cdot\Delta\boldsymbol{G},\ \boldsymbol{B}_{S_Z} = 1, \Delta\boldsymbol{B}_{S_Z} = \beta\boldsymbol{\varphi}\cdot\Delta\boldsymbol{G},$$

$$\Delta\boldsymbol{C}_{S_Z} = \boldsymbol{\varphi}\cdot\Delta\boldsymbol{P},\ \boldsymbol{\varphi} = \frac{\partial L_F^{r-1}h(\boldsymbol{X})}{\partial \boldsymbol{X}}.$$

Considering an VSC law below

$$v = -\boldsymbol{B}_{S_Z}^{-1}\left[\boldsymbol{A}_{S_Z} + a_s S_Z + b_s \operatorname{sgn}(S_Z)\right] \qquad (a_s \ge 0, b_s > 0) \tag{35}$$

an inequality below can be derived from the matching condition (c2), Eqs. (31) and (34).

$$\begin{aligned}
S_Z\dot{S}_Z &= S_Z\left\{\Delta\boldsymbol{A}_{S_Z} + \Delta\boldsymbol{C}_{S_Z} w - a_s S_Z - b_s \operatorname{sgn}(S_Z) - \Delta\boldsymbol{B}_{S_Z}\boldsymbol{B}_{S_Z}^{-1}\left[\boldsymbol{A}_{S_Z} + a_s S_Z + b_s \operatorname{sgn}(S_Z)\right]\right\} \\
&\le \|S_Z\|\|\Delta\boldsymbol{A}_{S_Z}\| + \|S_Z\|\|\Delta\boldsymbol{C}_{S_Z} w\| - a_s\|S_Z\|^2 - b_s\|S_Z\| + \|\Delta\boldsymbol{B}_{S_Z}\|\left(\|\boldsymbol{B}_{S_Z}^{-1}\boldsymbol{A}_{S_Z}\|\|S_Z\| + a_s\|S_Z\|^2 + b_s\|S_Z\|\right) \\
&\le \|S_Z\|\|\boldsymbol{\varphi}\|(f_m - \|\alpha\|g_m) + \|S_Z\|\|\boldsymbol{\varphi}\| p_m w_m - a_s\|S_Z\|^2 \\
&\quad - b_s\|S_Z\| + \|\beta\boldsymbol{\varphi}\| g_m\left(\|\boldsymbol{B}_{S_Z}^{-1}\boldsymbol{A}_{S_Z}\|\|S_Z\| + a_s\|S_Z\|^2 + b_s\|S_Z\|\right) \\
&= -\|S_Z\|^2 a_s\left(1 - \|\beta\boldsymbol{\varphi}\|g_m\right) - \|S_Z\|\left\{b_s\left(1 - \|\beta\boldsymbol{\varphi}\|g_m\right)\right. \\
&\quad \left. -\left[\|\varphi\|(f_m - \|\alpha\|g_m + p_m w_m) + \|\beta\boldsymbol{\varphi}\|\|\boldsymbol{B}_{S_Z}^{-1}\boldsymbol{A}_{S_Z}\|g_m\right]\right\}
\end{aligned} \tag{36}$$

It is noticed from Eq. (36) that if the perturbation boundary g_m of uncertain part $\Delta\boldsymbol{G}$ satisfies

$$g_m < \left\|\beta\boldsymbol{\varphi}\right\|^{-1} \tag{37}$$

then defining

$$b_s > \frac{\left\|\boldsymbol{\varphi}\right\|\left(f_m - \left\|\alpha\right\| g_m + p_m w_m\right) + \left\|\beta\boldsymbol{\varphi}\right\| \left\|\boldsymbol{B}_{S_Z}^{-1}\boldsymbol{A}_{S_Z}\right\| g_m}{1 - \left\|\beta\boldsymbol{\varphi}\right\| g_m} \tag{38}$$

may lead to the following inequality:

$$S_Z \dot{S}_Z < 0 \tag{39}$$

Namely, the convergence condition of the sliding mode is achieved.

From the above verification, the desired sliding mode is achievable under the VSC law (35), as long as the matching condition (c2) and the constraints (38) are satisfied. Since Eqs. (31) and (35) are the switching function and the control law over the new coordinate **X**, they should be transferred back to the original coordinate **Z** by adopting the inverse transformation **Z**=ψ(**X**). Finally, the DDRC law can be achieved by substituting the VSC law over the original coordinate into the disturbance decoupling state feedback control law (Eq. (18) or Eq. (19)).

To summarize, for an uncertain affine nonlinear system, if the disturbance decoupling condition (17) or (20) and the matching conditions of (c1) and (c2) hold respectively for the certain part and the uncertain part, the DDRC method with the combination of NDD and VSC theories can be figured out as the following design procedure:

Step 1. According to the NDD theory of affine nonlinear systems, the feedback control law (Eq. (18) or (19)) and the coordinate transformation (Eqs. (12) and (13)) are derived to transfer the original system into the linearized decoupling normal form (Eq. (15)) over the new coordinate.

Step 2. Give the VSC matching conditions (c1) and (c2) for the uncertain part of the affine nonlinear systems.

Step 3. Utilize the linearized decoupling normal form (Eq. (15)) over the new coordinate to design the switching function (Eq. (31)), and determine its coefficients accordingly.

Step 4. Design the VSC law (Eq. (35)) based on the perturbation boundary (37) of the uncertainty part, and the convergence condition of the sliding mode (39).

Step 5. Define the coordinate transformation (12) to transfer the switching function (Eq. (31)) and the VSC law (Eq. (35)) from the new coordinate **Z** back to the original coordinate **X**.

Step 6. Substitute the VSC law (Eq. (18) or (19)) over the original coordinate into the feedback control law, and yield the DDRC method.

A block diagram of the closed-loop system for the aforementioned DDRC method is shown in Figure 8, which includes two feedback loops. The nonlinear loop (i.e., the NDD loop) is used to achieve the disturbance decoupling and the partial linearization, regarding the system output y from the disturbance w. On the other hand, the linear loop (i.e., the VSC loop) is used to restrain the system's uncertainty and regulate the closed-loop dynamic performance.

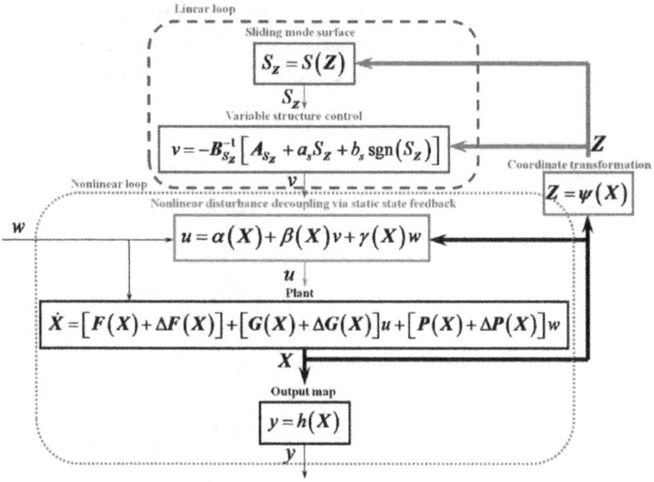

Fig. 8. Block diagram of closed-loop system for DDRC method

4. LFS AACC system

In this section, the proposed DDRC method will be used to design the LFS AACC system with respect to the driving and the braking conditions.

4.1 LFS AACC system for driving condition

Recall the procedure in 2.2, the disturbance decoupling problem on the LFS dynamics model without the impact of the uncertainty is considered (i.e., for the uncertain items of Eq. (7) let $\Delta F_a(X)=0$, $\Delta G_a(X)=0$). On the purpose of LFS AACC system, the following affine nonlinear system with the output variable is defined:

$$\begin{cases} \dot{X} = F_a(X) + G_a(X)\alpha_{th} + P_a(X)w \\ y = h(X) = \varepsilon_d \end{cases} \tag{40}$$

By adopting the NDD theory of certain affine nonlinear system, the relative degree of system (40) is calculated as

$$L_{F_a}h(X) = \varepsilon_v, L_{G_a}h(X) = [1 \quad 0 \quad 0 \quad 0]G_a = 0, L_{G_a}L_{F_a}h(X) = [0 \quad 1 \quad 0 \quad 0]G_a \neq 0.$$

Obviously, the relative degree is $r = 2$, which results in the following matrix

$$\Omega_a(X) = \begin{bmatrix} dh(X) \\ dL_{F_a}h(X) \end{bmatrix} = \begin{bmatrix} 1 & 0 & 0 & 0 \\ 0 & 1 & 0 & 0 \end{bmatrix} \tag{41}$$

Then, it is easy to verify that

$$\Omega_a(X)P_a = \begin{bmatrix} 1 & 0 & 0 & 0 \\ 0 & 1 & 0 & 0 \end{bmatrix} P_a = \begin{bmatrix} 0 \\ p_{a1} \end{bmatrix} \neq \mathbf{0} \tag{42}$$

That is to say, the disturbance decoupling from system (40) can not be achieved by the state feedback (18), because the necessary and sufficient condition (17) is not satisfied. Thus, one can turn to the state feedback (19) with measurable disturbance. Note that if

$$\gamma_a = -\left(\frac{p_{a1}}{g_{a1}}\right) \tag{43}$$

then the necessary and sufficient condition (20) is satisfied, i.e.,

$$\Omega_a(\mathbf{X})\left[\mathbf{G}_a\gamma_a + \mathbf{P}_a\right] = \begin{bmatrix} 1 & 0 & 0 & 0 \\ 0 & 1 & 0 & 0 \end{bmatrix}\left[\mathbf{G}_a\gamma_a + \mathbf{P}_a\right] = \mathbf{0} \tag{44}$$

By Eq. (19), the decoupling state feedback is obtained as

$$\alpha_{th} = \alpha_a(\mathbf{X}) + \beta_a(\mathbf{X})v_{ua} + \gamma_a(\mathbf{X})w = \frac{-f_{a2}(\omega_t,\omega_{ed}) + v_{ua} - p_{a1}w}{g_{a1}(\omega_t,\omega_{ed})} \tag{45}$$

and the corresponding coordinate transformation with r=2 dimensions is

$$\mathbf{Z}_a = \boldsymbol{\psi}_a(\mathbf{X}) = \begin{bmatrix} z_{a1} \\ z_{a2} \end{bmatrix} = \begin{bmatrix} h(\mathbf{X}) \\ L_{\mathbf{F}_a}h(\mathbf{X}) \end{bmatrix} = \begin{bmatrix} \varepsilon_d \\ \varepsilon_v \end{bmatrix} \tag{46}$$

where

$$L_{\mathbf{F}_a}^2 h(\mathbf{X}) = f_{a2}, L_{\mathbf{P}_a}L_{\mathbf{F}_a}h(\mathbf{X}) = p_{a1}, L_{\mathbf{G}_a}L_{\mathbf{F}_a}h(\mathbf{X}) = g_{a1}.$$

Additionally, in order to complete the coordinate transformation, the remaining n-r=2 dimensional coordinates μ_{a1}, μ_{a2} should satisfy the following condition:

$$\frac{\partial \mu_{ai}}{\partial \mathbf{X}}\mathbf{G}_a = \begin{bmatrix} \frac{\partial \mu_{ai}}{\partial \varepsilon_d} & \frac{\partial \mu_{ai}}{\partial \varepsilon_v} & \frac{\partial \mu_{ai}}{\partial \omega_t} & \frac{\partial \mu_{ai}}{\partial \omega_{ed}} \end{bmatrix}\begin{bmatrix} 0 \\ g_{a1} \\ 0 \\ g_{a2} \end{bmatrix} = 0 \qquad (i = 1,2) \tag{47}$$

The purpose is to ensure the diffeomorphism relationship of the coordinate transformation between the original and the new one (in other words, it is a one-to-one continuous coordinate transformation between the original and the new one, the same is for the inverse transformation). Obviously, one solution of the partial differential Eq. (47) is

$$\begin{aligned} \mu_{a1} &= \omega_t \\ \mu_{a2} &= -\varepsilon_v + \alpha_n t_h\left(b\omega_t\omega_{ed} + c\omega_{ed}^2 + d\frac{\omega_t^3}{\omega_{ed}}\right) \end{aligned} \tag{48}$$

Hence, the transformation of the remaining 2 dimensional coordinates is

$$\boldsymbol{\mu}_a = \boldsymbol{\phi}_a(\mathbf{X}) = \begin{bmatrix} \mu_{a1}(\mathbf{X}) \\ \mu_{a2}(\mathbf{X}) \end{bmatrix} \tag{49}$$

Up to now, the decoupling state feedback (Eq. (45)) and the coordinate transformation (Eqs. (46) and (49)) have been obtained for the certain part of the LFS dynamics model under the driving condition.
Further consideration on the uncertain part of model (7) will be continued. On the basis of the design procedure (Step2) in 3.2, the matching conditions (c1) and (c2) have to be verified at first, and

$$\begin{aligned} L_{\Delta F_a} h(\mathbf{X}) &= [1 \quad 0 \quad 0 \quad 0] \Delta \mathbf{F}_a = 0 \\ L_{\Delta G_a} h(\mathbf{X}) &= [1 \quad 0 \quad 0 \quad 0 \quad 0] \Delta \mathbf{G}_a = 0 \end{aligned} \tag{50}$$

It should be noticed from 1.2 and 1.3 that the uncertain items $\Delta \mathbf{F}_a(\mathbf{X})$, $\Delta \mathbf{G}_a(\mathbf{X})$ and the disturbance w are subject to the following limited upper boundaries:

$$\begin{aligned} \|\Delta \mathbf{F}_a(\mathbf{X})\| &\le f_{am} = 203 \\ \|\Delta \mathbf{G}_a(\mathbf{X})\| &\le g_{am} = 0.031 \\ \|w\| &\le w_{am} = 2 \end{aligned} \tag{51}$$

By substituting the decoupling state feedback $u=a_{th}$ (Eq. (45)) into model (7), and making use of the coordinate transformations (46) and (49), a linearized subsystem below can be achieved, in which the certain part is completely decoupled from the disturbance.

$$\begin{cases} \begin{bmatrix} \dot{z}_{a1} \\ \dot{z}_{a2} \end{bmatrix} = \overbrace{\begin{bmatrix} 0 & 1 \\ 0 & 0 \end{bmatrix} \begin{bmatrix} z_{a1} \\ z_{a2} \end{bmatrix} + \begin{bmatrix} 0 \\ 1 \end{bmatrix} v_{ua}}^{\text{Certain part}} + \overbrace{\begin{bmatrix} 0 \\ \Delta f_{a2} - \dfrac{f_{a2}}{g_{a1}} \Delta g_{a1} \end{bmatrix} + \begin{bmatrix} 0 \\ \dfrac{\Delta g_{a1}}{g_{a1}} \end{bmatrix} v_{ua} + \begin{bmatrix} 0 \\ -\dfrac{p_{a1}}{g_{a1}} \Delta g_{a1} \end{bmatrix} w}^{\text{Part of uncertain and disturbance}} \\ y = \varepsilon_d \end{cases} \tag{52}$$

Besides, a nonlinear dynamic internal subsystem without separating from the disturbance and the uncertainty is yielded

$$\dot{\boldsymbol{\mu}}_a = \mathbf{Q}_a(\mathbf{Z}_a, \boldsymbol{\mu}_a) + \Delta \mathbf{Q}_a(\mathbf{Z}_a, \boldsymbol{\mu}_a) + [\mathbf{K}_a(\mathbf{Z}_a, \boldsymbol{\mu}_a) + \Delta \mathbf{K}_a(\mathbf{Z}_a, \boldsymbol{\mu}_a)] w \tag{53}$$

where

$$\mathbf{Q}_a(\mathbf{Z}_a, \boldsymbol{\mu}_a) = \begin{bmatrix} a\mu_{a1}^2 + \dfrac{\mu_{a2} + z_{a2}}{\alpha_n t_h} + l \\ -\left(2a\mu_{a1} + \dfrac{1}{t_h}\right)\left(\alpha_n t_h a \mu_{a1}^2 + \mu_{a2} + z_{a2} + \alpha_n t_h l\right) \end{bmatrix}, \quad \mathbf{K}_a(\mathbf{Z}_a, \boldsymbol{\mu}_a) = \begin{bmatrix} 0 \\ -p_{a1} \end{bmatrix}.$$

Based on the analysis of the extreme operating conditions in 2.1, it can be noticed that the items $\Delta\mathbf{Q}_a$, $\Delta\mathbf{K}_a$ are constants with limited upper boundaries.
For the certain part of Eq. (52), it is clear that the state variables z_{a1}, z_{a2} have been completely decoupled from the disturbance w. In order to enhance the system's robustness from the remaining uncertain part and the disturbance within the linearized decoupling subsystem (52), we may design the following switching function over the new coordinate by making use of Eq. (52).

$$S_{aZ} = \boldsymbol{C}_a \begin{bmatrix} z_{a1} \\ z_{a2} \end{bmatrix} \tag{54}$$

where $\boldsymbol{C}_a$=[c_{a1} 1] is a coefficient matrix to be determined. Once the system is controlled towards the sliding mode, it obeys

$$S_{aZ} = c_{a1} z_{a1} + z_{a2} = 0 \Rightarrow z_{a2} = -c_{a1} z_{a1} \tag{55}$$

and the order of Eq. (52) can be reduced to

$$\dot{z}_{a1} = z_{a2} \tag{56}$$

Clearly, the disturbance and the uncertainty have been separated from Eq. (56). In this way, substituting Eq. (56) into Eq. (55) yields

$$\dot{z}_{a1} + c_{a1} z_{a1} = 0 \tag{57}$$

By the Laplace transform, an eigenvalue equation of Eq. (57) is obtained as

$$s + c_{a1} = 0 \tag{58}$$

To achieve a desired dynamic performance and a stable convergence of the sliding mode, the coefficient c_{a1} can be determined by employing the pole assignment method. That is, the eigenvalue of Eq. (58) should be assigned strictly in the negative half plane. Without loss of generality, it can be chosen herein as c_{a1}=1.
The VSC law is designed below by the procedure (Step4) of 3.2, in order to guarantee that the desired sliding mode occurs within a finite time. First, a VSC law is obtained on the basis of Eq. (35):

$$v_{ua} = -\boldsymbol{B}_{S_{aZ}}^{-1} \left[\boldsymbol{A}_{S_{aZ}} + a_{as} S_{aZ} + b_{as} \operatorname{sgn}(S_{aZ}) \right] \tag{59}$$

where $\boldsymbol{A}_{S_{aZ}} = c_{a1}\dot{z}_{a1}, \boldsymbol{B}_{S_{aZ}} = 1$. For determining the coefficients a_{as}, b_{as}, the perturbation boundary of g_{am} should be verified such that

$$g_{am} < \left\| \beta_a \boldsymbol{\varphi}_a \right\|^{-1} \tag{60}$$

where $\boldsymbol{\varphi}_a$=[0 1 0 0]. According to Eq. (45) and the analysis of 3.2, it is easy to obtain

$$\left\| \beta_a \boldsymbol{\varphi}_a \right\|^{-1} = \left(\max \left| \frac{1}{g_{a1}(\omega_t, \omega_{ed})} \right| \right)^{-1} = 0.98 \tag{61}$$

Clearly, the condition of Eq. (60) is satisfied. Then, the parameter b_{as} will be determined by the inequality (38). Recalling the analysis results of 3.1, $\left\| \alpha_a \right\| = \max \left| -\frac{f_{a2}(\omega_t, \omega_{ed})}{g_{a1}(\omega_t, \omega_{ed})} \right| = 16.33$ is given. On this basis, it is reasonable to suppose that the absolute value of the extreme relative velocity tracking error is max$|\varepsilon_v|$=35m/s. It can be presented as a scenario that the leading vehicle moves forward with a maximum velocity 35m/s relative to the statical controlled vehicle (assuming this given value is an actual maximum velocity). The values above will be substituted into the right hand side of the inequality (38), and we have

$$\frac{\|\boldsymbol{\varphi}_a\|(f_{am}-\|\alpha_a\|g_{am})+\|\beta_a\boldsymbol{\varphi}_a\|\|\boldsymbol{B}_{S_{aZ}}^{-1}\boldsymbol{A}_{S_{aZ}}\|g_{am}}{1-\|\beta_a\boldsymbol{\varphi}_a\|g_{am}}=210.25 \tag{62}$$

Then, the parameter b_{as}=250 can be determined, and a_{as}=10 is achieved separately by the condition of a_{as}>0.

By the procedure (Step5) in 3.2, the coordinate transformations $\boldsymbol{Z}_a=\psi_a(\boldsymbol{X})$ and $\boldsymbol{\mu}_a=\phi_a(\boldsymbol{X})$ will be used to transfer the new coordinates ($\boldsymbol{Z}_a$, $\boldsymbol{\mu}_a$) back to the original coordinate $\boldsymbol{X}$. In this way, the switching function over the original coordinate becomes

$$S_{aZ}=c_{a1}z_{a1}+z_{a2}\ \overset{\boldsymbol{Z}_a=\boldsymbol{\psi}_a(\mathrm{X})}{\Rightarrow}\ S_{aX}=c_{a1}\varepsilon_d+\varepsilon_v \tag{63}$$

the VSC law (57) over the original coordinate has the form

$$v_{ua}=-\left[c_{a1}\varepsilon_v+a_{as}S_{aX}+b_{as}\,\mathrm{sgn}(S_{aX})\right] \tag{64}$$

With substitutions of S_{aX} and v_{ua} into Eq. (45), a AACC system based on the DDRC method is finally obtained as

$$\alpha_{th}=\frac{-f_{a2}(\omega_t,\omega_{ed})}{g_{a1}(\omega_t,\omega_{ed})}-\frac{\left[c_{a1}\varepsilon_v+a_{as}(c_{a1}\varepsilon_d+\varepsilon_v)+b_{as}\,\mathrm{sgn}(S_{aX})\right]+p_{a1}w}{g_{a1}(\omega_t,\omega_{ed})} \tag{65}$$

The control laws designed above only satisfy the convergence stability and the robustness of the linearized decoupling subsystem. In order to ensure the stability of the total system, the stability of the remaining nonlinear internal dynamic subsystem has to be verified, so that the problem of tracking control can be solved completely. Based on ref. [38], the study on the stability of nonlinear internal dynamic subsystem can be turned into the study on its zero dynamics correspondingly. Therefore, let $\Delta\boldsymbol{Q}_a=\Delta\boldsymbol{K}_a=0$, i.e., ignore the tiny impact of the uncertain part. Then the zero dynamics of the nonlinear internal dynamic subsystem (53) owing to z_{a1}, z_{a2}, w=0 is obtained as follows

$$\begin{cases}\dot{\mu}_{a1}=a\mu_{a1}^2+\dfrac{\mu_{a2}}{\alpha_n t_h}+l\\[2ex] \dot{\mu}_{a2}=-\left(2a\mu_{a1}+\dfrac{1}{t_h}\right)\left(\alpha_n t_h a\mu_{a1}^2+\mu_{a2}+\alpha_n t_h l\right)\end{cases} \tag{66}$$

To verify the asymptotic stability of Eq. (66) at the equilibrium point (z_{a1}, z_{a2}, μ_{a1}, μ_{a2})=0, a candidate Lyapunov function is chosen:

$$V_a(\mu_{a1},\mu_{a2})=-(\alpha_n\mu_{a1}+\mu_{a2})^2 \tag{67}$$

The time derivative with respect to the Lyapunov function Eq. (67) is

$$\begin{aligned}\frac{dV_a}{dt} &= -2(\alpha_n \mu_{a1} + \mu_{a2})(\alpha_n \dot{\mu}_{a1} + \dot{\mu}_{a2}) \\ &= 2a\mu_{a1}\left(\alpha_n t_h a \mu_{a1}^2 + \mu_{a2} + \alpha_n t_h l\right) \times \left[\alpha_n \omega_t + \alpha_n t_h \left(b\omega_t \omega_{ed} + c\omega_{ed}^2 + d\frac{\omega_t^3}{\omega_{ed}}\right)\right]\end{aligned} \tag{68}$$

Because $a, b, c, d, \alpha_n, t_h, l, \omega_t, \omega_{ed} > 0$ and $\dot{\omega}_t > 0$ under the driving condition of the vehicle acceleration, we have

$$\alpha_n t_h a \mu_{a1}^2 + \mu_{a2} + \alpha_n t_h l = \alpha_n t_h \dot{\mu}_{a1} = \alpha_n t_h \dot{\omega}_t > 0, \text{ (if } \dot{\omega}_t \neq 0\text{)} \tag{69}$$

In addition, it is easy to verify

$$\alpha_n \omega_t + \alpha_n t_h \left(b\omega_t \omega_{ed} + c\omega_{ed}^2 + d\frac{\omega_t^3}{\omega_{ed}}\right) > 0 \quad \text{(if } \omega_t \neq \omega_{ed} \neq 0\text{)} \tag{70}$$

Therefore, $\frac{dV_a}{dt} > 0$. The following inequality is satisfied:

$$V_a \frac{dV_a}{dt} < 0 \qquad \text{(is } \omega_t \neq \omega_{ed} \neq 0 \text{ and } \dot{\omega}_t \neq 0\text{)} \tag{71}$$

The zero dynamics is asymptotically stable.

4.2 LFS AACC system for braking condition

The design of LFS AACC system under the braking condition is similar to under the driving condition. Regarding the purpose of the LFS AACC system (8), the output can be defined as $y=h(\mathbf{X})=\varepsilon_d$. Then, the relative degree is obtained as $r=2$, and the decoupling state feedback is achieved according to Eq. (19) as

$$u_b = \alpha_d(\mathbf{X}) + \beta_d(\mathbf{X})v_{ud} + \gamma_d(\mathbf{X})w = \frac{-f_{d2}(\omega_t, \omega_{ed}, a_b) + v_{ud} - p_{d1}w}{g_{d1}(\omega_t, a_b)} \tag{72}$$

The corresponding coordinate transformation is given as

$$\mathbf{Z}_d = \boldsymbol{\psi}_d(\mathbf{X}) = \begin{bmatrix} z_{d1} \\ z_{d2} \end{bmatrix} = \begin{bmatrix} h(\mathbf{X}) \\ L_{\mathbf{F}_d} h(\mathbf{X}) \end{bmatrix} = \begin{bmatrix} \varepsilon_d \\ \varepsilon_v \end{bmatrix} \tag{73}$$

$$\boldsymbol{\mu}_d = \boldsymbol{\phi}_d(\mathbf{X}) = \begin{bmatrix} \mu_{d1}(\mathbf{X}) \\ \mu_{d2}(\mathbf{X}) \\ \mu_{d3}(\mathbf{X}) \end{bmatrix} = \begin{bmatrix} \omega_t \\ \omega_{ed} \\ \varepsilon_v - \alpha_n t_h d_d a_b \end{bmatrix} \tag{74}$$

Taking further account of the influence from system's uncertainty, we have

$$\begin{aligned} L_{\Delta\mathbf{F}_d} h(\mathbf{X}) &= [1 \quad 0 \quad 0 \quad 0]\Delta\boldsymbol{F}_d = 0 \\ L_{\Delta\mathbf{G}_d} h(\mathbf{X}) &= [1 \quad 0 \quad 0 \quad 0 \quad 0]\Delta\boldsymbol{G}_d = 0 \end{aligned} \tag{75}$$

That is to say, the matching condition (c1) is satisfied with respect of uncertain items $\Delta F_d(X)$, $\Delta G_d(X)$. Besides, on the analyses of 2.2 and 2.3, the uncertain items $\Delta F_d(X)$, $\Delta G_d(X)$ and the disturbance w are subject to the following limited upper boundaries:

$$\begin{aligned} \|\Delta \boldsymbol{F}_d(\boldsymbol{X})\| &\le f_{dm} = 192 \\ \|\Delta \boldsymbol{G}_d(\boldsymbol{X})\| &\le g_{dm} = 0.029 \end{aligned} \tag{76}$$

By substituting the decoupling state feedback (72) into model (8), and making use of the coordinate transformations (73) and (74), a linearized subsystem (77) can be achieved, in which the certain part is completely decoupled from the disturbance.

$$\begin{cases} \begin{bmatrix} \dot z_{d1} \\ \dot z_{d2} \end{bmatrix} = \overbrace{\begin{bmatrix} 0 & 1 \\ 0 & 0 \end{bmatrix}\begin{bmatrix} z_{d1} \\ z_{d2} \end{bmatrix} + \begin{bmatrix} 0 \\ 1 \end{bmatrix} v_{ud}}^{\text{Certain part}} + \overbrace{\begin{bmatrix} 0 \\ \Delta f_{d2} - \frac{f_{d2}}{g_{d1}}\Delta g_{d1} \end{bmatrix} + \begin{bmatrix} 0 \\ \frac{\Delta g_{d1}}{g_{d1}} \end{bmatrix} v_{ud} + \begin{bmatrix} 0 \\ -\frac{p_{d1}}{g_{d1}}\Delta g_{d1} \end{bmatrix} w}^{\text{Part of uncertain and disturbance}} \\ y = \varepsilon_d \end{cases} \tag{77}$$

Additionally, a nonlinear internal dynamic subsystem with the influence of the disturbance and uncertainty is presented

$$\dot{\boldsymbol{\mu}}_d = \boldsymbol{Q}_d(\boldsymbol{Z}_d, \boldsymbol{\mu}_d) + \Delta \boldsymbol{Q}_d(\boldsymbol{Z}_d, \boldsymbol{\mu}_d) + \left[\boldsymbol{K}_d(\boldsymbol{Z}_d, \boldsymbol{\mu}_d) + \Delta \boldsymbol{K}_d(\boldsymbol{Z}_d, \boldsymbol{\mu}_d)\right] w \tag{78}$$

where

$$\boldsymbol{Q}_d(\boldsymbol{Z}_d, \boldsymbol{\mu}_d) = \begin{bmatrix} a_d\mu_{d1}^2 + b_d\mu_{d1}\mu_{d2} + c_d\mu_{d2}^2 + \dfrac{-\mu_{d3} + z_{d2}}{\alpha_n t_h} - \vartheta_d \\ e_d\mu_{d1}^2 + f_d\mu_{d1}\mu_{d2} + g_d\mu_{d2}^2 + h_d\mu_{d2} + i_d \\ -\left(2\dfrac{a_d}{d_d}\mu_{d1} + \dfrac{b_d}{d_d}\mu_{d2} + \dfrac{1}{t_h d_d}\right) \times \left(a_d\mu_{d1}^2 + b_d\mu_{d1}\mu_{d2} + c_d\mu_{d2}^2 + \dfrac{-\mu_{d3} + z_{d2}}{\alpha_n t_h} - \vartheta_d\right) \\ -\left(\dfrac{b_d}{d_d}\mu_{d1} + 2\dfrac{c_d}{d_d}\mu_{d2}\right) \times \left(e_d\mu_{d1}^2 + f_d\mu_{d1}\mu_{d2} + g_d\mu_{d2}^2 + h_d\mu_{d2} + i_d\right) \end{bmatrix}$$

$$\boldsymbol{K}_d(\boldsymbol{Z}_d, \boldsymbol{\mu}_d) = \begin{bmatrix} 0 \\ 0 \\ -p_{d1} \end{bmatrix}.$$

According to the analysis of 2.1, items ΔQ_d, ΔK_d are the constants with limited upper boundaries.

Similarly, the VSC law can be designed as

$$v_{ud} = -\boldsymbol{B}_{S_{dz}}^{-1}\left[\boldsymbol{A}_{S_{dz}} + a_{ds}S_{dz} + b_{ds}\,\mathrm{sgn}(S_{dz})\right] \tag{79}$$

where the sliding mode surface is

$$S_{dz} = c_{d1}z_{d1} + z_{d2} \tag{80}$$

By ignoring the tedious calculation process, the parameters are given directly as $\boldsymbol{A}_{S_{dz}} = c_{d1}\dot{z}_{d1}, \boldsymbol{B}_{S_{dz}} = 1$, $c_{d1} = 1$, $a_{ds} = 10$, $b_{ds} = 185$. By transferring v_{ud} back to the original coordinate and substituting it into Eq. (72), the AACC law is finally obtained as

$$u_b = -\frac{f_{d2}(\omega_t, \omega_{ed}, a_b)}{g_{d1}(\omega_t, a_b)} - \frac{\left[c_{d1}\varepsilon_v + a_{ds}(c_{d1}\varepsilon_d + \varepsilon_v) + b_{ds}\operatorname{sgn}(S_{dX})\right] + p_{d1}w}{g_{d1}(\omega_t, a_b)} \tag{81}$$

where $S_{aX} = c_{d1}\varepsilon_d + \varepsilon_v$, which is a sliding mode surface over the original coordinate.

The remaining nonlinear internal dynamic subsystem (78) should be verified as well to ensure the stability of the total system. At first, if z_{d1}, z_{d2}, w=0 and the impact of uncertain items $\Delta\boldsymbol{Q}_d$, $\Delta\boldsymbol{K}_d$ can be neglected, then the zero dynamics becomes

$$\begin{cases} \dot{\mu}_{d1} = a_d\mu_{d1}^2 + b_d\mu_{d1}\mu_{d2} + c_d\mu_{d2}^2 - \dfrac{\mu_{d3}}{\alpha_n t_h} - \vartheta_d \\ \dot{\mu}_{d2} = e_d\mu_{d1}^2 + f_d\mu_{d1}\mu_{d2} + g_d\mu_{d2}^2 + h_d\mu_{d2} + i_d \\ \dot{\mu}_{d3} = -\left(2\dfrac{a_d}{d_d}\mu_{d1} + \dfrac{b_d}{d_d}\mu_{d2} + \dfrac{1}{t_h d_d}\right) \times \left(a_d\mu_{d1}^2 + b_d\mu_{d1}\mu_{d2} + c_d\mu_{d2}^2 - \dfrac{\mu_{d3}}{\alpha_n t_h} - \vartheta_d\right) \\ \qquad -\left(\dfrac{b_d}{d_d}\mu_{d1} + 2\dfrac{c_d}{d_d}\mu_{d2}\right) \times \left(e_d\mu_{d1}^2 + f_d\mu_{d1}\mu_{d2} + g_d\mu_{d2}^2 + h_d\mu_{d2} + i_d\right) \end{cases} \tag{82}$$

Then, a candidate Lyapunov function is chosen as

$$V_d(\mu_{d1}, \mu_{d2}, \mu_{d3}) = \mu_{d2} + \left(\frac{2\pi\alpha_n t_h d_d r_t}{60 i_g i_0}\mu_{d1} + \int \mu_{d3} dt\right) \tag{83}$$

Since z_{d2}=0, it is easy to obtain

$$V_d(\mu_{d1}, \mu_{d2}, \mu_{d3}) = \mu_{d2} = \omega_{ed} > 0 \qquad (\text{if } \omega_{ed} \neq 0) \tag{84}$$

The time derivative with respect to the Lyapunov function Eq. (83) is

$$\frac{dV_d}{dt} = \dot{\mu}_{d2} + \left(\frac{2\pi\alpha_n t_h d_d r_t}{60 i_g i_0}\dot{\mu}_{d1} + \mu_{d3}\right) = \dot{\mu}_{d2} = \dot{\omega}_{ed} \tag{85}$$

For the braking condition, the engine operates under the decelerating mode, hence

$$\frac{dV_d}{dt} = \dot{\omega}_{ed} < 0 \ \ (\text{if } \dot{\omega}_{ed} \neq 0) \tag{86}$$

Assembling Eqs. (84) and (85), the following inequality is hold

$$V_d\frac{dV_d}{dt} < 0 \ \ (\text{if } \omega_{ed} \neq 0 \text{ and } \dot{\omega}_{ed} \neq 0) \tag{87}$$

Thus, the zero dynamics of the nonlinear internal dynamic subsystem (78) is asymptotically stable as long as z_{d1}, z_{d2}, w=0.

5. Simulation and analysis

Base on above analysis of the control system under the driving/braking conditions, the LFS AACC system applying the DDRC method can be designed as the block diagram in Figure 9. The system consists of three parts: the controlled object of a convoy with two vehicles, DDRC system, and the input/output signals.

In order to verify the control performance of the LFS AACC system, a typical driving cycle of the leading vehicle's aceeleration/deceleration, velocity, as well as the road grade are given in Figure 10. The road grade changes from 0°~+3° to 0°~-3° in a period of 80s~90s and 110s~120s, respectively. Furthermore, the conditions from the high-speed to low-speed SG, and two cases of mass equaling 10,000kg and 25,000kg are included. The initial errors at 0s for the inter-vehicles relative distance and relative velocity are set to 0m and 0m/s, respectively. Table 1 and the solid lines in Figures 11 and 12 are the coefficients and the simulation results, respectively for the proposed control system. In contrast, the coefficients and some simulation results of an upper LQ+lower PID hierarchical control system proposed in ref. [1] are also presented respectively in Table 2 and by the dotted lines in Figures 11 and 12. The comparison results of the throttle angle, desired input voltage of EBS, engine speed, automatic transmission gear position, relations of relative distance/relative velocity tracking error verses time scale, as well as the phase chart of the relative distance/relative velocity tracking error are shown in Figures 11 and 12 in sequences of (a)~(f).

Driving condition	c_{a1}=1	a_{as}=10	b_{as}=250
Braking condition	c_{d1}=1	a_{ds}=10	b_{ds}=185

Table 1. Control parameters of DDRC system

Conditions	Upper layer LQ parameters		Lower layer PID parameters
	Q	R	P, I, D
Driving	[7 0,0 4]	10	800, 560, 15
Braking			350, 150, 20

Table 2. Control parameters of hierarchical control system

As illustrated by Figures 11 (a)~(d), for the proposed control system, the throttle angle and the EBS desired input voltage exhibit smooth response characteristic, rapid convergence and small oscillation, even at the moment of gear switching. However, for the hierarchical control system, it shows intense and long time oscillations especially at low-speed condition (shown as dashed border subfigures inside the Figures 11 (a) and (b)), which have impacts on the vehicle's comfortability severely.

This is because the small parameters are adopted by the proposed control system as the consequence of applying DDRC method (shown as Tables 1), and thus the unmodeled high frequency oscillation can be effectively eliminated, in contrast with the hierarchical control system adopting large parameters (shown as Tables 2). Moreover, during the time period of 0s ~ 73s and 130s ~ 200s in Figures 11(e) and 12(e), the simulation results of the proposed control system indicate that the errors of the relative distance and the relative velocity are constrained within the range of ± 0.02m and -0.05m/s~0.02m/s, respectively. The tracking accuracy of the proposed control system is enhanced and almost frees from the disturbance of the leading vehicle's acceleration/deceleration. However, for the hierarchical control system, it is affected obviously by the change of the leading vehicle's acceleration/ deceleration, and touches the maximum value of ± 0.1m. Finally, the comparison between (e) and (f) in Figures 11 and 12 demonstrates a superior robustness for the proposed control system in spite of the uncertainties caused by the road grade, gear position and the vehicle mass. Particularly, while the road grade changes between ± 3° in the time period of 80s~120s, the tracking error of the relative distance and the relative velocity for the proposed control system are less than ± 0.05m and -0.04m/s ~ 0.02m/s, in contract to larger than ± 0.15m and ± 0.05m/s of the hierarchical control system.

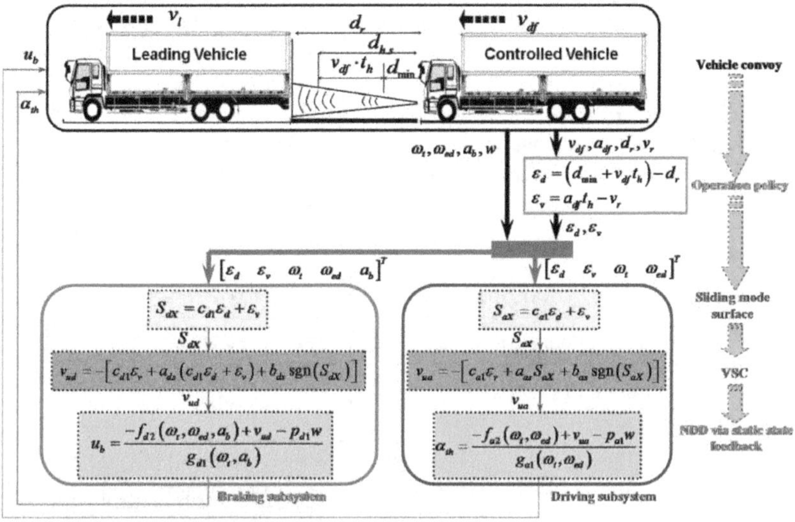

Fig. 9. LFS ACC system using the DDRC method

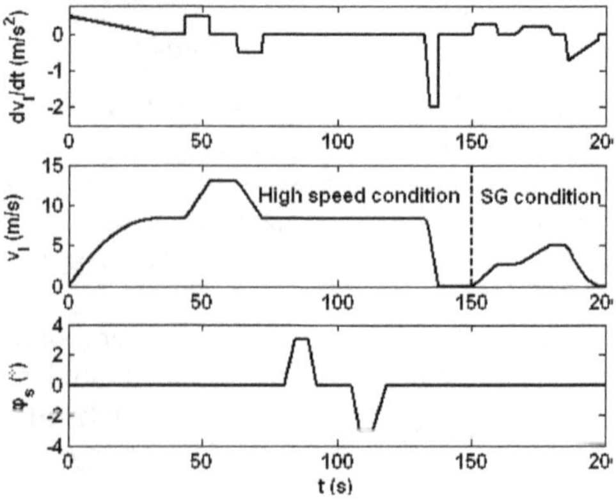

Fig. 10. Profile of leading vehicle driving cycle and road grade

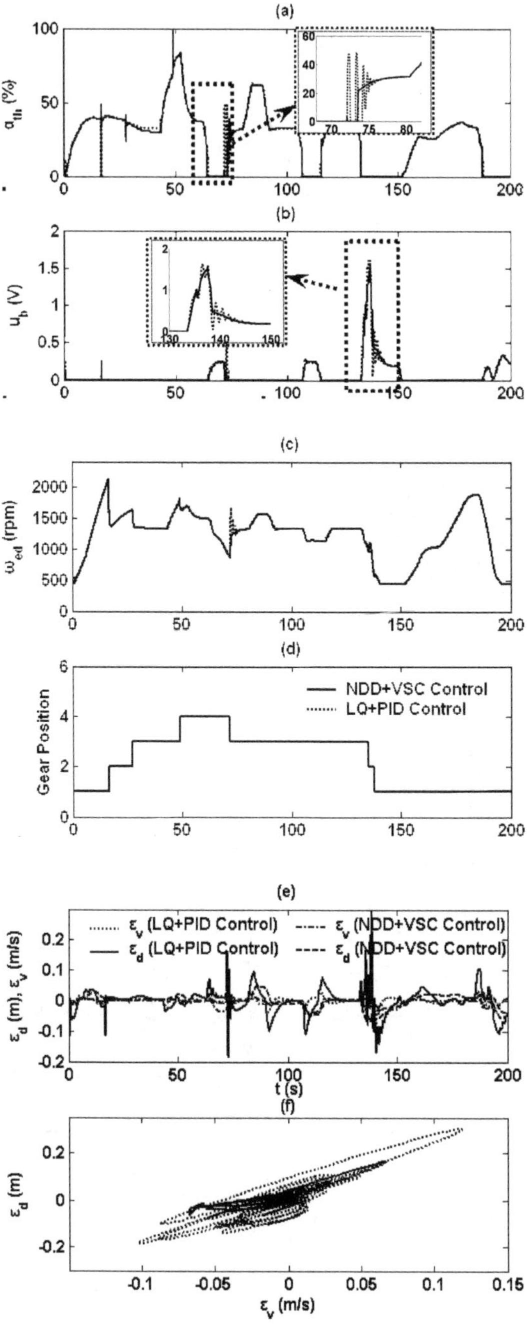

Fig. 11. Simulation results (mass is 10,000 kg)

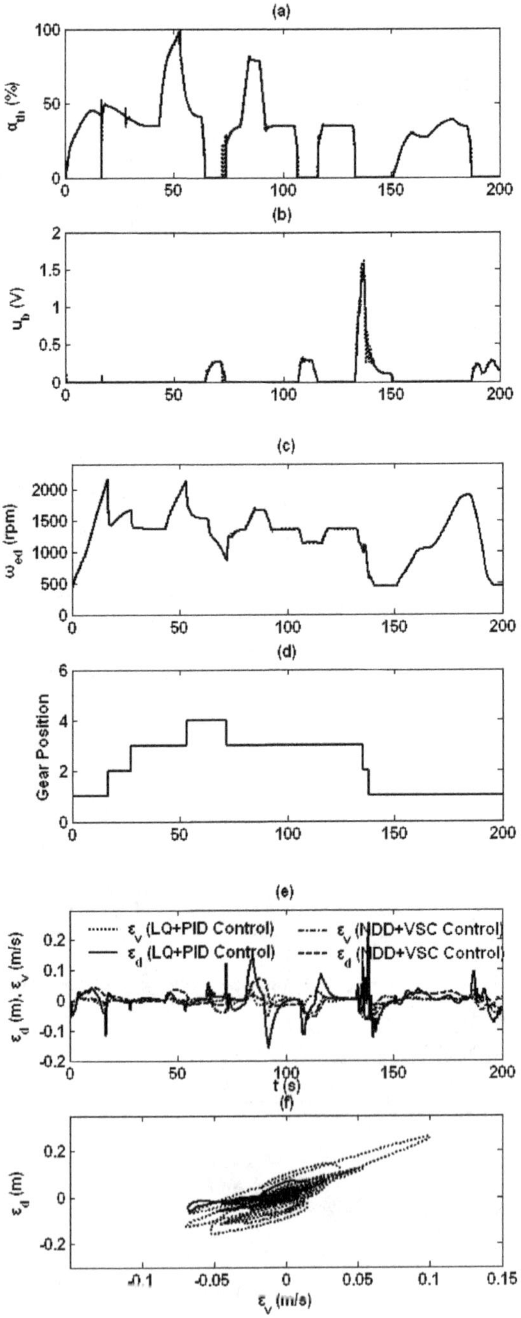

Fig. 12. Simulation results (mass is 25,000 kg)

From above analysis and the simulation results, it seems that the influence of nonlinearity, external disturbance and the variable uncertainties have been eliminated by adopting the proposed DDRC method for the LFS AACC system, and it results in a significant improvement of the tracking accuracy, robustness, as well as the response characteristics of the actuator system (i.e., the throttle angle and the EBS desired input voltage). In addition, the control structure and the parameters are simplified, and easy to determine in comparison with the hierarchical control algorithm.

6. Conclusion

In this study, an LFS nonlinear dynamics model is proposed by integrating the dynamics of the inter-vehicles and the controlled vehicle. Then, a DDRC method is developed, and used to design the LFS AACC system. Finally, the control performance is verified by the numerical simulation under a typical driving cycle. The simulation results confirm the followings:

1. The proposed LFS model not only can describe the vehicle's strong nonlinearity at low-speed conditions and the uncertainty induced by the complex traffic environment and the road condition, but also is able to express the strong coupling characteristics due to frequent change of the leading vehicle's acceleration/deceleration at high-speed condition. Particularly, the dynamics of the inter-vehicles and the controlled vehicle are lumped together within a universal state space equation.
2. The tracking accuracies at high-speed and low-speed SG condition, as well as the robustness to the external disturbance and the model parameter uncertainty have been improved simultaneously, because the DDRC method is applied in the design of the LFS ACC system.
3. The actuators' high frequency oscillation caused by the unmodeled part has been restrained through using small parameters, and this leads to a control system with simplified structure.

7. Appendixes

Appendix 1. Definition of the matrix items in Eq. (1)

$$f_{av1}(\mathbf{X})=\left\{\left[\tau_1\left(\frac{\omega_t}{\omega_{ed}}\right)^2+\tau_2\left(\frac{\omega_t}{\omega_{ed}}\right)+\tau_3\right]\left(\frac{\omega_{ed}}{60}\right)^2\frac{t_1\left(\frac{\omega_t}{\omega_{ed}}\right)+t_2}{g_g}\frac{i_{g_1}i_0\eta_k}{r_t}-\frac{\eta_1\left(\frac{\omega_t}{\eta_2}\right)^2+M(\eta_r+\sin\varphi_s)g_g}{g_g}\right\}\frac{i_{g_1}i_0}{\sigma_C}$$

$$f_{av2}(\mathbf{X})=\left\{(k_2\omega_{ed}+k_4)g_g-\left[\tau_1\left(\frac{\omega_t}{\omega_{ed}}\right)^2+\tau_2\left(\frac{\omega_t}{\omega_{ed}}\right)+\tau_3\right]\left(\frac{\omega_{ed}}{60}\right)^2\right\}\frac{\eta_2}{I_e}$$

$$g_{av1}(\mathbf{X})=0$$

$$g_{av2}(\mathbf{X})=(k_1\omega_{ed}+k_3)\frac{g_g\eta_2}{I_e}$$

Appendix 2. Definition of the matrix items in Eq. (2)

$$f_{dv1}(\mathbf{X})=\left\{\left[\tau_{d1}\left(\frac{\omega_t}{\omega_{ed}}\right)^2+\tau_{d2}\left(\frac{\omega_t}{\omega_{ed}}\right)+\tau_{d3}\right]\left(\frac{\omega_{ed}}{60}\right)^2\frac{i_{g_1}i_0\eta_k}{r_t}+Ma_b-\frac{\eta_1\left(\frac{\omega_t}{\eta_2}\right)^2+M(\eta_r+\sin\varphi_s)g_g}{g_g}\right\}\frac{i_{g_1}i_0}{\sigma_C}$$

$$f_{dv2}(\mathbf{X})=\left\{(k_2\omega_{ed}+k_4)g_g-\left[\tau_{d1}\left(\frac{\omega_t}{\omega_{ed}}\right)^2+\tau_{d2}\left(\frac{\omega_t}{\omega_{ed}}\right)+\tau_{d3}\right]\left(\frac{\omega_{ed}}{60}\right)^2\right\}\frac{\eta_2}{I_e}$$

$$f_{dv3}(\mathbf{X})=-\frac{1}{t_r}a_b$$

$$g_{dv1}(\mathbf{X})=g_{dv2}(\mathbf{X})=0$$

$$g_{dv3}(\mathbf{X})=-\frac{k_b+k_a a_b^2 v}{t_r}$$

Appendix 3. Definition of the matrix items in Eq. (7)

$$f_{a1}(\varepsilon_v)=\varepsilon_v$$

$$f_{a2}(\omega_t,\omega_{ed})=\left[\alpha_n t_h\left(2a\omega_t+b\omega_{ed}+3d\frac{\omega_t^2}{\omega_{ed}}\right)+\alpha_n\right]\dot{\omega}_t+\alpha_n t_h\left(b\omega_t+2c\omega_{ed}-d\frac{\omega_t^3}{\omega_{ed}^2}\right)$$
$$\left(e\omega_t^2+f\omega_t\omega_{ed}+g\omega_{ed}^2+h\omega_{ed}+i\right)$$

$$f_{a3}(\omega_t,\omega_{ed})=a\omega_t^2+b\omega_t\omega_{ed}+c\omega_{ed}^2+d\frac{\omega_t^3}{\omega_{ed}}-\vartheta$$

$$f_{a4}(\omega_t,\omega_{ed})=e\omega_t^2+f\omega_t\omega_{ed}+g\omega_{ed}^2+h\omega_{ed}+i$$

$$g_{a1}(\omega_t,\omega_{ed})=\alpha_n t_h\left(b\omega_t+2c\omega_{ed}-d\frac{\omega_t^3}{\omega_{ed}^2}\right)(j\omega_{ed}+k)$$

$$g_{a2}(\omega_{ed})=(j\omega_{ed}+k)$$

$$p_{a1}=-1$$

$$\Delta f_{a2}(\omega_t,\omega_{ed})=\left[\alpha_n t_h\left(2a\omega_t+b\omega_{ed}+3d\frac{\omega_t^2}{\omega_{ed}}\right)+\alpha_n\right]\Delta f_{av1}+\alpha_n t_h\left(b\omega_t+2c\omega_{ed}-d\frac{\omega_t^3}{\omega_{ed}^2}\right)\Delta f_{av2}$$

$$\Delta g_{a1}(\omega_t,\omega_{ed})=\alpha_n t_h\left(b\omega_t+2c\omega_{ed}-d\frac{\omega_t^3}{\omega_{ed}^2}\right)\Delta g_{av2}$$

$$\Delta f_{a3}=\Delta f_{av1},\Delta f_{a4}=\Delta f_{av2},\Delta g_{a2}=\Delta g_{av2}$$

where $a,b,c,d,e,f,g,h,i,j,k,\vartheta$ are constant coefficients, their specific values can be referred to ref. [16].

Appendix 4. Definition of the matrix items in Eq. (8)

$$f_{d1}(\varepsilon_v) = \varepsilon_v$$

$$f_{d2}(\omega_t, \omega_{ed}, a_b) = \left[\alpha_n t_h (2a_d\omega_t + b_d\omega_{ed}) + \alpha_n\right]\dot{\omega}_t + \alpha_n t_h (b_d\omega_t + 2c_d\omega_{ed})\dot{\omega}_{ed} + \alpha_n t_h d_d j_d a_b$$

$$f_{d3}(\omega_t, \omega_{ed}, a_b) = a_d\omega_t^2 + b_d\omega_t\omega_{ed} + c_d\omega_{ed}^2 + d_d a_b - \vartheta_d$$

$$f_{d4}(\omega_t, \omega_{ed}) = e_d\omega_t^2 + f_d\omega_t\omega_{ed} + g_d\omega_{ed}^2 + h_d\omega_{ed} + i_d$$

$$f_{d5}(a_b) = j_d a_b$$

$$g_{d1}(\omega_t, a_b) = \alpha_n t_h d_d \left(k_d a_b^2 \omega_t + l_d\right)$$

$$g_{d2}(\omega_t, a_b) = k_d a_b^2 \omega_t + l_d$$

$$p_{d1} = -1$$

$$\Delta f_{d2}(\omega_t, \omega_{ed}) = \left[\alpha_n t_h (2a_d\omega_t + b_d\omega_{ed}) + \alpha_n\right]\Delta f_{dv1} + \alpha_n t_h (b_d\omega_t + 2c_d\omega_{ed})\Delta f_{dv2} + \alpha_n t_h d_d \Delta f_{dv3}$$

$$\Delta g_{d1}(\omega_t, a_b) = \alpha_n t_h d_d \left(k_d a_b^2 \omega_t + l_d\right)\Delta g_{dv3}$$

$$\Delta f_{d3} = \Delta f_{dv1}, \Delta f_{d4} = \Delta f_{dv2}, \Delta f_{d5} = \Delta f_{dv3}, \Delta g_{d2} = \Delta g_{dv3}$$

where $a_d, b_d, c_d, d_d, e_d, f_d, g_d, h_d, i_d, j_d, k_d, l_d, \vartheta_d$ are constant coefficients, their specific values can be referred to ref. [16].

Appendix 5. The vehicle parameters are as follows:

$i_0 = 5.571$ - final reduction ratio;

$i_{g_1} = 3.49$ - first position gear ratio of the automatic transmission;

$r_t = 0.507$ - effective tire radius (m);

$I_e = 3.189$ - rotational inertia of the engine flywheel (kg m^2);

$\eta_k = 0.98$ - total transmission efficiency;

$\eta_r = 0.01$ - rolling resistance coefficient;

$M = 10{,}000$ - vehicle nominal mass (kg);

$\varphi_s = 0$ - nominal road grade (°);

$k_1 = 5.2\times10^{-3}, k_2 = -0.25, k_3 = -1.1, k_4 = 145$ - engine fitting coefficients;

$t_1 = -0.85, t_2 = 1.75, \tau_1 = -7.19\times10^{-2}, \tau_2 = 3.97\times10^{-2}\,\tau_3 = 3.68\times10^{-2}$ - torque converter fitting coefficients for the forward transmit condition;

$\tau_{d1} = -2.1\times10^{-2}, \tau_{d2} = 6.76\times10^{-2}, \tau_{d3} = -4.59\times10^{-2}$ - torque converter fitting coefficients for the reverse transmit condition;

$t_r = 0.2$ - time constant of the dynamic response for the braking system;

$k_a = -4.3\times10^{-3}, k_b = 0.29$ - fitting coefficients of the heat fading efficiency model for the braking system;

η_1, η_2, σ_C - constant coefficients:

$$\eta_1 = (0.232 g_g)\left(\frac{0.377 r\cdot 60}{3.6 i_g i_0 \cdot 2\pi}\right)^2, \quad \eta_2 = \frac{60}{6.283}, \quad \sigma_C = \left(\frac{M}{g_g\cdot 18.8}\right) + \left(\frac{M\cdot 1.55}{g_g^2\cdot 18.8}\right);$$

$g_g = 9.8\text{m}/\text{s}^2$.

8. Acknowledgment

We would like to thanks the data of vehicle supported by Tsinghua University, and the supports from the Young Scientists Fund of National Natural Science Foundation of China (51007003) and National Natural Science Foundation of China (51075010).

9. References

[1] Hedrick, J.K.; McMahon, D.H.; Swaroop, D. (1993). Vehicle Modeling and Control for Automated Highway Systems, *PATH Technical Report*, pp.1-73,UBC-ITS-PRR-93-24, Jan 01,1993

[2] Hedrick, J.K. (1998). Nonlinear Controller Design for Automated Vehicle Application, *Control '98. UKACC International Conference on (Conf. Publ. No. 455)*, pp.23-32,Swansea, UK, Sep 1-4,1998

[3] Rajamani, R.; Tan, H. S.; Law, B. K. and Zhang, W. B. (2000). Demonstration of Integrated Longitudinal and Lateral Control for the Operation of Automated Vehicles in Platoons. *IEEE Transactions on Control Systems Technology*, Vol.8, No.4, (July 2000), pp. 695-708, ISSN 1063-6536

[4] Yi, K.; Moon, I.; Kwon, Y. D. (2001). A vehicle-to-vehicle distance control algorithm for stop-and-go cruise control. *Intelligent Transportation Systems, 2001. Proceedings. 2001 IEEE,* pp. 478-482, ISBN: 0-7803-7194-1, Oakland, CA, USA, 2001

[5] Omae, M. (1999). Study on the vehicle platoon control system, *Doctor Dissertation,* Tokyo: University of Tokyo, 1999

[6] Fritz, A.; Schienlen, W. (1999). Automatic Cruise Control of a Mechatronically Steered Vehicle Convoy. *Vehicle System Dynamics,* Vol.32, (1999), pp. 331–344

[7] Schienlen, W.; Fritz, A. (1999). Nonlinear Cruise Control Concepts for Vehicle in Convoy. *Vehicle System Dynamics Supplement,* Vol.33,(1999), pp.256-269

[8] Naranjo, J.E.; Gonzalez, C.; Garcia, R.; de Pedro, T. (2006). ACC+Stop&go maneuvers with throttle and brake fuzzy control. *IEEE Transactions on Intelligent Transportation Systems,* Vol.7 ,No.4,(2006), pp. 213–225, ISSN: 1524-9050

[9] Daniele, C.; Schutter, B. De. (2008). Adaptive Cruise Control for a SMART Car: A Comparison Benchmark for MPC-PWA Control Methods. *IEEE Transactions on Control Systems Technology,* Vol.16, No.2, (March 2008), pp. 365-372, ISSN: 1063-6536

[10] Bifulco, G.N.; Simonelli, F.; Di Pace, R. (2008). Experiments toward a human-like adaptive cruise control, *Intelligent Vehicles Symposium,* pp. 919-924, ISBN 978-1-4244-2568-6, Eindhoven University of Technology, Eindhoven, The Netherlands, June 4-6, 2008

[11] Acarman, T.; Liu, Y. and Ozguner, U. (2006). Intelligent cruise control stop and go with and without communication, *Proceedings of the American Control Conference,* pp. 4356–4361, ISBN: 1-4244-0209-3, Minneapolis, Minnesota, USA, June 14-16, 2006

[12] Martinez, J. J. and Canudas-de-Wit, C. (2007). A Safe Longitudinal Control for Adaptive Cruise Control and Stop-and-Go Scenarios. *IEEE Transactions on Control Systems Technology,* Vol.15, No.2, (March 2007), pp.246-258, ISSN : 1063-6536

[13] Venhovens, P.; Naab, K.; Adiprasito, B. (2000). Stop and go cruise control, *Proceedings of Seoul 2000 FISITA World Automotive Congress,* pp.1-8, Seoul Korea, June 12-15, 2000

[14] Yamamura, Y.; Tabe, M.; Kanehira, M. (2001). Development of an adaptive cruise control system with stop and go capability,*SAE Technical Paper*, Detroit, MI, USA, March, 2001
[15] Bin,Y; Li, K. Q.; Ukawa, H.; Handa, M. (2006). Modeling and Control of Nonlinear Dynamic System for Heavy-Duty Trucks. *Proceedings of the Institution of Mechanical Engineers, Part D, Journal of Automobile Engineering,* Vol.220, No.10, Z(2006), pp. 1423-1435
[16] Bin, Y.; Li, K. Q.; Feng, N. L. (2008). Feedback Linearization Tracking Control of Vehicle Longitudinal Acceleration under Low-Speed Conditions. *Journal of Dynamic Systems, Measurement, and Control,* Vol.130, (2008), pp. 1-12
[17] Li, K. Q.; Bin, Y.; Ukawa, H.; Handa ,M. (2006). Study on Stop and Go Cruise Control of Heavy-Duty Vehicles. *Transaction of JSAE,* Vol.37, No.2, (2006), pp. 145-150, ISSN:0919-1364
[18] Bin,Y.; Li, K. Q,; Ukawa, H.; Handa, M. (2009). Nonlinear Disturbance Decoupling Control of Heavy-Duty Truck Stop and Go Cruise Systems. *Vehicle System Dynamics,* Vol.47, No.1, (January 2009), pp. 29-55
[19] Thomas D. Gillespie. (1992). Fundamentals of Vehicle Dynamics, Warrendale, *Society of Automotive Engineers, Inc,* 1992
[20] Swaroop, D.; Hetirick, J.K.; Chien, C.C.; Ioannou, P. (2004). A Comparison of Spacing and Headway Control Laws for Automatically Controlled Vehicles. *Vehicle System Dynamics,* Vol.23, No.8, (2004), pp. 597-625
[21] Bengtsson, J. (2001). Adaptive Cruise Control and Driver Modeling. *Research thesis, Department of automatic control, Lund Institute of Technology,* ISSN 0280–5316, Sweden
[22] Isidori, A.; Krener, A.; Gori-Giorgi, C.; Monaco, S. (1981). Nonlinear Decoupling via Feedback: A Differential Geometric Approach. *IEEE Transactions on Automatic Control,* Vol.26, No.2, (1981), pp. 331-345, ISSN: 0018-9286
[23] Nijmeijer, H. (1994). On dynamic state feedback in nonlinear control, *IEE Colloquium on Nonlinear Control,* pp.5/1~5/2, London, UK, May 24,1994
[24] Xia, X H. (1997). *Disturbance Decoupling Control.* Science Press, Beijing, 1997
[25] Morse, A.; Wonham, W. (1971). Status of noninteracting control. *IEEE Transactions on Automatic Control,* Vol.16, No.6, (Dec1971), pp. 568-581, ISSN: 0018-9286
[26] Conte, G.; Perdon, A. M. (1994). The disturbance decoupling problem by dynamic feedback for systems over a principal ideal domain, *Proceedings of the 33rd IEEE Conference on Decision and Control,* pp. 1276-1279, ISBN: 0-7803-1968-0, Lake Buena Vista, FL , USA, Dec 14-16 ,1994
[27] Xia, X H. (1993). Companion of Controlled invariant Distribution and Description of DDP Control Law, *Science in China,* pp. 130-136, Ser.A, 1993,
[28] Young, K.D. (1999). Variable structure systems, sliding mode and nonlinear control, *Springer,* London, 1999
[29] Hu, Y. M. (2003). *Variable Structure Control Theory and Application,* Science Press, Beijing
[30] Cheng, D. Z. (1988). *Geometric Theory of Nonlinear System.* Science Press, Beijing
[31] Byrnes, C.I.; Isidori, A.(1998). Output regulation for nonlinear systems: an overview, *Proceedings of the 37th IEEE Conference on Decision and Control,* pp.3069-3074, Tampa, FL, UNITED STATES, Dec 16-18, 1998
[32] Fliess, M.; Tevine, J.; Martin, P.; Rouchon, P.(1994). Nonlinear control and Lie-Backlund transformations: towards a new differential geometric standpoint, *1994*

Proceedings of the 33rd IEEE Conference on Decision and Control, pp.339-344, ISBN 0-7803-1968-0, Lake Buena Vista, FL , USA , Dec 14-16,1994

[33] Cheng, D. Z. (1987). Geometric Approach to Nonlinear Systems Part 1. Geometric Method and Geometric Preliminary, *Control Theory and Application,* Jan 1-9,1987

[34] Han, Z. Z.; Liu, J. H, et al.(1994). Characters of Nonlinear Control Systems (II). *Control and Decision,*Vol.9, No.5, (1994), pp. 91-97

[35] Wang, Y. F.; Xia, X. H.; Gao, W. B. (1994). Parameter Variations in Nonlinear Decoupling, *American Control Conference,* pp. 2700 - 2704 , ISBN: 0-7803-1783-1, June 29- July 1, 1994

[36] Isidori, A. (1985). *Nonlinear Control Systems,* Spronger Verlag,ISBN 0-387-15595-3, Berlin, Heidelberg

[37] Gao, W. B. (1988). *Nonlinear Control System Introduction.* Science Press, Beijing

[38] Slotine, J.; Li, W. (1991). *Applied Nonlinear Control,* Prentice-Hall Inc, ISBN 0-13-040890-5,Englewood Cliffs, New Jersey

Part 2

Control of Structures, Mechanical and Electro-Mechanical Systems

7

Robust Control of Mechanical Systems

Joaquín Alvarez[1] and David Rosas[2]
[1]*Scientific Research and Advanced Studies Center of Ensenada (CICESE)*
[2]*Universidad Autónoma de Baja California*
Mexico

1. Introduction

Control of mechanical systems has been an important problem since several years ago. For free-motion systems, the dynamics is often modeled by ordinary differential equations arising from classical mechanics. Controllers based on feedback linearization, adaptive, and robust techniques have been proposed to control this class of systems (Brogliato et al., 1997; Slotine & Li, 1988; Spong & Vidyasagar, 1989).
Many control algorithms proposed for these systems are based on models where practical situations like parameter uncertainty, external disturbances, or friction force terms are not taken into account. In addition, a complete availability of the state variables is commonly assumed (Paden & Panja, 1988; Takegaki & Arimoto, 1981; Wen & Bayard, 1988). In practice, however, the position is usually the only available measurement. In consequence, the velocity, which may play an important role in the control strategy, must be calculated indirectly, often yielding an inaccurate estimation.
In (Makkar et al., 2007), a tracking controller that includes a new differentiable friction model with uncertain nonlinear terms is developed for Euler-Lagrange systems. The technique is based on a model and the availability of the full state. In (Patre et al., 2008), a similar idea is presented for systems perturbed by external disturbances. Moreover, some robust controllers have been proposed to cope with parameter uncertainty and external disturbances. H_∞ control has been a particularly important approach. In this technique, the control objective is expressed as a mathematical optimization problem where a ratio between some norms of output and perturbation signals is minimized (Isidori & Astolfi, 1992). It is used to synthesize controllers achieving robust performance of linear and nonlinear systems.
In general, the control techniques mentioned before yield good control performance. However, the mathematical operations needed to calculate the control signal are rather complex, possibly due to the compensation of gravitational, centrifugal, or Coriolis terms, or the need to solve a Hamilton-Jacobi-Isaacs equation. In addition, if an observer is included in the control system, the overall controller may become rather complex.
Another method exhibiting good robustness properties is the sliding mode technique (Perruquetti & Barbot, 2002; Utkin, 1992). In this method, a surface in the state space is made attractive and invariant using discontinuous terms in the control signal, forcing the system to converge to the desired equilibrium point placed on this surface, and making the controlled dynamics independent from the system parameters. These controllers display good performance for regulation and tracking objectives (Utkin et al., 1999; Weibing & Hung, 1993;

Yuzhuo & Flashner, 1998). Unfortunately, they often exhibit the chattering phenomenon, displaying high-frequency oscillations due to delays and hysteresis always present in practice. The high-frequency oscillations produce negative effects that may harm the control devices (Utkin et al., 1999). Nevertheless, possibly due to the good robust performance of sliding mode controllers, several solutions to alleviate or eliminate chattering have been developed for some classes of systems (Bartolini et al., 1998; Curk & Jezernik, 2001; Erbatur & Calli, 2007; Erbatur et al., 1999; Pushkin, 1999; Sellami et al., 2007; Xin et al., 2004; Wang & Yang, 2007).

In the previous works, it is also assumed that the full state vector is available. However, in practice it is common to deal with systems where only some states are measured due to technological or economical limitations, among other reasons. This problem can be solved using observers, which are models that, based on input-output measurements, estimate the state vector.

To solve the observation problem of uncertain systems, several approaches have been developed (Davila et al., 2006; Rosas et al., 2006; Yaz & Azemi, 1994), including sliding mode techniques (Aguilar & Maya, 2005; Utkin et al., 1999; Veluvolu et al., 2007). The sliding mode observers open the possibility to use the equivalent output injection to identify disturbances (Davila et al., 2006; Orlov, 2000; Rosas et al., 2006).

In this chapter, we describe a control structure designed for mechanical systems to solve regulation and tracking objectives (Rosas et al., 2010). The control technique used in this structure is combined with a discontinuous observer. It exhibits good performance with respect to parameter uncertainties and external disturbances. Because of the included observer, the structure needs only the generalized position and guarantees a good convergence to the reference with a very small error and a control signal that reduces significantly the chattering phenomenon. The observer estimates not only the state vector but, using the equivalent output injection method, it estimates also the plant perturbations produced by parameter uncertainties, non-modeled dynamics, and other external torques. This estimated perturbation is included in the controller to compensate the actual disturbances affecting the plant, improving the performance of the overall control system.

The robust control structure is designed in a modular way and can be easily programed. Moreover, it can be implemented, if needed, with analog devices from a basic electronic circuit having the same structure for a wide class of mechanical systems, making its analog implementation also very easy (Alvarez et al., 2009). Some numerical and experimental results are included, describing the application of the control structure to several mechanical systems.

2. Control objective

Let us consider a mechanical system with $n-$degree of freedom (DOF), modeled by

$$M(q)\ddot{q} + C(q,\dot{q})\dot{q} + G(q) + \Phi(q,\dot{q},\ddot{q})\theta + \gamma(t) = u = \tau_0 + \Delta_\tau. \tag{1}$$

$q \in \mathbb{R}^n, \dot{q} = dq/dt, \ddot{q} = d^2q/dt^2$ denote the position, velocity, and acceleration, respectively; M and C are the inertia and Coriolis and centrifugal force matrices, G is the gravitational force, $\Phi\theta$ includes all the parameter uncertainties, and γ, which we suppose bounded by a constant σ, that is, $||\gamma(t)|| < \sigma$, denotes a external disturbance. τ_0 and Δ_τ are control inputs. Note that, under this formulation, the terms M, C, and G are well known. If not, it is known that they can be put in a form linear with respect to parameters and can be included in $\Phi\theta$ (Sciavicco & Siciliano, 2000).

We suppose that τ_0, which may depend on the whole state $(q, \dot{q})$, denotes a feedback controller designed to make the state $(q, \dot{q})$ follow a reference signal $(q_r, \dot{q}_r)$, with an error depending on the magnitude of the external disturbance γ and the uncertainty term $\Phi\theta$, but keeping the tracking error bounded. We denote this control as the "nominal control". We propose also to add the term Δ_τ, and design it such that it confers the following properties to the closed-loop system.

1. The overall control $u = \tau_0 + \Delta_\tau$ greatly reduces the steady-state error, provided by τ_0 only, under the presence of the uncertainty θ and the disturbance γ.
2. The controller uses only the position measurement.

Note that, for the nominal control, the steady state error is normally different to zero, usually large enough to be of practical value, and the performance of the closed-loop system may be poor. The role of the additional control term Δ_τ is precisely to improve the performance of the system driven by the nominal control.
The nominal control can be anyone that guarantees a bounded behavior of system (1). In this chapter we use a particular controller and show that, under some conditions, it preserves the boundedness of the state. In particular, suppose the control aim is to make the position q track a smooth signal q_r, and define the plant state as

$$e_1 = q - q_r, \quad e_2 = \dot{q} - \dot{q}_r. \tag{2}$$

Suppose also that the nominal control law is given by

$$\tau_0 = -M(\cdot)\left[K_p e_1 + K_v e_2 - \ddot{q}_r(t)\right] + C(\cdot)(e_2 + \dot{q}_r) + G(\cdot), \tag{3}$$

where K_p and K_v are $n \times n$-positive definite matrices. However, because the velocity is not measured, we need to use an approximation for the velocity error, which we denote as $\hat{e}_2 = \dot{\hat{q}} - \dot{q}_r$. This will be calculated by an observer, whose design is discussed in the next section. Suppose that the exact velocity error and the estimated one are related by $e_2 = \hat{e}_2 + \epsilon_2$. Then, if we use the estimated velocity error, the practical nominal control will be given by

$$\hat{\tau}_0 = -M(\cdot)(K_p e_1 + K_v \hat{e}_2 - \ddot{q}_r) + \hat{C}(\cdot)(\hat{e}_2 + \dot{q}_r) + G(\cdot). \tag{4}$$

Moreover, the approximated Coriolis matrix $\hat{C}$ can be given the form

$$\hat{C}(\cdot) = C(q, \dot{\hat{q}}) = C(\cdot, \hat{e}_2 + \dot{q}_r) = C(\cdot, e_2 + \dot{q}_r) - \Delta C(\cdot),$$

where $\Delta C = \mathcal{O}(\|\epsilon_2\|)$. Then the state space representation of system (1), with the control law (4), is given by

$$\begin{aligned} \dot{e}_1 &= e_2, \\ \dot{e}_2 &= -K_p e_1 - K_v e_2 + \xi(e, t) + \Delta u, \end{aligned} \tag{5}$$

where

$$\xi(\cdot) = -M^{-1}\left[(\hat{C} - MK_v)\epsilon_2 + \Delta C(e_2 + \dot{q}_r) + \Phi\theta + \gamma\right], \tag{6}$$

and $\Delta u = M^{-1}(\cdot)\Delta_\tau$ is a control adjustment to robustify the closed-loop system. When $\Delta u = 0$, a well established result is that, if

$$||\xi(e,t)|| < \rho_1||e|| + \rho_0, \;\; \rho_i > 0, \tag{7}$$

then there exist matrices K_p and K_v such that the state e of system (5) is bounded (Khalil, 2002). In fact, the bound on the state e can be made arbitrarily small by increasing the norm of matrices K_p and K_v.

The control objective can now be established as design a control input Δu that, depending only on the position, improves the performance of the control $\hat{\tau}_0$ by attenuating the effect of parameter uncertainty and disturbances, concentrated in ξ.

Note that disturbances acting on system (5) satisfy the matching condition (Khalil, 2002). Hence, it is theoretically possible to design a compensation term Δu to decouple the state e_1 from the disturbance ξ. The problem analyzed here is more complicated, however, because the velocity is not available.

In the next Section we solve the problem of velocity estimation using two observers that guarantee convergence to the states (e_1, e_2). Moreover, an additional property of these observers will allow us to have an estimation of the disturbance term ξ. This estimated perturbation will be used in the control Δu to compensate the actual disturbances affecting the plant.

3. Observation of the plant state

In this section we describe two techniques to estimate the plant state, yielding exponentially convergent observers.

3.1 A discontinuous observer

Discontinuous techniques for designing observers and controllers have been intensively developed recently, due to their robustness properties and, in some cases, finite-time convergence. In this subsection we describe a simple technique, just to show the observer performance.

The observer has been proposed in (Rosas et al., 2006). It guarantees exponential convergence to the plant state, even under the presence of some kind of uncertainties and disturbances.

Let us consider the system (5). The observer is described by

$$\begin{bmatrix} \dot{\hat{e}}_1 \\ \dot{\hat{e}}_2 \end{bmatrix} = \begin{bmatrix} \hat{e}_2 + C_2\epsilon_1 \\ -K_p e_1 - K_v\hat{e}_2 + \Delta u + C_1\epsilon_1 + C_0\mathrm{sign}(\epsilon_1) \end{bmatrix}, \tag{8}$$

where $\hat{e}_1 \in \mathbb{R}^n$ and $\hat{e}_2 \in \mathbb{R}^n$ are the states of the observer, $\epsilon_1 = e_1 - \hat{e}_1$. C_0, C_1, and C_2 are diagonal, positive-definite matrices defined by

$$C_i = \mathrm{diag}\{c_{i1}, c_{i2}, \ldots, c_{in}\} \qquad \text{for } i = 0, 1, 2.$$

The signum vector function $\mathrm{sign}(\cdot)$ is defined as

$$\mathrm{sign}(v) = [\mathrm{sign}(v_1), \mathrm{sign}(v_2), \ldots, \mathrm{sign}(v_n)]^T.$$

Then, the dynamics of the observation error $\epsilon = (\epsilon_1, \epsilon_2) = (e_1 - \hat{e}_1, e_2 - \hat{e}_2)$, are described by

$$\begin{bmatrix} \dot{\epsilon}_1 \\ \dot{\epsilon}_2 \end{bmatrix} = \begin{bmatrix} \epsilon_2 - C_2\epsilon_1 \\ -C_1\epsilon_1 - K_v\epsilon_2 - C_0\text{sign}(\epsilon_1) + \xi(e,t) \end{bmatrix}. \tag{9}$$

An important result is provided by (Rosas et al., 2006) for the case where $\rho_1 = 0$ (see equation (7)). Under this situation we can establish the conditions to have a convergence of the estimated state to the plant state.

Theorem 1. *(Rosas et al., 2006) If (7) is satisfied with $\rho_1 = 0$, then there exist matrices C_0, C_1, and C_2, such that system (9) has the origin as an exponentially stable equilibrium point. Therefore,* $\lim_{t\to\infty} \hat{e}(t) = e(t)$.

The proof of this theorem can be found in (Rosas et al., 2006). In fact, a change of variables given by $v_1 = \epsilon_1, v_2 = \epsilon_2 - C_2\epsilon_1$, allows us to express the dynamics of system (9) by

$$\begin{aligned} \dot{v}_1 &= v_2, \\ \dot{v}_2 &= -(C_1 + K_vC_2)v_1 - (C_2 + K_v)v_2 - C_0\text{sign}(v_1) + \xi(e,t), \end{aligned} \tag{10}$$

where v_1 and v_2 are vectors with the form

$$v_i = (v_{i1}, v_{i2}, \ldots, v_{in})^T; \; i = 1, 2.$$

Then system (10) can be expressed as a set of second-order systems given by

$$\begin{aligned} \dot{v}_{1i} &= v_{2i}, \\ \dot{v}_{2i} &= -\tilde{c}_{1i}v_{1i} - \tilde{c}_{2i}v_{2i} - c_{0i}\text{sign}(v_{1i}) + \xi_i(\cdot), \end{aligned} \tag{11}$$

where $\tilde{c}_{1i} = c_{1i} + k_{vi}c_{2i}$, $\tilde{c}_{2i} = c_{2i} + k_{vi}$, for $i = 1, \ldots, n$, and $|\xi_i| \leq \beta_i$, for some positive constants β_i. The conditions to have stability of the origin are given by

$$\tilde{c}_{1i} > 0, \tag{12}$$

$$\tilde{c}_{2i} > 0, \tag{13}$$

$$c_{0i} > 2\lambda_{\max}(P_i)\sqrt{\frac{\lambda_{\max}(P_i)}{\lambda_{\min}(P_i)}}\left(\frac{\tilde{c}_{1i}\beta_i}{\theta}\right), \tag{14}$$

for some $0 < \theta < 1$, where P_i is a 2×2 matrix that is the solution of the Lyapunov equation $A_i^T P_i + P_i A_i = -I$, and the matrix A_i is defined by

$$A_i = \begin{bmatrix} 0 & 1 \\ -\tilde{c}_{1i} & -\tilde{c}_{2i} \end{bmatrix}.$$

System (10) displays a second-order sliding mode (Perruquetti & Barbot, 2002; Rosas et al., 2010) determined by $v_1 = \dot{v}_1 = \ddot{v}_1 = 0$. To determine the behavior of the system on the sliding surface, the equivalent output injection method can be used (Utkin, 1992), hence

$$\ddot{v}_1 = -u_{eq} + \xi(e,t) = 0, \tag{15}$$

where u_{eq} is related to the discontinuous term $C_0\text{sign}(v_1)$ of equation (10). The equivalent output injection u_{eq} is then given by (Rosas et al., 2010; Utkin, 1992)

$$u_{eq} = \xi(e,t). \tag{16}$$

This means that the equivalent output injection corresponds to the perturbation term, which can be recovered by a filter process (Utkin, 1992). In fact, in this reference it is shown that the equivalent output injection coincides with the slow component of the discontinuous term in (10) when the state is in the discontinuity surface. Hence, it can be recovered using a low pass filter with a time constant small enough as compared with the slow component response, yet sufficiently large to filter out the high rate components.

For example, we can use a set of n second-order, low-pass Butterworth filter to estimate the term u_{eq}. These filters are described by the following normalized transfer function,

$$F_i(s) = \frac{\omega_{c_i}^2}{s^2 + 1.4142\omega_{c_i}s + \omega_{c_i}^2}, \qquad i = 1,\ldots,n, \tag{17}$$

where ω_{c_i} is the cut-off frequency of each filter. Here, the filter input is the discontinuous term of the observer, $c_{0_i}\text{sign}(v_{1i})$. By denoting the output of the filter set of as $x_f \in \mathbb{R}^n$, and choosing a set of constants ω_{c_i} that minimizes the phase-delay, it is possible to assume

$$\lim_{t\to\infty} x_f = \tilde{\xi}(\cdot) \approx \xi(\cdot), \tag{18}$$

where $\|\tilde{\xi}(\cdot) - \xi(\cdot)\| \leq \tilde{\rho}$ for $\tilde{\rho} \ll \rho_0$.

3.2 An augmented, discontinuous observer

A way to circumvent the introduction of a filter is to use an augmented observer. To simplify the exposition, consider a 1-DOF whose tracking error equations have the form of system (5). An augmented observer is proposed to be

$$\begin{aligned}
\dot{\hat{e}}_1 &= w_1 + c_{21}(e_1 - \hat{e}_1),\\
\dot{w}_1 &= c_{11}(e_1 - \hat{e}_1) + c_{01}\text{sgn}(e_1 - \hat{e}_1),\\
\dot{\hat{e}}_2 &= w_2 + c_{22}(w_1 - \hat{e}_2) - K_p e_1 - K_v \hat{e}_2 + \Delta u,\\
\dot{w}_2 &= c_{12}(w_1 - \hat{e}_2) + c_{02}\text{sgn}(w_1 - \hat{e}_2).
\end{aligned} \tag{19}$$

If we denote the observation error as $\epsilon_1 = e_1 - \hat{e}_1$, $\epsilon_2 = e_2 - \hat{e}_2$, we arrive at

$$\begin{aligned}
\dot{\epsilon}_1 &= -c_{21}\epsilon_1 - w_1 + e_2,\\
\dot{w}_1 &= c_{11}\epsilon_1 + c_{01}\text{sgn}(\epsilon_1),\\
\dot{\epsilon}_2 &= -(K_v + c_{22})\epsilon_2 - w_2 - c_{22}(w_1 - e_2) + \xi,\\
\dot{w}_2 &= c_{12}(w_1 - e_2 + \epsilon_2) + c_{02}\text{sgn}(w_1 - e_2 + \epsilon_2).
\end{aligned} \tag{20}$$

A change of variables given by

$$\begin{aligned}
v_{11} &= \epsilon_1,\\
v_{12} &= -c_{21}\epsilon_1 - w_1 + e_2,
\end{aligned}$$

$$v_{21} = w_1 - e_2 + \epsilon_2,$$
$$v_{22} = \dot{v}_{21} = -c_{22}v_{21} - K_v\epsilon_2 + \dot{w}_1 - \dot{e}_2 - w_2 + \xi$$

converts the system to

$$\begin{aligned}
\dot{v}_{11} &= v_{12}, \\
\dot{v}_{12} &= -c_{11}v_{11} - c_{21}v_{12} - c_{01}\mathrm{sgn}(v_{11}) + \dot{e}_2, \\
\dot{v}_{21} &= v_{22}, \\
\dot{v}_{22} &= -\tilde{c}_{12}v_{21} - c_{22}v_{22} - c_{02}\mathrm{sgn}(v_{21}) + \tilde{\xi},
\end{aligned} \tag{21}$$

where $\tilde{c}_{12} = c_{12} - K_v c_{22}$ and $\tilde{\xi}$ is a disturbance term that we suppose bounded. Under some similar conditions discussed in the previous section, particularly the boundedness of $\dot{e}_2$ and $\tilde{\xi}$, we can assure the existence of positive constants c_{ij} such that v_{ij} converges to zero, so $\hat{e}_1$ converges to e_1, w_1 and $\hat{e}_2$ to e_2, and w_2 converges to the disturbance ξ. This observer Hence we propose to use the redesigned control Δu, or Δ_τ, as (see equation (5))

$$\Delta u = -w_2 \ \rightarrow -\xi, \quad \Delta_\tau = -M(\cdot)w_2$$

to attenuate the effect of disturbance ξ in system (5) or in system (1), respectively.

4. The controller

As we mentioned previously, we propose to use the nominal controller (4) because the velocity is not available from a measurement. We can use any of the observers previously described, and replace the velocity e_2 by its estimation, $\hat{e}_2$. The total control is then given by

$$\tau = \tau_0 + \Delta_\tau = -M(\cdot)\left[\nu + K_p e_1 + K_v\hat{e}_2 - \ddot{q}_r(t)\right] + C(\cdot)(\hat{e}_2 + \dot{q}_r) + G(\cdot), \tag{22}$$

where ν is the redesigned control. This control adjustment is proposed to be $\nu = x_f$, where x_f is the output of filter (17), if the first observer is used (system (8)), or $\nu = w_2$, where w_2 is the last state of system (19), if the second observer is chosen.
The overall structure is shown in figure 1 when the first observer is used.
A similar structure is used for the second observer. An important remark is that the nominal control law (a PD-controller with compensation of nonlinearities in this case) can be chosen independently; the analysis can be performed in a similar way. However, this nominal controller must provide an adequate performance such that the state trajectories remain bounded.

5. Control of mechanical systems

To illustrate the performance of the proposed control structure we describe in this section its application to control some mechanical systems, a Mass-Spring-Damper (MSD), an industrial robot, and two coupled mechanical systems which we want them to work synchronized.

5.1 An MSD system

This example illustrates the application of the first observer (equation (8), Section 3.1).
Consider the MSD system shown in figure 2. Its dynamical model is given by equation (1),

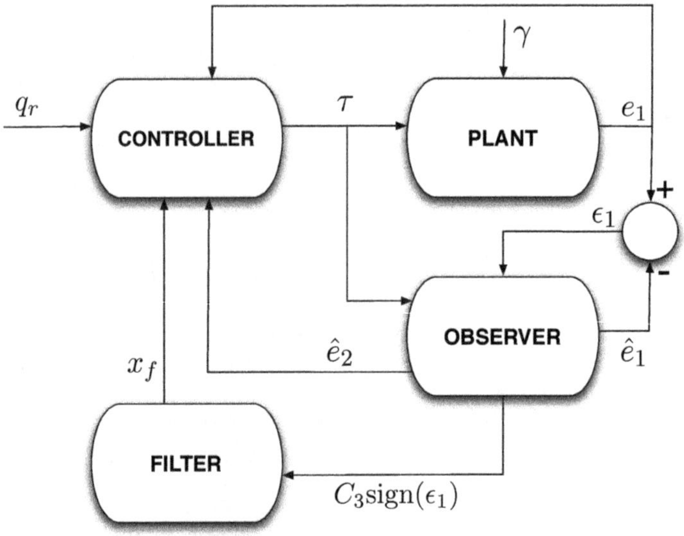

Fig. 1. The robust control structure.

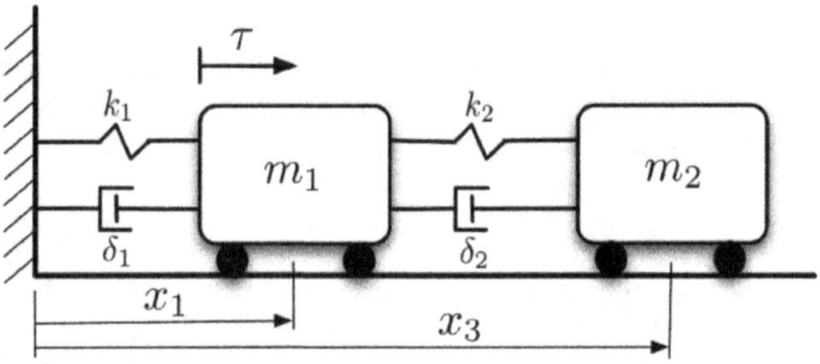

Fig. 2. Mass-spring-damper mechanical system.

with

$$M = \begin{pmatrix} m_1 & 0 \\ 0 & m_2 \end{pmatrix}, \quad C = \begin{pmatrix} \delta_1 + \delta_2 & -\delta_2 \\ -\delta_2 & \delta_2 \end{pmatrix}, \quad G = \begin{pmatrix} (k_1 + k_2)x_1 - k_2 x_3 \\ k_2(x_3 - x_1) \end{pmatrix}, \quad u = \begin{pmatrix} \tau \\ 0 \end{pmatrix},$$

where $x_1 = q_1$, $x_3 = q_2$. Consider that parameters k_i, δ_i, and m_i, for $i = 1,2$, are known. Note also that the system is underactuated, and only one control input is driving the system at mass m_1. Therefore, we aim to control the position of mass 1 (x_1), and consider that the action of the second mass is a disturbance. Hence, the model of the controlled system is again given by equation (1), but now with $M = m_1$, $C = \delta_1$, $G = k_1 q$. If we denote $x_1 = q$, $x_2 = \dot{q}$, and $x = (x_1, x_2, x_3, x_4) = (x_1, \dot{x}_1, x_3, \dot{x}_3)$ (see figure 2), then

$$\Gamma(x, \dot{x}; \theta) = \Phi(x, \dot{x})\theta + \gamma = k_2(x_1 - x_3) + \delta_2(x_2 - x_4),$$

where x_3 and x_4 are the solutions of the system

$$\dot{x}_3 = x_4,$$
$$\dot{x}_4 = -\frac{k_2}{m_2}(x_3 - x_1) - \frac{\delta_2}{m_2}(x_4 - x_2),$$

groups the effect of uncertainty and disturbance terms $\Phi\theta + \gamma$ of equation (1).
Now denote as $e_1 = x_1 - q_r$, $\hat{e}_2 = \hat{x}_2 - \dot{q}_r$, then the nominal control input τ_0 is proposed as equation (3), that is,

$$\tau_0 = -m_1 \left[K_p e_1 + K_v \hat{e}_2 - \ddot{q}_r(t)\right] + k_1 x_1 + \delta_1 \hat{x}_2, \tag{23}$$

where K_p and K_v are positive constants. Because the velocity is not measured, in (23) we have used the estimation $\hat{x}_2 = \hat{e}_2 + \dot{q}_r$, delivered by the observer given by (8).
With an adequate selection of the constants K_p and K_v we can guarantee that the perturbation $\Gamma(\cdot)$ in (1) is bounded (see Section 2 and (Khalil, 2002)). Therefore, from equation (16), $u_{eq} = \Gamma(\cdot)$.
Using the filter (17), we can recover an estimation of the disturbance, denoted as x_f. Therefore, the redesigned control will be $\Delta_\tau = m_1 x_f$ which, added to (23), adjusts the nominal control input to attenuate the effect of the disturbance Γ.
A numerical simulation was performed with plant parameter values $k_1 = 10\left[k_g m/sec^2\right]$, $k_2 = 20\left[k_g m/sec^2\right]$, $\delta_1 = \delta_2 = 0.1\left[k_g m/sec\right]$, $m_1 = 1\left[kg\right]$, and $m_2 = 4\left[kg\right]$. The observer parameter values were set to $c_1 = 2$, $c_2 = 2$, and $c_0 = 3$, with controller gains $K_p = K_v = 10$, and filter frequencies $\omega_c = 500[rad/sec]$. In this simulation the nominal control τ_0 was applied from 0 to 15 sec. The additional control term Δ_τ is activated from 15 to 30 sec. The aim is to track the reference signal $q_r(t) = 0.25\sin(t)$.
Figure 3 shows the response of this controlled system.
Figures a) and b) show the convergence of the observer state to the plant state, in spite of disturbances produced by the mass m_2. Figure c) shows the disturbance identified by this observer. The response of the closed-loop system is presented in Figures d), e), and f). Here we see a tracking error when the additional control term Δ_τ is not present (from 0 to 15 seconds). However, when this term is incorporated to the control signal, at $t = 15$ sec, the tracking error tends to zero. It is important to note that, contrary to typical sliding mode controllers, the control input (Figure 3.f) does not contain high frequency components of large amplitude.

5.2 An industrial robot

This is an example of the application of the first observer (Section 3.1) to a real system.
In this section we show the application of the described technique to control the first two joints of a Selective Compliant Assembly Robot Arm (SCARA), shown in figure 4, used in the manufacturing industry, and manufactured by Sony®.
In this experiment we have an extreme situation because all parameters are unknown. The control algorithm was programed in a PC using the Matlab® software, and the control signals are applied to the robot via a data acquisition card for real-time PC-based applications, the DSpace® 1104. The desired trajectory, which was the same for both joints, is a sinusoidal signal given by $q_r(t) = \sin(t)$.

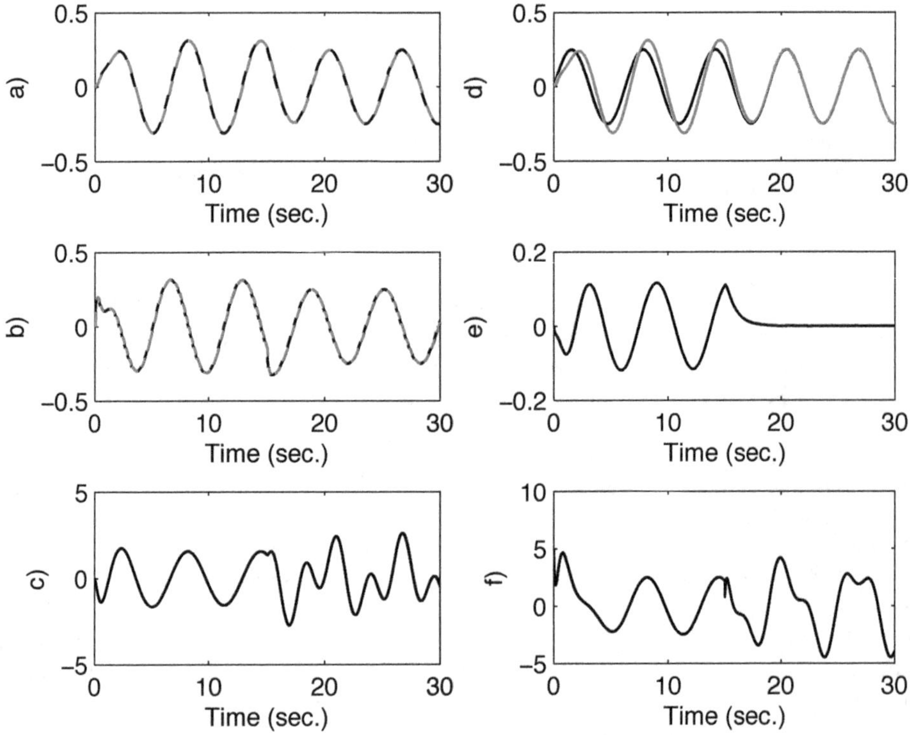

Fig. 3. Response of the closed-loop MSD system. a) x_1 (red) and $\hat{x}_1 = \hat{e}_1 + q_r$ (black); b) x_2 (red) and $\hat{x}_2 = \hat{e}_2 + \dot{q}_r$ (black), c) identified disturbance, x_f, d) reference q_r (black) and position x_1 (red); e) error $e_1 = x_1 - q_r$; f) control $\tau = \tau_0 + \Delta_\tau$.

In the design of the observer (8) the following matrices were selected,

$$C_0 = \begin{bmatrix} 300 & 0 \\ 0 & 300 \end{bmatrix}, \quad C_1 = C_2 = \begin{bmatrix} 25 & 0 \\ 0 & 25 \end{bmatrix}, \quad M^{-1} = \begin{bmatrix} 55.549 & 0 \\ 0 & 55.549 \end{bmatrix}.$$

A cut-off frequency $\omega_{ci} = 75$ rad/seg was selected for the filter(17). The control law is given by the controller (22), where

$$K_p = \begin{bmatrix} 668 & 0 \\ 0 & 391 \end{bmatrix}, K_v = \begin{bmatrix} 379 & 0 \\ 0 & 49 \end{bmatrix}.$$

Note that a nominal value of matrix M was used. Differences between nominal and the actual matrix $M(q)$ are supposed to be included in the perturbation term, as well as the Coriolis, centrifugal, and friction forces, external disturbances, parametric variations and coupling effects.

The perturbation terms $\xi_i(\cdot)$ for $i = 1, 2$ that correspond to perturbations present in the two joints are displayed in Figure 5.

Fig. 4. A SCARA industrial robot.

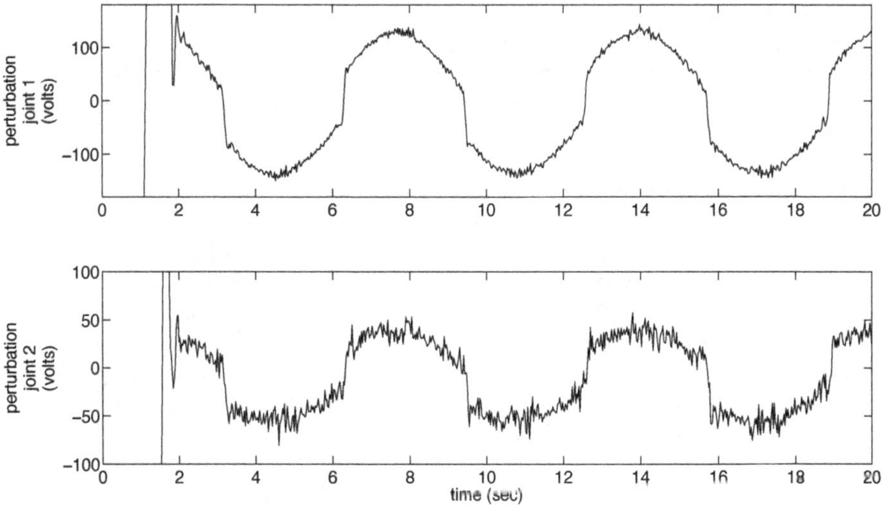

Fig. 5. Identified perturbation terms in the joints of an industrial robot. Up: joint 1 perturbation. Down: joint 2 perturbation.

To verify the observer performance, the observation errors $e_i = \theta_i - \hat{\theta}_i$, for $i = 1, 2$, are displayed in Figure 6, showing small steady-state values.

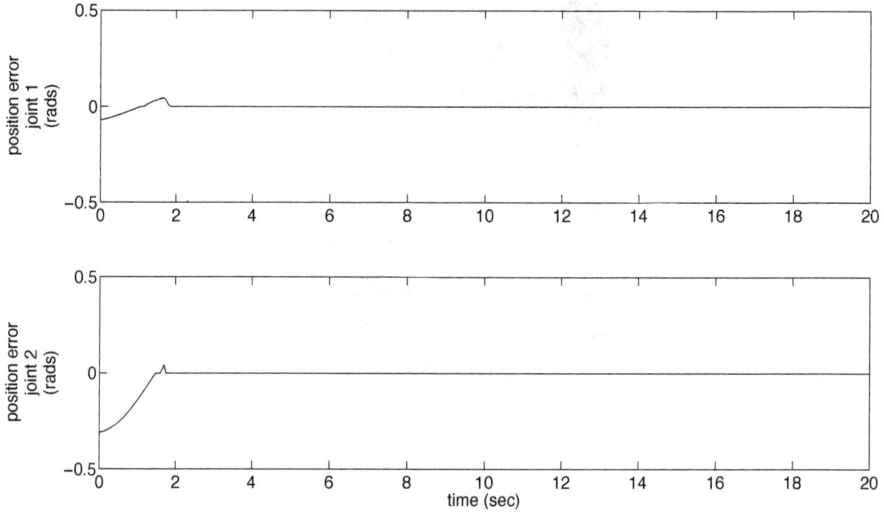

Fig. 6. Observation position errors of the industrial robot.

Figure 7 shows the system output and the reference. Control inputs for joints 1 and 2 are displayed in Figure 8.
Although these control inputs exhibit high frequency components with small amplitude, they do not produce harmful effects on the robot. Also, it is interesting to note that the control input levels remain in the dynamic range allowed by the robot driver, that is, between −12 V and +12 V.

5.3 Two synchronized mechanical systems

This example illustrates the practical performance of the proposed technique, using the augmented observer given by (19). It refers to a basic problem of synchronization.
Synchronization means correlated or corresponding-in-time behavior of two or more processes (Arkady et al., 2003). In some situations the synchronization is a natural phenomenon; in others, an interconnection system is needed to obtain a synchronized behavior or improve its transient characteristics. Hence, the synchronization becomes a control objective and the synchronization obtained in this way is called controlled synchronization (Blekhman et al., 1997). Some important works in this topic are given by (Dong & Mills, 2002; Rodriguez & Nijmeijer, 2004; Soon-Jo & Slotine, 2007).
In this subsection we present a simple application of the control technique to synchronize two mechanisms connected in the basic configuration, called master-slave (see figure 9).
The master system is the MSD described in Section 5.1, manufactured by the company ECP®, model 210, with only the first mass activated. The slave is a torsional system from the same company, with the first and third disks connected. The master sends its position x to the slave, and the synchronization objective is to make the slave track the master state, that is, the

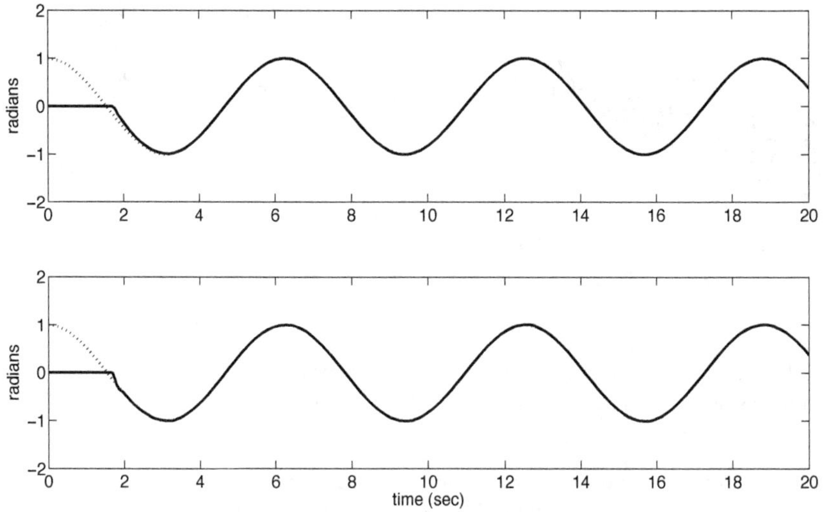

Fig. 7. Reference signal (dotted line) and position (solid line) for each joint of the industrial robot. Up: joint 1. Down: joint 2.

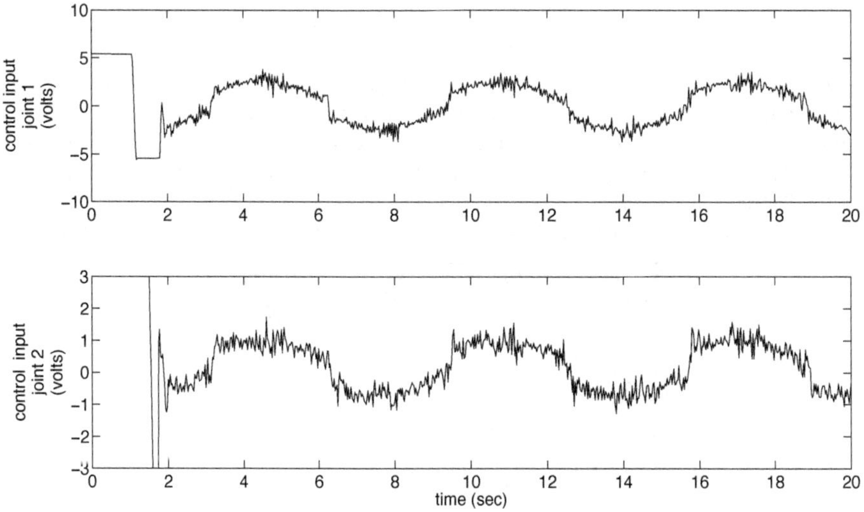

Fig. 8. Control input for each joint of the industrial robot.

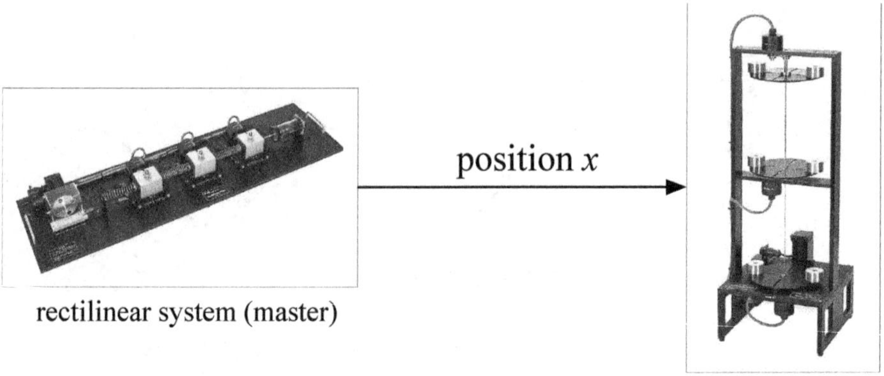

Fig. 9. Two synchronized mechanisms in a master/slave configuration. The master is the rectilinear system, model 210, from ECP®. The slave is the torsional system, model 205, from the same company.

angular position θ and velocity $\dot{\theta}$ of the torsional system must follow the position x and the velocity $\dot{x}$ of the master, respectively. The relation between the two states is 1cm of the master corresponds to 1rad of the slave.
The rectilinear system is modeled by

$$m\ddot{x} + c_m\dot{x} + k_m x + \gamma_m(t) = F(t),$$

where x is the position of the mass; m, c_m, and k_m are the mass, damping, and spring coefficients, respectively, and F is an external force driving the system. The torsional system is described as

$$J\ddot{\theta}_1 + c_t\dot{\theta}_1 + k_t(\theta_1 - \theta_2) + \gamma_t(t) = \tau_0 + \Delta_\tau,$$

where θ_1 and θ_2 are the angular positions of the first and third disks, respectively; J, c_t, and k_t are the inertia, damping, and spring coefficients of the first disk. γ_m and γ_t are external disturbances possibly affecting the systems. The force driving the MSD system is set as $F(t) = 1.5\sin(1.5\pi t)$. All positions are available, but the velocities are estimated with the second observer (19) (see Section 3.2).
The nominal values of the coefficients are given in Table 1.

System	Parameter	Value	Units
MSD	m	1.27	kg
	k_m	200	N/m
	c_m	2.1	N/m/sec
Torsional	J	0.0108	Kg-m^2
	c_t	0.007	N-m/rad/sec
	k_t	1.37	N-m/rad
Observer	$c_{11}, c_{12}, c_{21}, c_{22}$	500	
	c_{01}	50	
	c_{02}	100	

Table 1. Parameter values for the synchronization example.

If we define the synchronization error as

$$e_1 = x - \theta, \quad e_2 = \dot{x} - \dot{\theta},$$

the control objective es to make $e = (e_1, e_2)$ converge to zero.
Let us consider the nominal control

$$\tau_0 = -J(k_p e_1 + k_v \hat{e}_2) + c_t \hat{\dot{\theta}}_1 + k_t \theta_1 - k_t \theta_2,$$

where $\hat{\dot{\theta}}_1$ and $\hat{e}_2$ are the estimated velocity and the estimated velocity error obtained from the observer. From the last equations it is possible to get the synchronization error dynamics as

$$\begin{aligned}\dot{e}_1 &= e_2 \\ \dot{e}_2 &= -k_p e_1 - k_v e_2 + \Delta u - \xi,\end{aligned}$$

where $\Delta u = J^{-1} \Delta_\tau$ and

$$\xi = (Jc_t - k_v)\epsilon_2 + J^{-1}\gamma_t(t) - m^{-1}\left(c_m \dot{x} + k_m x - F(t) + \gamma_m(t)\right),$$

with $\epsilon_2 = e_2 - \hat{e}_2$.
We have then formulated this synchronization problem in the same framework allowing us to design a robust controller. Therefore, we can use one of the observers described previously, and use a redesign control $\Delta_\tau = J\hat{\xi}$.
We describe the results obtained from this controller to synchronize these devices. Figure 10 shows its performance, using the augmented observer (19).

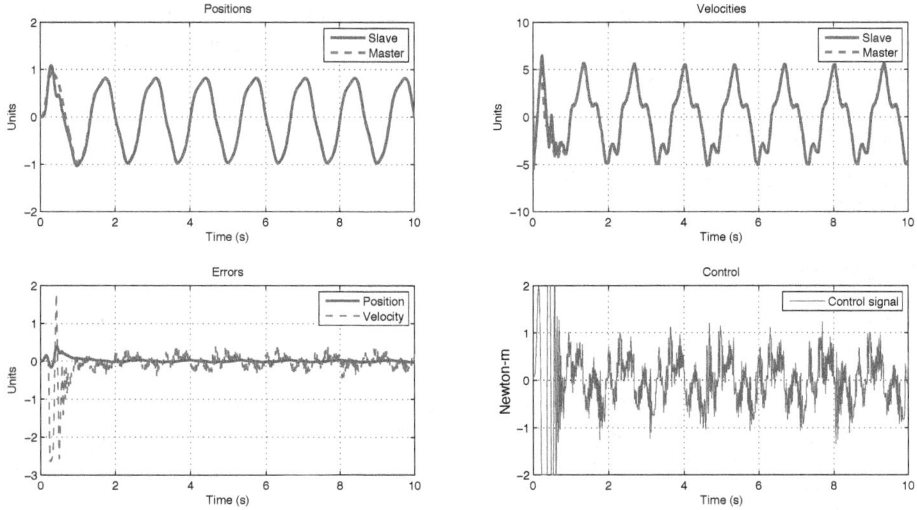

Fig. 10. Responses of the synchronized mechanisms (Figure 9). One unit corresponds to 1 cm (1 rad) for the position, or 1 cm/sec (1 rad/sec) for the velocity, of the master (slave) system.

This figure shows how the slave (torsional) system synchronizes with the master (rectilinear) system in about 1 sec. In 2 sec the synchronization error (position and velocity) is very small.

The control input designed for the slave is saturated at ± 2 N-m, and after 1 sec maintains its values between -1 and $+1$ N-m. This is accomplished even under the presence of the disturbance introduced by the third disk, which is not modeled.

6. Conclusions

A robust control structure for uncertain Lagrangian systems with partial measurement of the state has been presented. This control structure allows us to solve tracking and regulation problems and guarantees the convergence to a small neighborhood of the reference signal, in spite of nonvanishing disturbances affecting the plant.

This technique makes use of robust, discontinuous observers with a simple structure. An important property of these observers is its ability to estimate the disturbances acting on the plant, which can be conveniently incorporated in the control signal to increase the robustness of the controller and decrease the steady-state tracking error. The observer structure can even be built with conventional analog circuits, as it is described in (Alvarez et al., 2009). An adequate tuning of the observer parameters guarantees the convergence to the reference signal in an operation region large enough to cover practical situations.

The numerical simulations and the experimental results described in this chapter exhibited a good performance of the proposed technique, and the control signal showed values inside practical ranges.

An interesting and important problem that has been intensively studied recently is the synchronization of dynamical systems. Synchronization of mechanical systems is important as soon as two or more mechanical systems have to cooperate. The control technique described in this chapter has been applied to the simplest configuration, that is, the master/slave synchronization, exhibiting a good performance. This same control strategy, based on robust observers, can be also successfully applied to synchronize arrays of mechanical systems, connected in diverse configurations. A more detailed application can be found in (Alvarez et al., 2010).

7. Acknowledgement

We thank Jonatan Peña and David A. Hernandez for performing the experiments of Section 5.2 and 5.3.

8. References

Aguilar, R. & Maya, R. (2005), State estimation for nonlinear systems under model uncertainties: a class of sliding-mode observers, J. Process Contr. Vol. (15): 363-370.

Alvarez, J., Rosas, D. & Peña, J. (2009), Analog implementation of a robust control strategy for mechanical systems, IEEE Trans. Ind. Electronics, Vol. (56), No. 9: 3377-3385.

Alvarez, J., Rosas, D., Hernandez, D. & Alvarez, E. (2010), Robust synchronization of arrays of Lagrangian systems, Int. J. of Control, Automation, and Systems, Vol. (8), No. 5:1039-1047.

Arkady, P., Michael, R. & Kurths, J. (2003), Synchronization. A Universal Concept in Nonlinear Sciences, Cambridge Press: Cambridge.

Bartolini, G., Ferrara, A. & Usani, E. (1998), Chattering avoidance by second-order sliding mode control, IEEE Trans. Aut. Ctl. Vol. (43), No. 2: 241-246.

Blekhman, I. I., Fradkov, A. L., Nijmeijer, H. & A. Y. Pogromsky, (1997) On self-synchronization and controlled synchronization, Systems & Control Letters. (31): 299-305.

Brogliato, B., Niculescu, S. I. & Orhant, P. (1997), On the control of finite-dimensional mechanical systems with unilateral constraints, IEEE Trans. Aut. Ctl., Vol. (42), No. 2: 200-215.

Curk, B. & Jezernik, K. (2001), Sliding mode control with perturbation estimation: Application on DD robot mechanism, Robot. Vol. (19): 641-648.

Davila, J., Fridman, L. & Poznyak, A. (2006), Observation and identification of mechanical systems via second order sliding modes, Int. J. Control, Vol. (79), No. 10: 1251-1262.

Dong, S. & Mills, J. K. (2002), Adaptive synchronize control for coordination of multirobot assembly tasks, IEEE Trans. on Robotics and Automation, Vol. (18), No. 4: 498-510.

Erbatur, K., & Calli, B. (2007), Fuzzy boundary layer tuning as applied to the control of a direct drive robot, in Proc. IECON: 2858–2863.

Erbatur, K., Okyay, M. & Sabanovic, A. (1999), A study on robustness property of sliding-mode controllers: A novel design and experimental investigations, IEEE Trans. Ind. Electron., Vol. (46), no. 5: 1012–1018.

Isidori, A., &Astolfi, A. (1992), Disturbance attenuation and H U221e control via measurement feedback in nonlinear systems, IEEE Trans. Aut. Ctl., Vol. (37), No. 9: 1283-1293.

Khalil, H. (2002) Nonlinear Systems, New Jersey: Prentice Hall.

Makkar, C., Hu, G., Sawyer, W. G. & Dixon, W. E. (2007), Lyapunov-based tracking control in the presence of uncertain nonlinear parametrizable friction, IEEE Trans. Aut. Ctl., Vol (52), No. 10: 1988-1994.

Orlov, I. (2000), Sliding mode observer-based synthesis of state derivative-free model reference adaptive control of distributed parameter systems, J. Dyn. Syst-T ASME, Vol. (122), No. 4: 725-731.

Paden, B. & Panja, R. (1988). Globally asymptotically stable PD+ controller for robot manipulators, Int. J. Control Vol (47), No. 6: 1697–1712.

Patre, P. M., MacKunis, W., Makkar, C. & Dixon, W. E. (2008), Asymptotic tracking for systems with structured and unstructured uncertainties, IEEE Trans. Control Syst. Technol., Vol. (16), No. 2: 373-379.

Perruquetti, W. & Barbot, J. (Eds), (2002), Sliding Mode Control in Engineering, New York: Marcel Dekker.

Pushkin, K. (1999), Existence of solutions to a class of nonlinear convergent chattering free sliding mode control systems, IEEE Trans. Aut. Ctl., Vol. (44), No. 8: 1620-1624.

Rodriguez, A. & Nijmeijer, H. (2004), Mutual synchronization of robots via estimated state feedback: a cooperative approach, IEEE Trans. on Control Systems Technology, Vol. (12), No. 4: 542-554.

Rosas, D., Alvarez, J. & Fridman, L. (2006), Robust observation and identification of nDOF Lagrangian systems, Int. J. Robust Nonlin., Vol. (17): 842-861.

Rosas, D., Alvarez, J. & Peña, J. (2010), Control structure with disturbance identification for Lagrangian systems, Int. J. Non-Linear Mech., doi:10.1016/j.ijnonlinmec.2010.08.005.

Sciavicco, L. & Siciliano, B. (2000) Modelling and Control of Robots Manipulators, London: Springer-Verlag.

Sellami, A., Arzelier, D., M'hiri, R. & Zrida, J. (2007), A sliding mode control approach for systems subjected to a norm-bounded uncertainty, Int. J. Robust Nonlin., Vol. (17): 327-346.

Slotine, J. J. & Li, W. (1988). Adaptive manipulator control: A case study, IEEE Trans. Aut. Ctl., Vol. (33): 995-1003.

Soon-Jo, C & Slotine, E. (2007). Cooperative robot control and synchronization of Lagrangian systems, in Proc. 46th IEEE Conference on Decision and Control, New Orleans.

Spong, M. W. & Vidyasagar, M. (1989), Robot Dynamics and Control, New York: Wiley.

Takegaki, M. & Arimoto, S. (1981). A new feedback method for dynamic control manipulators, J. Dyn. Syst. Trans. ASME, Vol (103): 119–125.

Utkin, V. (1992), Sliding Modes in Control and Optimization, New York: Springer-Verlag.

Utkin, V., Guldner, J. & Shi, J. (1999), Sliding Mode Control in Electromechanical Systems, London, U.K.: Taylor & Francis.

Veluvolu, K., Soh, Y. & Cao, W. (2007), Robust observer with sliding mode estimation for nonlinear uncertain systems, IET Control Theory A., Vol. (5): 1533-1540.

Xin, X. J., Jun, P. Y. & Heng, L. T. (2004), Sliding mode control whith closed-loop filtering architecture for a class of nonlinear systems, IEEE T. Circuits-1, Vol. (51), No. 4: 168-173.

Wang, X. & Yang, G. (2007), Equivalent sliding mode control based on nonlinear observer for nonlinear non-minimum-phase systems, J. Dyn. Control. Syst., Vol. (13), No. 1: 25-36.

Weibing, G. & Hung, J. C., (1993), Variable structure control of nonlinear systems: A new approach, IEEE Trans. Ind. Electronics, Vol. (40), No. 1: 45-55.

Wen, J. & Bayard, D. (1988). New class of control law for robotic manipulators. Part 1: non-adaptive case, Int. J. Control, Vol (47), No. 5: 1361–1385.

Yaz, E. & Azemi, A. (1994), Robust/adaptive observers for systems having uncertain functions with unknown bounds, Proc. 1994 American Control Conference, Vol. (1): 73-74.

Yuzhuo, W. & Flashner, H., (1998), On sliding mode control of uncertain mechanical systems, in Proc. IEEE Aerosp. Conf., Aspen, CO, 85–92.

8

Discussion on Robust Control Applied to Active Magnetic Bearing Rotor System

Rafal P. Jastrzebski[1], Alexander Smirnov[1], Olli Pyrhönen[1] and Adam K. Piłat[2]

[1]*Dept. of Electrical Engineering, LUT Energy, Lappeenranta University of Technology*
[2]*Dept. of Automatics, AGH University of Science and Technology, Krakow*
[1]*Finland*
[2]*Poland*

1. Introduction

Since the 1980s, a stream of papers has appeared on system uncertainties and robust control. The robust control relies on $\mathcal{H}_\infty$ control and μ synthesis rather than previously favored linear-quadratic Gaussian control. However, highly mathematical techniques have been difficult to apply without dedicated tools. The new methods have been consolidated in the practical applications with the appearance of software toolboxes, such as Robust Control Toolbox from Matlab. This chapter focuses on the application of this toolbox to the active magnetic bearing (AMB) suspension system for high-speed rotors.

AMBs are employed in high-speed rotating machines such as turbo compressors, flywheels, machine tools, molecular pumps, and others (Schweitzer & Maslen, 2009). The support of rotors using an active magnetic field instead of mechanical forces of the fluid film, contact rolling element, or ball bearings enables high-speed operation and lower friction losses. Other major advantages of AMBs include no lubrication, long life, programmable stiffness and damping, built-in monitoring and diagnostics, and availability of automatic balancing. However, AMB rotor system forms an open-loop unstable, multiple-input multiple-output (MIMO) coupled plant with uncertain dynamics that can change over time and that can vary significantly at different rotational speeds. In practical systems, the sensors are not collocated with the actuators, and therefore, the plant cannot always be easily decoupled. Additionally, the control systems face a plethora of external disturbances.

The major drawback of an AMB technology is a difficulty in designing a high-performance reliable control and its implementation. For such systems, the μ and $\mathcal{H}_\infty$ control approaches offer useful tools for designing a robust control (Moser, 1993; Zhou et al., 1996).

The high-performance and high-precision control for the nominal plant without uncertainties can be realized by using model-based, high-order controllers. In the case of control synthesis, which is based on the uncertain plant model, there is a tradeoff between the nominal performance (time- and frequency-domain specifications) and the robustness. The modeled uncertainties cannot be too conservative or otherwise obtaining practical controllers might be not feasible (Sawicki & Maslen, 2008). Moreover, too complex uncertainty models lead to increased numerical complexity in the control synthesis. The models applied for the control

synthesis of AMBs can vary from a point mass (Oliveira et al., 2006) to very complex MIMO plants (Li, Lin, Allaire & Luo, 2006).
The literature presents different weighting or interconnection design schemes. Each of the schemes has its contradictive objectives and tradeoffs. For the point mass levitated systems, the load uncertainty is typically applied. As an example, Li, Lin, Allaire & Luo (2006) present an $\mathbf{S}/\mathbf{T}/\mathbf{KS}$ scheme, where the $\mathbf{S}$, $\mathbf{T}$, $\mathbf{K}$, and $\mathbf{G}$ are the sensitivity, complementary sensitivity, controller, and plant transfer functions. The corresponding weights are tuned using engineering judgment and manual trial and error simulations. Losch (2002) splits the available design schemes to signal-based and the loop-shaping schemes. The signal-based schemes are considered to be more complex and conservative. The loop-shaping schemes, for example, discussed by Losch (2002) include $\mathbf{KS}/\mathbf{SG}/\mathbf{T}$ for the control of the rigid rotor and $\mathbf{KS}/\mathbf{SG}/\mathbf{T}/\mathbf{S}$ for the control of the flexible rotor. Another loop-shaping procedure is developed by Glover & McFarlane (1989). It applies robust stabilization of normalized coprime factorization of the plant using two weights: pre- and post-compensators. Skogestad & Postlethwaite (2005) give a general recommendation on the selection of these weights.
This chapter reviews different weighting schemes for building the robust control of AMB systems. The presentation starts with the point mass levitation and then undertakes non-gyroscopic and gyroscopic coupled AMB rotor systems. The aim of the robust control is to stabilize the rotor suspension independently to the assumed uncertainties. The robustness must be satisfied in the full range of the operating frequencies and for the selected range of the state variables. The work studies how to select the optimal control weighting functions for selected schemes based on genetic algorithms and experimental data obtained from the test rig. The Linear Parameter-Varying (LPV) technique is applied to suppress the influence of the variable rotational speed on the plant dynamics, thus reducing the uncertainty set. The real-time controller operating conditions are considered. The nonlinear simulations of the synthesized controllers and the accurate plant models in Simulink are compared with experimental results.

2. Suspension of the point mass

2.1 Introduction

The main component of the AMB system is an electromagnet that is used for the levitation purposes to keep the ferromagnetic object (e.g. rotor) levitated. The electromagnetic force value is controlled by the coil current steered by the external regulator. The introduction to the robust control is described by the example of Active Magnetic Suspension (AMS), which is also referred as Active Magnetic Levitation (AML). The robust approach can be applied to the uncertainty of the electromagnetic actuator and the levitated object mass. The controller synthesis and experiments are devoted to the MLS2EM (InTeCo, 2008) system (see Fig. 1) that extends the standard single electromagnet AML and represents one axis of the typical four horse-shoe AMB configuration.

2.2 Why robust control is required

In the classical state-feedback control approach for locally linearized AML model (Pilat, 2002) the mass uncertainty affects the control quality and object position. For the designed state-feedback controller with different closed-loop properties the 90 % mass perturbation has been introduced and presented with Bode diagrams in Fig. 2. One can find the influence of the mass change on the phase and amplitude depending on the designed controller properties.

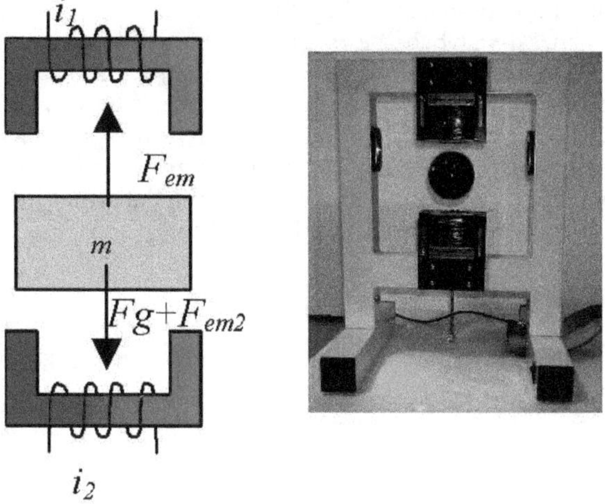

Fig. 1. Dual electromagnet Active Magnetic Levitation System - concept and test-rig.

The closed-loop characteristics remain unchanged due to the fixed and non-robust structure of the controller.

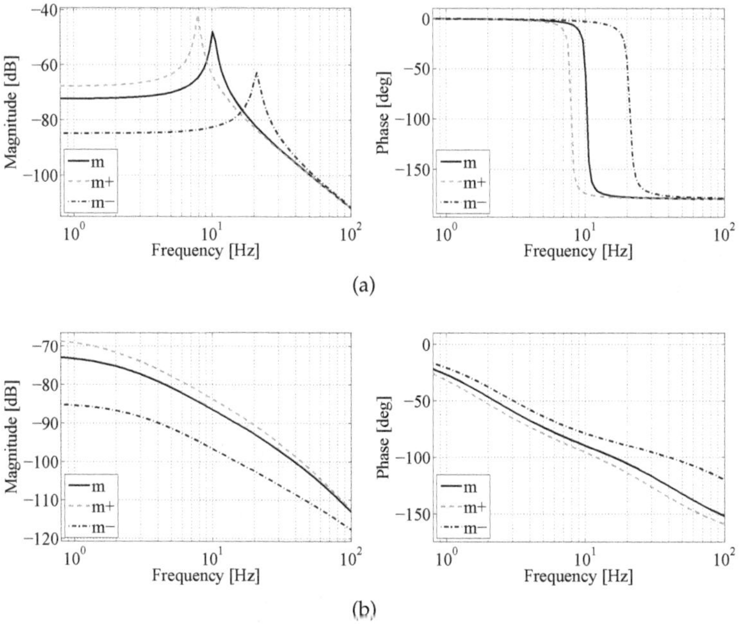

Fig. 2. Influence on the mass perturbation for the state feedback controller: a) for k = 250 $\mathrm{N\,m^{-1}}$, c = 0.2 $\mathrm{N\,s\,m^{-1}}$, b) for for k = 250 $\mathrm{N\,m^{-1}}$, c = 20 $\mathrm{N\,s\,m^{-1}}$.

The robust controller can be realized in the intelligent form by the application of the Fuzzy-Logic approach (Pilat & Turnau, 2005), where the controller is pre-tuned and optimized at the modelling and simulation stage, or by the application of an on-line adopted neural network (Pilat & Turnau, 2009), where the weights and biases are updated while the real-time control is pending. Another approach is based on the linear control theory and parameter uncertainty. Some applications to the magnetic levitation and bearing systems can be found in (Fujita et al., 1995; Gosiewski & Mystkowski, 2008; Mystkowski & Gosiewski, 2009). The following section will present a robust controller design to stabilize the levitated object independently to its mass uncertainty. More detailed, simulation results and comparison to the state feedback controller can be found in (Pilat, 2010).

2.3 AML modelling and control

2.3.1 Nonlinear and linear AML model

The open loop structurally unstable model of the current driven single electromagnet AML (Pilat, 2009) is given by Equation (1).

$$\ddot{x_1} = -K_{em} \frac{(i_0 + i)^2}{m(x_{10} + x_1)^2} + g, \tag{1}$$

where: x_1 - object displacement with respect to the x_{10} [m], x_{10} - nominal object distance from the electromagnet surface [m] (x_1>0), x_2 - object velocity [m s^{-1}], m - object mass [kg], g - gravity acceleration [m s^{-2}], K_{em} - actuator constant describing its construction [N m^2 A^{-2}], i - coil current [A], i_0 nominal coil current for the object distance x_{10}. This research will use the laboratory setup (Fig. 1b) characterized by the following parameter values: m = 0.056 kg, K_{em} = 5.594·10^{-5} N m^2 A^{-2}. By analyzing the nonlinear model one can observe that the variable mass affects the system dynamics so that heavier objects require an increase in the coil current when the actuator construction remains the same. It means that the controller should react to the variable load using the robustness property. The steady-state coil current depends on the nominal object distance and the levitated object mass and the actuator design 2.

$$i_0(x_{10}, m) = x_{10}\sqrt{mgK_{em}^{-1}}. \tag{2}$$

One can notice that the mass variation with respect to the nominal object mass is a source of demand for the coil current change. This should be satisfied automatically by the controller. To perform the controller synthesis for a chosen object position a linear model is required. The nonlinear model is linearized in the steady-state point $\boldsymbol{x}_0 = [0\ 0]^T$ resulting in the linear model in the form $\dot{\boldsymbol{x}} = \mathbf{A}\boldsymbol{x} + \mathbf{B}\boldsymbol{u}$, where:

$$\mathbf{A} = \begin{bmatrix} 0 & 1 \\ m^{-1}\alpha_0 & 0 \end{bmatrix}, \quad \mathbf{B} = \begin{bmatrix} 0 \\ m^{-1}\beta_0 \end{bmatrix} \tag{3}$$

with: $\alpha_0 = 2K_{em}i_0^2x_{10}^{-3}$ kg s^{-2}, $\beta_0 = -2K_{em}i_0x_{10}^{-2}$ kg m A^{-1} s^{-2}.

2.3.2 Robust controller design

The $\mathcal{H}_2$, $\mathcal{H}_\infty$ and μ-synthesis theory allows to perform an analysis and synthesis of the robust control systems (Battachatyya et al., 1995; Gu et al., 2005a; Kwakernaak, 1993; 2002) in the case of model-system uncertainties and perturbations. In the AML, the exact physical value of the levitated object mass is not known, but can be measured before an experiment. When applying the AML in real applications the mass value can vary. It can be assumed that the mass value is known with a certain, known interval. Thus, we can represent the mass as follows:

$$m = \overline{m}(1 + p_{\mathrm{m}}\delta_{\mathrm{m}}), \tag{4}$$

where $\overline{m}$ is the nominal value of m, and p_{m} and δ_{m} represent the relative perturbation on the object mass. The $\delta_{\mathrm{m}} \in [-1, 1]$ allows to perturb the mass vs. nominal value with a given ratio $p_{\mathrm{m}} \in [0, 1]$ corresponding to the percentage uncertainty. Let G_{ML0} denote the open-loop dynamics of the AMS taking into account the uncertainty of the levitated object mass. Thus, the AMS dynamics is given in the following form:

$$\begin{bmatrix} \dot{x}_1 \\ \dot{x}_2 \\ y_{\mathrm{m}} \\ y \end{bmatrix} = \mathbf{G}_{\mathrm{ML0}} \begin{bmatrix} x_1 \\ x_2 \\ u_{\mathrm{m}} \\ u \end{bmatrix}, \tag{5}$$

where:

$$\mathbf{G}_{\mathrm{ML0}} = \begin{bmatrix} \mathbf{A} & \mathbf{B}_1 & \mathbf{B}_2 \\ \mathbf{C}_1 & \mathbf{D}_1 & \mathbf{0} \\ \mathbf{C}_2 & \mathbf{D}_2 & \mathbf{0} \end{bmatrix}, \mathbf{A} = \begin{bmatrix} 0 & 1 \\ \overline{m}^{-1}\alpha_0 & 0 \end{bmatrix}, \mathbf{B}_1 = \begin{bmatrix} 0 \\ -p_{\mathrm{m}} \end{bmatrix}, \mathbf{B}_2 = \begin{bmatrix} 0 \\ \overline{m}^{-1}\beta_0 \end{bmatrix}, \tag{6}$$

$$\mathbf{C}_1 = \begin{bmatrix} \overline{m}^{-1}\alpha_0 \; 0 \end{bmatrix}, \mathbf{C}_2 = \begin{bmatrix} 1 \; 0 \end{bmatrix}, \mathbf{D}_1 = -p_{\mathrm{m}}, \mathbf{D}_2 = \overline{m}^{-1}\beta_0.$$

Note that the G_{ML0} depends only on the nominal AML parameters and the possible perturbation of a nominal object mass. The objective is to design the robust feedback controller $K(s)$ applied in the form:

$$u(s) = K(s)y(s). \tag{7}$$

The stability (8) of the nominal plant model as well as closed-loop robust stability (9) must be fulfilled.

$$\left\| \begin{bmatrix} W_p(1 + \mathbf{G}_{\mathrm{ML0}}K)^{-1} \\ W_u K(1 + \mathbf{G}_{\mathrm{ML0}}K)^{-1} \end{bmatrix} \right\|_{\infty} < 1 \tag{8}$$

$$\left\| \begin{bmatrix} W_p(1 + F_u(\mathbf{G}_{\mathrm{ML0}}, \delta_{\mathrm{m}})K)^{-1} \\ W_u K(1 + F_u(\mathbf{G}_{\mathrm{ML0}}, \delta_{\mathrm{m}})K)^{-1} \end{bmatrix} \right\|_{\infty} < 1 \tag{9}$$

The closed loop system with the designed controller, mass uncertainty and added weighting functions is presented in Fig. 3. The performance criterion is to have transfer functions from d to e_p and e_u small in the sense of $||\cdot||_{\infty}$ for all possible mass uncertainties. The weighting functions are used to reflect the relative significance of the performance requirement over different frequency ranges.

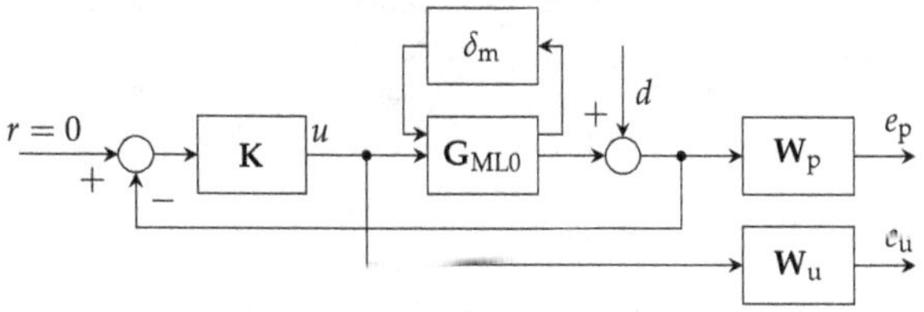

Fig. 3. AML closed loop system with an uncertain mass.

Thus, a key point in the controller design is to develop the sensitivity function to satisfy the required closed-loop performance over a specified frequency range. There are many possible approaches to propose the weighting functions, for example they can be chosen as follows:

$$W_p(s) = \frac{w_{n0}}{w_{d1}s + w_{d0}}. \tag{10}$$

The control weighting function $W_u(s)$ is chosen as a scalar value of 10^{-3}. By adjusting the values of w_{n0}, w_{d1}, and w_{d0} the performance of the robust controller could be tuned up.
The robust μ-synthesis based on the D-K iteration procedure involving a set of optimizations produces the controller in a continuous form. The resulting controller order can be high and depend on the mass perturbation, formulation of the weighting function, and the number of iterations executed to find the optimal controller. The obtained 3rd order controller has the following parameters: a_2=-1.473·10^6, a_1=-8.457·10^7, a_0 = -8.552·10^8, b_2 = 1.648·10^3, b_1 = 3.014·10^5, b_0 = 3.012·10^4 and it is given by equation (11).

$$K(s) = \frac{a_2s^2 + a_1s + a_0}{s^3 + b_2s^2 + b_1s + b_0}. \tag{11}$$

2.3.3 Real-time experiments

The realization of the AML controller is carried out using the MATLAB/Simulink and additional toolboxes. When steered from the PC-based platform, the I/O board is installed in the PC and RTW/RTWT toolboxes are applied to provide a real-time simulation in the Windows environment. When the control unit is based on the dSPACE controller and the Control Desk toolbox, the real-time controller is executed on the target embedded platform.
The dual electromagnet AML system driven by a frequency-based current hardware feedback controller was used to test the performance of the robust controller. The MLS2EM system was steered from the PC with a FastDAQ custom I/O board (Pilat & Piatek, 2008) from MATLAB/Simulink via RTWT at a sampling frequency of F_S = 4 kHz. The extra force generated in the programmable way and produced by the lower electromagnet was attracting the levitated object and therefore simulating mass uncertainty. To show the performance of the robust controller, the experimental data has been filtered to remove the high frequencies from the measured signals.
In the case of a step-type load representing a narrow mass change of 15 % the object is brought down to the desired level in 100 ms. The maximal overshoot versus desired object position is equal to 317 μm while for the triangular load corresponding to the low-frequency mass change of 33% is equal to 237 μm.

2.3.4 Conclusions to AML robust control design

The analytical robust control approach requires a good model of the system at the operating point. The parameter uncertainty does not cancel the structural nonlinearities, but is satisfactory for the required control performance. In some cases, the obtained high-order controller structure could not be realized by the hardware resources. In this case, the order reduction under special attendance of the controller quality is required.

3. Modelling of the AMB rotor systems

The second case study plant is a laboratory test stand with an AMB-supported custom rotor. The machine was originally a solid rotor induction motor for general industrial high-speed applications with the rated speed 12000 rpm. The original machine was produced by Rotatek Finland Oy. The AMB setup consist of two radial actuators and one axial actuator. The control

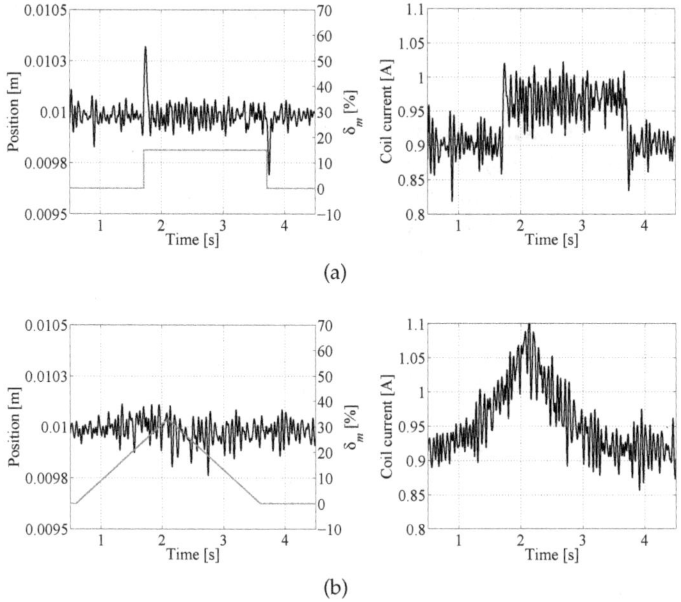

Fig. 4. Real-time experimens: a) narrow load change, b) slow load change.

layout comprises the inner current control loop and the outer position control loop. This section focuses on the radial suspension.

The studied AMB system is non-symmetric and non-collocated. The rotor is of a long rotor type without a significant gyroscopic effect. The machine is subcritical, that is, the maximum rotational speed is below the first flexible bending mode. From the radial position control point of view, the measured outputs are rotor displacements in two axes in two sensor planes and the applied control signals are four control currents of two radial eight-pole magnetic bearings. The system parameters are presented in Table 1.

Current stiffness and position stiffness	$k_i = 268\ \mathrm{N\,A^{-1}}$ and $k_x = 992\ \mathrm{N\,mm^{-1}}$
Rotor mass	46.2 kg
Rotor transverse moment of inertia	$4.8\ \mathrm{kg\,m^2}$
Rotor polar moment of inertia	$0.041\ \mathrm{kg\,m^2}$
Damping ratio of 1-3 flexible modes	0.0041, 0.0022, 0.0043
DC link voltage	150 V
Bias current and maximum currents	2.5 A and 10 A
Equivalent coil inductance and resistance	$L = 0.042$ H and $R = 0.43\ \Omega$
Equivalent average modulation delay	$\tau_{\mathrm{PWM}} = 25\ \mu\mathrm{s}$
Nominal magnetic air-gap lengths	0.6 mm

Table 1. Key AMB system parameters and their nominal values.

The technical details of the plant are given by Jastrzebski (2007), Jastrzebski & Pöllänen (2009) and Jastrzebski et al. (2010). The plant model comprises the actuator model and the rotor model.

3.1 Modelling of an AMB radial actuator

For each input-output channel, a complete nominal actuator model consists of a 2nd-order system with a pulse width modulation (PWM) delay and a motion-induced back electromotive force. The magnetic force relation for a single axis in each actuation plane in the close vicinity of the operating point is assumed to be

$$f = k_i i_c + k_x x, \tag{12}$$

where k_i and k_x denote the current stiffness and the position stiffness. i_c and x are the control current and the position at the location of the bearings, respectively. Each of the inner current control loops is modeled as

$$\begin{bmatrix} \dot{i}_c \\ \dot{u} \end{bmatrix} = \mathbf{A}_a \cdot \begin{bmatrix} i_c \\ u \end{bmatrix} + \mathbf{B}_{ar}\dot{x} + \mathbf{B}_a i_{c,ref}, \quad i_c = \mathbf{C}_a \begin{bmatrix} i_c \\ u \end{bmatrix}, \tag{13}$$

$$\mathbf{A}_a = \begin{bmatrix} -\frac{R}{L} & \frac{1}{L} \\ -\frac{G_p}{\tau_{PWM}} & -\frac{1}{\tau_{PWM}} \end{bmatrix}, \quad \mathbf{B}_{ar} = \begin{bmatrix} -\frac{k_i}{L} \\ 0 \end{bmatrix}, \quad \mathbf{B}_a = \begin{bmatrix} 0 \\ \frac{G_p + G_{ff}}{\tau_{PWM}} \end{bmatrix}, \quad \mathbf{C}_a = \begin{bmatrix} 1 \\ 0 \end{bmatrix}. \tag{14}$$

$i_{c,ref}$ is the reference control current provided by the position control loop. G_p and G_{ff} are the proportional and feed-forward gains of the inner controllers.

3.2 Modeling of a mechanical subsystem

The rotor is modeled using a finite element method (FEM) custom code (Jastrzebski, 2007). The FEM model has 32 nodes, which corresponds to 128 degrees of freedom. The FEM code model is tuned to better correlate with the results of an experimental modal analysis of the free-free rotor and the results of frequency responses of the AMB levitated rotor (Jastrzebski et al., 2010). It is sufficient to retain only few lowest frequency modes. We apply the reduced unsupported rotor model for the controller synthesis. The model retains three flexible bending modes calculated at standstill in each plane (in the xz and yz planes). The equation of motion for the rotor spinning with the rotational speed Ω in the modal coordinates is

$$\mathbf{M}^m \ddot{\eta}^m + (\mathbf{D}^m + \Omega \mathbf{G}^m)\dot{\eta}^m + \mathbf{K}^m \eta^m = \boldsymbol{f}^m. \tag{15}$$

The matrices of the mechanical system description $\mathbf{M}^m$, $\mathbf{K}^m$, $\mathbf{G}^m$ and $\mathbf{D}^m$ are the diagonal mass matrix, the diagonal stiffness matrix, the skew-symmetric gyroscopic matrix, and the damping matrix, respectively. $\boldsymbol{f}^m$ and η^m are the vector of the modal forces acting on the rotor and the vector of modal coordinates. In fact, the first four coordinates correspond to the rigid rotor modes in the center of gravity coordinates. This reduced rotor model has in total ten coordinates.

In order to include the bearing stiffness matrices $\mathbf{K}_i$ and $\mathbf{K}_x$ in the rotor model, a transformation $\mathbf{C}_f$ from the position of actuators to the center of mass is applied. Additionally, the model has to provide rotor displacements in the position of sensors and velocities at the location of bearings. Thus, another transformation matrixes are necessary $\mathbf{C}_s$ and $\mathbf{C}_b$.

Finally, after removing the superscript 'm' for modal, the state space equations of the rotor-bearing system has the following form

$$\begin{aligned}\mathbf{A}_{\mathrm{r}} &= \begin{bmatrix} \mathbf{0} & \mathbf{I} \\ -\mathbf{M}^{-1}\left(\mathbf{K}-\mathbf{C}_{\mathrm{f}}^{T}\mathbf{K}_{x}\mathbf{C}_{\mathrm{f}}\right) & -\mathbf{M}^{-1}\left(\mathbf{D}+\Omega\mathbf{G}\right)\end{bmatrix}, \\ \mathbf{B}_{\mathrm{r}} &= \begin{bmatrix} \mathbf{0} \\ -\mathbf{M}^{-1}\mathbf{C}_{\mathrm{f}}^{T}\mathbf{K}_{i}\end{bmatrix}, \\ \mathbf{C}_{\mathrm{rs}} &= \begin{bmatrix}\mathbf{C}_{\mathrm{s}} & \mathbf{0}\end{bmatrix}, \\ \mathbf{C}_{\mathrm{rb}} &= \begin{bmatrix}\mathbf{0} & \mathbf{C}_{\mathrm{b}}.\end{bmatrix}\end{aligned} \tag{16}$$

3.3 Complete nominal plant model

The resulting equation for the full system, which combines the rotor and actuator has the following form

$$\mathbf{A} = \begin{bmatrix} \mathbf{A}_{\mathrm{a}} & \mathbf{B}_{\mathrm{ar}}\mathbf{C}_{\mathrm{rb}} \\ \mathbf{B}_{\mathrm{r}}\mathbf{C}_{\mathrm{a}} & \mathbf{A}_{\mathrm{r}}\end{bmatrix}, \quad \mathbf{B} = \begin{bmatrix}\mathbf{B}_{\mathrm{a}} \\ \mathbf{0}\end{bmatrix}, \quad \mathbf{C} = \begin{bmatrix}\mathbf{0} & \mathbf{C}_{\mathrm{r}}\end{bmatrix}. \tag{17}$$

The open-loop transfer function of the plant in the Laplace domain using the state variable form can be written as

$$\mathbf{y} = \mathbf{G}(s)\,\boldsymbol{u} = \mathbf{C}\left(s\mathbf{I}-\mathbf{A}\right)^{-1}\mathbf{B}\boldsymbol{u}. \tag{18}$$

$\mathbf{G}(s)$ is a transfer function matrix of the plant. $\boldsymbol{u}$ and $\boldsymbol{y}$ are the vectors of the control currents and the measured displacements, respectively. $\mathbf{A}$, $\mathbf{B}$, and $\mathbf{C}$ are the state matrix, the input matrix, and the output matrix in the state-space representation, respectively. The combined actuator and rotor models form a coupled plant, which has 28 states. The coupling between the transversal and tilting rotor movements is caused by the radial actuators. The coupling between the xz and yz planes appears as a result of the gyroscopic coupling (Jastrzebski, 2007). In order to decrease the condition number of the plant, the MIMO coupled plant model applies a similarity transformation leading to a normalized per-unit (pu) system. Such a per-unit plant is less prone to numerical problems when designing a controller.

3.4 Modeling of uncertainties

We divide uncertainties into dynamic perturbations and disturbance signals (Gu et al., 2005b). The disturbances originate from the inverter, motor and the load transmitted forces, as well as sensor and actuator noise. These disturbances are difficult to measure and model but some rough estimations can be applied. The dynamic perturbations comprise unstructured uncertainties, when the perturbations are only considered by upper and lower bounds, and the structured uncertainties when the perturbations appear in particular parameters (Skogestad & Postlethwaite, 2005). The former ones are unmodelled dynamics of the base and truncated high-frequency modes of the rotor. The letter ones are neglected nonlinearities of the actuators and sensors and other variations of nominal system parameters.
The structured uncertainties in the actuator include:

- variable current stiffness and position stiffness because of modeling inaccuracies, actuator nonlinearities, and changes of the operational point (± 10 %)
- variation of electrical parameters of the actuator (± 10 %)

The effects of hysteresis and time delays (of the modulation, digital control, and sensors) can be neglected for the applied system components.

The structured uncertainties when considering mechanical models and position sensors are:

- variable mass resulting from external low-frequency loads depending on applications, e.g., in compressors and pumps (± 10 %)
- variable sensor gain and offset (± 5 %)
- uncertain sensor locations (± 1 %)
- variation of the rotational speed
- uncertainties in the modal mass and damping matrices (± 2 %)

The uncertainty in the sensor locations emulates uncertainty of the mode shapes of the bearings, which are more difficult to implement. The most notable variations occur because of changes in the operational speed and shifting of the operational point. The shifting occurs for the nonzero reference position, in the presence of sensing errors, rotor runout, and external forces.

All or some of the dynamic perturbations can be lumped into a single perturbation block Δ. Δ is referred to as an unstructured uncertainty and it is complex whereas the parametric uncertainties are assumed to be real.

Differences between the measured frequency responses of the test-rig and the nominal plant model that are significant and otherwise not covered by the structured uncertainties (Jastrzebski et al., 2010) are modeled as an unstructured uncertainty. In particular, the structural resonance of the base of the machine at about 1130 rad/s (180 Hz), is modeled using an output multiplicative uncertainty $\mathbf{\Delta} = \mathbf{\Delta}_\mathrm{o}$.

The uncertain plant with a multiplicative output uncertainty in each input-output channel is

$$\mathbf{G}_\mathrm{p} = (\mathbf{I} + w_\mathrm{o}\mathbf{\Delta}_\mathrm{o})\,\mathbf{G},\ \|\mathbf{\Delta}_\mathrm{o}\|_\infty \leq 1. \tag{19}$$

$w_\mathrm{o}(s)$ is an uncertainty scalar weight with appropriately selected coefficients a_i such as

$$|w_\mathrm{o}(j\omega)| \geq l_\mathrm{o}(\omega)\,\forall\omega,\ l_\mathrm{o}(\omega) = \max_{\bar{\sigma}}\left(\left(\mathbf{G}_\mathrm{p} - \mathbf{G}\right)\mathbf{G}^{-1}(j\omega)\right), \tag{20}$$

$$w_\mathrm{o}(j\omega) = \frac{a_0 s^2 + a_1 s + a_2 s^2}{s^2 + a_3 s + a_4 s^2}. \tag{21}$$

$\|.\|_\infty$ and $\bar{\sigma}$ denote the $\mathcal{H}_\infty$ norm and the maximum singular value (Skogestad & Postlethwaite, 2005), respectively. When the uncertain parts are separated from the dynamics, the system can be presented in a well-known upper linear fractional transformation (LFT) $F(\mathbf{M}, \mathbf{\Delta})$, where $\mathbf{M}$ represents a standard interconnection of the system with uncertainties taken out. Now, $\mathbf{\Delta}$ consists of both the unstructured and parametric uncertainties. The uncertain block $\mathbf{\Delta}$ is a diagonal matrix.

The analysis and design are more difficult when the structural uncertainties are real numbers. Unfortunately, the use of the lumped full model also results in a pessimistic analysis and a conservative design (Gu et al., 2005b). Therefore, a proper selection of modeled uncertainties is not straightforward.

After analyzing the suspension of the point mass, which can be treated equivalently to the axial suspension of the rotor, we focus on the radial suspension.

4. $\mathcal{H}_\infty$ control of the AMB rotor system with insignificant gyroscopic effect

Different weighting schemes are applicable to form a cost function subject to the $\mathcal{H}_\infty$ norm in (sub)optimization problems. Perhaps the most commonly applied schemes are the $\mathbf{S}/\mathbf{KS}$ and $\mathbf{S}/\mathbf{T}$ schemes. The $\mathbf{S}/\mathbf{KS}$ scheme can achieve nominal performance in tracking or disturbance rejection and robust stability against the additive perturbations. The weighted mixed sensitivity $\mathbf{S}/\mathbf{T}$ scheme can achieve nominal performances and robust stability against multiplicative perturbations. However, in the aforementioned schemes there is a danger of pole-zero cancellation between the nominal model and the controller (Sefton & Glover, 1990). They are also limited by the condition of the number of the right-half plane poles. In the perturbed system the number should be the same as in the nominal one (Lunz, 1989). In response to these limitations, another weighting scheme features robust stabilization against normalized coprime factor perturbation of the nominal plant. The $\mathcal{H}_\infty$ loop-shaping design relaxes the right-half plane restrictions and produces no pole-zero cancellation. The solution is obtained directly without the need for iterations.

4.1 Loop-shaping Glover-McFarlane control of an AMB rotor system

A loop-shaping $\mathcal{H}_\infty$ design procedure was introduced by Glover & McFarlane (1989). Later, it was extended to the two-degrees of freedom problem by Limebeer et al. (1993). The approach gained its popularity as it does not require a γ-iteration and provides a result by solving two Riccati equations.

To achieve a controller based on a loop-shaping technique, two weights should be selected. This is a pre-compensator $\mathbf{W}_1$ and a post-compensator $\mathbf{W}_2$. They alter the open-loop transfer function of the plant $\mathbf{G}$ to the desired shape $\mathbf{G}_\mathrm{s}$. Selection of weights depends on the performance and robustness criteria. Additionally, weights can be selected based on the presented multiplicative uncertainties. Structured uncertainty is not supported directly by the method. In a case where there are many sources of uncertainties, other methods prove to be conservative or too difficult to apply. Hence, multiplicative uncertainty approximated on the representative set of plants is a useful solution.

After selecting weights and multiplying the nominal plant from left and right, the system is stabilized with an $\mathcal{H}_\infty$ controller $\mathbf{K}_\mathrm{s}$ see Fig. 5(a). The final controller $\mathbf{K}$ is obtained as

$$\mathbf{K} = \mathbf{W}_1\mathbf{K}_\mathrm{s}\mathbf{W}_2. \tag{22}$$

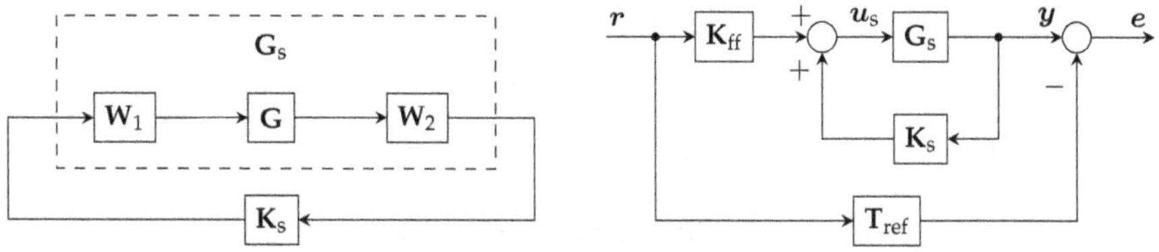

(a) Glover-McFarlane controller structure (b) Two degrees-of-freedom design problem

Fig. 5. Loop-shaping controllers

As a next step, a feedforward part is added. For that, a reference transfer function $\mathbf{T}_\mathrm{ref}$ should be chosen. The feedforward controller $\mathbf{K}_\mathrm{ff}$ is obtained by minimizing the following problem

$$\|(\mathbf{I} - \mathbf{G}_\mathrm{s}\mathbf{K}_\mathrm{s})^{-1}\mathbf{G}_\mathrm{s}\mathbf{K}_\mathrm{ff} - \mathbf{T}_\mathrm{ref}\|_\infty \le \gamma \tag{23}$$

The described method is based mainly on the weight selection. The pre-compensator is usually a low-pass filter. Additional features can be included in the weight such as a notch filter, which is particularly useful in the described application to suppress the flexible modes. The post-compensator is used to emphasize one output over the other. As in the AMB system, all the outputs are equivalent, and this weight is a constant diagonal matrix. The last weight $\mathbf{T}_{\text{ref}}$ should describe the desired transfer function of a closed-loop plant. Thus, a first-order transfer function with a steady state gain equals one, and a crossover frequency is chosen to correspond to the desired bandwidth of the system.

This procedure for an AMB system was applied by Fujita et al. (1993), where the authors give a review how to choose weights based on the multiplicative uncertainties in the system. The applied model of the system was relatively simple accounting only for rigid modes. The loop-shaping method was combined with a μ-synthesis procedure by Lanzon & Tsiotras (2005) to guarantee performance specifications and tolerate structured uncertainties. The resulting controller was successfully applied to the AMB system.

In this work, for the controller synthesis, the procedure suggested by (Skogestad & Postlethwaite, 2005, ch. 9.4.2) is applied. The process is the same as described earlier with an addition of calculation gains to ensure the desired steady-state response. The reference function $\mathbf{T}_{\text{ref}}$ is chosen as

$$\mathbf{T}_{\text{ref}} = \mathbf{I}_{4\times4}\frac{1}{\frac{1}{\omega_{\text{bw}}}s+1}, \tag{24}$$

where $\omega_{\text{bw}} = 215$ rad/sec is the bandwidth of the closed-loop system.

The pre-compensator transfer function is chosen to be a low-pass filter with a DC gain of 78.1 dB. Additionally, the weight includes a notch filter as a second-order transfer function. The damping frequency is $1.664 \cdot 10^3$ rad s^{-1} and the damping ration is 0.08. The final transfer function is as follows

$$\mathbf{W}_1 = \mathbf{I}_{4\times4}\frac{s+110}{s+0.01365}\cdot\frac{\left(\frac{s}{1.664\cdot10^3}\right)^2+\frac{0.3\cdot0.08}{1.664\cdot10^3}s+1}{\left(\frac{s}{1.664\cdot10^3}\right)^2+\frac{0.3}{1.664\cdot10^3}s+1}. \tag{25}$$

Using the weight (25) presented in Fig. 6(a) and the reference function (24), a two-degrees of freedom controller is synthesised. The order of the controller is reduced to fit the real-time implementation using a Schur method (Safonov & Chiang, 1988). The evaluation of the controller with a μ-analysis is presented in Fig. 6(b).

The plot shows that the controller is capable of handling the modeled structured uncertainty. All the values are below one. As it was expected, the highest values are spotted near the first flexible mode. However, the use of a notch filter helps to alleviate the problem. The experimental evaluation of the controller is discussed in section 4.6.

4.2 $\mathcal{H}_\infty$ signal-based control of an AMB rotor system

For the simple weighting schemes in the frequency domain, for example, such as the $\mathbf{S}/\mathbf{KS}$ mixed sensitivity problem, which provides good tracking and limits control energy, we are not able to include more complex specifications. The more versatile schemes are signal-based $\mathcal{H}_\infty$ approaches. However, the more complex the resulting lower LFT becomes, the more difficult the selection of the multiple design weights and the more complex and difficult the numerical solution of the minimization problem are. We modify the Skogestad & Postlethwaite (2005) scheme by lifting up the restrictions on all of the states but instead adding application-specific

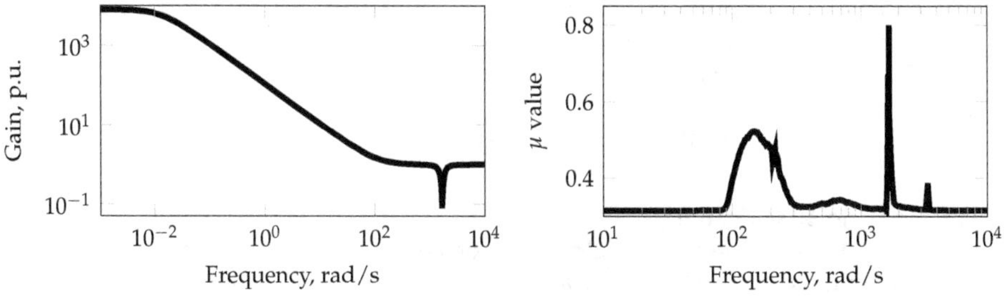

(a) Pre-compensator shape in the frequency domain

(b) μ-analysis

Fig. 6. $\mathcal{H}_\infty$ loop-shaping design

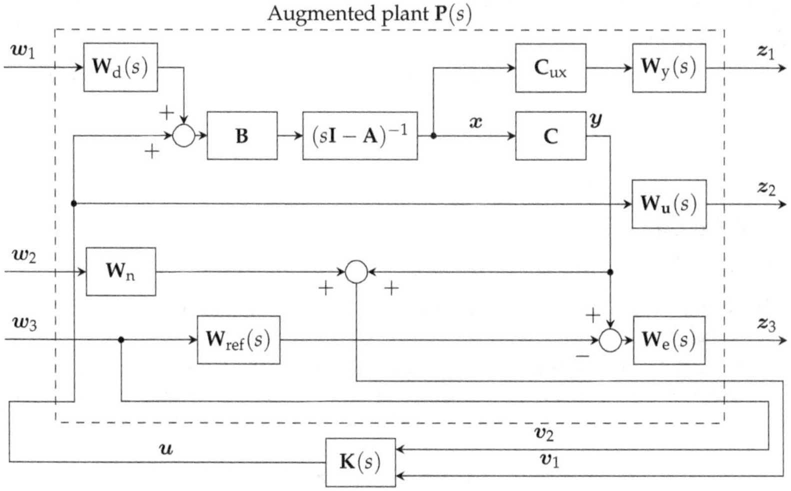

Fig. 7. 2DOF $\mathcal{H}_\infty$ signal-based design problem.

voltage limitation and displacement limitations at critical locations other than sensor planes. Now, a magnetic bearing system can be described using a general control configuration (Fig. 7). The stabilizing controller can be found by minimizing the $\mathcal{H}_\infty$ norm from the exogenous inputs $\boldsymbol{w} = [\boldsymbol{w}_1, \boldsymbol{w}_2, \boldsymbol{w}_3]^\mathrm{T}$ to the exogenous outputs $\boldsymbol{z} = [\boldsymbol{z}_1, \boldsymbol{z}_2, \boldsymbol{z}_3]^\mathrm{T}$. The inputs to the controller $\boldsymbol{v}_1$ and $\boldsymbol{v}_2$ are the vector of the position reference signals and the vector of the distorted signals received from the displacement sensors, respectively. The augmented plant input vectors $\boldsymbol{w}_1$, $\boldsymbol{w}_2$ and $\boldsymbol{w}_3$ are the vector of the input distortion signals, the vector of the output distortion signals, and the vector of the reference signals, respectively. The augmented plant output vectors $\boldsymbol{z}_1$, $\boldsymbol{z}_2$, and $\boldsymbol{z}_3$ are the vector of the voltages and displacements obtained using the output matrix $\mathbf{C}_{ux}$, weighted system input signals, and the vector of the weighted position error signals, respectively.

The signal limitations result in the unitary weight for the normalized plant special outputs $\mathbf{W}_y = \mathbf{I}$. The sensor noise spectrum is approximated by the first-order high-pass filter $\mathbf{W}_\mathrm{n}$ with the dc gain and the high-frequency gain equal to 0.2 % and 5 % of the measuring range. The crossover frequency is 250 Hz.

The weights $\mathbf{W}_d(s)$, $\mathbf{W}_u(s)$, and $\mathbf{W}_e(s)$ are defined as first-order transfer functions multiplied by a 4×4 unitary matrices. The coefficients of these functions are treated as design parameters. Applying the $\mathcal{H}_\infty$ control problem, the admissible controller $\mathbf{K}$ is found, if one exists, so that for $\gamma > 0$

$$\|\mathbf{F}_l(\mathbf{P},\mathbf{K})\|_\infty = \max_\omega \bar{\sigma}\left(\mathbf{F}_l\left(\mathbf{P},\mathbf{K}\right)(j\omega)\right) \leq \gamma. \tag{26}$$

4.3 Control design specification

For all of the schemes, the appropriate choice of the weighting functions, which provide guaranteed stability, robustness margin, and tracking nominal performance, is required. The structure and order of the weights should deliver enough flexibility but without too much added complexity in the optimization. The order of the weights together with the order of the nominal plant decide if and how easily the satisfactory solution can be obtained using necessary numerical procedures.

When defining the control design specification the major points are:

- closed-loop stability
- limitations of actuators, i.e., maximum coil current and limited DC link voltage and as a result, limited force slue rate
- no steady-state error
- sufficient input disturbance rejection and noise rejection of the sensors (output)
- robust stability and robust performance
- minimization of the output sensitivity peak

Additionally, the minor objectives are: desired step responses and the closed-loop bandwidth within the desired range.

The most of the listed objectives are easily tested. However, in order to test robust stability, the structural singular value μ has to be computed (Gu et al., 2005b; Skogestad & Postlethwaite, 2005; Zhou, 1998)

$$\mu_\Delta^{-1}(\mathbf{M}) := \min_{\boldsymbol{\Delta}\in\boldsymbol{\Delta}_s} \left\{\bar{\sigma}(\boldsymbol{\Delta}) : \det\left(\mathbf{I} - \mathbf{M}\boldsymbol{\Delta}\right) = 0\right\}. \tag{27}$$

$\mathbf{M}$ is the interconnected closed-loop system transfer function matrix and $\boldsymbol{\Delta} \in \boldsymbol{\Delta}_s$ represents uncertainties. $\mathbf{M}(s)$ is formed with respect to the uncertainty set $\boldsymbol{\Delta}_s$

$$\boldsymbol{\Delta}_s = \left\{diag\left[\delta_1 I_{1r}, \cdots, \delta_s I_{rs}, \Delta_1, \cdots, \Delta_f\right] : \delta_i \in C, \Delta_j \in C^{m_j \times m_j}\right\}, \tag{28}$$

where $\sum_{i=1}^{s} r_i + \sum_{j=1}^{f} m_j = n$ with $\mathbf{M} \in C^{n\times n}$. n equals to the dimension of the block $\boldsymbol{\Delta}$. s and f are the dimensions of the scalar and full uncertainty blocks, respectively.

The structural singular value of $\mathbf{M}(s)$ is a measure of the robust stability of the uncertain system

$$\mu_\Delta\left(\mathbf{M}(s)\right) := \sup_{\omega\in R} \mu_\Delta\left(\mathbf{M}(j\omega)\right). \tag{29}$$

For normalized uncertainties, the system in a standard configuration is robustly stable if $\mathbf{M}(s)$ is stable and $\mu_\Delta\left(\mathbf{M}(s)\right) < 1$. The robust performance requires that the closed-loop control system performs satisfactorily even in the presence of the defined plant uncertainties. The robust performance problem can be solved by generalizing to the robust stabilization problem with the uncertainty block replaced by $\tilde{\Delta} \in \tilde{\Delta}_s := \text{diag}\{\Delta, \Delta_p\}$, where the uncertainties are normalized and the fictious performance uncertainty block is bounded by the norm $\|\Delta_p\|_\infty \leq 1$. Δ_p is unstructured with appropriate dimensions defined by the exogenous inputs and error outputs of the system $\mathbf{M}$ to represent system performance specifications.

4.4 Weighting functions as design parameters

An elegant solution to alleviate the weight selection procedure is the μ-synthesis approach. For the system with a specified uncertainty set, the algorithm gives the weights that result in a robustly stable controller obtained by an $\mathcal{H}_\infty$ synthesis. The main drawback is that there is no analytical solution for the problem. The procedure is iterative and computationally expensive. It results in a controller of a very high order. What is more, the performance requirements are again specified as initial weights, and the designer should also choose a specific weighting scheme. Last but not least, the resulting order of the controller depends on the complexity of the applied weighting scheme, plant order, and applied uncertainties. Detailed interconnections lead to controllers, which are difficult to implement and are not transparent.

For complex systems, such as the flexible AMB rotor system, finding appropriate performance weights by trial and error is very time consuming. To find the weights that produce a design meeting the multiple requirements, we could use the optimization based on the method of inequalities (Whidborne et al., 1994) or the linear matrix inequalities (Scherer et al., 1997). Another option for such a multibjective design is to apply a basic genetic algorithm (GA) (Jastrzebski et al., 2010).

For a signal-based weighting scheme, the coefficients of the weights $\mathbf{W}_d(s)$, $\mathbf{W}_u(s)$, and $\mathbf{W}_e(s)$ are limited by its minimum and maximum selected values because of numerical reasons. Also for numerical reasons and to prevent unwanted pole-zero cancellation (Gu et al., 2005b) the stable and minimum-phase weights are applied. For continuous-time weights in the Laplace domain both the zeros and poles of a minimum phase weight must be strictly inside the left-half s-plane.

4.5 Genetic algorithm approach to multiobjective synthesis

The $\mathcal{H}_\infty$ optimization and the μ-synthesis result in the complex controllers of the higher order than the plant. In an effort to obtain a lower-order controller, we could reduce the plant model by truncating the high-frequency modes beyond the actuator bandwidth prior to the controller synthesis. In the iterative design, the resulting lower-order controller could be tested in each iteration together with the higher-order non-reduced plant against the multi-objective performance function. An alternative procedure to obtain a lowest-order controller is to use the detailed plant model for the synthesis and to apply the controller-order reduction afterwards. Both approaches replace a direct design of the low-order controller.

For the signal-based weighting scheme, some of the signal weights are kept constant while the others, which are the free parameters in the optimizations, are varied in order to reach the optimal design in the multi-objective control design problem. The basic genetic algorithm search is improved by limiting the feasible solution space. This improves the numerical conditioning, and the weights without physical relevance are excluded from the solutions (Jastrzebski et al., 2010).

The design objectives are normalized by the desired limiting values and are proportional to the square of the following performance indices:

- Output sensitivity peak $M_S = \|\mathbf{S}_\mathrm{o}\|_\infty$ and the closed-loop bandwidth (the frequency where $\bar{\sigma}(\mathbf{S}_\mathrm{o})$ first crosses 0.7 from below.
- High controller gain (a small maximum singular value of the sensitivity) at low frequencies $\bar{\sigma}(\mathbf{S}_\mathrm{o}(\omega))$, where $\omega \to 0$.
- Input disturbance attenuation $M_{T\mathrm{i}} = \| \mathbf{K}_\mathrm{fb}\mathbf{G}\mathbf{S}_\mathrm{i}\ \mathbf{G}\mathbf{S}_\mathrm{i} \|_\infty$ and output disturbance attenuation $M_{T\mathrm{o}} = \| \mathbf{G}\mathbf{K}_\mathrm{fb}\mathbf{S}_\mathrm{o}\ \mathbf{K}_\mathrm{fb}\mathbf{S}_\mathrm{o} \|_\infty$.
- Value of γ.

The norms $M_{T\mathrm{i}}$ and $M_{T\mathrm{o}}$ minimize the usage of control signals and the plant output signals in the presence of the input and output distortion signals, respectively. The sensitivity functions are defined as

$$\mathbf{S}_\mathrm{o} = (\mathbf{I} + \mathbf{G}\mathbf{K})^{-1}, \quad \mathbf{S}_\mathrm{i} = (\mathbf{I} + \mathbf{K}\mathbf{G})^{-1}. \tag{30}$$

After applying GA and obtaining a final $\mathcal{H}_\infty$ controller the closed-loop uncertain system is

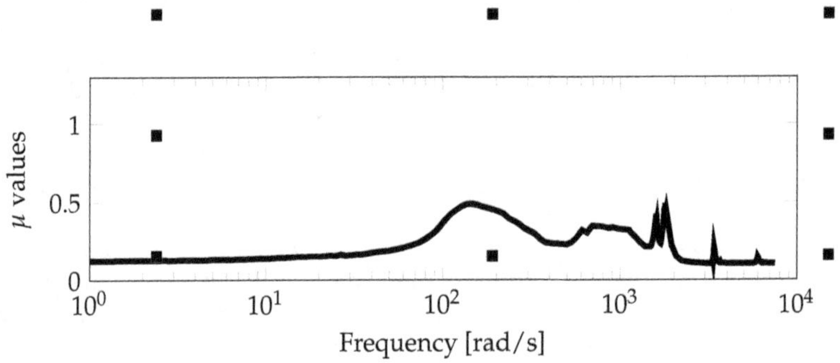

Fig. 8. μ analysis for robust stability.

tested for robust stability (Fig. 8) and performance. In order to limit design conservativeness in $\mathcal{H}_\infty$ control the uncertainties in the plant model, which is applied for design synthesis, are limited to the uncertain speed. In the case of the structured uncertainty, the computation of the structural singular value μ has to be applied and the μ synthesis remains an open problem. When applying the weights obtained using the GA to the μ synthesis, the μ synthesis cannot considerably improve the initial γ value.

4.6 Control validation

The controller achieved in section 4.1 is applied for radial AMBs in the test rig. First, the frequency responses are compared. The output sensitivity function for the B-end of the rotor is measured. The results are presented in Fig. 9. The theoretical values coincide the values obtained from the prototype. One peak that is not presented in the theoretical model corresponds to the natural frequency of the foundation. The foundations were not taken into account in the described synthesis method. Additionally, the values vary between 100 and 300 rad s^{-1}. This can be explained by the water-bed effect. The surface below one and above one closed by the curve must be equal. Thus, these lower values compensate the higher frequency peak.

The next experiment was carried out in the time domain. Two type of step responses are measured; the reference step response and an input disturbance step response. The

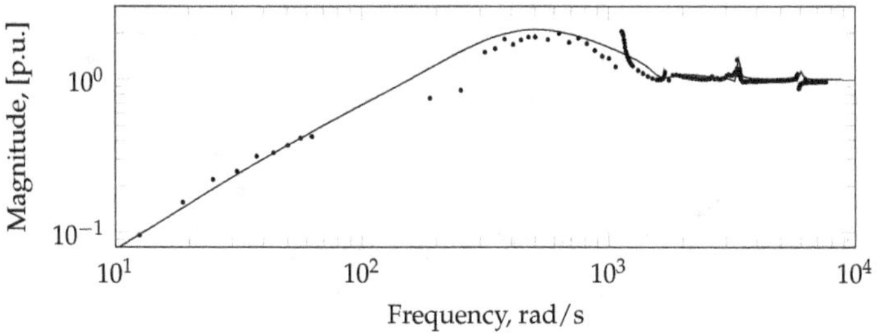

Fig. 9. Output sensitivity function.

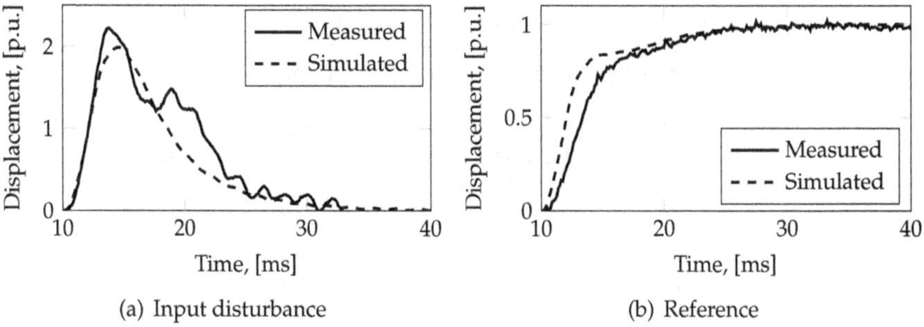

Fig. 10. Step responses.

results of the measurements are presented in Fig. 10. The reference response shows a good correspondence in the settling time. The disagreement with rise time can be explained by the presented nonlinearities of the system or position of the rotor away from the operational point. Disturbance response shows slightly higher maximum amplitude. Additional oscillations come from the first flexible mode, which is difficult to suppress by the feedback.

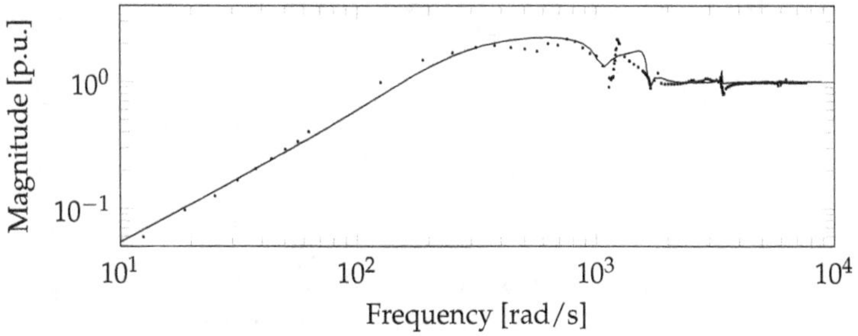

Fig. 11. Output sensitivity function of the H_∞ control.

Similarly, the step responses of the signal-based $\mathcal{H}_\infty$ control (from section 4.2) are presented in Fig. 12. The measured positions for the step responses are filtered by the controller with a relatively low bandwidth of about 110 rad/s. The measured output sensitivity function (Fig. 11) does not differ significantly from the analytical result. The peak unaccounted in the analytically computed values is caused by the structural mode of the base. For the rotational speed in the range from 0 to 6000 rpm the output sensitivity peek varies from 2.618 to 2.625 pu.

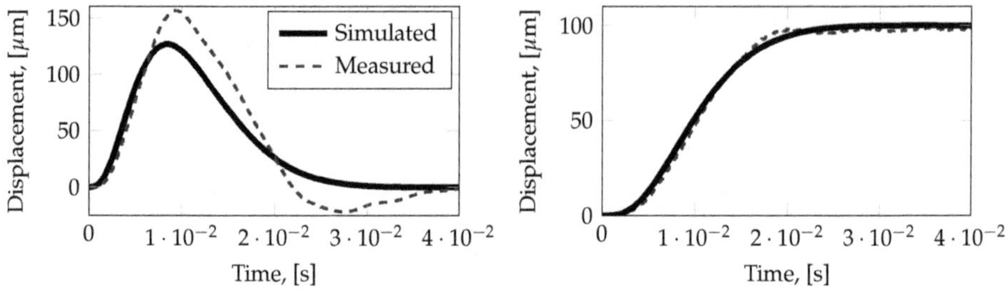

(a) Input disturbance 1 A.

(b) Reference 100 μm.

Fig. 12. Step responses of the $\mathcal{H}_\infty$ signal-based design problem.

5. LPV method applied to a gyroscopic AMB rotor system

The rotating speed of the rotor in AMBs is a source of significant uncertainty. What is more important is that it affects the frequency of the flexible modes; these are known to be challenging to suppress with the feedback control (Li, Lin & Allaire, 2006). Especially, the problem is significant for highly gyroscopic systems. The system is considered as a gyroscopic one if a polar moment of inertia is greater than the diametral one $I_p > I_d$ or the rotational speed is significant (Schweitzer & Maslen, 2009). A good illustration to the problem is a Campbell diagram presented in Fig. 13.

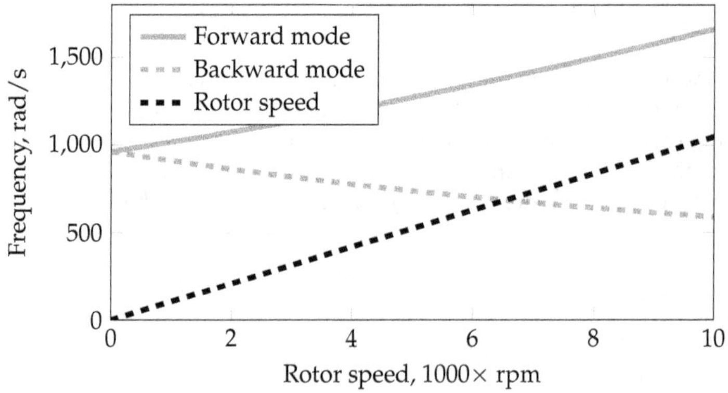

Fig. 13. Campbell diagram.

The significant splitting of the first flexible mode causes the corresponding peak to shift considerably in the frequency response. That affects the controller significantly as it must stabilize the system all the way from the start and up to the nominal speed. The most challenging part of the acceleration curve is around the points where the rotor crosses the flexible mode. In Fig. 13 this happens around 6500 rpm at that point the structural mode gets in resonance with the rotor speed resulting in a significant oscillation magnitude. To overcome this problem, a set of different controllers are synthesized for different rotational speeds. In that case a problem during the switch appears as different controllers have different levels of signals for the same operational point. The problem gets even more significant in MIMO systems. This drawback is treated with bumpless switch techniques (Li (2007); Turner

& Walker (2000)). Another approach to avoid bumps is to interpolate the controllers along with a changing parameter, which is the rotor speed in this case. The last method provides some restrictions, such that interpolated controllers should have the same order and structure. The interpolated controllers are called gain-scheduled controllers (Leith & Leithead, 2000). In particular, the implementation of the AMBs can be presented as a system where the rotor speed is a linear varying parameter. Thus, it is referred to as a category of LPV systems, for which a special LPV gain-scheduling methods can be applied. These methods are free of the above-mentioned drawbacks and provide a unified approach for controller synthesis.

An idea to systematically utilize the rotor speed for the controller adjustment in AMBs was proposed by different authors in different ways. One of the first examples is presented in the work of Matsumura et al. (1996). The authors synthesize a robust loops-shaping controller, which is able to reject sinusoidal disturbance with the rotor rotational frequency. It is carried out by adopting additional boundary constraints for an $\mathcal{H}_\infty$ problem. The model used by the authors contained only rigid modes and the rotor under consideration was without unbalance.

Lu et al. (2008) applied an LPV technique for an AMB system. Their model also contained only rigid modes, and additionally, a special technique was used to identify uncertainty and provide weighting functions for the controller synthesis. The authors presented the controller in a set of parameter-dependent LMIs via a Lyapunov function. The basic controller was a general $\mathcal{H}_\infty$ problem with weighting functions.

The problem of LPV controllers was also investigated in the work of Li (2007), where the author compared an LFT approach with a Lyapunov function approach and additionally, with a "frozen" $\mathcal{H}_\infty$ controller. The model used was highly accurate, including not only higher-frequency modes but also structural resonances resulting in a nominal model with as many as 48 states. The author provided the comparison based only on the theoretical γ values of an $\mathcal{H}_\infty$ controllers.

Here, the system model in an LPV form is presented. Based on the Lyapunov function approach to an LPV gain-scheduling a controller synthesis procedure is described. The achieved controllers are compared with the optimal $\mathcal{H}_\infty$ controllers based on the maximum singular values. Additionally, simulations with a non-linear model and unbalance presented in the rotor are discussed. An LPV model of an AMB system is obtained by the same linearization around the operational point as an ordinary AMB model. The system is assumed to be in the operational point in the center of magnetic forces. Only small deviations from that point are considered as a rotor displacement. The rotor movement is translated to the center of mass resulting in a system with five degrees of freedom. The system is decoupled between the z and x, y axes, providing four states for the radial case. The states are displacements in the x and y and rotations around the x and y axes. They are respectively denoted as $\boldsymbol{q}_c^T = [x\ y\ \alpha\ \beta]$. It can be seen that the model (16) and the following (17) has the form of an LPV system

$$\begin{aligned} \dot{\boldsymbol{x}} &= \mathbf{A}(\Omega)\boldsymbol{x} + \mathbf{B}\boldsymbol{u}, \\ \boldsymbol{y} &= \mathbf{C}\boldsymbol{x}. \end{aligned} \tag{31}$$

In general, there are two approaches to the controller synthesis for the LPV plants. The first approach is based on a Lyapunov function. A quadratic Lyapunov function was used to achieve a set of parameter dependent LMIs by Becker & Packard (1994). Later, less conservative results were obtained by incorporating boundaries on parameters variation rates by Wu et al. (1996). As LMIs in this approach are parameter dependent, in general, there are an infinite number of them to solve. Usually, it is suggested to grid the space of varying parameters and achieve a solution for a limited number of points. The method is proposed for a small number of varying parameters. In an AMB controller synthesis one parameter can be considered as varying. However, the order of the system is rather high and griding with more than five points results in an unrealistically long synthesis time (Li, 2007). Another drawback is that an implementation requires a matrix inversion in real time that is quite challenging with the desired sampling rate on available microcontrollers.

The second one is based on a small gain theorem. The plant is considered as a linear time invariant (LTI) system, which is closed by the feedback loop with a varying parameter. Thus, the full system can be presented as a lower fractional transformation (LFT) of an LTI part and a parameter as presented in Fig. 14(a). Solutions for continuous- and discrete-time cases in a form of LMIs were presented by Apkarian & Gahinet (1995). The solution is conservative compared with the first approach as the realness of parameters is not used. Helmersson (1995) provided an additional research to reduce conservatism by introducing a rate of variation of parameters, which, however, leads to infinite dimensional solvability conditions. A more detailed overview of the research in that field is given by (Leith & Leithead, 2000).

In this work the first approach is taken and in particular, its extension to an affine system proposed by Apkarian et al. (1995). It can be seen from (16) that the system provides a convex set on the speed parameter Ω. Thus, the problem of infinite LMIs is avoided by solving them only at vertexes of the varied parameter. An additional benefit is that the controller implementation is simple and does not require matrix inversion. However, the system considered by Apkarian et al. (1995) neglects the varying state, input, and output transformations, and provides sufficient results under the assumption of a slow-varying parameter as discussed by Leith & Leithead (2000). The slow-varying parameter assumption is valid for an AMB system as the speed variation is relatively slow compared with state variations.

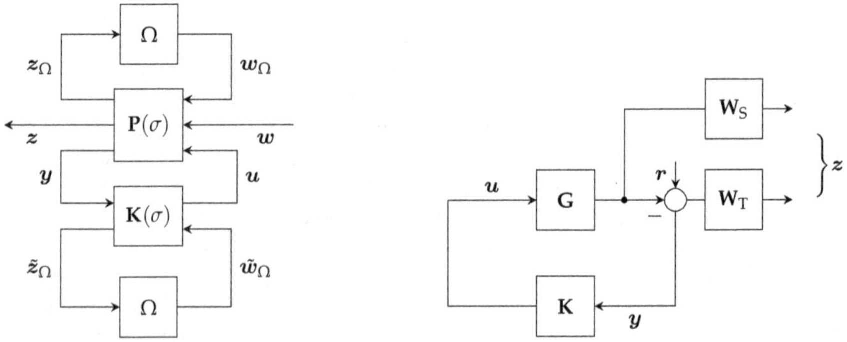

(a) LPV controller structure

(b) Mixed sensitivity control problem

Fig. 14. Controller structures.

The general linear $\mathcal{H}_\infty$ problem is to find a controller $\mathbf{K}$ such that it minimizes (26). The generalized plant $\mathbf{P}$ is obtained from the original plant by providing additional exogenous inputs w and outputs z with specified weights to tune the desired system. The particular scheme for the mixed sensitivity problem is presented in Fig. 14(b). The following weights were used to shape the plant to the desired objectives

$$\mathbf{W}_\mathrm{S} = \mathbf{I}_{4\times4} \cdot 0.5 \frac{s+144}{s+0.144}, \quad \mathbf{W}_\mathrm{T} = \mathbf{I}_{4\times4} \cdot 0.5 \frac{s+0.01}{s+10}. \tag{32}$$

The general rule is that the weight for the sensitivity function is a low-pass filter and for the complementary sensitivity one is a high-pass filter.
Having the generalized plant $\mathbf{P}$ in the form

$$\mathbf{P}(s) = \mathbf{D} + \mathbf{C}(s\mathbf{I} - \mathbf{A})^{-1}\mathbf{B} \tag{33}$$

we follow the authors of (Apkarian et al., 1995) and solve the following LMIs

$$\left(\begin{array}{c|c} \mathcal{N}_{\mathrm{R}} & 0 \\ \hline 0 & \mathbf{I} \end{array}\right)^T \left(\begin{array}{cc|c} \mathbf{A}_i\mathbf{R} + \mathbf{R}\mathbf{A}_i^T & \mathbf{R}\mathbf{C}_{1i}^T & \mathbf{B}_{1i} \\ \mathbf{C}_{1i}\mathbf{R} & -\gamma\mathbf{I} & \mathbf{D}_{11i} \\ \hline \mathbf{B}_{1i}^T & \mathbf{D}_{11i}^T & -\gamma\mathbf{I} \end{array}\right) \left(\begin{array}{c|c} \mathcal{N}_{\mathrm{R}} & 0 \\ \hline 0 & \mathbf{I} \end{array}\right) < 0, \quad i = 1, \ldots, r, \tag{34}$$

$$\left(\begin{array}{c|c} \mathcal{N}_{\mathrm{S}} & 0 \\ \hline 0 & \mathbf{I} \end{array}\right)^T \left(\begin{array}{cc|c} \mathbf{A}_i\mathbf{S} + \mathbf{S}\mathbf{A}_i^T & \mathbf{S}\mathbf{B}_{1i} & \mathbf{C}_{1i}^T \\ \mathbf{B}_{1i}^T\mathbf{S} & -\gamma\mathbf{I} & \mathbf{D}_{11i}^T \\ \hline \mathbf{C}_{1i} & \mathbf{D}_{11i} & -\gamma\mathbf{I} \end{array}\right) \left(\begin{array}{c|c} \mathcal{N}_{\mathrm{S}} & 0 \\ \hline 0 & \mathbf{I} \end{array}\right) < 0, \quad i = 1, \ldots, r, \tag{35}$$

$$\begin{pmatrix} \mathbf{R} & \mathbf{I} \\ \mathbf{I} & \mathbf{S} \end{pmatrix} \geq 0, \tag{36}$$

where the bases of the null spaces of $(\mathbf{B}_2^T, \mathbf{D}_{12}^T)$ and $(\mathbf{C}_2, \mathbf{D}_{21})$ are denoted $\mathcal{N}_{\mathrm{R}}$ and $\mathcal{N}_{\mathrm{S}}$, respectively. Next, the unique solution $\mathbf{X}_{\mathrm{cl}}$ of the matrix equation $\mathbf{\Pi}_2 = \mathbf{X}_{\mathrm{cl}}\mathbf{\Pi}_1$ should be computed, where

$$\mathbf{\Pi}_2 = \begin{pmatrix} \mathbf{S} & \mathbf{I} \\ \mathbf{N}^T & \mathbf{0} \end{pmatrix}, \quad \mathbf{\Pi}_1 = \begin{pmatrix} \mathbf{I} & \mathbf{R} \\ \mathbf{0} & \mathbf{M}^T \end{pmatrix} \tag{37}$$

and the matrices $\mathbf{M}$ and $\mathbf{N}$ are such that

$$\mathbf{M}\mathbf{N}^T = \mathbf{I} - \mathbf{R}\mathbf{S}. \tag{38}$$

The controllers for each vertex can be found by solving the following LMI

$$\begin{pmatrix} \mathbf{A}_{\mathrm{K}i}^T\mathbf{X}_{\mathrm{cl}} + \mathbf{X}_{\mathrm{cl}}\mathbf{A}_{\mathrm{K}i} & \mathbf{X}_{\mathrm{cl}}\mathbf{B}_{\mathrm{K}i} & \mathbf{C}_{\mathrm{K}i}^T \\ \mathbf{B}_{\mathrm{K}i}^T\mathbf{X}_{\mathrm{cl}} & -\gamma\mathbf{I} & \mathbf{D}_{\mathrm{K}i}^T \\ \mathbf{C}_{\mathrm{K}i} & \mathbf{D}_{\mathrm{K}i} & -\gamma\mathbf{I} \end{pmatrix} < 0. \tag{39}$$

Having the state-space matrices for each vertex $\mathbf{A}_{\mathrm{K}i}$, $\mathbf{B}_{\mathrm{K}i}, \mathbf{C}_{\mathrm{K}i}, \mathbf{D}_{\mathrm{K}i}$ the controller for the particular point is obtained as

$$\begin{bmatrix} \mathbf{A}_{\mathrm{K}}(\Omega) & \mathbf{B}_{\mathrm{K}}(\Omega) \\ \mathbf{C}_{\mathrm{K}}(\Omega) & \mathbf{D}_{\mathrm{K}}(\Omega) \end{bmatrix} = \sum_{i=1}^{r} \alpha_i \begin{bmatrix} \mathbf{A}_{\mathrm{K}i} & \mathbf{B}_{\mathrm{K}i} \\ \mathbf{C}_{\mathrm{K}i} & \mathbf{D}_{\mathrm{K}i} \end{bmatrix}, \tag{40}$$

where α_i is such that

$$\Omega = \left\{ \sum_{i=1}^{r} \alpha_i \omega_i : \alpha_i \geq 0, \sum_{i=1}^{r} \alpha_i = 1 \right\}. \tag{41}$$

The r denotes the total number of vertices and ω_i the particular vertex. The parameter Ω is measured in real time and the controllers are updated on each step. For the controller testing, we use the system with the Campbell diagram (see Fig. 13) presented above. The polar moment of inertia $I_{\mathrm{p}} = 10.6$ kg m^2 is greater than the diametral moment $I_{\mathrm{d}} = 0.59$ kg m^2. However, the speed varies from 0 to 10 000 rpm, and thus, the system has significant gyroscopic effect. The controller is synthesized using the above-mentioned weighting functions (32). As the main objective is the stability of the system, a maximum singular value of sensitivity functions is evaluated. A good starting point for a comparison is an output sensitivity function $\mathbf{S}_o$ (Li, Lin & Allaire, 2006). Additionally, an output complementary sensitivity function $\mathbf{T}_o$ is used for the evaluation.

$$\mathbf{T}_o = \mathbf{GK}(\mathbf{I}+\mathbf{GK})^{-1}. \tag{42}$$

The evaluation of the controller is carried out in each point of a variation parameter. It means that the closed loop transfer functions (30) and (42) are calculated at each rotor speed and their peak value is found. The peak values of the MIMO system are defined as maximum singular values in the same fashion as in (26). The achieved results are presented in Fig. 15.

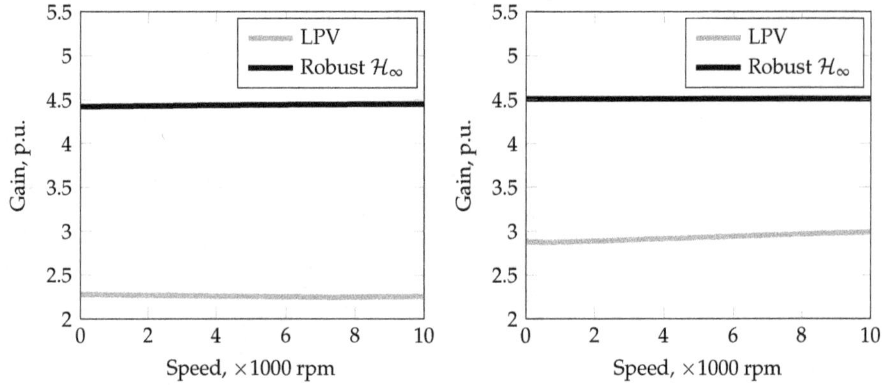

(a) Output sensitivity

(b) Output complementary sensitivity

Fig. 15. Maximum values of sensitivity functions.

It is seen that an LPV controller provides a stable system with low values of sensitivity functions. For comparison a robust $\mathcal{H}_\infty$ controller is synthesized using the same weights and the same structure. In this synthesis, speed is treated as a structured uncertainty. In Fig. 15 it is seen that the robust controller has higher peak values and additionally, the values do not change over the parameter variation. The LPV controller peak values are smaller and have some deviation. In general, Fig. 15 shows that the LPV controller provides a greater stability margin.

The previous assessment was based on a theoretical model and provides the basic insight into the stability margins. For a deeper evaluation, simulations with a non-linear model are carried out. The rotor for the simulations is considered to have an imbalance of 0.01 kg, and a system with three flexible modes is used. The force-current relations are non-linear; they include the actuator delay and are based on look-up tables from the switch-reluctance network model.

A typical case of the rotor acceleration is simulated. The speed increases linearly from zero up to the maximum value. The beginning and ending phases of acceleration are smoothed to avoid unrealistic sharp edges. The results are evaluated for an LPV and a robust $\mathcal{H}_\infty$ controllers. The displacements at the A-end in the x direction are presented in Fig. 16.

The LPV controller shows worse performance for the transient response. The magnitude of oscillations is significantly higher around two times. The oscillations take place around the

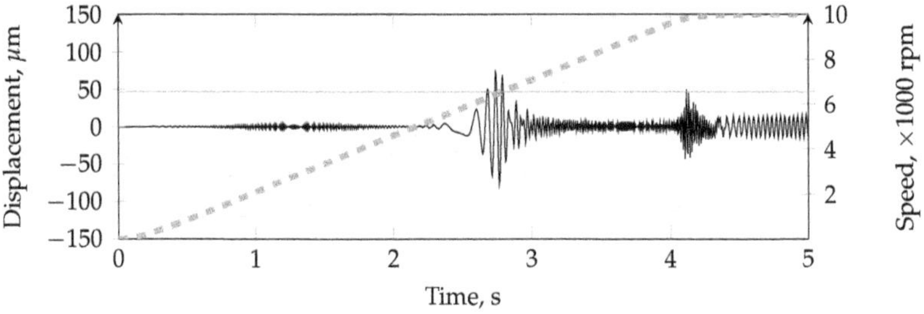

(a) Robust $\mathcal{H}_\infty$ controller

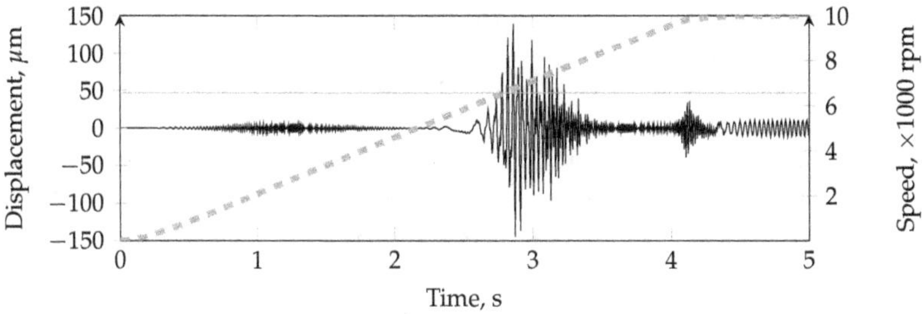

(b) LPV controller

Fig. 16. Rotor acceleration responses.

point of 6500 rpm where the system crosses the first flexible mode. The second point where the system experiences oscillations is close to the maximum speed and it can be explained by the deceleration of the rotor. The LPV controller has a lower magnitude of oscillations around this point; the difference is 35 %. Such a behavior can be explained by an adaptive nature of an LPV controller. In each step, the gains are modified according to the rotational speed. During the acceleration process, the system does not have enough time to adapt. This results in a higher amplitude of oscillations. During the later deceleration phase, the coefficients do not change that fast and performance is better. The speed of the parameter variation is a significant problem for the LPV controllers, and usually the main point of conservatism in that approach (Leith & Leithead, 2000).
The second simulation experiment in the steady state proves that LPV controller provides a better performance. In this experiment, a step disturbance to the x channel of the rotor A-end is applied at the maximum rotational speed. The simulation results are presented in Fig. 17. The magnitude of the disturbance response for an LPV controller is about three times smaller than that of a robust controller. Additionally, the LPV controller does not have coupling between different ends, so the disturbance does not propagate through the system.

6. Real-time operating conditions

The AMB-based system requires hard-real time controllers. In the case of a robust control strategy, the control law is of higher complexity than other solutions. Therefore, the implementation of the control law must fulfill the requirements of the target control system such as finite precision of the arithmetic and number format and available computational

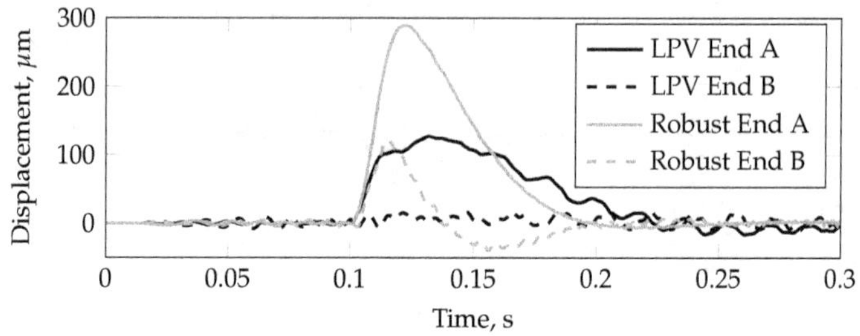

Fig. 17. Step disturbance response for controllers in the x direction.

power. The digital control realization requires a digital controller that matches the continuous form in the operating frequency range. The controllers for the radial suspension of the AMB rotor system are tested using a dSpace DS1005-09 digital control board and a DS4003 Digital Input/Output system board as a regulation platform. The Simulink and Real-time Workshop software are applied for automatic program code generation. The selected sampling rate is 10 kHz. The resolution of the applied ADCs is 16 bits. The control setup limits the maximum number of states of the implemented controllers to 28 states.

7. Conclusions

The chapter discusses options and feasible control solutions when building uncertain AMB rotor models and when designing a robust control for the AMB rotor systems. The review of the AMB systems is presented. The recommendations for difficult weight selection in different weighting schemes are given. Design-specific problems and trade-offs for each controller are discussed. It is shown that the operating conditions of the selected real-time controllers satisfy the control quality requirements. The resulting order of the controller depends on the complexity of the applied weighting scheme, plant order, and applied uncertainties. The detailed interconnections lead to controllers, which are difficult to implement and are not transparent. However, the too simple weighting schemes cannot provide sufficient design flexibility with respect to the multi-objective specification. For the systems with considerably gyroscopic rotors and high rotational speeds, the LPV method provides a significantly better solution than nonadaptive robust control methods.

8. Acknowledgement

This chapter was partially founded by AGH Research Grant no 11.11.120.768

9. References

Apkarian, P. & Gahinet, P. (1995). A convex characterization of gain-scheduled H_∞ controllers, *Automatic Control, IEEE Transactions on* 40(5): 853–864.

Apkarian, P., Gahinet, P. & Becker, G. (1995). Self-scheduled H_∞ control of linear parameter-varying systems: a design example, *Automatica* 31(9): 1251–1261.

Battachatyya, S. P., Chapellat, H. & Keel, L. H. (1995). *Robust Control The Parametric Approach*, Prentice Hall.

Becker, G. & Packard, A. (1994). Robust performance of linear parametrically varying systems using parametrically-dependent linear feedback, *Systems & Control Letters* 23(3): 205–215.

Fujita, M., Hatake, K. & Matsumura, F. (1993). Loop shaping based robust control of a magnetic bearing, *Control Systems Magazine, IEEE* 13(4): 57–65.

Fujita, M., Namerikawa, T., Matsamura, F. & Uchida, K. (1995). mi-synthesis of an electromagnetic suspension system, *IEEE Transactions on Automatic Control* 40: 530–536.

Glover, K. & McFarlane, D. (1989). Robust stabilization of normalized coprime factor plant descriptions with H_∞-bounded uncertainty, *Automatic Control, IEEE Transactions on* 34(8): 821–830.

Gosiewski, Z. & Mystkowski, A. (2008). Robust control of active magnetic suspension: Analytical and experimental results, *Mechanical Systems and Signal Processing* 22: 1297–1303.

Gu, D., Petkov, P. & Konstantinov, M. (2005a). *Robust Control Design with MATLAB*, Springer.

Gu, D.-W., Petkov, P. & Konstantinov, M. (2005b). *Robust Control Design with MATLAB*, Springer, Leipzig, Germany.

Helmersson, A. (1995). *Methods for robust gains scheduling*, PhD thesis, Linkoping University.

InTeCo (2008). *MLS2EM, Magnetic Levitation User's Guide*, InTeCo, Poland.

Jastrzebski, R. (2007). *Design and Implementation of FPGA-based LQ Control of Active Magnetic Bearings*, PhD thesis, LUT, Finland.

Jastrzebski, R., Hynynen, K. & Smirnov, A. (2010). *H*-infinity control of active magnetic suspension, *Mechanical Systems and Signal Processing* 24(4): 995–1006.

Jastrzebski, R. & Pöllänen, R. (2009). Centralized optimal position control for active magnetic bearings - comparison with decentralized control, *Electrical Engineering* 91(2): 101–114.

Kwakernaak, H. (1993). Robust control and hinf-optimization tutorial paper, *Automatica* 29: 253–273.

Kwakernaak, H. (2002). H2-optimization theory and applications to robust control design, *Annual Reviews in Control* 26: 45–56.

Lanzon, A. & Tsiotras, P. (2005). A combined application of H infin; loop shaping and mu;-synthesis to control high-speed flywheels, *Control Systems Technology, IEEE Transactions on* 13(5): 766–777.

Leith, D. J. & Leithead, W. E. (2000). Survey of gain-scheduling analysis and design, *International Journal of Control* 73(11): 1001–1025.

Li, G. (2007). *Robust stabilization of rotor-active magnetic bearing systems*, PhD thesis, University of Virginia.

Li, G., Lin, Z. & Allaire, P. (2006). Uncertainty classification of rotor-amb systems, *Proc. of* 11th *International Symposium on Magnetic Bearings*.

Li, G., Lin, Z., Allaire, P. & Luo, J. (2006). Modeling of a high speed rotor test rig with active magnetic bearings, *Journal of Vibration and Acoustics* 128: 269–281.

Limebeer, D. J. N., Kasenally, E. M. & Perkins, J. D. (1993). On the design of robust two degree of freedom controllers, *Automatica* 29(1): 157–168.

Losch, F. (2002). *Identification and Automated Controller Design for Active Magnetic Bearing Systems*, Swiss Federal Institute of Technology, ETH Zurich.

Lu, B., Choi, H., Buckner, G. D. & Tammi, K. (2008). Linear parameter-varying techniques for control of a magnetic bearing system, *Control Engineering Practice* 16(10): 1161–1172.

Lunz, J. (1989). *Robust Multivariable Feedback Control*, Prentice Hall, London.

Matsumura, F., Namerikawa, T., Hagiwara, K. & Fujita, M. (1996). Application of gain scheduled H_∞ robust controllers to a magnetic bearing, *Control Systems Technology, IEEE Transactions on* 4(5): 484–493.

Moser, A. (1993). Designing controllers for flexible structures with H-infinity/μ-synthesis, *IEEE Control Systems* pp. 79–89.

Mystkowski, A. & Gosiewski, Z. (2009). Uncertainty modeling in robust control of active magnetic suspension, *Solid State Phenomena* 144: 22–26.

Oliveira, V., Tognetti, E. & Siqueira, D. (2006). Robust controllers enhanced with design and implementation processes, *IEEE Trans. on Education* 49(3): 370–382.

Pilat, A. (2002). *Control of Magnetic Levitation Systems*, PhD thesis, AGH University of Science and Technology.

Pilat, A. (2009). Stiffness and damping analysis for pole placement method applied to active magnetic suspension (in polish), *Automatyka* 13: 43–54.

Pilat, A. (2010). mi-synthesis of robust controller for active magnetic levitation system, *MSM 2010 : Mechatronic Systems and Materials : 6th international conference : 5-8 July, Opole, Poland.*

Pilat, A. & Piatek, P. (2008). Multichannel control and measurement board with parallel data processing (in polish), *in* L. Trybus & S. Samolej (eds), *Recent advances in control and automation*, Academic Publishing House EXIT, pp. 00–00.

Pilat, A. & Turnau, A. (2005). Self-organizing fuzzy controller for magnetic levitation system, *Computer Methods and Systems, Krakï£¡w, Poland*, pp. 101–106.

Pilat, A. & Turnau, A. (2009). Neural adapted controller learned on-line in real-time, *14 International Conference on Methods and Models in Automation and Robotics, 19-21 August, Miedzyzdroje, Poland.*

Safonov, M. G. & Chiang, R. Y. (1988). A Schur Method for Balanced Model Reduction, *American Control Conference, 1988*, pp. 1036–1040.

Sawicki, J. & Maslen, E. (2008). Toward automated amb controller tuning: Progress in identification and synthesis, *Proc. of* 11th *International Symposium on Magnetic Bearings*, pp. 68–74.

Scherer, C., Gahinet, P. & Chilali, M. (1997). Multiobjective output-feedback control via LMI optimization, *IEEE Transations on Automatic Control* 42(7): 896–911.

Schweitzer, G. & Maslen, E. (2009). *Magnetic Bearings: Theory, Design, and Application to Rotating Machinery*, Springer, New York.

Sefton, J. & Glover, K. (1990). Pole/zero cancellations in the general [infinity] problem with reference to a two block design, *Systems and Control Letters* 14(4): 295–306.

Skogestad, S. & Postlethwaite, I. (2005). *Multivariable Feedback Control Analysis and Design*, 2 edn, John Wiley & Sons Ltd., England.

Turner, M. C. & Walker, D. J. (2000). Linear quadratic bumpless transfer, *Automatica* 36(8): 1089–1101.

Whidborne, J., Postlethwaite, I. & Gu, D.-W. (1994). Robust controller design using H_∞ loop-shaping and the method of inequalities, *IEEE Transations on Control Systems Technology* 2(2): 455–461.

Wu, F., Yang, X. H., Packard, A. & Becker, G. (1996). Induced L2-norm control for LPV systems with bounded parameter variation rates, *International Journal of Robust and Nonlinear Control* 6(9-10): 983–998.

Zhou, K. (1998). *Essentials of Robust Control*, Prentice-Hall, Upper Saddle River, NJ.

Zhou, K., Doyle, J. & Glover, K. (1996). *Robust and Optimal Control*, Prentice-Hall, Englewood Cliffs, NJ.

9

Robust Control of Electro-Hydraulic Actuator Systems Using the Adaptive Back-Stepping Control Scheme

Jong Shik Kim, Han Me Kim and Sung Hwan Park
School of Mechanical Engineering, Pusan National University
Republic of Korea

1. Introduction

Conventional hydraulic actuator (CHA) systems have been widely used as power units because they can generate very large power compared to their size. In general, a CHA system consists of an electric motor, a pump, a reservoir, various valves, hoses, which are used to transfer the working fluid and an actuator. CHA systems, however, have some problems such as environmental pollution caused by the leakage of the working fluid, maintenance load, heavy weight and limited installation space. These shortcomings can be overcome by compactly integrating the components of CHA systems and by applying a suitable control scheme for the electric motor. To overcome these shortcomings of CHA systems, electro-hydraulic actuator (EHA) systems have been developed, having merits such as smaller size, higher energy efficiency and faster response than existing CHA systems (Kokotovic, 1999). However, for the robust position control of EHA systems, system uncertainties such as the friction between the piston and cylinder and the pump leakage coefficient have to be considered.

To solve these system uncertainty problems of EHA systems and to achieve the robustness of EHA systems with system disturbance and bounded parameter uncertainties, Wang et. al. presented a sliding mode control and a variable structure filter based on the variable structure system (Wang, 2005). Perron et. al proposed a sliding mode control scheme for the robust position control of EHA systems showing volumetric capacity perturbation of the pump (Perron, 2005). However, these control methods have some chattering problem due to the variable structure control scheme. The chattering vibrates the system and may reduce the life cycle of the system. Jun et. al. presented a fuzzy logic self-tuning PID controller for regulating the BLDC motor of EHA systems which has nonlinear characteristics such as the saturation of the motor power and dead-zone due to the static friction (Jun, 2004). Chinniah et. al. used a robust extended Kalman filter, which can estimate the viscous friction and effective bulk modulus, to detect faults in EHA systems (Chinniah, 2006). Kaddissi et. al. applied a robust indirect adaptive back-stepping control (ABSC) scheme to EHA systems having perturbations of the viscous friction coefficient and the effective bulk modulus due to temperature variations (Kaddissi, 2006). However, in spite of the variation of the effective bulk modulus due to the temperature and pressure variations, Chinniah et. al. considered only the case of constant effective bulk modulus and Kaddissi et. al. used EHA systems that are not controlled by an electric motor but by a servo valve.

In this chapter, an ABSC scheme was proposed for EHA systems to obtain the desired tracking performance and the robustness to system uncertainties. Firstly, to realize a stable back-stepping control (BSC) system with a closed loop structure and to select new state variables, EHA system dynamics are represented with state equations and error equations. Defining the Lyapunov control functions, we can design a BSC system, which can guarantee exponential stability for the nominal system without system uncertainties. However, the BSC system cannot achieve robustness to system uncertainties. To overcome the drawback of the BSC system, an ABSC scheme for EHA position control systems with classical discrete disturbance observer was proposed. To evaluate the tracking performance and robustness of the proposed EHA position control system, both BSC and ABSC schemes were evaluated by computer simulation and experiment.

2. System modeling of EHA system

Figure 1 shows the simplified schematic diagram of an EHA system that consists of an electric servo motor, bi-directional gear pump and actuator. The servo motor rotates the gear pump, which, in turn, generates the flow rate. The pressure generated by the flow rate changes the position of the piston rod. The movement direction of the piston is related to the rotational direction of the servo motor. The chamber volumes of the actuator depend on the cross sectional area and the displacement of the piston as follows

$$\begin{cases} V_A(t) = V_{0A} + Ax(t) \\ V_B(t) = V_{0B} - Ax(t) \end{cases} \tag{1}$$

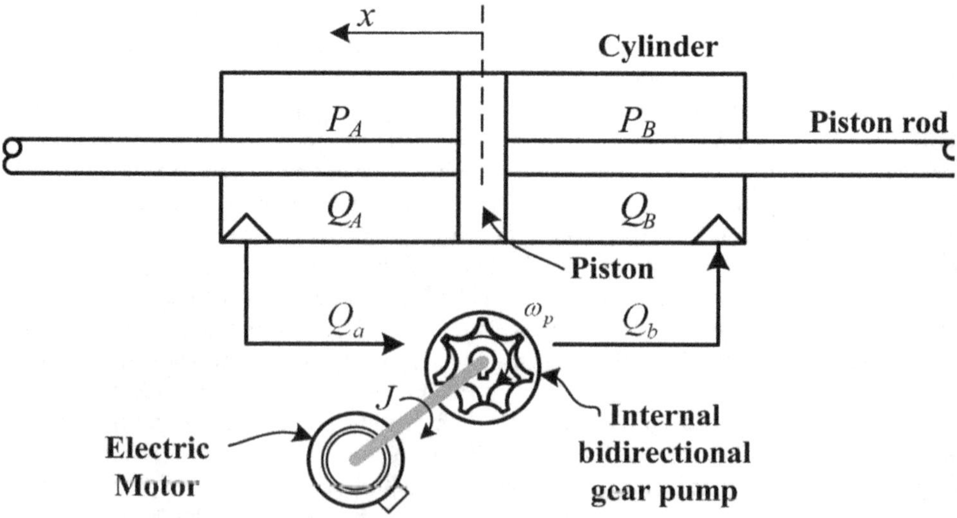

Fig. 1. Simplified schematic diagram of an EHA system

where V and V_0 are the chamber volume and the initial chamber volume, respectively, A and x are the pressure area of a double rod hydraulic cylinder and displacement of the piston, respectively, and subscripts 'A' and 'B' denote the chamber notations of the actuator. Considering the fluid compressibility and continuity principle for the actuator, the flow rate equations of both ports of the actuator can be represented as (Merritt, 1967)

$$\begin{cases} Q_A = A\dot{x} + \dfrac{V_{0A} + Ax}{\beta_e}\dot{P}_A + LP_A \\ Q_B = A\dot{x} - \dfrac{V_{0B} - Ax}{\beta_e}\dot{P}_B - LP_B \end{cases} \tag{2}$$

where Q is the flow rate in the actuator, β_e is the effective bulk modulus of the working fluid, and L and P are the actuator external leakage coefficient and the pressure in the chamber, respectively.

It is assumed that there is no fluid leakage of conduits because the conduits of EHA systems are very short and hard. Then, (2) can be expressed as

$$\begin{cases} Q_A = A\dot{x} + \dfrac{V_{0A} + Ax}{\beta_e}\dot{P}_A \\ Q_B = A\dot{x} - \dfrac{V_{0B} - Ax}{\beta_e}\dot{P}_B \end{cases} \tag{3}$$

The electric motor, directly connected to the hydraulic pump, changes the flow direction and adjusts the flow rate through the ports. In addition, the pressure generated by the continuous supply of flow in the actuator can produce a minute fluid leakage of the pump. Hence, the equations for the fluid leakage of the pump are expressed as

$$\begin{cases} Q_a = C_p\omega_p - L_f P_L \\ Q_b = -Q_a \end{cases} \tag{4}$$

where Q is the flow rate of the pump, whose subscripts a and b denote the ports of the pump, C_p is the volumetric capacity of the pump, ω_p is the rotational velocity of the electric motor, L_f is the leakage factor of the pump and the load pressure $P_L = P_A - P_B$. From (4), the inflow and outflow of the pump are expressed as functions of the rotational velocity ω_p.

In addition, the actuator dynamic equation of EHA systems is expressed as

$$(P_A - P_B)A = M\ddot{x} + F_f + F_{ex} \tag{5}$$

where M and x are the mass and displacement of the piston, respectively, F_f is the friction force between the cylinder and piston and F_{ex} is the external disturbance force.

In order to substitute (3) into (5), the derivative of (5) is expressed as

$$(\dot{P}_A - \dot{P}_B)A = M\dddot{x} + \dot{F}_f + \dot{F}_{ex} \tag{6}$$

In addition, it is assumed that the conduits connected between the actuator ports and the pump ports are very short. Then, the flow rates in (3) and (4) can be represented as $Q_A = Q_a$

and $Q_B = Q_b$. Substituting (1) through (4) into (6), therefore, the dynamic equation of EHA systems can be represented as

$$\ddot{x} = -\frac{1}{M}\left\{\beta_e A^2\left(\frac{1}{V_A}+\frac{1}{V_B}\right)\dot{x} + \dot{F}_f + \dot{F}_{ex}\right\} + \frac{\beta_e A}{M}\left(\frac{1}{V_A}+\frac{1}{V_B}\right)\left(L_f P_L - C_p\omega_p\right) \tag{7}$$

To represent the characteristics of the friction F_f between the piston and cylinder, the LuGre friction model is considered. The LuGre friction model is based on bristles analysis, which is represented with the average deflection force of bristles stiffness. The deflection displacement equation of bristles z, which is actually unmeasurable by experiment, is expressed as (Choi, 2004)(Lee, 2004)

$$\frac{dz}{dt} = \dot{x} - \frac{\sigma_0 |\dot{x}|}{g(\dot{x})} z \tag{8}$$

where σ_0 is the bristles stiffness coefficient, z is the unmeasurable internal state and the nonlinear function $g(\dot{x})$ depends on the material property, grade of lubrication and temperature; that is

$$g(\dot{x}) = F_c + F_s e^{-(\dot{x}/v_{sv})^2} \tag{9}$$

where F_c, F_s and v_{sv} represent the Coulomb friction force, static friction force, and Stribeck velocity between the cylinder and piston, respectively.

If the relative velocity of the contact materials increases gradually, the friction force decreases instantaneously and then it increases gradually again; this effect is called the Stribeck effect and the relative velocity is the Stribeck velocity. This phenomenon depends on the material property, grade of lubrication and temperature. The friction force F_f can be represented with the average deflection z and the velocity of the piston $\dot{x}$ as follows

$$F_f = \sigma_0 z + \sigma_1 \dot{z} + \mu \dot{x} \tag{10}$$

where σ_1 and μ represent the bristles damping and viscous friction coefficients, respectively.

3. Controller design for the EHA position control systems

The EHA position control system consists of the inner loop for the angular velocity control of the servo motor/pump and the outer loop for the position control of the piston. For the velocity control of the motor in the inner loop, Kokotovic et al. applied an adaptive control scheme so that the EHA position control systems can have robustness (Kokotovic, 1999). Habibi et. al. presented that if the inner loop dynamics are stable, the control gains of the PID velocity controller in the inner loop can have relatively large values and then the disturbance effect can be sufficiently rejected (Habibi, 1999). The velocity controller in the inner loop is very important because it regulates the electric motor. However, the case of (Kokotovic, 1999) is very complicated and the case of (Habibi, 1999), although it is theoretically possible, has a physical limitation that increases the control gains of the inner loop controller. Therefore, it is desirable to handle the controller in the outer loop rather than in the inner loop to improve the performance and robustness of EHA position control systems.

In this chapter, the BSC and ABSC schemes based on EHA system dynamics are considered as the position controller. Firstly, to design a BSC system, (7) is transformed to a general form (Slotine, 1999) as follows

$$\dddot{x} = f + bu \tag{11}$$

where

$$f = -\frac{1}{M}\left\{\beta_e A^2\left(\frac{1}{V_A}+\frac{1}{V_B}\right)\dot{x} + \dot{F}_f + \dot{F}_{ex} - \beta_e L_f A\left(\frac{1}{V_A}+\frac{1}{V_B}\right)P_L\right\},$$

$$b = -\frac{\beta_e A(V_A + V_B)C_p}{MV_A V_B},$$

$$u = \omega_p$$

Now, let (11) represent state equations as follows

$$\begin{cases} \dot{x}_1 = x_2 \\ \dot{x}_2 = x_3 \\ \dot{x}_3 = f + bu \end{cases} \tag{12}$$

And, in order to design the BSC system, new state variables are defined as follows

$$z_1 = x_1 - x_d \tag{13}$$

$$z_2 = x_2 - \alpha_1(z_1) \tag{14}$$

$$z_3 = x_3 - \alpha_2(z_1, z_2) \tag{15}$$

where x_d is the desired position input, and α_1 and α_2 are the functions for new state variables, which can be obtained through the following BSC design procedure.

Step 1.

From (13), the state equation for z_1 can be described as

$$\dot{z}_1 = z_2 + \alpha_1(z_1) - \dot{x}_d \tag{16}$$

$\alpha_1(z_1)$ is the virtual control which should be selected to guarantee the stability of the control system through the Lyapunov control function(LCF) which is defined as

$$V_1(z_1) = \frac{1}{2}z_1^2 \tag{17}$$

Then,

$$\dot{V}_1(z_1) = z_1\dot{z}_1 = z_1[\alpha_1(z_1) - \dot{x}_d] + z_1 z_2 \tag{18}$$

From (18), if $\alpha_1(z_1) = -k_1 z_1 + \dot{x}_d$, (16) can be exponentially stable when $t \to \infty$. And $k_1(>0)$ is a design parameter.

Step 2.
From (14), the state equation for z_2 can be described as

$$\dot{z}_2 = z_3 + \alpha_2(z_1, z_2) - \dot{\alpha}_1(z_1) \tag{19}$$

where

$$\dot{\alpha}_1(z_1) = \frac{\partial \alpha_1}{\partial z_1}\dot{z}_1 + \frac{\partial \alpha_1}{\partial \dot{x}_d}\ddot{x}_d = -k_1\dot{z}_1 + \ddot{x}_d = -k_1(z_2 - k_1 z_1) + \ddot{x}_d$$

Since (19) includes the information of (16), the second LCF for obtaining the virtual control to guarantee the stability of the control system can be selected as

$$V_2(z_1, z_2) = V_1(z_1) + \frac{1}{2}z_2^2 \tag{20}$$

Then,

$$\dot{V}_2(z_1, z_2) = \dot{V}_1(z_1) + \dot{z}_2 z_2 = -k_1 z_1^2 + z_2 z_3 + z_2[z_1 + \alpha_2(z_1, z_2) - \dot{\alpha}_1(z_1)] \tag{21}$$

If the virtual control α_2 in the last term of (21) is defined as

$$\alpha_2(z_1, z_2) = -k_2 z_2 - z_1 + \dot{\alpha}_1(z_1)$$

where $k_2(>0)$ is a design parameter, then another expression of α_2 can be rearranged as

$$\alpha_2(z_1, z_2) = -(k_1 + k_2)z_2 - (1 - k_1^2)z_1 + \ddot{x}_d \tag{22}$$

Therefore

$$\dot{V}_2 = z_2 z_3 - k_1 z_1^2 - k_2 z_2^2 \tag{23}$$

Step 3.
From (15), the state equation for z_3 is described as

$$\dot{z}_3 = \dot{x}_3 - \dot{\alpha}_2(z_1, z_2) = f + bu - \dot{\alpha}_2(z_1, z_2) \tag{24}$$

where

$$\dot{\alpha}_2(z_1, z_2) = \frac{\partial \alpha_2}{\partial z_1}\dot{z}_1 + \frac{\partial \alpha_2}{\partial z_2}\dot{z}_2 + \frac{\partial \alpha_2}{\partial \dot{\alpha}_1}\ddot{\alpha}_1 = -\dot{z}_1 - k_2\dot{z}_2 + \ddot{\alpha}_1 \tag{25}$$

and

$$\ddot{\alpha}_1 = \frac{\partial \dot{\alpha}_1}{\partial z_1}\dot{z}_1 + \frac{\partial \dot{\alpha}_1}{\partial z_2}\dot{z}_2 + \frac{\partial \dot{\alpha}_1}{\partial \ddot{x}_d}\dddot{x}_d = k_1^2\dot{z}_1 - k_1\dot{z}_2 + \dddot{x}_d \tag{26}$$

Substituting (16), (19), and (26) into (25), (25) can be rearranged as

$$\dot{\alpha}_2(z_1, z_2) = (k_1^2 - 1)\dot{z}_1 - (k_1 + k_2)\dot{z}_2 + \dddot{x}_d \tag{27}$$

Since (24) uses the information of z_1 and z_2 due to the property of the design procedure of the back-stepping control, the third LCF for (15) can be defined as

$$V_3(z_1, z_2, z_3) = V_2(z_1, z_2) + \frac{1}{2} z_3^2 \tag{28}$$

Then,

$$\dot{V}_3(z_1, z_2, z_3) = \dot{V}_2 + z_3 \dot{z}_3 = -k_1 z_1^2 - k_2 z_2^2 + z_3(z_2 + f + bu - \dot{\alpha}_2) \tag{29}$$

If the last term of (29) for satisfying the system stability is defined as

$$-k_3 z_3 = z_2 + f + bu - \dot{\alpha}_2 \tag{30}$$

then the BSC law can be selected as

$$u = \frac{1}{b}(\dot{\alpha}_2 - k_3 z_3 - z_2 - f) \tag{31}$$

From (31), if the information of f is assumed to be known, the negative semi-definite of $\dot{V}_3$ can be obtained by substituting (31) into (29) as

$$\dot{V}_3(z_1, z_2, z_3) = \dot{V}_2 + z_3 \dot{z}_3 = -k_1 z_1^2 - k_2 z_2^2 - k_3 z_3^2 \le 0 \tag{32}$$

From (32), it is found that EHA position control systems using the BSC law of (31) can guarantee exponential stability.

If system uncertainties can be exactly known, the BSC law of (31) can achieve the desired tracking performance and the robustness to the system uncertainties of EHA systems. However, the BSC law of (31) will cause a tracking error and does not achieve the robustness to the system uncertainties because the value of f cannot be exactly known. To improve the tracking performance and the robustness to the system uncertainties, the value of f, in which system uncertainties are included , should be estimated.

Therefore, in this chapter, an ABSC scheme is proposed, which is the BSC scheme with the estimator of f. In order to design the ABSC system, the BSC law of (31) is modified as

$$u = \frac{1}{b}(\dot{\alpha}_2 - k_3 z_3 - z_2 - \hat{f}) \tag{33}$$

where $\hat{f}$ is the estimator of the system uncertainties.

Substituting (33) into (12), (12) is modified as

$$\begin{cases} \dot{x}_1 = x_2 \\ \dot{x}_2 = x_3 \\ \dot{x}_3 = \tilde{f} + \dot{\alpha}_2 - k_3 z_3 - z_2 \end{cases} \tag{34}$$

where $\tilde{f} = f - \hat{f}$.

From (13), (14), and (15), these equations are the error equations for the velocity, acceleration and jerk of the piston, which include $\alpha_1(z_1)$ and $\alpha_2(z_1,z_2)$ that guarantee the exponential stability of EHA position control systems. Substituting these equations into (34), the error dynamics can be represented as

$$\begin{cases} \dot{z}_1 = z_2 - k_1 z_1 \\ \dot{z}_2 = z_3 - k_2 z_2 - z_1 \\ \dot{z}_3 = \tilde{f} - k_3 z_3 - z_2 \end{cases} \tag{35}$$

From (35), the LCF is defined as

$$V_4 = \frac{1}{2}z_1^2 + \frac{1}{2}z_2^2 + \frac{1}{2}z_3^2 + \frac{1}{2\gamma}\tilde{f}^2 \tag{36}$$

where γ is a positive constant.
The derivative of (36) can be described as

$$\dot{V}_4 = z_1\dot{z}_1 + z_2\dot{z}_2 + z_3\dot{z}_3 + \frac{1}{\gamma}\tilde{f}\dot{\tilde{f}} = -k_1 z_1^2 - k_2 z_2^2 - k_3 z_3^2 + \tilde{f}(z_3 - \frac{1}{\gamma}\dot{\tilde{f}}) \leq 0 \tag{37}$$

From (37), an estimation rule to guarantee the system stability can be obtained as

$$\dot{\hat{f}} = \dot{f} - \gamma z_3 \tag{38}$$

Equation (38) uses the information of z_3, which depends on the information of z_1 and z_2. Therefore, (38) closely relates to α_1 and α_2, which guarantee the stability of BSC systems. However, (38) cannot be used to the estimation rule because the value of f is unknown. On the other hand, if f is assumed as a lumped uncertainty, system uncertainty f can be estimated by $\hat{f} = -\gamma z_3$. However, since the value of f for the EHA system is changed according to the operating condition, it cannot be assumed as the lumped uncertainty. Therefore, to obtain the value of f, the classical discrete disturbance observer scheme was used. Assuming that the sampling rate of the control loop is very fast, the classical discrete disturbance observer expressed by the difference equation is induced from (31) as follows

$$f(k-1) = bu(k) - \dot{\alpha}_2(k) + k_3 z_3(k) + z_2(k) \tag{39}$$

To analyze the stability of the proposed control scheme, (38) is substituted into (37). Then,

$$\dot{V}_4 = -k_1 z_1^2 - k_2 z_2^2 - k_3 z_3^2 = -\mathbf{z}^{\mathrm{T}}\mathbf{K}\mathbf{z} < 0 \tag{40}$$

where $\mathbf{K}$ is the diagonal matrix of k_1, k_2 and k_3, $\mathbf{z}=[z_1\ z_2\ z_3]^{\mathrm{T}}$, and $\dot{V}_4 = 0$ if $\mathbf{z} = 0$.
If $\mathbf{z}$ is bounded, (40) can be defined as

$$\Phi(t) = \mathbf{z}^{\mathrm{T}}\mathbf{K}\mathbf{z} \geq 0 \tag{41}$$

Integrating (41) from 0 to t, the following result can be obtained

$$\int_0^t \Phi(\tau)d\tau = V_4(\mathbf{z}(0),\tilde{f}(0)) - V_4(t) \tag{42}$$

Applying Barbalat's Lemma(Krstic, 1995) to (42), we can obtain that $\Phi(t) \to 0$ as $t \to \infty$. Therefore,

$$\lim_{t\to\infty} \int_0^t \Phi(\tau)d\tau \le V_4(\mathbf{z}(0),\tilde{f}(0)) < \infty \tag{43}$$

4. Computer simulation

In order to evaluate the validity of the proposed control scheme for EHA position control systems, a sinusoidal reference input was considered as follows

$$x_d = \sin(0.25\pi t) + \sin(0.05\pi t) \ \text{[cm]} \tag{44}$$

This sinusoidal reference input is suitable for evaluating the tracking performance and the robustness of EHA position control systems because it reflects the various changes in the magnitudes of the velocity and position of the piston. Table 1 shows the system parameters of the EHA system which are used to computer simulation. Figure 2 shows the block diagram of the EHA position control system.

Notation	Description	Unit
V_0	Initial volume of the chamber	3.712×10^{-4} m^3
A	Pressure area of the piston	5.58×10^{-3} m^2
M	Piston mass	5 kg
β_e	Effective bulk modulus	1.7×10^3 MPa
L_f	Leakage factor of the pump	3.16×10^{-16} m^3/Pa
σ_0	Bristles stiffness coefficient	5.77×10^6 N/m
σ_1	Bristles damping coefficient	2.28×10^4 N/m/s
$\omega_{p\max}$	Maximum speed of the motor	178 rad/s
C_p	Volumetric capacity of the pump	1.591×10^{-6} m^3/rad
μ_0	Coulomb friction coefficient	370 N
μ_1	Static friction	217 N
μ_2	Viscous friction coefficient	2318 N/m/s
v_{sv}	Stribeck velocity	0.032 m/s

Table 1. System parameters of the EHA

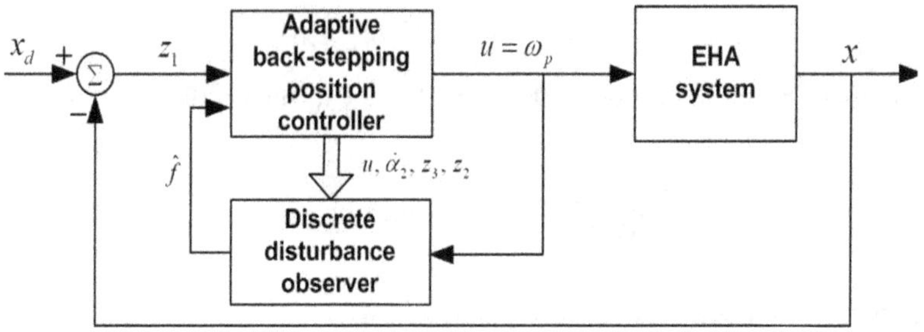

Fig. 2. Block diagram of the EHA position control system

Figure 3 shows the tracking errors of the BSC and ABSC systems for the sinusoidal reference. This result shows that the ABSC system has better tracking performance than the BSC system and has error repeatability precision of higher reliability than the BSC system. In addition, in both position and control schemes relatively large tracking errors occur at the nearly zero velocity regions. This is due to the effect of dynamic friction characteristics, which produce an instantaneous large force at the nearly zero velocity regions. For the transient response region of the initial operation of EHA position control systems, the ABSC system with the estimator for system uncertainties yields approximately 40% improvement compared with the BSC system without the estimator because the f in (31) including system uncertainties is estimated by (43), as shown in Fig. 4. Figure 4 shows the estimated value $\hat{f}$ for the system uncertainties of EHA systems obtained by the proposed adaptive rule. The estimated value plat a role in the consideration of nonlinearity and uncertainties included in EHA systems.

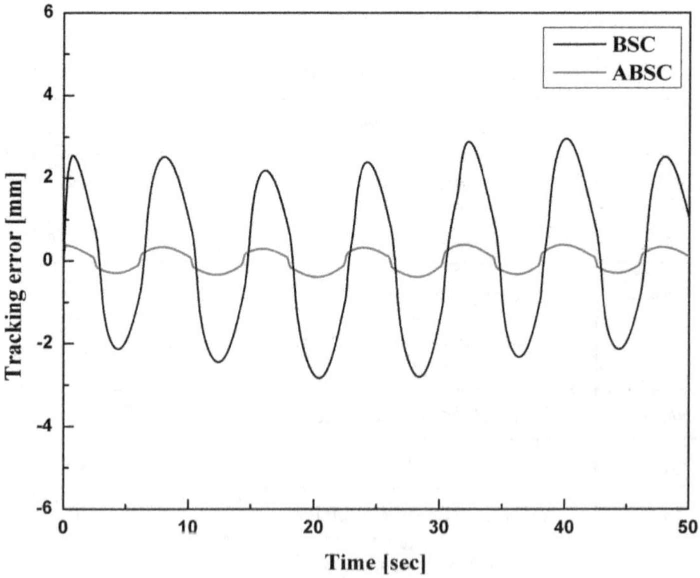

Fig. 3. Tracking errors of the BSC and ABSC systems for the sinusoidal reference input

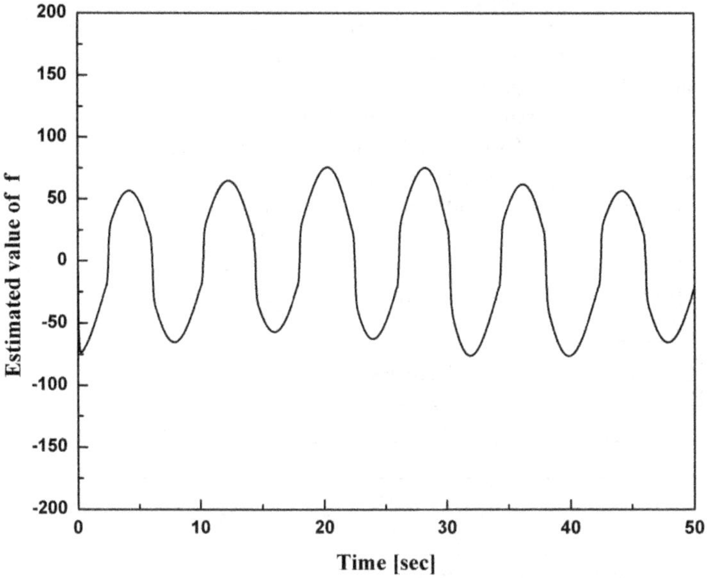

Fig. 4. Estimated value for the system uncertainties of the ABSC system for the sinusoidal reference input

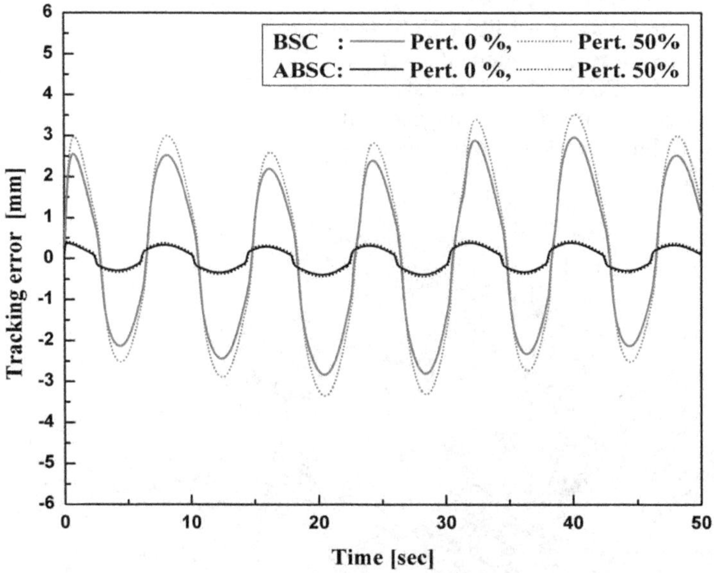

Fig. 5. Tracking errors of the BSC and ABSC systems with the perturbation of the system parameters

Figure 5 shows the tracking errors of the BSC and ABSC systems having perturbations of the system parameters such as the Coulomb friction, viscous friction and pump leakage coefficient in the EHA system for the sinusoidal reference input. It was assumed that the system parameters have a perturbation of 50%. From Fig. 5, it was found that the perturbations of the system parameters of the EHA system are closely related with the tracking performance of the EHA system. Table 2 shows the tracking RMS errors of the BSC and ABSC systems according to the perturbation of the system parameters. The variations of the tracking RMS errors due to the 50% perturbation of the system parameters for the BSC and ABSC systems are 17.6% and 3.02%, respectively. These results show that the proposed position control scheme has the desired robustness to system uncertainties such as the perturbation of the viscous friction, Coulomb friction and pump leakage coefficient.

Control scheme	Perturbation ratio	RMS value
BSC	0%	1.878 mm
	50%	2.209 mm
ABSC	0%	0.265 mm
	50%	0.273 mm

Table 2. Tracking RMS errors of the BSC and ABSC systems according to the perturbations of the system parameters

5. Experimental results and discussion

Figure 6 shows the experimental setup of the EHA system. To evaluate the effectiveness of the proposed control system, the PCM-3350(AMD Geode processor, 300MHz) was used. The control algorithms were programmed by Turbo-C++ language on MS-DOS, in order to directly handle the PCM-3718 as a data acquisition board. The PCM-3718 is a fully multifunctional card with PC/104 interface. In addition, to measure the position of the piston, an LVDT(linear variable differential transformer) sensor was used. The sampling rate was set to 1 kHz.

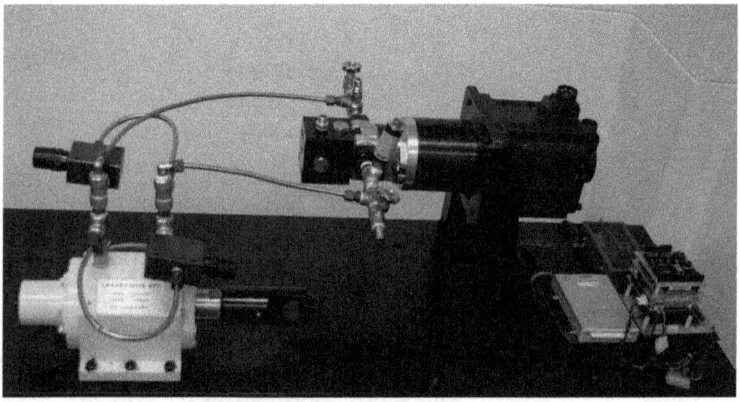

Fig. 6. Experimental setup of the EHA system

Figure 7 shows the tracking errors of the BSC and ABSC systems for the sinusoidal reference input, which was used in the computer simulation. The tracking error of the BSC system is relatively large when the direction of the piston is changed because the BSC system cannot compensate the friction of the EHA system. In addition, the tracking error of the BSC varies according to the direction of the piston because of the system uncertainties of the EHA system. However, the ABSC system has better tracking performance than the BSC system because the ABSC system can effectively compensate the system uncertainties as well as the nonlinear friction effects by using the estimated value $\hat{f}$, which is shown in Fig. 8.

Figure 9 shows the speed of the motor as the control input for the sinusoidal reference input. Figure 10 shows the tracking errors of the BSC and ABSC systems for the square wave type reference input. The characteristics of the transient responses of the BSC and the ABSC systems are almost same. In the BSC system, however, steady-state error occurs relatively large in the backward direction. This shows that the BSC system cannot compensate the system uncertainties of the EHA system. But we can show that the ABSC system can effectively compensate the system uncertainties regardless of the piston direction. Figure 11 shows the estimated value $\hat{f}$ for the system uncertainties of the ABSC system for the square wave type reference input. The estimated value $\hat{f}$ for the system uncertainties makes the desired tracking performance and robustness to the EHA system with system uncertainties. Figure 12 shows the speed of the motor as the control input for the square wave type reference input.

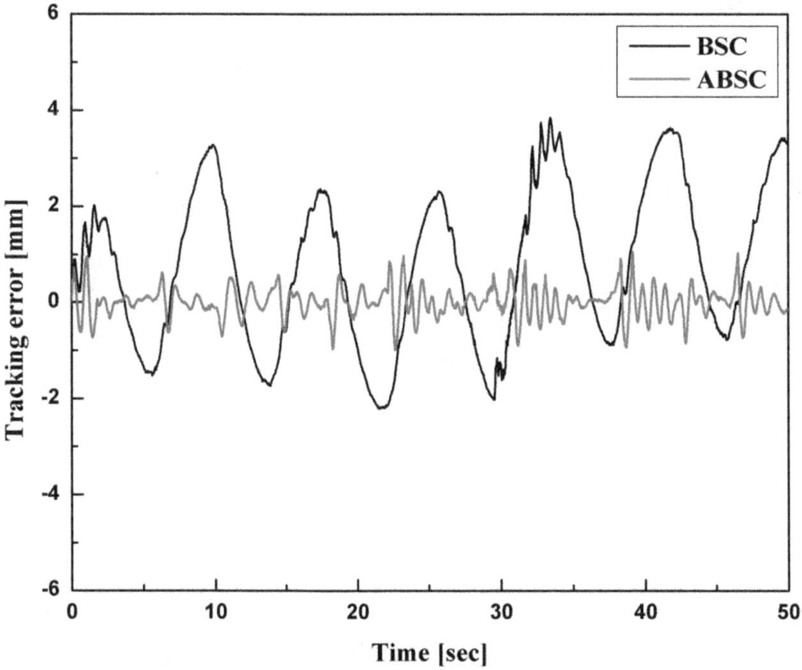

Fig. 7. Tracking errors of the BSC and ABSC systems for the sinusoidal reference input

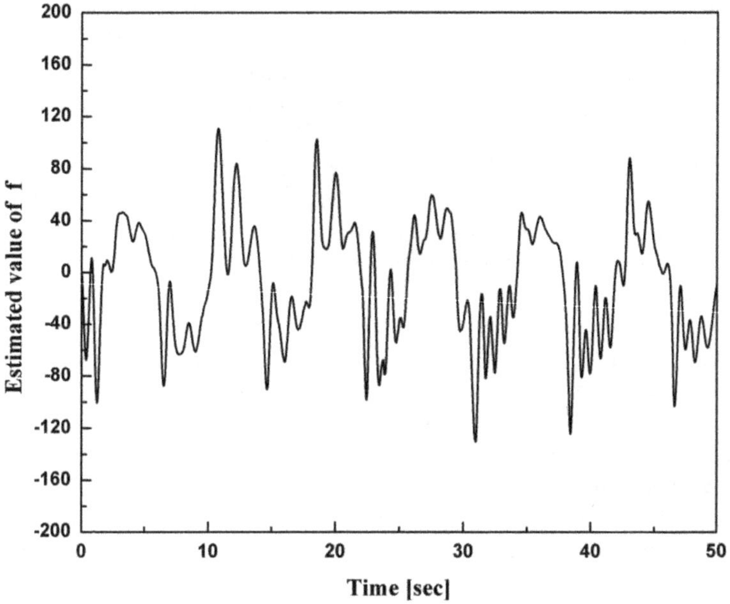

Fig. 8. Estimated value for the system uncertainties of the ABSC system for the sinusoidal reference input

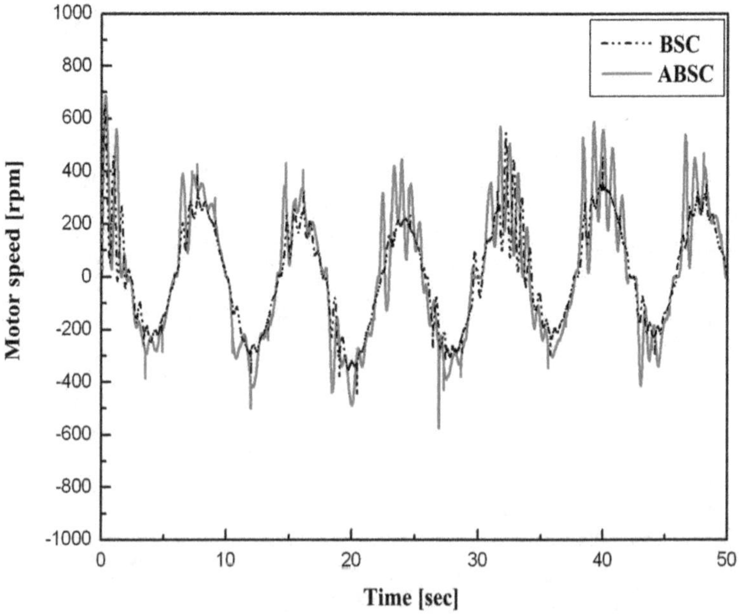

Fig. 9. Speed of the motor as the control input for the sinusoidal reference input

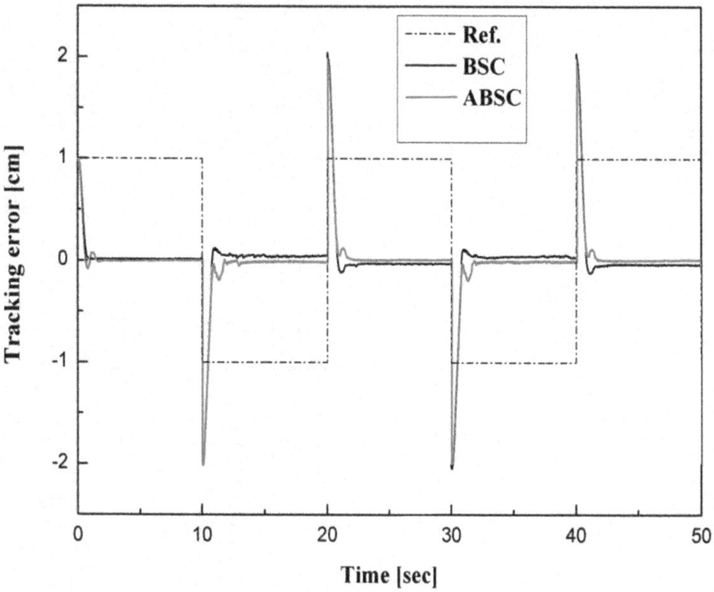

Fig. 10. Tracking errors of the BSC and ABSC systems for the square wave type reference input

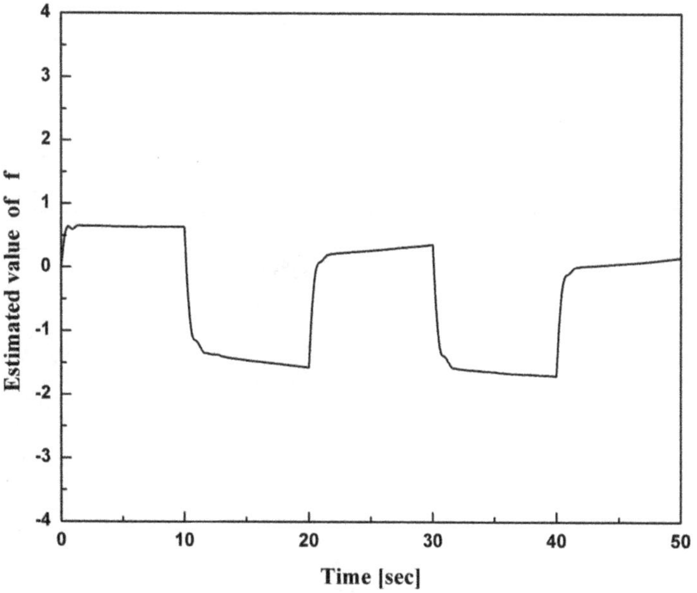

Fig. 11. Estimated value for the system uncertainties of the ABSC system for the square wave type reference input

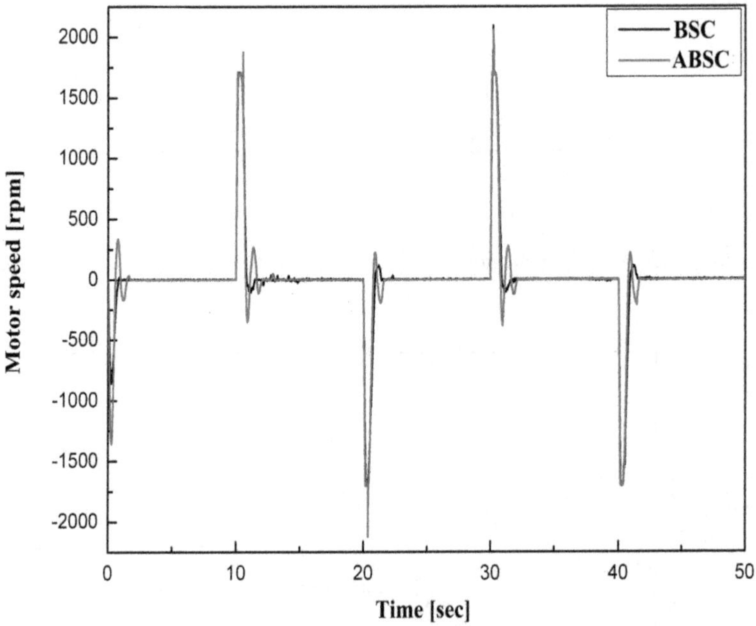

Fig. 12. Speed of the motor as the control input for the square wave type reference input

Table 3 shows the tracking RMS errors of the BSC and ABSC systems for the sinusoidal reference input and the square wave type reference input at steady-state. From Table 3, it was found that using the ABSC system instead of the BSC system yields about 5 times improvement in the tracking performance of the EHA position control system.

Control system	Sinusoidal reference input	Square wave type reference input at steady state
BSC	1.762 mm	0.395 mm
ABSC	0.309 mm	0.114 mm

Table 3. Tracking RMS errors of the BSC and ABSC systems

6. Conclusion

A robust position control of EHA systems was proposed by using the ABSC scheme, which has robustness to system uncertainties such as the perturbation of viscous friction, Coulomb friction and pump leakage coefficient. Firstly, a stable BSC system based on the EHA system dynamics was derived. However, the BSC scheme had a drawback: it could not consider system uncertainties. To overcome the drawback of the BSC scheme, the ABSC scheme was proposed having error equations for the velocity, acceleration and jerk of the piston, respectively, which were induced by the BSC scheme. To evaluate the performance and robustness of the proposed EHA position control system, BSC and ABSC schemes were implemented in a computer simulation and experiment. It was found that the ABSC scheme can yield the desired tracking performance and the robustness to system uncertainties.

7. References

Y. Chinniah, R. Burton and S. Habibi (2006), Failure monitoring in a high performance hydrostatic actuation system using the extended kalman filter, *Int. J. Mechatronics 16(10)* , pp. 643-653.

J. J. Choi, J. S. Kim and S. I. Han (2004), Pre-sliding friction control using the sliding mode controller with hysteresis friction compensator, *KSME Int'l J. 18(10)*, pp. 1755-1762.

S. Habibi and A. Goldenberg (2000), Design of a new high-performance electro-hydraulic actuator, IEEE Trans. *Mechatronics 5(2)*, pp. 158-164.

L. Jun, F. Yongling, Z. Guiying, G. Bo and M. Jiming (2004), Research on fast response and high accuracy control of an airborne brushless DC motor, *Proc. 2004 IEEE Int. Conf. Robotics and Biomimetics*, Shenyang, China, pp. 807-810.

C. Kaddissi, J. P. Kenne and M. Saad (2006), Indirect adaptive control of an electro-hydraulic servo system based on nonlinear backstepping, *IEEE Int. Symposium Ind. Electron*, Montreal, Quebec, Canada, pp. 3147-3153.

V. V. Kokotovic, J. Grabowski, V. Amin and J. Lee (1999), Electro hydraulic power steering system, *Int. Congress & Exposition*, Detroit, Michigan, USA, pp. 1-4.

M. Krstic, I. Kanellakopoulos and P. Kokotovic (1995), Nonlinear and Adaptive Control Design, *Wiley Interscience*, New York, USA.

K. J. Lee, H. M. Kim and J. S. Kim (2004), Design of a chattering-free sliding mode controller with a friction compensator for motion control of a ball-screw system, *IMechE J. of Systems and Control Engineering*, 218, pp. 369-380.

H. E. Merritt (1967), Hydrostatic Control Systems, Wiley, New York, USA.

M. Perron, J. de Lafontaine and Y. Desjardins (2005), Sliding-mode control of a servomotor-pump in a position control application, *IEEE Conf. Electrical and Computer Eng*, Saskatoon, Canada, pp. 1287-1291.

J. J. Slotine and W. Li (1991), Applied Nonlinear Control, *Pearson Education*, New Jersey, USA.

S. Wang, R. Burton and S. Habibi (2005), Sliding mode controller and filter applied to a model of an electro-hydrostatic actuator system, *ASME Int. Mechanical Engineering Congress & Exposition*, Orlando, Florida, USA, pp. 1-10.

10

A Decentralized and Spatial Approach to the Robust Vibration Control of Structures

Alysson F. Mazoni, Alberto L. Serpa and Eurípedes G. de O. Nóbrega
University of Campinas - UNICAMP
Brazil

1. Introduction

Designing active controllers for minimizing mechanical vibration of structures is a challenging task which presents several levels of difficulties. Due to the continuous nature of the structures, they have an infinite number of degrees of freedom which leads to infinite vibration modes. This requires a model reduction and modal truncation considering the controller objectives, in order to achieve a viable numerical model which may allow the designed controller to perform satisfactorily within the frequency range of interest (Zhou & Doyle, 1997). But for real structures, even for truncated models, it may be expected a significant number of vibration modes to consider, conducting to mathematical and computational issues, besides the natural consequences of the reduction of the model order leading to unexpected behavior due to the controller feedback.

Considering the now vast literature in the vibration control area, there is no consensus regarding the most suitable control design method. Several techniques seem to give similar results, as shown in the works of Baz & Chen (2000); Bhattacharya et al. (2002); Hurlebaus et al. (2008). Linear matrix inequalities methods, due to powerful yet simple formulation and computational solution to implement the theory of robust control, present nowadays a slight predominance (Boyd et al., 1994; Zhou & Doyle, 1997). Several recent works that use this approach may be cited such as Barrault et al. (2007; 2008); Cheung & Wong (2009); Halim et al. (2008).

The $\mathcal{H}_\infty$ control technique emerged in the last decades as a robust control technique in the context of multiple-inputs and multiple-outputs (MIMO) feedback problems. The usual formulation involves the minimization of the $\mathcal{H}_\infty$ norm from the disturbances inputs to the performance outputs, corresponding to the minimization of the worst possible response. Vibration control of structures is a well reported application using this approach (Gawronski, 2004). Usually, performance outputs are selected based on the interest points distributed over the structure, and taken for the formulation of the objective function in the minimization problem.

However, the control problem, stated as the transfer matrix between the vibration actuator and sensor positions, has a known drawback. Because it does not clearly impose the desired behavior on the whole structure, it is not possible to guarantee the vibration level minimization beyond the sensor isolated position points. This approach may present acceptable reduction levels for simple structures, but more comprehensive methods are needed to achieve good results with real engineering structures, guaranteeing a vibration reduction through regions of the structure instead of isolated points.

The overall vibration energy distribution is then necessary to be considered, which renders the control problem always a non-collocated one. Additionally, real structures require in general a significant number of transducers, increasing the complexity of the system due to the number of transfer function combinations of inputs and outputs.

The spatial $\mathcal{H}_\infty$ control looks for an equivalent worst case output performance norm, in order to have a weighted performance over an specific region of the structure, instead of points. Addressing regions of interest instead of points, this methodology is attractive to the vibration control area. Particularly, for the common case of using a finite element model for the formulation of the spatial $\mathcal{H}_\infty$ control, it results in a simple formulation.

Some works have discussed the spatial $\mathcal{H}_\infty$ control, specially in the case of plate vibration (Halim, 2002; 2007; Halim et al., 2008). In these works, the spatial $\mathcal{H}_\infty$ design is solved trough a convenient algebraic manipulation which converts the spatial norm formulation to an equivalent ordinary $\mathcal{H}_\infty$ control problem.

Decentralized control is another promising approach recently studied for the vibration problem. Its basic architectural idea is to adopt several distributed controllers with lesser authority, instead of a big controller for the whole structure. Each controller accesses a subset of inputs and outputs, being responsible for a region of the structure. Decentralized control has been used for sound irradiation control of plates in Bianchi et al. (2004), with semi-active control in Casadei et al. (2010), using an optimal controller with static feedback in Jiang & Li (2010) and with decentralized velocity feedback in Zilletti et al. (2010). It is obviously useful for big structures in particular, where its constructive robustness represent an immediate advantage, since it may be implemented using independent microcontrollers and the system can easily accommodate actuator or sensor failures. Another advantage is the numerical simplicity of the controller algorithms, since each one deals with a smaller number of inputs and outputs. One problem is to decouple the controllers in order to avoid mutual undesired interference.

The purpose of this work is to compare an application of the spatial norm and the decentralized approaches to the vibration control of a plate including the $\mathcal{H}_\infty$ control technique, and adopting a linear matrix inequalities formulation.

The finite element method is used here to determine the vibration model of a plate. The plate is divided in Mindlin finite elements generating a discretized finite dimensional model that captures the vibration modes (Ferreira, 2008). The finite element method is suitable to determine the mass and stiffness matrices using interpolation functions of each finite element of the mesh, and the assemblage of these results for all the elements leads to a representation of the structure. This model is then used to generate the state-space model used to design the active controller.

This chapter is divided according to the following main topics: Structural modeling, where the main aspects of the dynamic equations, modal analysis fundamentals to describe the model, and model reduction are described; $\mathcal{H}_\infty$ control, where the optimization problem to minimize the $\mathcal{H}_\infty$ norm and aspects of multi-variable control are discussed; Spatial $\mathcal{H}_\infty$ control technique, where a more global and spatial vibration performance along the structure is considered as vibration reduction objective; Decentralized control, where controllers are designed in an independent form in order to reduce the design effort and also to increase the reliability in case of failures, is presented. Finally, the concluding remarks are presented.

The notation used in this work is: matrices are denoted by uppercase bold (**M**, **K**, **A** etc); vectors are denoted by lowercase bold (**x**, **z**, **y** etc); transposition of a matrix is denotes by the apostrophe (transpose of $\mathbf{C}$ is denoted by $\mathbf{C}'$ etc); time is denoted by variable t; frequency is denoted by ω.

2. Mechanical structures modeling

2.1 Dynamic equation

The movement equation of a generic structure can be written as

$$\mathbf{M}\ddot{\mathbf{q}}(t) + \mathbf{D}\dot{\mathbf{q}}(t) + \mathbf{K}\mathbf{q}(t) = \mathbf{B}_0\mathbf{f}(t), \tag{1}$$

where $\mathbf{q}(t)$ denotes the displacements, $\mathbf{M}$ is the mass matrix, $\mathbf{D}$ is the damping matrix, $\mathbf{K}$ is the stiffness matrix, $\mathbf{f}(t)$ is the vector of all external forces and $\mathbf{B}_0$ is a localization matrix for the external forces.

The main features of the dynamic response of a vibrating structure (Gawronski, 2004) are: 1) presence of resonance (amplification of response in specific frequencies); 2) the vibration models are decoupled (they can be excited independently); 3) the total response can be obtained by the summation of each mode contribution; 4) the impulse response consists of harmonic components, which are related to complex poles with small real parts; and 5) the system is controllable and observable.

2.2 Modal model

The structural model described in Eq. (1) can be represented also in modal coordinates (Ewins, 2000; Gawronski, 2004). The advantages of this kind of description are that the modal properties become evident such as the natural frequencies and damping factors for each structural mode.

The solution for the undamped free vibration is given by $\mathbf{q}(t) = \bar{\mathbf{q}}e^{j\omega t}$. Substituting this solution in the undamped free vibration movement equation it is obtained the eigen-problem given by

$$\mathbf{K}\bar{\mathbf{q}} = \omega^2\mathbf{M}\bar{\mathbf{q}}. \tag{2}$$

A structural system with n degrees of freedom presents n natural frequencies and n vibration modes. These natural frequencies and modes are determined through the solution of the eigen-problem related to the characteristic equation given by

$$det(\mathbf{K} - \omega^2\mathbf{M}) = 0 \tag{3}$$

The natural frequencies ω_i can be stored in a diagonal matrix $\mathbf{\Omega}$ given by

$$\mathbf{\Omega} = diag[\omega_1 \;\; \omega_2 \;\; \dots \;\; \omega_n], \tag{4}$$

and the vibration modes $\boldsymbol{\phi}_i$ can be stored in the matrix $\mathbf{\Phi}$ according to

$$\mathbf{\Phi} = [\boldsymbol{\phi}_1 \;\; \boldsymbol{\phi}_2 \;\; \dots \;\; \boldsymbol{\phi}_n]. \tag{5}$$

The model represented by the matrices $\mathbf{K}$ and $\mathbf{M}$ is the spatial model. The model denoted by the matrices $\mathbf{\Omega}$ and $\mathbf{\Phi}$ is the modal model.

A very important property is the orthogonality that allows the diagonalization of mass and stiffness matrices, i.e.,

$$\mathbf{\Phi}'\mathbf{M}\mathbf{\Phi} = diag[m_1 \;\; m_2 \;\; \dots \;\; m_n] = diag[m_i], \tag{6}$$

$$\mathbf{\Phi}'\mathbf{M}\mathbf{\Phi} = diag[k_1 \;\; k_2 \;\; \dots \;\; k_n] = diag[k_i]. \tag{7}$$

A specific situation which is mathematically convenient is the proportional damping where $\mathbf{D} = \alpha\mathbf{M} + \beta\mathbf{K}$. In this case it can be verified directly that the damping matrix is also diagonalized since **M** and **K** can be diagonalized, i.e.,

$$\mathbf{\Phi}'\mathbf{D}\mathbf{\Phi} = \alpha\mathbf{\Phi}'\mathbf{M}\mathbf{\Phi} + \beta\mathbf{\Phi}'\mathbf{K}\mathbf{\Phi} = diag[d_1 \;\; d_2 \;\; \dots \;\; d_n] = diag[d_i] \tag{8}$$

Considering a coordinate transformation given by $\mathbf{p}(t) = \mathbf{\Phi}\mathbf{q}(t)$, and pre-multiplying the Eq. (1) by $\mathbf{\Phi}$, it is possible to obtain for proportional damping

$$\mathbf{\Phi}'\mathbf{M}\mathbf{\Phi}\ddot{\mathbf{p}}(t) + \mathbf{\Phi}'\mathbf{D}\mathbf{\Phi}\dot{\mathbf{p}}(t) + \mathbf{\Phi}'\mathbf{K}\mathbf{\Phi}\mathbf{p}(t) = \mathbf{\Phi}'\mathbf{B}_0\mathbf{f}(t), \tag{9}$$

which can be rewriten as

$$diag[m_i]\ddot{\mathbf{p}}(t) + diag[d_i]\dot{\mathbf{p}}(t) + diag[k_i]\mathbf{p}(t) = \mathbf{\Phi}'\mathbf{B}_0\mathbf{f}(t) \tag{10}$$

One can verify that Eq. (10) corresponds to a set of uncoupled second order differential equations similar to the movement equation of the one degree of freedom system. Each decoupled equation corresponds to a specific vibration mode of the system and can be written as

$$m_i\ddot{p}_i(t) + d_i\dot{p}_i(t) + k_ip_i(t) = \bar{f}_i(t), \tag{11}$$

or in a standard form of second order system as

$$\ddot{p}_i(t) + 2\xi\omega_i\dot{p}_i(t) + \omega_i^2p_i(t) = \gamma\omega_i^2\bar{f}_i(t). \tag{12}$$

It is possible to write for the i-mode the corresponding conjugate pair of poles

$$-\xi_i\omega_i \pm j\omega_i\sqrt{1-\xi_i^2} \tag{13}$$

where ω_i is the natural frequency and ξ_i is the non-dimensional damping factor, both related to the i vibration mode.

The modal model is a convenient way to include damping in models obtained by the finite element method, for example. The damping factor of each mode can be included independently. The proportional damping is not a mandatory hypothesis in this work since the control techniques can be applied to non-proportional damping also.

2.3 State-space model

The Eq. (1) can be rewriten as

$$\ddot{\mathbf{q}}(t) + \mathbf{M}^{-1}\mathbf{D}\dot{\mathbf{q}}(t) + \mathbf{M}^{-1}\mathbf{K}\mathbf{q}(t) = \mathbf{M}^{-1}\mathbf{B}_0\mathbf{f}(t). \tag{14}$$

Two kinds of external forces may be present in the active vibration control problem: the disturbance forces, denoted by $\mathbf{w}(t)$, and the control forces, denoted by $\mathbf{u}(t)$. Two kinds of outputs of the system can be defined: the measured outputs, denoted here by $\mathbf{y}(t)$, and the performance outputs, denoted by $\mathbf{z}(t)$.

Defining the state-space vector as $\mathbf{x}(t) = [\mathbf{q}(t) \;\; \dot{\mathbf{q}}(t)]'$, which corresponds to the displacements and velocities in this case, it is possible to write the state-space model in the form

$$\dot{\mathbf{x}}(t) = \mathbf{A}\mathbf{x}(t) + \mathbf{B}_1\mathbf{w}(t) + \mathbf{B}_2\mathbf{u}(t), \tag{15}$$

$$\mathbf{z}(t) = \mathbf{C}_1\mathbf{x}(t) + \mathbf{D}_{11}\mathbf{w}(t) + \mathbf{D}_{12}\mathbf{u}(t), \tag{16}$$

$$\mathbf{y}(t) = \mathbf{C}_2\mathbf{x}(t) + \mathbf{D}_{21}\mathbf{w}(t) + \mathbf{D}_{22}\mathbf{u}(t), \tag{17}$$

where the state-space matrix $\mathbf{A}$ is given by

$$\mathbf{A} = \begin{bmatrix} \mathbf{0} & \mathbf{I} \\ -\mathbf{M}^{-1}\mathbf{K} & -\mathbf{M}^{-1}\mathbf{K} \end{bmatrix}. \tag{18}$$

The matrices $\mathbf{B}_1$ and $\mathbf{B}_2$ are constructed with the structure $[\mathbf{0}\ \ \mathbf{M}^{-1}\mathbf{B}_0]'$ where the appropriate position matrix $\mathbf{B}_0$ is used for $\mathbf{w}(t)$ and for $\mathbf{u}(t)$. It is convenient to mention that the number of columns of $\mathbf{B}_1$ is the number of disturbances and the number of columns of $\mathbf{B}_2$ is the number of control forces.

The matrices $\mathbf{C}_1$, $\mathbf{D}_{11}$ and $\mathbf{D}_{12}$ are constructed to define the performance output in terms of the displacements, velocities and accelerations, or linear combinations of these values. The number of lines of $\mathbf{C}_1$ is the number of performances outputs to be monitored.

The matrices $\mathbf{C}_2$, $\mathbf{D}_{21}$ and $\mathbf{D}_{22}$ are constructed to specify the measured output also in terms of the displacements, velocities and accelerations. The number of lines of $\mathbf{C}_2$ is the number of measures.

This dynamic system can be represented in a compact form according to

$$\begin{bmatrix} \dot{\mathbf{x}}(t) \\ \mathbf{z}(t) \\ \mathbf{y}(t) \end{bmatrix} = \begin{bmatrix} \mathbf{A} & \mathbf{B}_1 & \mathbf{B}_2 \\ \mathbf{C}_1 & \mathbf{D}_{11} & \mathbf{D}_{12} \\ \mathbf{C}_2 & \mathbf{D}_{21} & \mathbf{D}_{22} \end{bmatrix} \begin{bmatrix} \mathbf{x}(t) \\ \mathbf{w}(t) \\ \mathbf{u}(t) \end{bmatrix}. \tag{19}$$

The transfer matrix of the system in Laplace domain variable s, relating each input to each output, can be writen as

$$\mathbf{P}(s) = \mathbf{C}(s\mathbf{I} - \mathbf{A})^{-1}\mathbf{B} + \mathbf{D}, \tag{20}$$

where

$$\mathbf{B} = [\mathbf{B}_1\ \ \mathbf{B}_2], \quad \mathbf{C} = \begin{bmatrix} \mathbf{C}_1 \\ \mathbf{C}_2 \end{bmatrix}, \quad \mathbf{D} = \begin{bmatrix} \mathbf{D}_{11} & \mathbf{D}_{12} \\ \mathbf{D}_{21} & \mathbf{D}_{22} \end{bmatrix}. \tag{21}$$

2.4 State-space model in modal form

Considering that in modal coordinates the differential equations are decoupled for each mode, it is possible to reorganize the state-space in a modal form. Based on the standard form given by the Eq. (12), a state-space model for each mode can be generated.

One usual form of modal model (Gawronski, 2004) considers the states defined as

$$\mathbf{x}_i = \begin{bmatrix} \omega_i p_i \\ \xi_i \omega_i p_i + \dot{p}_i \end{bmatrix}. \tag{22}$$

For this case, the state-space matrix for the i-mode is given by

$$\mathbf{A}_i = \begin{bmatrix} -\xi_i\omega_i & \omega_i \\ -\omega_i & -\xi_i\omega_i \end{bmatrix}. \tag{23}$$

The state-space matrix will be a block diagonal matrix with the contribution of each mode in the form

$$\mathbf{A} = diag(\mathbf{A}_i). \tag{24}$$

This formulation is used in this work through the function `canon` with the option `modal` in the MATLAB® software.

2.5 Model reduction

A real structure is a continuous system with infinite degrees of freedom. It is necessary to have a finite dimensional representation for the system. This representation can be obtained by techniques such as finite elements or direct experimental identification. These two approaches lead to models that are finite dimensional but that can present a number of degrees of freedom yet considered excessive large. In this case, in order to have a feasible numerical treatment and feasible controller design, it is necessary to have a reduced order model.
The model reduction can be performed according to some techniques (Qu, 2004). The most usual and simple technique is the model truncation, where a number of modes is kept under a critical frequency value of interest. Upper frequency modes are simply discarded. This technique is adequate for the objectives of this work, and it is adopted here. Obviously the lost information can affect the dynamic representation of the structure and bring undesirable effects, such as spillover, implying the use of additional performance filtering to the model. In most situations, the interest in the dynamic response of the structure is limited to a specific range of frequencies, and the model reduction can be performed considering this information. In the present case, the model reduction is conducted using the function `modreal` of the software MATLAB. This function performs the model reduction selecting the frequency ordered blocks of the modal model corresponding to the indicated frequency range, i.e., the selection is based on the blocks of the Eq. (24).

3. Structural and control models - plate vibration

It is considered in this work a finite element model of a plate. The MATLAB codes given in Ferreira (2008) were employed to obtain the mass and stiffness matrices considering the Mindlin plate formulation. The plate finite element has four nodes and three degrees of freedom in each node: rotations in axes x and y and displacement in axis z. The plate in this work was considered with all boundaries free. The finite element mesh is shown in Figure 1, and Table 1 shows the physical parameters used in the finite element model of the plate.
This finite element model presents 90 nodes with 3 degrees of freedom per node. This leads to a model of 270 degrees of freedom and 540 states. This model was reduced to a model with 24 states for control design purposes.
This model is used in this work to evaluate the spatial and decentralized $\mathcal{H}_\infty$ control techniques. There are, in this plate model, three convenient orientations for the transducers: horizontal, vertical and with an orientation of 45 degrees (representing identical actuation in the degrees of freedom in x and y directions of the same node). The placement of these sensors and actuators are indicated in Figure 1.

Height	1 m
Width	1 m
Thickness	2 mm
Density	2710 kg/m^3
Poisson Modulus	0.33
Young Modulus	70 GPa

Table 1. Physical properties of the plate

In order to have a more realistic dynamic system in the simulations, damping should be taken into account. In this case, it was included a modal damping of 3×10^{-6} to all vibration modes of the plate.

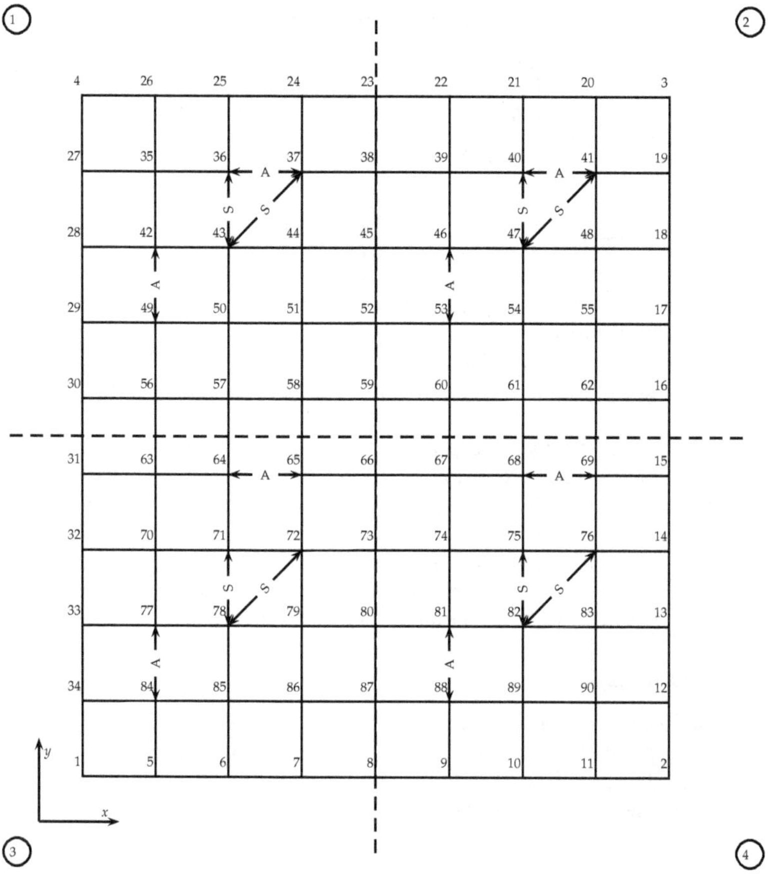

Fig. 1. Finite element mesh for the plate with four partitions - A denotes actuators and S denotes sensors

It is considered that the actuators and sensors are piezoelectric (PZT). The actuator receives a voltage and apply a pair of opposite moments in nearby nodes. The sensor generates a voltage proportional to its deformation, i.e., proportional to the difference between angles in nearby nodes. Figure 2 shows schematically the actuator and sensor representation used in this work.

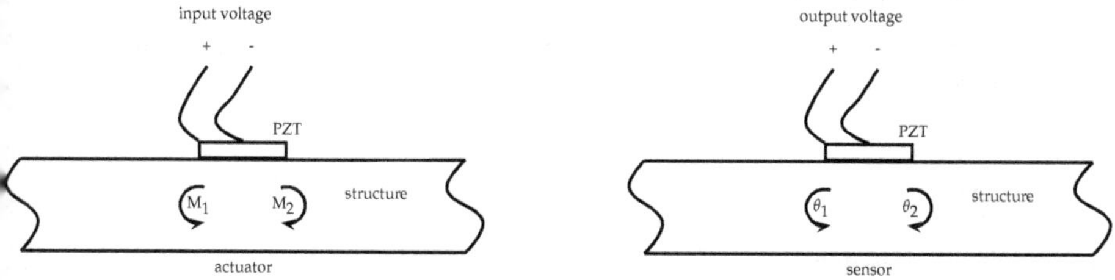

Fig. 2. PZT actuator and sensor relations to the respective degrees-of-freedom

	Actuators			Sensors		
	Number	DOF	Nodes	Number	DOF	Nodes
Disturbance	1 (w)	⊙	86			
Partition 1	2 (u_1)	↔	36 - 37	1 (z_1)	⤢	43 - 37
	3 (u_2)	↕	49 - 42	2 (y_1)	↕	43 - 36
Partition 2	4 (u_3)	↔	40 - 41	3 (z_2)	⤢	47 - 41
	5 (u_4)	↕	53 - 46	4 (y_2)	↕	47 - 40
Partition 3	6 (u_5)	↔	64 - 65	5 (z_3)	⤢	78 - 72
	7 (u_6)	↕	84 - 77	6 (y_3)	↕	78 - 71
Partition 4	8 (u_7)	↔	68 - 69	7 (z_4)	⤢	82 - 76
	9 (u_8)	↕	88 - 81	8 (y_4)	↕	82 - 75

Table 2. Definition and placement of actuators and sensors for the mesh in the Figure 1.

Table 2 shows actuators, sensors and nodes location for the mesh of Figure 1. The arrows indicate the respective degrees of freedom. The partition reveals which actuators and sensors are used in each local model for the case of the decentralized control. The disturbance is considered a force in the z direction applied in the node 86. Actuators numbered from 2 to 9 are chosen as control inputs. Sensors 2, 4, 6 and 8 are measuring outputs. The performance parameters are the sensors numbered as 1, 3, 5 and 7. The uncontrolled system was normalized to have an $\mathcal{H}_\infty$ norm equal to 1 (normalized plant).

4. $\mathcal{H}_\infty$ control formulation

The $\mathcal{H}_\infty$ control design method consists of designing a controller transfer function $\mathbf{K}(s)$ in a closed loop with a plant $\mathbf{P}(s)$ in order to minimize the $\mathcal{H}_\infty$ norm of the closed loop transfer function $\mathbf{T}(s)$ from the disturbance $\mathbf{w}$ to the performance $\mathbf{z}$ in the frequency domain ω. The loop is usually represented as in Figure 3.

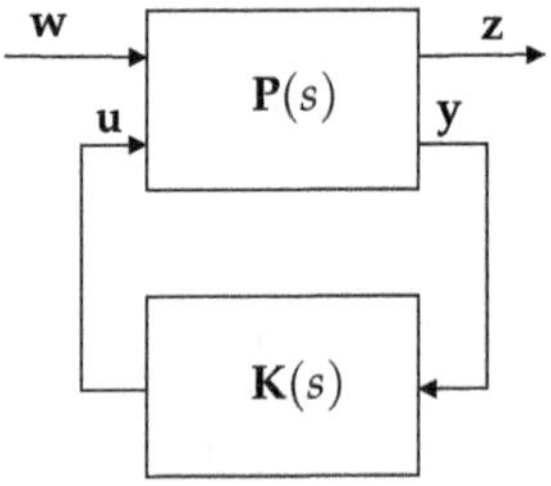

Fig. 3. $\mathcal{H}_\infty$ closed loop diagram

The $\mathcal{H}_\infty$ norm of a system, from the disturbance input $\mathbf{w}(t)$ to the performance output $\mathbf{z}(t)$ (Skelton et al., 1998), can be defined as

$$J_\infty = \|\mathbf{T}(s)\|_\infty = \frac{\int_0^\infty \mathbf{z}'(t)\mathbf{z}(t)\,dt}{\int_0^\infty \mathbf{w}'(t)\mathbf{w}(t)dt}. \tag{25}$$

The $\mathcal{H}_\infty$ norm can be calculated as

$$\|\mathbf{T}(s)\|_\infty = \sup_\omega \bar{\sigma}(\mathbf{T}(j\omega)),$$

where $\bar{\sigma}$ is the maximum singular value of the transfer function $\mathbf{T}(s)$ (Zhou & Doyle, 1997). This is a measure in the frequency domain of the worst response of $\mathbf{T}(s)$. If the worst response, in the sense of the higher amplitude, is achieved to an acceptable level, the performance is evidently guaranteed for all cases.

Weighting functions are used in this work to compel the performance output and control signals to follow the specified frequency distributions. In general, low-pass weighting functions $W_z(s)$ are used to balance the performance output levels and high-pass functions $W_u(s)$ are applied to the control forces. Commonly used filter functions (Zhou & Doyle, 1997) are:

$$W_p(s) = \left(\frac{s\sqrt[k]{M} + \omega_c}{s + \omega_c \sqrt[k]{\epsilon}} \right)^k, \qquad W_u(s) = \left(\frac{s + \omega_c \sqrt[k]{M}}{s\sqrt[k]{\epsilon} + \omega_c} \right)^k,$$

where ω_c is the cut frequency, k is the filter order, M is the gain at pass band and ϵ is the gain at rejection band.

Specifying the correct weighting functions for each problem is very important in the controller design process. They define the frequency regions where the disturbance signals response should be minimized and where the control signals should be effective, avoiding the excitation of neglected vibration modes in the model, which is fundamental to avoid the spillover effect (Balas, 1978).

An $\mathcal{H}_\infty$ controller design problem can be written as an optimization problem. The controller $\mathbf{K}(s)$ can be obtained by the minimization of the $\mathcal{H}_\infty$ norm of the closed-loop $\mathbf{T}(s)$, i.e.,

$$\begin{array}{rl} \min_{\mathbf{K}(s)} & \|\mathbf{T}(s)\|_\infty \\ \text{subjected to} & \mathbf{K}(s) \text{ stable} \\ & \mathbf{T}(s) \text{ stable.} \end{array}$$

This optimization problem can be considered a global design, since it involves all the inputs and outputs of the plant. Provided an acceptable level of vibration, a sub-optimal solution of this problem may be obtained solving the associated Riccati equations or by the solution of a linear matrix inequality problem (Boyd et al., 1994; Zhou & Doyle, 1997). The solution of this problem can be obtained using the MATLAB Robust Control Toolbox with the `hinfsyn` function for example.

5. Spatial $\mathcal{H}_\infty$ control

5.1 Spatial $\mathcal{H}_\infty$ norm

The $\mathcal{H}_\infty$ norm may be generalized considering a spatial distribution for the performance parameters. This can lead to a weighted response over the specified spatial region.

The spatial $\mathcal{H}_\infty$ norm (Skelton et al., 1998) for a dynamic system considering the disturbance input $\mathbf{w}(t)$ to the spatial performance output $\mathbf{z}(r,t)$ can be defined as

$$J_\infty = \frac{\int_0^\infty \int_{\mathcal{R}} \mathbf{z}'(t,r)\mathbf{Q}(r)\mathbf{z}(t,r)\, drdt}{\int_0^\infty \mathbf{w}'(t)\mathbf{w}(t)\, dt}, \tag{26}$$

where $\mathcal{R}$ denotes the spatial region and $\mathbf{Q}(r)$ is a spatial weighting function.

5.2 Spatial and non-spatial $\mathcal{H}_\infty$-control parallel

The spatial $\mathcal{H}_\infty$ norm allows to generalize the $\mathcal{H}_\infty$ control design problem. Consider a system in which the performance output $\mathbf{z}(r,t)$ depends both on space (r) and time (t), whilst the measured output $\mathbf{y}(t)$ depends only on time. The state space model may be described as:

$$\begin{aligned} \dot{\mathbf{x}}(t) &= \mathbf{A}\mathbf{x}(t) + \mathbf{B}_1\mathbf{w}(t) + \mathbf{B}_2\mathbf{u}(t) \\ \mathbf{z}(t,r) &= \mathbf{C}_1(r)\mathbf{x}(t) + \mathbf{D}_{11}(r)\mathbf{w}(t) + \mathbf{D}_{12}(r)\mathbf{u}(t) \\ \mathbf{y}(t) &= \mathbf{C}_2 x(t) + \mathbf{D}_{21}\mathbf{w}(t) + \mathbf{D}_{22}\mathbf{u}(t). \end{aligned} \tag{27}$$

It is possible to notice that r stands for a vector position and can represent two or three-dimensional problems. The definition of the spatial norm is a multiple integral depending on the problem dimensionality according to the Eq. (26).
The purpose of control design is to obtain a dynamic controller given by

$$\begin{aligned} \dot{\mathbf{x}}_k(t) &= \mathbf{A}_k\mathbf{x}_k(t) + \mathbf{B}_k y(t) \\ \mathbf{u}(t) &= \mathbf{C}_k\mathbf{x}_k(t) + \mathbf{D}_k\mathbf{y}(t), \end{aligned}$$

which reduces the particular norm of interest.
The spatial $\mathcal{H}_\infty$ problem is solved through the conversion to an equivalent punctual $\mathcal{H}_\infty$ with a modified performance output $\tilde{\mathbf{z}}(t)$, which is responsible for taking into account the desired vibration region. The ordinary $\mathcal{H}_\infty$ norm based on $\tilde{\mathbf{z}}(t)$ according to Equation (25) is

$$J_\infty = \frac{\int_0^\infty \tilde{\mathbf{z}}'(t)\tilde{\mathbf{z}}(t)\,dt}{\int_0^\infty \mathbf{w}'(t)\mathbf{w}(t)\,dt}. \tag{28}$$

Comparing equations (28) and (26) it is possible to establish the equivalence

$$\tilde{\mathbf{z}}'(t)\tilde{\mathbf{z}}(t) = \int_{\mathcal{R}} \mathbf{z}'(t,r)\mathbf{Q}(r)\mathbf{z}(r,t)\,dr. \tag{29}$$

This equivalence allows to convert the spatial $\mathcal{H}_\infty$ control design problem into the standard $\mathcal{H}_\infty$ problem with the modified performance output.
From Equation (27):

$$\mathbf{z}(t,r) = [\mathbf{C}_1(r)\ \ \mathbf{D}_{11}(r)\ \ \mathbf{D}_{12}(r)] \begin{bmatrix} \mathbf{x} \\ \mathbf{w} \\ \mathbf{u} \end{bmatrix},$$

and the equivalent punctual output

$$\tilde{\mathbf{z}}(t) = \mathbf{\Gamma} \begin{bmatrix} \mathbf{x} \\ \mathbf{w} \\ \mathbf{u} \end{bmatrix}. \tag{30}$$

Using Equation (29), it is possible to write

$$\begin{bmatrix} \mathbf{x} \\ \mathbf{w} \\ \mathbf{u} \end{bmatrix}' \mathbf{\Gamma}'\mathbf{\Gamma} \begin{bmatrix} \mathbf{x} \\ \mathbf{w} \\ \mathbf{u} \end{bmatrix} =$$

$$= \int_R \begin{bmatrix} \mathbf{x} \\ \mathbf{w} \\ \mathbf{u} \end{bmatrix}' \begin{bmatrix} \mathbf{C}_1'(r) \\ \mathbf{D}_{11}'(r) \\ \mathbf{D}_{12}'(r) \end{bmatrix} \mathbf{Q}(r)\, [\mathbf{C}_1(r)\ \ \mathbf{D}_{11}(r)\ \ \mathbf{D}_{12}(r)] \begin{bmatrix} \mathbf{x} \\ \mathbf{w} \\ \mathbf{u} \end{bmatrix} dr,$$

$$\begin{bmatrix} \mathbf{x} \\ \mathbf{w} \\ \mathbf{u} \end{bmatrix}' \mathbf{\Gamma}'\mathbf{\Gamma} \begin{bmatrix} \mathbf{x} \\ \mathbf{w} \\ \mathbf{u} \end{bmatrix} =$$

$$= \begin{bmatrix} \mathbf{x} \\ \mathbf{w} \\ \mathbf{u} \end{bmatrix}' \int_{\mathcal{R}} \begin{bmatrix} \mathbf{C}_1'(r) \\ \mathbf{D}_{11}'(r) \\ \mathbf{D}_{12}'(r) \end{bmatrix} \mathbf{Q}(r) \left[\mathbf{C}_1(r) \;\; \mathbf{D}_{11}(r) \;\; \mathbf{D}_{12}(r)\right] dr \begin{bmatrix} \mathbf{x} \\ \mathbf{w} \\ \mathbf{u} \end{bmatrix}.$$

The equivalence results in the following equality

$$\mathbf{\Gamma}'\mathbf{\Gamma} =$$

$$= \int_{\mathcal{R}} \begin{bmatrix} \mathbf{C}_1'(r) \\ \mathbf{D}_{11}'(r) \\ \mathbf{D}_{12}'(r) \end{bmatrix} \mathbf{Q}(r) \left[\mathbf{C}_1(r) \;\; \mathbf{D}_{11}(r) \;\; \mathbf{D}_{12}(r)\right] dr. \tag{31}$$

By defining a spatial weighting function $\mathbf{Q}(r)$, the matrix $\mathbf{\Gamma}'\mathbf{\Gamma}$ can be found from Equation (31) and $\mathbf{\Gamma}$ may be determined. One should notice that $\mathbf{\Gamma}$ is the transformation that allows the punctual $\mathcal{H}_\infty$ problem to represent equivalently the spatial $\mathcal{H}_\infty$ problem.
Using Equation (30), the performance output $\tilde{\mathbf{z}}$ is defined as

$$\tilde{\mathbf{z}} = \mathbf{\Gamma} \begin{bmatrix} \mathbf{x} \\ \mathbf{w} \\ \mathbf{u} \end{bmatrix} = \left[\mathbf{\Pi} \;\; \mathbf{\Theta}_1 \;\; \mathbf{\Theta}_2\right] \begin{bmatrix} \mathbf{x} \\ \mathbf{w} \\ \mathbf{u} \end{bmatrix},$$

in which $\mathbf{\Pi}$, $\mathbf{\Theta}_1$ and $\mathbf{\Theta}_2$ are simultaneously defined as matrix partitions of $\mathbf{\Gamma}$ according to the signal dimensions.
So, the final plant model is written as

$$\begin{aligned} \dot{\mathbf{x}}(t) &= \mathbf{A}\mathbf{x}(t) + \mathbf{B}_1\mathbf{w}(t) + \mathbf{B}_2\mathbf{u}(t) \\ \tilde{\mathbf{z}}(t) &= \mathbf{\Pi}\mathbf{x}(t) + \mathbf{\Theta}_1\mathbf{w}(t) + \mathbf{\Theta}_2\mathbf{u}(t) \\ \mathbf{y}(t) &= \mathbf{C}_2\mathbf{x}(t) + \mathbf{D}_{21}\mathbf{w}(t) + \mathbf{D}_{22}\mathbf{u}(t). \end{aligned}$$

5.3 Calculation of Γ

Equation (31) defines $\mathbf{\Gamma}'\mathbf{\Gamma}$ as an integral of a square matrix of order $n + n_w + n_u$, where n is the number of plant states, n_w is the number of disturbances and n_u is the number of control signals. $\mathbf{\Gamma}$ has dimensions $p \times (n + n_w + n_u)$, where the number of lines p represents the number of performance outputs, i.e., the number of lines of $\tilde{\mathbf{z}}$. The number of elements of $\mathbf{\Gamma}$ is $p \times (n + n_w + n_u)$ and the number of elements of $\mathbf{\Gamma}'\mathbf{\Gamma}$ is $(n + n_w + n_u) \times (n + n_w + n_u)$. Since, $\mathbf{\Gamma}'\mathbf{\Gamma}$ is symmetric, the number of unknowns elements are $(n + n_w + n_u)(n + n_w + n_u + 1)/2$. A convenient choice is $p = n + n_w + n_u$, which amounts to a square matrix for $\mathbf{\Gamma}$, and in this case a Cholesky factorization can be applied in $\mathbf{\Gamma}'\mathbf{\Gamma}$ to obtain $\mathbf{\Gamma}$. Another possibility to determine Γ involves a specific situation related to finite element models as described in the next section.

5.4 Γ for the case of constant spatial weighting

Taking the spatial weighting function constant inside every element allows some simplifying results. In this case the spatial performance output can be discretized for the degrees of freedom that are the model states and the spatial performance output can be interpolated from the degrees of freedom. The integral of Equation (31) that defines $\mathbf{\Gamma}'\mathbf{\Gamma}$ may be approximated as

$$\mathbf{\Gamma}'\mathbf{\Gamma} \approx \sum_i f(r_i) \begin{bmatrix} \mathbf{C}_1'(r_i) \\ \mathbf{D}_{11}'(r_i) \\ \mathbf{D}_{12}'(r_i) \end{bmatrix} \mathbf{Q}(r_i) \left[\mathbf{C}_1(r_i) \ \mathbf{D}_{11}(r_i) \ \mathbf{D}_{12}(r_i)\right], \tag{32}$$

by supposing an integration method such as the gaussian quadrature (Bathe, 1995), where the values $f(r_i)$ represent the contribution to the specific degree of freedom. In this case, $f(r_i)$ can be considered the gauss weightings and r_i the respective integration points (in this case the degrees of freedom).

If the finite element mesh is homogeneous in terms of the element size, a simplification of a constant value of the integrand inside each element can be used leading to less calculations. The integral in Equation (31) becomes a summation according to

$$\mathbf{\Gamma}'\mathbf{\Gamma} = \sum_i \begin{bmatrix} \mathbf{C}_{1i}' \\ \mathbf{D}_{11i}' \\ \mathbf{D}_{12i}' \end{bmatrix} Q_i \left[\mathbf{C}_{1i} \ \mathbf{D}_{11i} \ \mathbf{D}_{12i}\right] A_i, \tag{33}$$

with A_i as an elementary length, area or volume, according to the dimension in the integral, and Q_i is the weighting function value related to point i in Equation (32). A simplification of notation, taking i to denote the corresponding r_i, was employed.

Defining $t_i = Q_i A_i$, it is possible to write Equation (33) as

$$\mathbf{\Gamma}'\mathbf{\Gamma} = \sum_i \left(\begin{bmatrix} \mathbf{C}_{1i}' \\ \mathbf{D}_{11i}' \\ \mathbf{D}_{12i}' \end{bmatrix} \sqrt{t_i} \right) \left(\sqrt{t_i} \left[\mathbf{C}_{1i} \ \mathbf{D}_{11i} \ \mathbf{D}_{12i}\right] \right).$$

This summation can be rewritten as

$$\mathbf{\Gamma}'\mathbf{\Gamma} = \left(\sum_i \sqrt{t_i} \begin{bmatrix} \mathbf{C}_{1i}' \\ \mathbf{D}_{11i}' \\ \mathbf{D}_{12i}' \end{bmatrix} \right) \left(\sum_i \sqrt{t_i} \left[\mathbf{C}_{1i} \ \mathbf{D}_{11i} \ \mathbf{D}_{12i}\right] \right) - \mathbf{X},$$

where

$$\mathbf{X} = \sum_i \sum_j^{i \neq j} t_i \begin{bmatrix} \mathbf{C}_{1i}' \\ \mathbf{D}_{11i}' \\ \mathbf{D}_{12i}' \end{bmatrix} \left[\mathbf{C}_{1j} \ \mathbf{D}_{11j} \ \mathbf{D}_{12j}\right].$$

Since finite element models are considered in this work, where the degrees of freedom are model states, the matrices $\left[\mathbf{C}_{1j} \ \mathbf{D}_{11j} \ \mathbf{D}_{12j}\right]$ are orthogonal. $\mathbf{C}_{1j}$ is a matrix of zeros with a one in the position j of the convenient degree of freedom. $\mathbf{D}_{11j}$ and $\mathbf{D}_{12j}$ are null since the displacement and velocities are the states. Acceleration outputs are not considered in this work. This yields $\mathbf{X} = \mathbf{0}$ and consequently

$$\mathbf{\Gamma}'\mathbf{\Gamma} = \left(\sum_i \sqrt{t_i} \begin{bmatrix} \mathbf{C}_{1i}' \\ \mathbf{D}_{11i}' \\ \mathbf{D}_{12i}' \end{bmatrix} \right) \left(\sum_i \sqrt{t_i} \left[\mathbf{C}_{1i} \ \mathbf{D}_{11i} \ \mathbf{D}_{12i}\right] \right)$$

where one can choose

$$\Gamma = \sum_i \sqrt{t_i} \left[\mathbf{C}_{1i} \ \mathbf{D}_{11i} \ \mathbf{D}_{12i}\right]. \tag{34}$$

In this way, a numerical definition of the output matrix $\mathbf{\Gamma}$ of the $\mathcal{H}_\infty$ spatial control is achieved for the particular case of finite element models, where the degrees of freedom are the states.

6. Decentralized $\mathcal{H}_\infty$ control

The decentralized control design problem can be obtained by imposing a block-diagonal structure to the controller. If the order of inputs and outputs in the transfer function respects physical proximity, a block diagonal structure for the controller can be obtained such as:

$$\mathbf{K}(s) = \begin{bmatrix} \mathbf{K}_1(s) & & & \\ & \mathbf{K}_2(s) & & \\ & & \ddots & \\ & & & \mathbf{K}_p(s) \end{bmatrix},$$

where $\mathbf{K}_i(s)$ are the local controllers.
It is difficult to formulate the decentralized control design with a problem structure that can be solved easily. When the optimization problem is formulated through linear matrix inequalities, the requirement to impose a particular structure in the decision variable $\mathbf{K}(s)$ represents a mathematical difficulty that can lead to a non-convex problem. This difficulty motivates the investigation of other approaches for the decentralized control.
One alternative is that the original plant can be divided in several local plants with their own inputs and outputs and with spatially close actuators and sensors. In this case, it is possible to design local controllers corresponding to each plant subdivision. The closed-loop can be generated by employing these controllers along with the original plant in all its input and output signals, i.e., it is possible to solve several optimization problems such as

$$\begin{array}{rl} \min_{\mathbf{K}_i(s)} & \|\mathbf{T}_i(s)\|_\infty \\ \text{subjected to} & \mathbf{K}_i(s) \text{ stable} \\ & \mathbf{T}_i(s) \text{ stable.} \end{array}$$

where the controllers $\mathbf{K}_i(s)$ are obtained. In this case, the closed-loop is a function of all controllers and of the global plant.
Through this approach no additional mathematical development is necessary, since the solution is taken as a combination of solutions of several simultaneous optimizations problems.

7. Simulated results

Using $\mathcal{H}_\infty$ control for both the centralized and decentralized designs the same configuration of actuators and sensors already described were adopted in order to permit to compare the results.
The control design is performed using the linear matrix inequalities formulation for the $\mathcal{H}_\infty$ controller design using the function `hinfsyn` of MATLAB 7.2 (default parameters).
The parameters of the weighting filters used in this work are shown in Table 3. The same filters were employed in all simulations of this work.
A simulation test is performed according to the presented configuration of inputs and outputs. A linear sine sweep of 10 s from 0 to 2 KHz is used as a disturbance signal in all cases.

	ω_c	k	M	ϵ
$W_z(s)$ - low-pass weight for performance	1500	1	0.1	0.001
$W_u(s)$ - high-pass weight for control force	2000	1	0.1	0.001

Table 3. Weighting filters parameters

7.1 Centralized control

The centralized control case is the ordinary punctual $\mathcal{H}_\infty$ applied to the finite element model of the plate described above. Control results for the centralized control are shown in time domain in Figure 4 and in frequency domain in Figure 5.

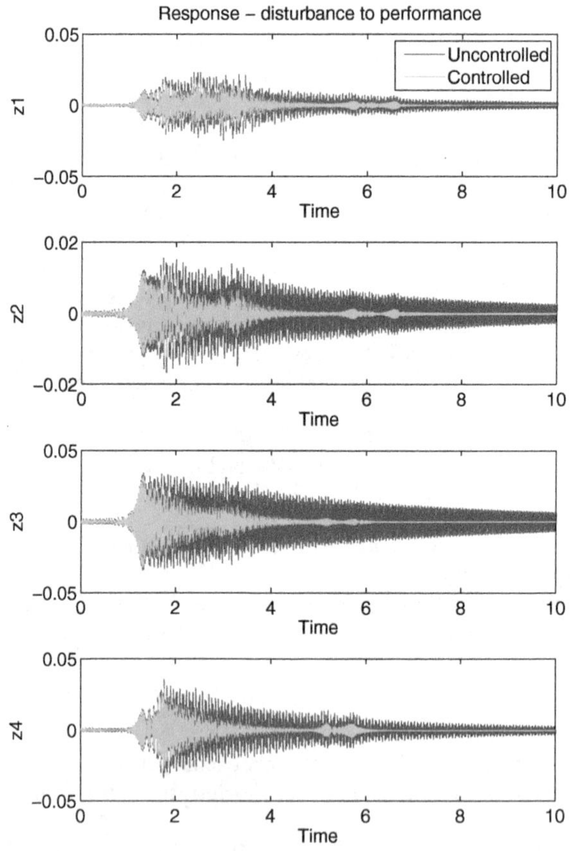

Fig. 4. Centralized control - control result from disturbance signal to spatial performance output

The time scale in Figure 4 is the duration of the sweep disturbance signal, and it may be interpreted as a frequency scale. It is possible to observe a good attenuation increasing as the

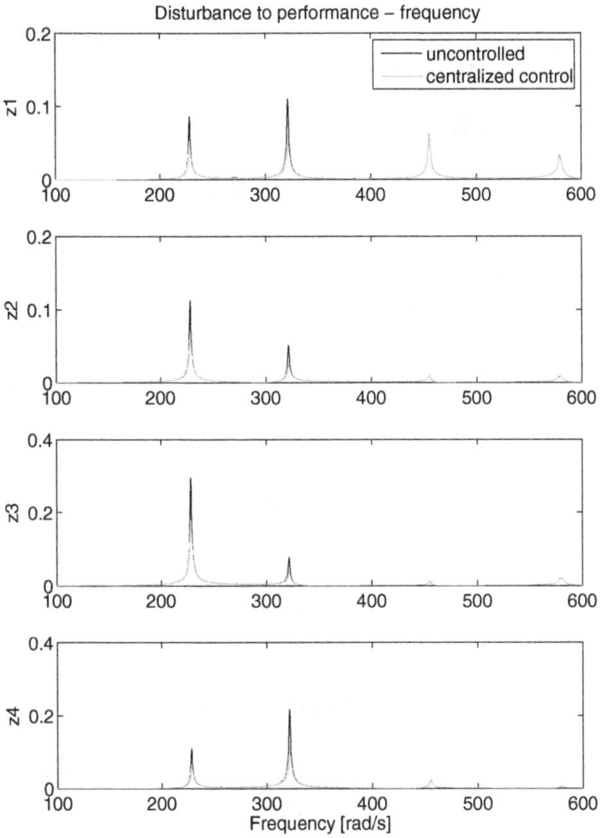

Fig. 5. Centralized control - control result from disturbance signal to spatial performance output in frequency domain

disturbance frequency increases. It is possible to notice also the presence of four predominant natural frequencies in the plate, but only in the attenuated response.
In the spectral response of Figure 5 it is possible to observe clearly the four natural frequencies, but only the first and the second peaks are attenuated, achieving a reduction of approximately 50% in the amplitude. The bigger reduction on the time response of Figure 4 for the highest frequencies is due to the low damping regularly found in these structures, and the respective transient response.

7.2 Decentralized control

Frequency and time domain results for the decentralized control in contrast with centralized control are shown in Figures 6 and 7.
In Figure 6 it is possible to see that the attenuation of the decentralized controller is practically the same, but just a bit less amplitude is present in the middle frequencies.

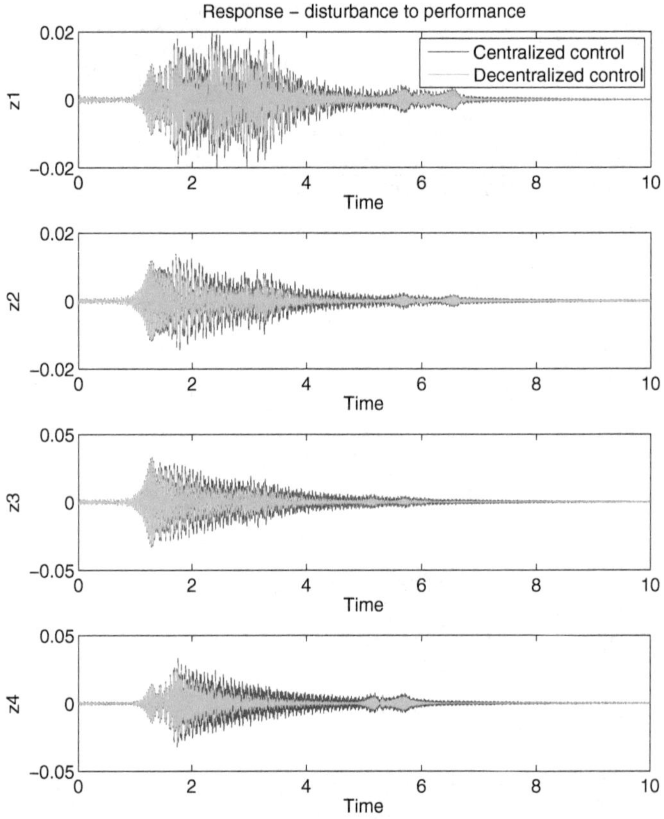

Fig. 6. Centralized and decentralized control - control result from disturbance signal to spatial performance output

In Figure 7 this slightly bigger attenuation is not present in any of the four peaks, with a complete superposition of the responses. Once again, the difference seen in Figure 6 is due to the low damping of the plate.

7.3 Spatial control

In the spatial control case the performance is the spatial output defined in the original design, which in this case is a constant and equal weighting of all the nodes except for the boundary of the plate.

The first four sensors are used as performance measurements with the same control loop design for the spatial performance defined for the whole plate, in order to compare it with $\mathcal{H}_\infty$ decentralized design. The control results obtained are shown in frequency and time response respectively in Figures 8 and 9.

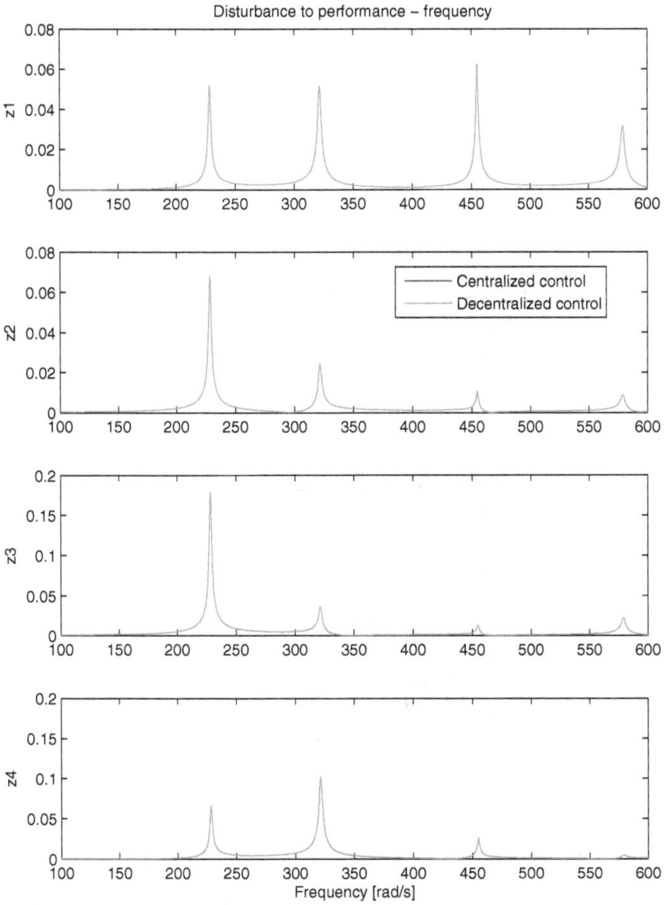

Fig. 7. Centralized and decentralized control - control result from disturbance signal to spatial performance output in frequency domain

In Figure 8 it is possible to notice that the spatial attenuation is bigger than in the decentralized controller results, in the low and middle frequency regions.

In Figure 9 the attenuation attained by the spatial controller is on the range around 10 and 20%, in comparison to the decentralized controller, which presented a similar result to the centralized controller on the order of 50%. This means that the spatial controller achieved indeed a good vibration attenuation result. But in the high frequency range, the two peaks once again were not attenuated.

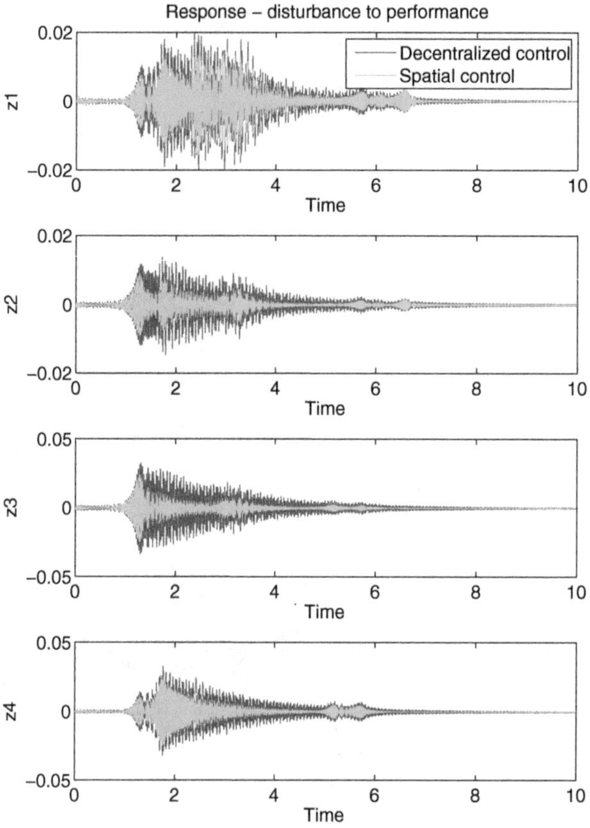

Fig. 8. Decentralized and spatial control - control results from disturbance signal to spatial performance outputs

7.4 Control signal comparison

The control signal levels for the spatial and decentralized controlled are presented in Figure 10 in the time domain. It is possible to have some insight into the behavior of the controllers results by analyzing these curves.

The closed loop frequency response, through the associated controllers efforts to attenuate the correspondent natural frequencies, is very clear on the curves of Figure 10. The spatial controller presented a bigger effort to attenuate the first and the second peaks, while the level of the decentralized controller does not reflect clearly the passage of the natural frequencies. That is the reason that made the spatial controller the better one. Other higher frequencies also presented controller effort, but the respective attenuation was not possible to be seen in the spectral responses in Figure 9. It would be interesting to further investigate if some other points of the region is presenting attenuation on these peaks.

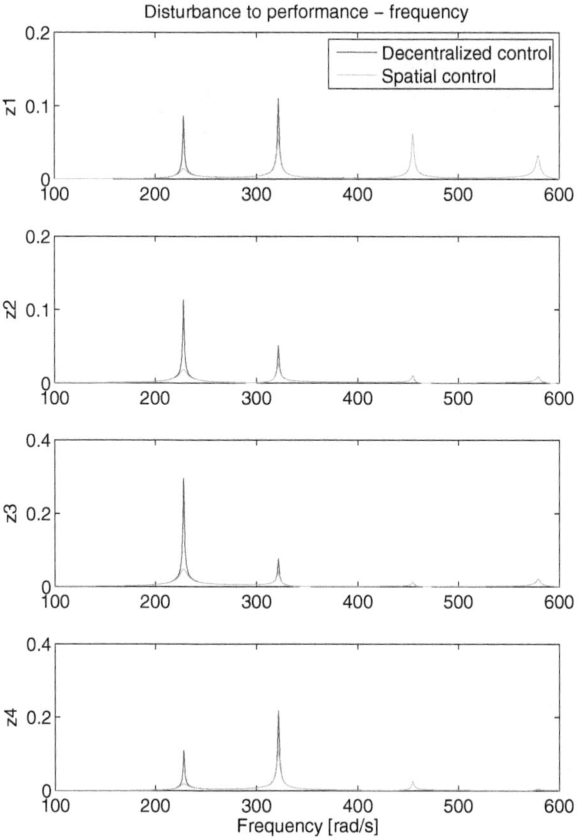

Fig. 9. Decentralized and spatial control - control results from disturbance signal to spatial performance outputs in frequency domain

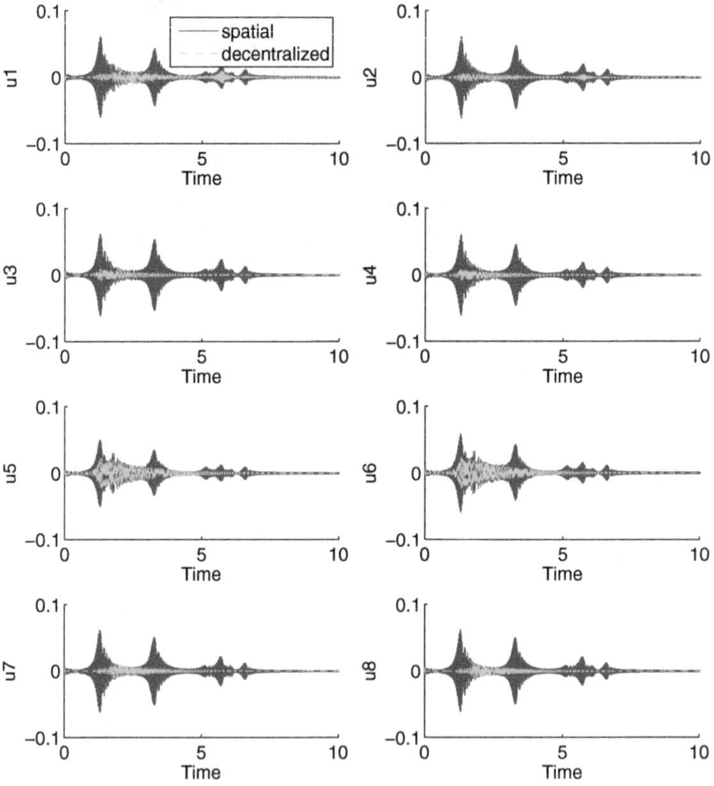

Fig. 10. Comparison of control signal in time domain between spatial and decentralized control

8. Concluding remarks

Two recently proposed $\mathcal{H}_\infty$ controller design methods dedicated to active structural vibration control were presented, and simulated results based on a finite element model of a plate were analyzed. The spatial norm based method aims to attenuate the vibration over entire regions of the structures, using the controller energy in a more effective way. The decentralized control method also tries to achieve a good energy distribution based on the application of the control effort through different controllers. A third controller, based on a standard $\mathcal{H}_\infty$ design for the complete plate, and using the same sensors and actuator, was evaluated also, to serve as a comparison base.

The decentralized control presented a similar behavior to the centralized one, but with a somewhat smaller control effort. Centralized control can demand more expensive equipment and is less robust in case of failures when compared to the decentralized approach. The results validate the option for a decentralized control as opposed to the regular centralized control.

The spatial control as compared to the decentralized control presented the better results in terms of attenuation. The analysis was based on the response on the same punctual performance points, instead of the complete region. But it is possible to affirm that a better attenuation on the complete region is present on the performance of this controller, based on the mathematical definition of the spatial norm.

A future investigation is related to the stability of the decentralized case, since each decentralized control can affect the others. In this work, this aspect was checked by the direct verification of the closed-loop stability, but only for the specific configuration of the four decentralized controllers considered here.

Also the choice of weighting function in the spatial control is an open problem, that heavily depends on the problem's practical requirements.

9. References

Balas, M. J. (1978). Feedback control of flexible systems, *IEEE Transactions on Automatic Control* 23: 673 - 679.

Barrault, G., Halim, D., Hansen, C. & Lenzi, A. (2007). Optimal truncated model for vibration control design within a specified bandwidth, *International Journal of Solids and Structures* 44(14-15): 4673 – 4689.

Barrault, G., Halim, D., Hansen, C. & Lenzi, A. (2008). High frequency spatial vibration control for complex structures, *Applied Acoustics* 69(11): 933 – 944.

Bathe, K.-J. (1995). *Finite Element Procedures (Part 1-2)*, Prentice Hall.

Baz, A. & Chen, T. (2000). Control of axi-symmetric vibrations of cylindrical shells using active constrained layer damping, *Thin-Walled Structures* 36(1): 1 – 20.

Bhattacharya, P., Suhail, H. & Sinha, P. K. (2002). Finite element analysis and distributed control of laminated composite shells using lqr/imsc approach, *Aerospace Science and Technology* 6(4): 273 – 281.

Bianchi, E., Gardonio, P. & Elliott, S. J. (2004). Smart panel with multiple decentralized units for the control of sound transmission. part iii: control system implementation, *Journal of Sound and Vibration* 274(1-2): 215 – 232.

Boyd, S., El Ghaoui, L., Feron, E. & Balakrishnan, V. (1994). *Linear Matrix Inequalities in System and Control Theory*, Vol. 15 of *Studies in Applied Mathematics*, SIAM.

Casadei, F., Ruzzene, M., Dozio, L. & Cunefare, K. A. (2010). Broadband vibration control through periodic arrays of resonant shunts: experimento investigation on plates, *Smart materials and structures* 19.

Cheung, Y. & Wong, W. (2009). H_∞ and H_2 optimizations of a dynamic vibration absorber for suppressing vibrations in plates, *Journal of Sound and Vibration* 320(1-2): 29 – 42.

Ewins, D. J. (2000). *Modal Testing: Theory, Practice and Application*, Research Studies Press, Ltd.

Ferreira, A. (2008). *MATLAB Codes for Finite Element Analysis: Solids and Structures*, Springer Publishing Company, Incorporated.

Gawronski, W. (2004). *Advanced Structural Dynamics and Active Control of Structures*, Springer-Verlag.

Halim, D. (2002). *Vibration analysis and control of smart structures*, PhD thesis, University of NewCastle – School of Electrical Engineering and Computer Science, New South Wales, Australia.

Halim, D. (2007). Structural vibration control with spatially varied disturbance input using a spatial method, *Mechanical Systems and Signal Processing* 21(6): 2496 – 2514.

Halim, D., Barrault, G. & Cazzolato, B. S. (2008). Active control experiments on a panel structure using a spatially weighted objective method with multiple sensors, *Journal of Sound and Vibration* 315(1-2): 1 – 21.

Hurlebaus, S., Stöbener, U. & Gaul, L. (2008). Vibration reduction of curved panels by active modal control, *Comput. Struct.* 86(3-5): 251–257.

Jiang, J. & Li, D. (2010). Decentralized guaranteed cost static output feedback vibration control for piezoelectric smart structures, *Smart Materials and Structures* 19(1): 015018.

Qu, Z.-Q. (2004). *Model Order Reduction Techniques with Applications in Finite Element Analysis*, Springer.

Skelton, R. E., Iwasaki, T. & Grigoriadis, K. M. (1998). *An Unified Algebraic Approach to Linear Control Design*, Taylor and Francis.

Zhou, K. & Doyle, J. C. (1997). *Essentials of Robust Control*, Prentice Hall.

Zilletti, M., Elliott, S. J. & Gardonio, P. (2010). Self-tuning control systems of decentralised velocity feedback, *Journal of Sound and Vibration* 329(14): 2738 – 2750.

Permissions

The contributors of this book come from diverse backgrounds, making this book a truly international effort. This book will bring forth new frontiers with its revolutionizing research information and detailed analysis of the nascent developments around the world.

We would like to thank Andrzej Bartoszewicz, for lending his expertise to make the book truly unique. He has played a crucial role in the development of this book. Without his invaluable contribution this book wouldn't have been possible. He has made vital efforts to compile up to date information on the varied aspects of this subject to make this book a valuable addition to the collection of many professionals and students.

This book was conceptualized with the vision of imparting up-to-date information and advanced data in this field. To ensure the same, a matchless editorial board was set up. Every individual on the board went through rigorous rounds of assessment to prove their worth. After which they invested a large part of their time researching and compiling the most relevant data for our readers. Conferences and sessions were held from time to time between the editorial board and the contributing authors to present the data in the most comprehensible form. The editorial team has worked tirelessly to provide valuable and valid information to help people across the globe.

Every chapter published in this book has been scrutinized by our experts. Their significance has been extensively debated. The topics covered herein carry significant findings which will fuel the growth of the discipline. They may even be implemented as practical applications or may be referred to as a beginning point for another development. Chapters in this book were first published by InTech; hereby published with permission under the Creative Commons Attribution License or equivalent.

The editorial board has been involved in producing this book since its inception. They have spent rigorous hours researching and exploring the diverse topics which have resulted in the successful publishing of this book. They have passed on their knowledge of decades through this book. To expedite this challenging task, the publisher supported the team at every step. A small team of assistant editors was also appointed to further simplify the editing procedure and attain best results for the readers.

Our editorial team has been hand-picked from every corner of the world. Their multi-ethnicity adds dynamic inputs to the discussions which result in innovative outcomes. These outcomes are then further discussed with the researchers and contributors who give their valuable feedback and opinion regarding the same. The feedback is then collaborated with the researches and they are edited in a comprehensive manner to aid the understanding of the subject.

Apart from the editorial board, the designing team has also invested a significant amount of their time in understanding the subject and creating the most relevant covers. They scrutinized every image to scout for the most suitable representation of the subject and create an appropriate cover for the book.

The publishing team has been involved in this book since its early stages. They were actively engaged in every process, be it collecting the data, connecting with the contributors or procuring relevant information. The team has been an ardent support to the editorial, designing and production team. Their endless efforts to recruit the best for this project, has resulted in the accomplishment of this book. They are a veteran in the field of academics and their pool of knowledge is as vast as their experience in printing. Their expertise and guidance has proved useful at every step. Their uncompromising quality standards have made this book an exceptional effort. Their encouragement from time to time has been an inspiration for everyone.

The publisher and the editorial board hope that this book will prove to be a valuable piece of knowledge for researchers, students, practitioners and scholars across the globe.

List of Contributors

Gianfranco Morani, Giovanni Cuciniello, Federico Corraro and Adolfo Sollazzo
Italian Aerospace Research Centre (CIRA), Italy

Bruno Ferreira, Aníbal Matos and Nuno Cruz
INESC Porto and University of Porto, Portugal

Abhijit Das, Frank L. Lewis and Kamesh Subbarao
Automation and Robotics Research Institute, The University of Texas at Arlington, USA

Benedikt Alt and Ferdinand Svaricek
University of the German Armed Forces Munich, Germany

Takuma Suzuki and Masaki Takahashi
Keio University, Japan

Yang Bin and Nenglian Feng
Beijing University of Technology, China

Keqiang Li
Tsinghua University, China

Joaquín Alvarez
Scientific Research and Advanced Studies Center of Ensenada (CICESE), Mexico

David Rosas
Universidad Autónoma de Baja California, Mexico

Rafal P. Jastrzebski, Alexander Smirnov and Olli Pyrhönen
Dept. of Electrical Engineering, LUT Energy, Lappeenranta University of Technology, Finland

Adam K. Piłat
Dept. of Automatics, AGH University of Science and Technology, Krakow, Poland

Jong Shik Kim, Han Me Kim and Sung Hwan Park
School of Mechanical Engineering, Pusan National University, Republic of Korea

Alysson F. Mazoni, Alberto L. Serpa and Eurípedes G. de O. Nóbrega
University of Campinas - UNICAMP, Brazil

Printed in the USA
CPSIA information can be obtained
at www.ICGtesting.com
JSHW011426221024
72173JS00004B/686

9 781632 402035